"OUR AIM
WAS MAN"

"OUR AIM WAS MAN"

Andrew's Sharpshooters in the American Civil War

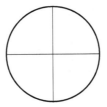

EDITED BY

Roberta Senechal de la Roche

University of Massachusetts Press

AMHERST AND BOSTON

ISBN 978-1-62534-248-5 (paper); 247-8 (cloth)

Designed by Dennis Anderson
Set in Electra and Adobe Jenson Pro
Printed and bound by Maple Press, Inc.

Cover design by Jack Harrison
Cover art: (top) Monument to the 1st Massachusetts Sharp Shooters at
Gettysburg National Military Park. Photo by David M. McLaughlin;
(bottom) Andrew's Sharpshooters honor guard for Brigadier General Frederick
West Lander, 1862. Research Your Civil War Ancestor,
www.researchonline.net/macw/unit5.htm#.WBpLrPorKUm.

Library of Congress Cataloging-in-Publication Data
A catalog record for this book is available from the Library of Congress.

British Library Cataloguing-in-Publication Data
A catalog record for this book is available from the British Library.

For Donald,
who was always there.

CONTENTS

PREFACE

The birth of this volume traces back to a close call on a hot July day many years ago. My mother was in the process of moving into a new house. When I arrived to help her one afternoon, nobody was there. The sky was darkening, distant thunder was sounding, and the wind was picking up. I noticed several open cardboard boxes outside on a deck, exposed to the coming downpour. One contained old letters, and I was interested to see that many were from a Civil War soldier named Moses Hill. I rushed the boxes inside just before the storm broke.

My mother later told me that Moses Hill was my great-great-grandfather, a Union Army volunteer from East Medway, Massachusetts, who died of disease before his three-year enlistment expired. I had a number of questions: What was his regiment? Where did he serve? What disease killed him? What happened to his wife and children after he died? She did not know.

Because I was concerned about the future of the letters, that night I announced to my mother that I was taking possession of them for the indefinite future. She readily agreed, perhaps in part because I was a history major in college and intended to go to graduate school and become a professional historian. So I left her house not merely with a box of letters, but with a heightened sense of the fragility of the past and the mortality of memory. I soon began transcribing the letters, hoping someday to publish them. The journey proved longer than I expected.

I learned from Moses Hill's letters that he was a sharpshooter, one of about a hundred men who joined the First Company Massachusetts Volunteer Sharpshooters—also known as "Andrew's Sharpshooters" (or "the Andrew Sharpshooters"). Although obviously he was a skilled marksman, only much later did I discover that he belonged to a very special breed of sharpshooter: a sniper who used a rifle with a telescopic sight to kill unsuspecting enemy soldiers across long distances. I also learned that during the Civil War both civilians and ordinary soldiers expressed considerable ambivalence about snipers. The use of rifles with telescopic sights in the military was new in 1861, and the practice of sniping was controversial. To some it seemed cowardly and unmanly—a violation of military honor. Others even viewed it as cold-blooded murder delivered from afar by someone hiding in the branches of a tree or lurking behind a pile of rubble. Yet the experience of snipers in the Civil War had received little attention from historians. I therefore decided the subject was worthy of a book.

But I came to see that however detailed and interesting Moses Hill's letters might be, I needed more voices to adequately capture the world of Andrew's Sharpshooters. Hill's letters covered only the sharpshooters' first year in the war. Although he was present during the Peninsula Campaign in the spring and summer of 1862, for example, he was unable to join his comrades when they took part in the Battle of Antietam that fall and later battles such as those at Fredericksburg and Gettysburg.

Letters, diaries, and memoirs of Civil War sharpshooters are scarce, and writings pertaining to snipers scarcer still (partly because they served in small units). So I felt extraordinarily fortunate to be able to locate sources for three more members of Andrew's Sharpshooters: Luke Emerson Bicknell, Egbert Oswald Hixon, and Ferdinand Joseph Fuller Crossman. Their writings allowed me to extend the narrative of the company to the end of 1863 (after which the available sources become extremely thin). They also better enabled me to address changes in the role of the sharpshooters over time, and the significance of those changes not only for them but for snipers in the Union army as a whole.

In my search for more information about Andrew's Sharpshooters to supplement my great-great-grandfather Moses Hill's letters, I accrued many more debts than I can adequately acknowledge here.

I am deeply grateful to all the individuals who enthusiastically shared photographs, letters, diaries, and family stories about Luke Bicknell, Egbert Hixon, and Ferdinand Crossman. I particularly wish to thank Susan L. Harnwell, webmaster for the Internet site "The 15th Massachusetts Volunteer Infantry in the Civil War, 1861–1865, with the 1st Co. Andrew Sharpshooters" (www.nextech.de/ma15mvi/). The website provides rosters, photographs, genealogical information, and the names of those who have contributed to it—a number of whom I was able to reach for further information. In addition,

Susan facilitated contact with various descendants of Andrew's Sharpshooters. Thanks to her, for example, I made the acquaintance of Carol Botteron, a descendant of Egbert Hixon. By a strange coincidence, Hixon turned out to be the only other sniper from Moses Hill's hometown, and his tentmate as well. Carol (and other Hixon descendants) made available his diary, letters, army pension records, photographs, and family stories handed down from one generation to the next. She read an early draft of my manuscript and offered many useful editorial suggestions as well.

Susan Harnwell likewise helped put me in touch with Evangeline (Bicknell) Dollemore, a descendant of Luke Bicknell, the best-educated and most prolific writer of the four Andrew's Sharpshooters whose stories are included here. I am indebted to her and her husband, Doug, for the two days I spent in their home, going through the letters Bicknell wrote to his fiancée during his service as well as his postwar writings—all of which yielded valuable information about the history of the sharpshooters. And I especially wish to thank yet another person I met through the 15th Massachusetts website: David M. McGlaughlin, whose short history of Andrew's Sharpshooters is available in that location. David provided welcome support and suggestions in the early stages of my project, and later made and donated an excellent photograph of the sharpshooters' monument at the Gettysburg battlefield for the cover of this volume.

Many others helped me reconstruct the sharpshooters' lives before, during, and after the war. Among them were Joe and Betty Hersey, whose house in Millis, Massachusetts, was once home to Moses Hill and his family. Harriet Van Dyke of South Sutton, Massachusetts, showed me the colonial-era home where Ferdinand Crossman and his wife lived and regaled me with historical details about the neighborhood. By a stroke of luck, even my innkeeper in Sutton, Martyn Bowden, turned out to be a specialist in the historical and cultural geography of New England who in various ways enriched my understanding of the prewar lives of the men described in this volume.

Others who contributed their time, local knowledge, and primary source materials to the project include Paul Brosnihan, former president of the Sutton Historical Society; Paul LaCroix, president of the Millis Historical Society; Steve Carter, caretaker of the historic Prospect Hill Cemetery in Millis; the staff at the town offices of Medway, Millis, Sutton, and Bellingham, Massachusetts; the staff at the Millis and Sutton town libraries; and Ralph Parmenter Bennett, who generously shared his research on his sharpshooter ancestor, Marcus Morton Parmenter.

Special thanks go to the libraries of Washington and Lee University and the University of Virginia for providing access to rare primary sources, and to the staff of the William L. Clements Library at the University of Michigan for their help with the Crossman Papers. In addition, I thank the Massachusetts Historical Society in Boston, whose Civil War collections for the state were invaluable to me, and the American Antiquarian Society in Worcester, Massachusetts, for allowing me access to the diaries of Ferdinand Crossman and his wife.

I am grateful as well to the University of Massachusetts Press, especially director Mary Dougherty, for support and useful advice throughout the entire publication process. I also warmly thank the two anonymous reviewers for their careful reading of the manuscript, the generous detail of their comments, and the many improvements to the book they suggested.

I benefited greatly, too, from the thorough reading of the manuscript by Civil War historian J. Holt Merchant, my colleague at Washington and Lee University. I received other useful advice and encouragement from historians Michael B. Chesson, Barton Myers, and Carol A. Reardon during the project's evolution. And I want to express my appreciation to the Class of 1956 Provost's Faculty Development Endowment and the Department of History at Washington and Lee University for the financial support they contributed to this project.

I finally thank my husband, sociologist Donald Black, who provided many incisive and insightful comments over the years and who brought his unmatched editorial skills to bear on the manuscript. Nor can I forget my thoughtful cat Victoria Regina, who continually assisted my work on the project by rearranging my notes, finding new locations for my pens, and walking across my computer keyboard when I was not looking.

"OUR AIM WAS MAN"

INTRODUCTION

After the outbreak of the Civil War in mid-April 1861, John Saunders, a tall, stout carpenter from Salem, Massachusetts, conceived of the idea of forming a hundred-man Union Army company of specially equipped elite sharpshooters—expert, highly skilled marksmen. From the outset, Saunders wanted his men to specialize as snipers: extremely accurate sharpshooters who fire from concealed positions and over long distances, using a rifle suitable for that purpose. According to the historian Gary Ecelbarger: "Saunders had obtained a custom-made, forty-pound telescopic rifle, able to strike a target consistently at 500 yards. . . . [He] showed his rifle to another sportsman, Governor [John Albion] Andrew, who was easily convinced that an entire company of soldiers carrying these guns would provide great benefit to the service—particularly in picking off enemy artillerists."[1]

On July 25, 1861, Governor Andrew telegraphed Washington, seeking approval for Saunders's proposition.[2] Four days later he received a positive response, and issued "Special Order 342" authorizing the formation of a sniper company with John Saunders as captain. Andrew also specified a test prospective recruits would have to pass: "No man will be accepted or mustered into service who cannot when firing at a rest, at a distance of two hundred yards put ten consecutive shots in a target, the average distance not to exceed five inches from the centre of the bull's eye to the ball." He further noted that the company would join a sharpshooter regiment that Colonel Hiram Berdan of New York had been authorized to form.[3] A grateful Saunders named his company in honor of the governor, and his riflemen, the press, and public thereafter called it Andrew's Sharpshooters (or sometimes the Andrew Sharpshooters).[4]

1

As early as the American Revolution, the U.S. military had occasionally used individual skilled marksmen to kill high-value targets, such as enemy officers and artillerymen. As one historian notes, however, the Civil War marked "the first time battalions of sharpshooters would be raised for the *specific* purpose of sniping and where they would have completely free rein over the battlefield."[5] Moreover, as the historian Earl J. Hess notes in his classic study *The Rifle Musket in Civil War Combat*, by 1861 "Americans led the world in the development of telescopic sights for long-range rifles." Thus the Civil War witnessed the first use of skilled marksmen who were trained to "perform the modern role of sniper."[6]

Disagreement exists as to just who first proposed an elite unit of skilled riflemen, equipped with the best weapons and clothed in distinctive uniforms, to perform this new role in the Union Army. Many credit Hiram Berdan, a wealthy and politically well-connected New York engineer and inventor who also enjoyed legendary renown as the nation's best rifle shot. In June 1861, Berdan—whom a contemporary described as having "much influence in many places and a certain necessary ruthlessness"—persuaded the federal government to commission him with the rank of colonel and authorize him to organize two regiments: the First and Second United States Sharp Shooters, popularly known as "Berdan's Sharpshooters."[7] They were said by one veteran of the First U.S.S.S. to be "the best known of any regiments in the Army."[8]

Colonel Berdan's recruitment flyers and newspaper announcements circulated widely throughout the North that summer, and the press (including the influential *New York Times* and *Harper's Weekly*) fueled the public's fascination with his riflemen. One former Berdan's Sharpshooter recalled the intense interest in the First U.S.S.S. regiment when it camped near Washington, D.C., in 1861: "During the splendid weather of the autumn months, visitors . . . came in untold numbers; they were constantly crowding in, not only from our own mighty North, but from all civilized quarters of the world. And not the least of the many objects of interest to be noted was that of the rifle practice. . . . The newspapers at the time were full of these target trials, and the shooting of the Sharpshooters furnished items for a long while to the dailies and illustrated journals."[9] Berdan proved an effective promoter, inviting numerous dignitaries—including President Abraham Lincoln and Major General George B. McClellan—to view his regiment's target practices. To the delight of the press and other spectators, he sometimes displayed his own famed shooting prowess as well.[10]

Although ten other Union sharpshooter units served during the Civil War, the Northern press devoted most of its coverage to Colonel Berdan's two

regiments.[11] As a result, to the public, "sharpshooters" quickly became virtually synonymous with "Berdan's Sharpshooters," and most historical accounts
of Union sharpshooters are disproportionately devoted to Berdan's men. With
few exceptions, other units typically receive, at best, brief sketches of their
actions.[12] This imbalance in historical treatment is likely due to the uneven
availability of source materials. Whereas primary sources such as letters,
diaries, and memoirs are typically extremely scarce for sharpshooter units,
Colonel Berdan's two regiments left a wealth of firsthand accounts, which,
combined with the generous press coverage of the time, has allowed them a
fuller portrayal.

During the Civil War, the term "sharpshooter" was generic, and was often
applied to any highly skilled rifleman. As Hess observes, "It is not always easy
to differentiate a sniper from a skirmisher in [wartime] accounts, for their
duties sometimes overlapped, and snipers were often detailed from the skirmish line." Still, Hess stresses, "the two were indeed separate military func-
tions."[13] Skirmishers were sent out beyond the front or flanks of their massed
infantry, moving in a line of widely spaced groups of four or five men and
trying to conceal their movements as much as possible. Sometimes they simply performed reconnaissance; at other times they might harass and slow an
advancing enemy's forces. If driven back by the enemy, skirmishers would
retreat to their main line of infantry and fight alongside them. This tactic
was not new in 1861, but had been used since the American Revolution.[14]
Though skirmishers on occasion might be ordered to try to kill enemy officers
or those manning cannons, that was not their primary function. Their most
important role was, as Hess notes, "in protecting the battle line by giving it
advance warning of enemy movements" and in delaying any advances by the
enemy.[15]

Civil War infantry regiments routinely trained their men to perform as
skirmishers if necessary, and, according to a veteran of the Twenty-Second
Massachusetts Infantry, common foot soldiers relished the role: "Instruction
in skirmish-drill was one of the daily duties of camp-life. . . . There is something about skirmishing to which the soldier takes instinctively, and the man
who shirks the ordinary drill seldom fails to be on the skirmish-line. The
officers took to it kindly, as well as the men."[16] And, as one historian notes,
"For many sharpshooters, much of their combat experience throughout the
Civil War would be the role of regular infantry, albeit with a greater propen-
sity for hitting their target than the average soldier."[17] Aside from their relatively higher level of marksmanship, Berdan's Sharpshooters enjoyed greater
firepower than their infantry counterparts. Most of Berdan's men used Sharps
rapid-firing, breech-loading rifles named for their original designer, Christian

Sharps. Under battlefield conditions, skilled marksmen using Sharps rifles averaged one shot every twelve seconds. In contrast, infantry averaged about one shot every two minutes with their muzzle-loading weapons.[18]

For most Union sharpshooter units, the functional line between regular infantry skirmishers and them was blurred from the outset and became less distinct over time.[19] The Union Army thus used Berdan's Sharpshooters as skirmishers rather than snipers. Although Berdan's men did on occasion serve as snipers to try to kill enemy artillerymen, pickets, and officers at long distances and from concealed positions, skirmishing remained their primary function.[20] Hess notes that after enjoying a wave of press attention for their skirmishing and sniping prowess during the siege of Yorktown in 1862, Berdan's Sharpshooters "served both as infantry and as skirmishers like most other infantry units." He adds, "Both regiments faded into obscurity as their roles changed from specialized skirmish outfits to that fulfilled by any other regiment. . . . Skirmishing could be performed by any number of regiments armed with rifle muskets."[21]

Sniping was different. The term "sniper" was not widely used in the United States until World War I, but some riflemen in the Civil War did specialize in shooting long distances from hidden positions. And some of these snipers were for the first time equipped with rifles with telescopes mounted on them—equipment that eventually became the hallmark of the modern military sniper.[22] Snipers went out to shoot in small groups or in pairs, and might also prowl as individuals "on their own hook," in the slang of the day. They were often called upon to kill valuable targets such as officers and artillerymen, and sometimes were also used to suppress harassing enemy fire from fortifications, rifle pits, or concealed skirmishers. And they usually were the ones charged with eliminating enemy snipers.

The few Union sharpshooter units that served primarily as snipers typically carried so-called target rifles: large, heavy weapons with octagonal barrels mounted with long telescopic sights (with a magnification of up to 25X). Target rifles were popular just before the war among hunters and competitive shooters, and some sharpshooter recruits were permitted to carry their own weapons when they joined the service. Hiram Berdan owned one, and many of his prospective recruits used them during their initial target-shooting trials.[23] A Massachusetts writer noted:

> They weighed from 20 to 70 pounds, and were necessarily fired from a rest. They were made by gunsmiths in various sections of the country to suit the individual, the one feature in common being that each was provided with a telescopic tube running the length of the barrel, at the front of which

Figure 1. Morgan James target rifle, c. 1860. Courtesy of West Point Museum Collections.

fine threads were crossed, allowing great nicety in sighting. The rifles were muzzle loaders, shooting a conical ball used with a patch [a small piece of cloth or paper between the ball and powder] and propelled with a very heavy charge of powder; an expert in their use could load, aim, and fire about once in two minutes.[24]

A sniper resting his target rifle on a tree branch or fence might be able to hit a target 1,000 or more yards away (versus the 500 to 800 yards for the Sharps breech-loading rifle carried by most of Colonel Berdan's men). A Maine sharpshooter might have exaggerated when he remarked, "With these [telescopic] sights one could see a ten-penny nail head half a mile away," but one Andrew's Sharpshooter who used a 25-pound target rifle wrote home after his first few weeks of target practice that at 550 yards he "could hit a Turkey twice out of three times," and that some of the men could "hit the bigness of a cracker most every time" at 220 yards. He added that they sometimes practiced shooting at targets a half mile distant. Another sniper claimed that he and his fellows could "hit a twenty five cent piece at a ¼ mile distance." And the author of an 1864 guide titled *Hints to Riflemen* observed that "with the target rifle and telescope sights, the feat has repeatedly been performed of firing a series of shots *without a single miss* into a flour barrel at three quarters of a mile."[25]

For a short time Colonel Berdan's First U.S.S.S. had two companies equipped with target rifles. But fearing that their weight would hinder his men's mobility in skirmishing and marching, Berdan eventually decided to get rid of all but a few of the big rifles. One veteran Berdan's Sharpshooter remarked: "It was soon found that there were objections to the use in the field of the fine guns so effective on the target ground. The great weight of some of them was of itself almost prohibitory, for, to a soldier burdened with the weight of his knapsack, haversack and canteen, blanket and overcoat, the additional weight of a target rifle—many of which weighed fifteen pounds each, and some as much as thirty pounds—was too much to be easily borne."[26] Adding to the weight, and slowing the process of loading the target rifles, were "false muzzles" and "starters," attached to the end of target rifle barrels for each reloading and removed before each shot. They helped give each bullet rammed down the barrel as perfect an alignment as possible and minimized damage to the rifle barrel as well. The false muzzles and the long telescopes also meant that target rifles could not be equipped with bayonets and used in hand-to-hand combat.[27] At ten pounds and free of such accessories, the Sharps rifles eventually issued to Berdan's men were deemed much more practical and versatile for his highly mobile skirmishers.

Andrew's Sharpshooters preferred the role of sniper and insisted on using telescoped target rifles, despite their weight and slow firing. But some writers have been critical of their choice. For example, Charles A. Stevens, a former captain in the First U.S.S.S. and author of an extensive history of Berdan's Sharpshooters published in 1892, wrote:

There were two companies of Andrew Sharpshooters of Massachusetts, . . . raised for Col. Berdan's Second Regiment, who were sent out as indepen-

Figure 2. Morgan James target rifle, c. 1860, showing the false muzzle
that had to be put on when loading the rifle, and the mounted telescope on top.
Courtesy of West Point Museum Collections.

dent companies. Berdan offered them Sharps rifles to march and skirmish with, but they preferred to carry the heavy telescopes. . . . [One company] was badly cut up at Antietam [in September 1862], in a close engagement where rapid loading and quick shooting with them was out of the question, their guns being little better in that affair than clubs, they losing 26 with their captain and lieutenant among the killed.[28]

Although Stevens was actually wrong about the type of rifle the two Massachusetts companies carried in late 1862, later historians echo his criticism of sniping with target rifles as "useless" compared to skirmishing with breechloaders.[29]

In any case, we know more about the snipers' rifles than we know about the men who shouldered them. Leaving aside Berdan's two regiments, accounts written by sharpshooters are very rare, and sniper accounts are rarer still. How did Union Civil War volunteers come to be snipers? How did they view their role in the military? In terms of personality, did they resemble the "ideal sniper" of the twentieth century—"a loner who shunned the limelight and often the company of his comrades alike," who was quiet, cautious, restrained in his habits, and averse to the playfulness and revelry of common infantrymen?[30] What were their families and social networks like before and after the war?

In this book I seek to recapture some of the character, experiences, and social life of the men who were among the first of a long line of American snipers armed with long-range weapons with telescopic sights. The letters, diaries, and memoirs of four members of Andrew's Sharpshooters (formally designated the First Company Massachusetts Sharpshooters) provide new details about these snipers' service. To be sure, much of what they say about their everyday life is typical of most Civil War foot soldiers: complaints about bad food, bad weather, boredom in camp, inadequate shelter, incompetent officers, incomprehensible orders, mind-numbing and physically punishing marches through mud or choking dust, and simple homesickness. Readers interested in the medical and environmental history of the common soldier will find many new details in these sharpshooters' writings. In particular, their experiences in their first year of service further illuminate the innovative work of Kathryn Shively Meier, who in Nature's Civil War: Common Soldiers and the Environment in 1862 Virginia compares the impact of the environment, disease, and rigors of campaigning on troops in the Shenandoah Valley Campaign that began in March 1862 and in the Peninsula Campaign from April to August of the same year. Andrew's Sharpshooters experienced extreme conditions in both settings, and many fell seriously ill in one—or in some cases, both—of the campaigns. Like other soldiers, the sharpshooters often responded to the varied challenges to their health, both physical and psychological, with what Meier terms "self care." These included attempts to find fresh water, foraging, buying, or stealing food to diversify their diet, improvising better shelters, and obtaining advice, moral support, and care from comrades and from their social networks back home (which sometimes included hometown family doctors who might send medicine).[31]

But the four Andrew's Sharpshooters also provide a composite sketch of their distinctive service in the war—in their own words. Their writings yield details specific to the camp life and training of the sniper company (descriptions of which are exceedingly scarce in the literature), their experience in battle, and their reactions to the evolution of their company over time. Finally, they offer brief glimpses into the experiences of their friends and families back in Massachusetts, and the strains the war placed on those at home.[32]

The Morality of the Sniper

Honorable warfare in the Western world had long involved open, reciprocal combat with roughly equal risks for the soldiers engaged in it. The fighting was symmetrical: soldiers on the field of battle exchanged bullets, blows, shells, or shot until one side retreated or surrendered. And all who voluntarily stepped into the line of fire were deemed courageous. Covert attacks—such as ambushes, hit-and-run tactics, shooting from under cover—were deemed cowardly and immoral, and all the more so if the victims were unarmed, asleep, relieving themselves, or otherwise unable to defend themselves. So because sniping at the time of the Civil War was covert, unequal, and asymmetrical, it violated long-standing conceptions of honorable combat.[33] Skirmishing was bad enough; one veteran of Gettysburg called it "savage—nay, devilish," and added, "To juke and hide and skulk for men and deliberately aim at and murder them one by one is far too bloodthirsty business for Christian men."[34] But at least skirmishers sometimes fought out in the open alongside infantrymen. Snipers were far worse. A man in the crosshairs of a rifle telescope had no chance whatsoever to defend himself. One Union soldier complained that "there was an unwritten code of honor among the infantry that forbade the shooting of men while attending to the imperative calls of nature, and these sharpshooting brutes were constantly violating that rule."[35] As Andrew's Sharpshooter Luke Bicknell remarked, sniping was "not anything like a square, open, stand up fight."[36] It was unequal and one-sided in the extreme: the target not only could not fight back, but with the new telescope technology, a sniper's shot could be so long that the victim might never even know the source of his injury or death. But it was not just the distance of the sniper's shot that troubled many Civil War officers and soldiers. The use of telescopic sights also meant that the process of killing and being killed became disturbingly "personal": snipers carefully singled out their targets and sometimes could clearly see their victims before they fired.[37]

To some degree, however, snipers faced what the historian Martin Pegler calls "a clear double standard" in the eyes of their fellow soldiers: a "love/hate relationship" consisting of a mix of "awe, disdain, and frequent contempt."[38] On the one hand, infantrymen expressed relief when, say, snipers helped protect them by suppressing enemy artillery fire. A contemporary writer was told, for example, that during the siege of Yorktown in the spring of 1862, "the Andrews Sharpshooters . . . in repeated instances held the enemy's batteries still, till counter works were established which could not have been erected, but for their aid." He adds that another much-appreciated contribution was to eliminate enemy snipers: "At Yorktown . . . on one occasion a party of our men working in the trenches were annoyed by a sharpshooter who had posted himself in a tree eight hundred yards distant, from which he could make their position an uncomfortable one, while it was impossible at that distance even to distinguish him with the naked eye among the branches of the tree. Two of the Andrews Sharpshooters were placed in the trench, a telescope sight was fixed upon him, and the first shot brought him down."[39] One Andrew's Sharpshooter, Moses Hill, proudly wrote to his wife: "We have protected them when they was building their breastworks and protected our batterys. . . . You don't know how much the soldiers think of us, and well they may."[40]

On the other hand, Civil War soldiers on both sides sometimes described snipers as cowards guilty of "slawtering men when it does no good." They particularly condemned the covert nature of sniper attacks. As one infantry-man wrote, "They could sneak around trees or lurk behind stumps, or cower in wells or in cellars, and from the safety of their lairs murder a few men." He added, "I hated sharpshooters, both Confederate and Union . . . and was always glad to see them killed."[41] In fact, snipers on both sides expected to be summarily executed if captured. A Union sniper at the Yorktown siege thus mentioned that "the enemy had announced their purpose to hang to the nearest tree every man caught with a telescopic rifle."[42]

One who expressed horror at sniping at Yorktown—and sniping in general— was the well-known artist Winslow Homer, then an illustrator for *Harper's Weekly* who accompanied the Sixty-First New York Infantry during the Peninsula Campaign of 1862. During the siege of Yorktown he persuaded a sniper to let him look through his rifle's telescope at Confederate soldiers on their fortifications, and years later, in a letter to a friend, sketched what he saw. Homer added his reaction: "The above impression struck me as being as near murder as anything I could think of in connection with the army & I always had a horror of that branch of the service."[43] He nevertheless seemed fascinated with snipers—enough so that the first oil painting of his notable career was titled *The Army of the Potomac—A Sharp-Shooter on Picket Duty.* First appearing as a print in *Harper's Weekly* in 1862, the powerful and chillingly beautiful image of a sniper concealed in a tree, finger on the trigger, has

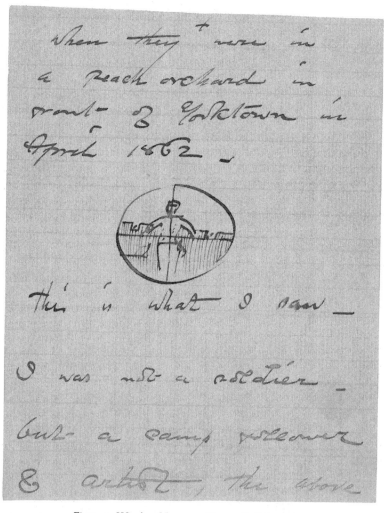

Figure 3. Winslow Homer to George G. Briggs, 1896.
Archives of American Art, Smithsonian Institution.

long been emblematic of the Civil War sniper (see illustration in chapter 5). As one art historian noted, "This is a picture without banners and glory." It portrays the sniper as "a cool and aloof figure who killed and terrorized without passion or warning. By denying others the opportunity to rise above the horrors of war through acts of courage and compassion, the sharpshooter diminished his own humanity. For the infantry soldier the sharpshooter was little more than a murderer—a cold and passionless extension of his distant and deadly weapon."[44]

The snipers' own feelings about the morality of their mode of warfare can never be known, but one attitude they did often voice was ambivalence. On the one hand, as a Berdan's Sharpshooter admitted, the skilled rifleman's role "had a peculiar fascination for these men. In fact, sharp shooting is the squirrel hunting of war; it is wonderful to see how self-forgetful the marksman grows—to see with what sportsmanlike eyes he seeks out the grander game, and with what coolness and accuracy he brings it down. At the moment he grows utterly indifferent to human life or human suffering, and seems intent only on cruelty and destruction; to make a good shot and hit his man, brings for the time being a feeling of intense satisfaction." But he also reflected: "Few, however, care to recall afterwards the look of the dying enemy, and there are none who would not risk as much to aid the wounded victim of their skill as they did to inflict the wound. War is brutalizing, but the heat of the actual conflict passed, soldiers are humane and merciful, even to their foes."[45]

Andrew's Sharpshooters sometimes expressed similarly mixed feelings about their deadly work. Moses Hill, for instance, commented disapprovingly that "some take pride in going out and shoot[ing] a man from the Rebel breastwork when it does no good at all." Others actively avoided killing defenseless men. It was said, for example, that one member of the company would "spare many a man entirely," and "fire to wound only as a rule while we prowled."[46] Hill himself reassured his wife that he did not kill for sport: "I shal not nor I have not shot anyone unless it is agoing to do some good for the Country." In his letters to his sweetheart, another Andrew's Sharpshooter, Luke Emerson Bicknell, recounted the company's actions and his part in them with enthusiasm. After one foray at Yorktown he reported excitedly, "I had the luck to hit one rebel myself." But many years later when he composed his memoir, Bicknell expressed more discomfort about his role in the war.[47]

Martin Pegler notes that Civil War sharpshooters' attitudes also changed over time: "They went through several very distinct phases: initial excitement followed within weeks or months by a realization of the deadly nature of their profession, and eventually a sense of fatalism over their ability to survive."[48]

Enthusiasm seemingly carried the Andrew's Sharpshooters from their lengthy training in the fall of 1861 and through a prolonged winter campaign in 1862. Full realization of the peculiar nature of sniping only occurred during the siege of Yorktown in 1862, when, according to Bicknell, some "got to perfectly hate their murderous work and to share in the sentiment then quite popular that sharpshooting was out of the pale of honorable warfare."[49] By the winter of 1862–63, some entered a more fatalistic phase—what Pegler calls "the most dangerous mental state for a sharpshooter to be in, as he would tend to become careless."[50] An extreme illustration was a daylong reckless sniper duel fought on the breastworks of Petersburg, Virginia, in 1864 (detailed in chapter 8). Ultimately, however, many apparently became largely indifferent to their form of warfare. As one sharpshooter from the Eighth Maine Infantry at Petersburg in 1864 summed it up, "As to sharpshooting the Rebs, we had been shot at so much and had had comrades shot down at our sides so often that we had come to have no more feeling or sentiment in regard to the matter than as if they had been wild animals."[51]

The surviving writings of Andrew's Sharpshooters mostly express a sense of quiet, unemotional, grimly enduring, and patient—and sometimes proud—workmanship. Only rarely did they pause to evaluate their role as snipers from a moral standpoint. Perhaps, as Lt. Col. Dave Grossman suggests in his book *On Killing*, the long-distance nature of sniping meant they suffered less guilt and other lasting emotional trauma in comparison to those who had to kill at much closer quarters.[52] Or perhaps what one historian has said of working-class Civil War soldiers in general applies to most snipers: that they unsentimentally approached their deadly work as "a job to be done, not thought about," where "demonstrations of concern were taboo," and where the "mind had no room for thoughts about the horrors of combat."[53]

"Good Shots and Good Fellows"

What Captain John Saunders promised Andrew's Sharpshooters recruits in the summer of 1861 was alluring. They would have special weapons: telescoped target rifles. Anyone who brought his own target rifle would be compensated with at least $50.[54] If a recruit had no rifle, he would be given a new one. Their "special service" as snipers would exempt them from most of the chores of common infantrymen, such as guard duty and drill (practicing open-field infantry maneuvers). Saunders promised them extra pay as well. And on long marches, their heavy rifles would be moved by wagon. As Luke Bicknell put it, "We knew that they could not be carried on the march . . . and we did not enlist to carry them, except in action, any more than the artillerist enlists to carry his guns upon his shoulder on the march."[55] Bicknell, an early recruit, listed other attractions of Saunders's unit: "The work of the company was to be picking off officers and artillerists in battle, or siege, and from the unwieldy character of our guns we were to be free from duty in line of battle and, from the same reason were to go scott free from drill and guard duty. . . . On account of the supposed extra-hazardous character of the service we were to receive twenty-five dollars per month."[56]

Some sharpshooters believed that sniping was safer than skirmishing because one was less exposed to enemy fire—and possibly this was true, although, for one reason or another, most of the early Andrew's Sharpshooters did not survive the war. Late in the war, a wounded sniper told his skirmisher friend that he "wanted me to take his [target] rifle to use as that would keep me from the close hardest fighting and most dangerous places." The skirmisher declined the offer, but soon was trying to buy his own target rifle, saying, "If I got me a good gun . . . [it] will save me a great deal of hard duty." He explained, "There were many of these rifles in our battalion [at the siege of Petersburg], but they were so clumsy that they could not be handled quickly and the men that had them were not expected to go up close as the rest of us were or as they used to express it, 'Take a front seat.' We with the Spencers [repeating rifles] were always shoved right up on the front line."[57]

Then there was the leadership style of Saunders himself. Sharpshooting reputedly attracted independent-minded men who wanted to fight without being under the constant supervision of an officer. Bicknell strongly praised Saunders for his "rooted aversion to all salutes, drills and parades," adding "he meant to have none of that about him."[58] Andrew's Sharpshooters were thus to be an elite body of snipers—more independent, better paid, and better treated than common infantrymen. The first company filled rapidly.

By early September 1861, approximately two hundred prospective snipers had gathered at Camp Schouler (named in honor of the Massachusetts adjutant general) in Lynnfield, a small town about eight miles west of Salem and twelve miles north of Boston. They assembled at a former racetrack, whose "level field made an admirable camping place, and afforded ample room for drilling."[59] Captain Saunders, one private noted, "meant to have a company of picked men mainly of American birth, good shots and good fellows."[60] Perhaps mindful of the weight of the target rifles, Saunders also carefully sought men who were unusually strong and sturdy. Moses Hill of East Medway, the seventy-sixth man to sign the company's roll in August, boasted to his wife: "A better Company never went into the Army. The Smartist & largest lot of men I never saw. We have a good meny men that weigh over two hundred pounds and some are six to six 3 in. high."[61]

The 107 Andrew's Sharpshooters who traveled south in September 1861 were distinctive in other ways as well. One nineteenth-century writer observed, "An older average age obtained in this company, it having special attractions for 'old gunners.' "[62] But the age difference was not large: whereas the average age of Union soldiers was twenty-five, with the largest age group between eighteen and twenty years (together accounting for over 36 percent of enlisted men), the First Andrew's Sharpshooters' average age was almost twenty-seven, with those between eighteen and twenty making up only 15 percent of the company. More than a third were thirty or older, including two officers in their fifties.[63]

The sharpshooters were also more urban and industrial than the average Union recruit. All but seven lived within a thirty-five-mile radius of Boston. Of the thirty Massachusetts communities that contributed sharpshooters, most were small to medium-sized towns. For example, Lowell, Lynn, and Stoneham—all cities with a heavy factory presence—accounted for nearly one-third of the recruits. And while 48 percent of Union Army soldiers listed farming as their occupation, only 13 percent of Andrew's Sharpshooters did so. Out of thirty-four sharpshooter occupations, skilled crafts, factory work, and unskilled nonfarm labor predominated.[64] Nearly 30 percent were shoemakers or bootmakers, most of whom had worked in the mills of Lowell, Lynn, and Stoneham. Finally, 15 percent of the sharpshooters had white-collar occupations, including six clerks, a lawyer, a publisher, several manufacturers and storekeepers, and even one "artist."[65]

Having filled their company quota of a hundred men by mid-August 1861, the Andrew's Sharpshooters departed for Washington, D.C., on September 3. They left behind at Camp Schouler many eager and qualified recruits, 102 of whom mustered into the Second Company Massachusetts Sharpshooters. By October 8, armed with target rifles, they too boarded railroad cars for the journey south. Captain Lewis Wentworth, a tinsmith from Salem (and quite possibly a friend of Captain Saunders), headed the Second Company, which was attached to the Twenty-Second Massachusetts Regiment for all three years of their enlistment.[66]

The first company of Andrew's Sharpshooters began as part of the Twentieth Massachusetts Regiment under the command of Brigadier General Frederick West Lander, who was born into a prosperous Salem family in 1821. Lander's biographer summed him up as "the prototype of the nineteenth-century American hero."[67] Another historian notes that "by 1861 he had garnered fame as a western surveyor, railroad engineer, Indian fighter, soldier-poet, and husband of the noted actress Jean Margaret Davenport."[68] One Massachusetts soldier termed Lander "a fine, dashing officer with horse to match." Colonel William R. Lee of the Twentieth Massachusetts Infantry said of him, "General L. is a frank soldier-like man, agreeable—very much so— . . . kind in his disposition, *but a man who will be obeyed.*"[69] Oliver Wendell Holmes (later a well-known member of the U.S. Supreme Court), a lieutenant in the same regiment, reported that most regarded him as "a first rate man."[70] And most described the tall, strapping, and handsome Lander as bold, aggressive, and fearless, the sort of general who preferred to lead from the front, a "daring officer, regardless of danger, and glorying in the strife when hottest around him."[71] He proved widely popular with his soldiers, and the Northern press lionized him early in the war.

General Lander was to the Andrew's Sharpshooters what Colonel Berdan was to his two regiments of marksmen: patron, protector, and promoter. While Berdan decided to use most of his men as skirmishers armed with Sharps rifles, Lander—an old Indian fighter and student of quasi-guerilla warfare—was attracted to the idea of having a sniper unit armed with target rifles.[72] He coveted the Andrew's Sharpshooters for his new brigade. He also enjoyed influential and useful connections in both Massachusetts and Washington in the summer of 1861. Although originally Governor Andrew had decreed that the Massachusetts sharpshooters would join one of Berdan's U.S.S.S. regiments, Lander was "an old time friend of Capt. Saunders" and knew Governor Andrew too, and he quickly and successfully lobbied to add the Andrew's Sharpshooters as an independent company under his own command.[73] By mid-September they and the rest of Lander's brigade—the Nineteenth and Twentieth Massachusetts Infantry, the Seventh Michigan Infantry, and a battery of First Rhode Island Light Artillery—assembled just outside Poolesville, Maryland, near the Potomac River and about thirty miles north of Washington, D.C. Here they served as part of General Charles P. Stone's Corps of Observation to help monitor Confederate activity on the Virginia side of the river.

General Lander sought to define an effective role for his sniper company; his biographer writes that he "reveled in the possibilities the sharpshooters offered with their long-range accuracy, their skills as artisans, and the strength and endurance locked within their large-framed bodies." Because he recognized that their target rifles could not be fitted with bayonets but still wanted the men to be ready for fighting in close quarters as well as from long distances, he also lobbied hard to have them equipped with Colt revolvers.[74] Andrew's Sharpshooters eventually accompanied Lander on an ambitious and unusual winter campaign in the mountains of northwestern Virginia to put General Thomas "Stonewall" Jackson to flight. In March 1862, however, Lander succumbed to an old, festering leg wound, leaving the men "orphaned." Bereft of their famous, enthusiastic, and powerful patron, Andrew's Sharpshooters would thereafter be shifted from one indifferent—or even hostile—commander to the next.[75]

Four Snipers

Of the four members of Andrew's Sharpshooters represented in this book, two—Moses Hill and Luke Bicknell—left long and detailed accounts of their first year in action. The writings of the other two men, Ferdinand Crossman and Egbert Hixon, though scantier, still yield valuable details about the sharpshooters' experiences in the war. In fact, Crossman's letters constitute the only available personal writings left by an Andrew's Sharpshooter for the period after July 1863.

Moses Hill

A stonemason and a settled married man with two children, Moses Hill was thirty-eight years old when he enlisted. The son of Moses Hill Sr. and Persis (Phipps) Hill, Moses was born March 22, 1823, in Bellingham, Massachusetts, a small town about twenty miles southwest of Boston. His father moved to the adjacent community of Medway, where the U.S. Census enumerator in 1850 listed his occupation as "stone mason" as well.[76] After his death in July 1855, the elder Hill's probate inventory suggested other skills. He owned a small sixteen-acre farm, stocked with a horse, a cow, two pigs, and a flock of chickens. In the barn—along with a plow, harnesses, a wagon, hay, and stonecutter's tools—lay carpenter's tools, iron bars, and blacksmith's bellows. Small amounts of crops were enumerated, including corn, potatoes, squash, and pumpkins, as well as the humble tin, wooden, and earthen bowls and plates on which they were served. In all, the probate inventory suggests that the younger Moses grew up in comfortable but modest circumstances. His father bequeathed all of his property to his wife, Persis. His main legacy to his son was the art of stonecutting and masonry.[77]

The younger Moses set up a small shop near his home, where he did stonecutting for a local clientele. Some of his work was for the funeral trade. In his letters to his wife, Eliza, he mentioned his skill at designing and lettering gravestones, for instance, and also instructed his wife about the sale of his "herse." But Medway was too small—just over 3,100 inhabitants in 1860—to provide steady income from his trade, so he was obliged to travel elsewhere for short-term contracts. Sometimes he had to be away from his family for weeks at a time.[78] By the time of the war, Moses and Eliza were therefore accustomed to a degree of separation.

The sixty-three Civil War letters written by Moses to his wife, his mother, and his two children (Lucina, or "Sis," and George, or "Bub") span the period of his enlistment in September 1861 to his hospitalization in Washington, D.C., a year later. Except for a few worried letters sent to him at the army hospital, none of his wife's wartime correspondence survives. While Moses urged his wife to save his letters, he confided that he destroyed hers—because he did not want to risk having them fall into enemy hands. Eliza also saved a number of letters from their courtship and early marriage, which allow at least a brief glimpse of their relationship and day-to-day routines before the war.

Hill counted himself a serious Christian, and comes across as a quiet man troubled by the bloody conflict in which he finds himself. His letters are plainspoken and bear all the grammatical and spelling defects of a man with a limited public school education. His voice is that of a steady and mature small-town skilled artisan. Moses described a good deal about camp life, marches, fellow sharpshooters, and officers, and his letters constitute the only detailed source for the activities of Andrew's Sharpshooters during the unit's 1862 winter campaign in northwestern Virginia. He was sparing, however, with descriptions of battles, perhaps to keep Eliza from worrying about him. And apart from brief complaints about the use of profanity among the rank and file, Moses revealed little about the more high-spirited behavior—including drinking and gambling—of some of his comrades, possibly to protect their reputations back home in Massachusetts.[79] Captain Saunders ultimately promoted him to corporal.

Luke Emerson Bicknell

Another Andrew's Sharpshooter, Luke Emerson Bicknell, also left detailed descriptions of his service. Born October 27, 1839, in Windsor, a small town of under nine hundred inhabitants in the hills of western Massachusetts, Luke was the only son of Loring and Mary (Pierce) Bicknell. His father was a moderately successful farmer, with real estate worth $1,000 in 1860, and employed a farm laborer and a female domestic servant. It is likely that he (like most farmers in the area) raised cattle for market and kept a dairy. Because Windsor had been bypassed by a new railroad, its economy was languishing, so Loring probably did not expect his son to follow in his footsteps. In any case, young Luke would seek his opportunity far beyond the Berkshire Hills.[80]

At fifteen, Luke moved to Boston and for several years worked in a clothing store, a printing office, and a bookbindery. He next attended Hinsdale Academy, located near his hometown of Windsor, then taught at a public school for a single term. In June 1860, the U.S. Census enumerator found him living at home with his parents and listed his occupation as "scholar." Later that year he moved to Chelsea, just outside of Boston, "to prepare himself to enter Harvard College the following year."[81] But the outbreak of war in April 1861 changed his plans. "A man of strong and decided convictions," on April 16, 1861, Luke immediately enlisted in the Eighth Massachusetts Infantry (nicknamed "The Minutemen of '61") for a three-month tour of duty. (The federal government expected the war to be short.) He volunteered again after his discharge from the Eighth Massachusetts in August, this time joining Andrew's Sharpshooters, and rose quickly from private to sergeant to lieutenant.[82]

The letters Luke sent home to his sweetheart, Lucretia Pierce, a schoolteacher in Windsor, have survived. Among other things, they provide details about the Andrew's Sharpshooters that Luke did not mention in a memoir he wrote many years after the war. Luke wrote the memoir, he said, out of a sense of duty to his comrades, and completed the final draft in early March 1883, in the quiet Hampshire County village of West Cummington, Massachusetts, not far from where he was born.[83] The memoir lacks the sense of immediacy of his wartime letters to Lucretia, but it remains an invaluable source on many of the military actions of Andrew's Sharpshooters up to the summer of 1863. He is also a little more forthcoming in the memoir than in his letters about some of the mischief committed by several of the younger sharpshooters.

Luke noted at the beginning of his memoir that it was difficult to remember much of what he would have wanted to include about his fellow sharpshooters: "When I came to undertake the task I found that I had forgotten so much that I must needs make the narrative as personal as it is." Thus much of his memoir focuses on his own actions—especially his performance as an officer in battle situations. Possibly because the passage of time contributed a romantic aura to his recollections, he presents himself as a bold and somewhat dashing officer, and passes lightly over the drudgery, dirt, and diseases the sharpshooters endured. Nor does he say much about the painful personal losses he suffered in the war. For example, although his good friend, George Whittemore Jr.—a Harvard College graduate and lawyer from Gloucester—died in battle in 1862, Luke wrote but two brief sentences marking his death.[84]

Both Luke's memoir and his letters to Lucretia reveal his idealism, aggressiveness—and sometimes rashness—during the war. After a mere two months in the service, he confidently remarked, "I do not think I was born to be shot." And he was not shy about giving several generals and the governor of Massachusetts his advice. For example, during the 1862 Peninsula Campaign in Virginia, Luke seems to have petitioned the Army of the Potomac's commander, General George McClellan (without the knowledge or consent of the Andrew's Sharpshooters officers), proposing major changes to his company's mission. An 1863 incident also suggests his aggressiveness. Luke was a candidate for lieutenant, but newly arrived sharpshooter recruits expressed concern over his possible promotion, saying he was too fond of "action" and too "inclined to take great risks in a fight." And Luke did not deny their charges: "I had brought in more wounded men, and got out of more tight scrapes, than any other man who had been entrusted to lead."[85] Then there was the Battle of Antietam in 1862, when Luke was grievously wounded. Although he could easily have qualified for a discharge, after a brief furlough (during which he married Lucretia), he insisted on returning to his company. Luke remained on active duty until the pain from his old wounds made it impossible for him to keep up with the army any longer, and he left for home with the rank of second lieutenant in July 1863.

Ferdinand Joseph Fuller Crossman

Two other Andrew's Sharpshooters left briefer and less detailed accounts. One was Ferdinand J. F. Crossman, born on April 22, 1834, the only child of Martin L. and Experience (Robbins) Crossman in the small Worcester County village of South Sutton. His mother died shortly after his birth, and his father gave him to Ferdinand's grandparents, Stephen and Susan Crossman, to raise. Ferdinand eventually inherited much of his grandfather's large holdings, for the 1860 U.S. Census recorded him as a farmer with $2,000 in real estate. He married Vermont-born Adelaide Isham in 1855, and by 1860 their household included two children, ages one and three.[86] Brief entries in a diary kept by Ferdinand and Adelaide from 1855 on reveal two very busy young parents. In addition to her household and childcare duties, Adelaide sewed garments to sell. Ferdinand supplemented his farm income by hauling timber to local sawmills, chopping and delivering firewood, and, in the winter, cutting and delivering blocks of ice from a nearby pond.[87]

Ferdinand enlisted August 10, 1862—one of about forty men raised to supplement the dwindling ranks of the Andrew's Sharpshooters' original 1861 volunteers. Two neighbors, twenty-three-year-old Chilon Houghton, a gunsmith and fellow farmer, and Ferdinand's close friend, twenty-six-year-old Lysander Martin, the only child of aging parents, enlisted with him. Martin and Ferdinand became tentmates, and Martin quickly became one of the most popular men in Andrew's Sharpshooters—"a general favorite," as Luke Bicknell put it.[88]

About fifty letters that Ferdinand wrote home to his wife, "Adda," from mid-June 1863 to early May 1864 survive. His letters pick up where Luke Bicknell's memoir leaves off, and are the only sharpshooter's source that details the actions of the company to nearly the end of their tour of duty in 1864. These letters, written in a large, heavy, energetic (and at times nearly illegible) script, reveal a somewhat higher level of education than Moses Hill's. Unfortunately, however, many of them contain only a few details about camp life or combat. For example, although Ferdinand fought at Fredericksburg, at Gettysburg, and at the Battle of the Wilderness, he wrote only a few short lines about his experiences in those engagements. And because illness kept him away from the company for extended periods, his account is not continuous. Even so, he does effectively communicate how the men of Andrew's Sharpshooters viewed their role late in their three-year tour of duty, and describes some of the company's later movements in Virginia and Maryland. Ferdinand's pen was stilled in May 1864 when he was captured by Confederate soldiers at the Battle of Spotsylvania Court House and shipped to Andersonville Prison in Georgia.

Egbert Oswald Hixon

The fourth sharpshooter represented here is Egbert Oswald Hixon, born August 1, 1824, to Isaac and Persis (Adams) Hixon of West Medway, Massachusetts. The family patriarch, Isaac (born in 1762), had fought in the American Revolution, and no doubt his nine sons and one daughter grew up on stories of his military exploits. Isaac lived until 1849, when at least one-half of his farm was sold at auction. His wife likely continued to live in the family home, perhaps helped by one of her older sons. In any case, Egbert received no land and only $50 from the land sale.[89] He thus faced a choice common among the offspring of eastern Massachusetts farmers at the time: move away or find employment as a wage earner in manufacturing. Egbert (and other younger members of the large and growing Hixon clan) took a job in one of the bootmaking factories established in Medway in the 1830s. By 1860 he had his own rapidly growing family that included his wife, Electa Louise (Morrill), and five children ranging in age from one to eleven.

Egbert's descendants remembered him as "a church man, singing bass in the Congregational Church at Medway. It is said that he was faithful to the last, singing in the church choir and doing his church duties on the Sunday before he started for war."[90] But he must have been hard-pressed to support six dependents on a bootmaker's wages. When the 1860 census enumerator visited the Hixon home, he left blank the spaces on the form that reported the value of real estate and personal property for the household.[91]

Immediately after the Confederate attack on Fort Sumter, Egbert joined the rush to enlist in three-month regiments. On April 15, 1861, he joined Company D of the Eighth Massachusetts Regiment. Since this was a light infantry company, he likely received intensive training in marksmanship and skirmish

Figure 4. Members of Company D, Eighth Massachusetts Infantry. Egbert Hixon is seated
second from the left. Courtesy of John Robinson.

tactics, skills that later would have made him an attractive recruit to Andrew's
Sharpshooters. In fact, Egbert was one of eighteen members of the Eighth
Massachusetts—including Luke Bicknell—who went on to join the sharp-
shooter company when their enlistments expired in early August.

Egbert's hometown of Medway provided what support it could to the
families of its men who left to serve in the war. His wife received $395, for
example, and Moses Hill's was given $330. That this aid plus a private's pay
(often woefully delayed) was not enough is indicated by the men's occasional
expressions of anxiety over whether those at home had enough food and fuel.
At one point in 1864, during his later service as an Ohio infantryman, Egbert
even described for his wife a telling and poignant dream of plenty he had one
night: "I done a great deal of managing for you. I bought you a store & a lot of
coal & wood & beef & pork & everything that you can think of almost. When
I woke up the sun was up high."[92]

In addition to Egbert's letters home after his service with Andrew's Sharpshooters, he kept a diary for a short time while he was with the company.

From March to August 1862—a period covering most of the Peninsula Campaign in Virginia—he jotted brief daily entries about the weather, the company's marches, and his activities. Except for a few terse but significant lines, the diary's main value is in tracing the company's movements during the campaign. Nine letters Egbert wrote home in 1864 also yield a few insights into his Civil War military experiences.

Several of Moses Hill's letters mention Hixon. They were the only "Medway Boys" in the sharpshooter company, and the thirty-five-year-old Egbert and thirty-eighty-year-old Moses would have been viewed as "old gunners." The two marched together and sometimes shared a tent, and their writings help shed light on the experiences of both. For example, although Moses typically did not mention his comrade's behavior (such as his occasional drinking and gambling) in his letters home, he did write that Egbert was very worried about his wife, Louise, whom he sometimes called his "little blue eyed darling wife." Egbert's worries over his wife's finances and poor health may help account for his desertion in early September 1862. His descendants also say that he himself was seriously ill (possibly with malaria) at the time. But, ever protective, Moses never mentioned Egbert's departure. In any case, Egbert somehow traveled to Cleveland, where his wife had taken work in her sister's millinery shop, changed his name to Egbert Hicks, and in 1863 enlisted to serve three years with the 124th Ohio Regiment.[93] Apparently, then, he did not desert Andrew's Sharpshooters out of fear of being wounded or killed.

From Sniper to Skirmisher

After serving for about a year, both the First and Second Company Massachusetts Sharpshooters were transformed from snipers into skirmishers. Over their bitter protests, they were armed with Sharps rifles—the same weapons that were carried by Berdan's Sharpshooters. By the end of 1862, virtually all of the recruitment promises Captain John Saunders had made to his sharpshooters were broken. They never received their extra pay. Those who brought their personal target rifles to war were never compensated. They were forced to perform ordinary infantry chores such as marching drills and picket duty. They also eventually lost their status as an independent company and were attached to a regular infantry regiment. In the Second Company, the snipers experienced even worse treatment. For instance, they were sometimes ordered to help construct entrenchments, shouldering shovels and axes instead of target rifles. As one private complained about such so-called fatigue-duty, "[I] am sorry to say that the 2nd Co Mass Sharpshooters were ordered to take shovels and go into the trenches with infantry which seemed to be very far from what we enlisted for."[94] And after the men of the sharp-shooter companies were forced to give up their target rifles, they soon found that they were no longer "free from duty in line of battle." In 1862 the Second Company sharpshooters received bayonets for their newly issued Sharps rifles, and were ordered to take part in bayonet drill—which prompted one of them to remark, "It appears that we are gradually being brought down to infantry tactics altho' we had the promise that our duty would be no different than it was before taking these new arms." The men protested by boycotting bayonet drill for several days.[95]

By September 1862, both sharpshooter companies had been "brought down" to the level of ordinary infantry. Although the Andrew's Sharpshooters understood the significance of the forced change from sniper to skirmisher, their writings do not dwell at great length on the transformation. They seem to have simply shouldered their new rifles and grimly resigned themselves to their new, more ordinary, and more dangerous form of fighting. In the end, only one of them wrote of the cost in blood these changes entailed.

Ironically, as the Union army reduced its commitment to snipers armed with telescoped rifles, the Confederacy gradually moved to augment theirs. The Confederate army increasingly deployed "true sniper detachments which delivered fire at extreme ranges." Their weapon of choice was the expensive, finely crafted, lightweight (10 pounds) English-made Whitworth muzzle-loading rifle, fitted with a telescope and accurate up to a thousand yards or more. Toward the end of the war, the Whitworth, equipped with a telescopic sight, became "the war's best sniper rifle." At least one firearms expert strongly urged the Union army to likewise adopt the Whitworths, but they never did.[96] Instead, Union commanders increasingly used their elite marksmen as quasi-infantry, a function scorned by pure snipers.

By the time Andrew's Sharpshooters mustered out of service in September and October 1864, they had seen significant action in the eastern theater of the Civil War. They had served in the ill-fated Peninsula Campaign of 1862 and fought at Antietam, Fredericksburg, Gettysburg, the Wilderness, Spotsylvania Court House, and Cold Harbor, among other battlefields. The few early recruits still in the ranks in 1864 were hardened and cynical men who impatiently counted the weeks and days remaining in their three-year enlistments. One was the South Sutton farmer, Ferdinand Crossman. When the issue of reenlistment of the "three-year men" arose in 1864, Ferdinand wrote to his wife, "I shall re-enlist if I am *Drunk* or crazy!"[97] Of the more than two hundred men who volunteered, only thirty-two returned to New England in the fall of 1864. Of these, fewer than twenty "survived their service with Andrew's Sharpshooters completely unscathed from start to finish."[98]

Editor's Note

Luke Bicknell's memoir was the product of a well-educated man with the leisure to carefully craft his narrative. His letters to his fiancée, Lucretia, were similarly well written. Neither source needed much editing. The same was not the case for Moses Hill, Egbert Hixon, and Ferdinand Crossman. These men often had to write in haste under unfavorable conditions—while sitting on the ground or a stump, often with only a knapsack or cracker box for a writing surface. The men also tried to squeeze as much as they could onto their small sheets of stationery, sometimes writing in the margins. Their cramped and hurried lines also lack paragraphing or punctuation. And since they had only received a brief common-school education, their writing is full of misspellings and awkward grammar.

I have left the prose of all four soldiers as close to the original as possible, but have added paragraphing, punctuation, and capitalization where needed for the sake of clarity. I have also corrected misspellings that might confuse the reader, such as when the word "of" is used for "off," "to" for "too," "here" for "hear," or "there" for "their." In cases where names of people or places are misspelled (for example, "General Macleland" instead of "General McClellan"), I have corrected the spelling as well. But except for a few rare instances where the wording might create confusion, I have left the men's grammar alone. Finally, I have left some sections of letters entirely uncorrected. For instance, when Moses Hill describes a battle or foxhunt, I decided that the sense of the breathless rush of events would be better conveyed by his sprawling run-on sentences. More generally, then, in order to preserve the quirkiness and distinctiveness of each sharpshooter's voice, I have tried to minimize editorial corrections and intrusions as much as possible.

BEFORE

In peace her sails fleck all the seas,
Her mills shake every river;
And where are scenes so fair as these
God and her true hands give her?

—Robert Lowell, "The Massachusetts Line" (1861)

Prewar writings by two of the four Andrew's Sharpshooters, Ferdinand Crossman (a farmer) and Moses Hill (a skilled stonecutter) have survived and give us brief glimpses into their everyday routines. Later, as Civil War soldiers, both men would express strong preferences for the role of the sniper over that of a skirmisher or common infantryman. Of course, these men are but two out of the dozens who served. But the normality of their lives clearly helps counter the notion that snipers were often aloof, antisocial loners. Both Ferdinand and Moses had extensive and active networks of kin and friends—people who would later provide moral support, clothing, cakes, pies, and sometimes medicine to the men off fighting in Virginia.

Ferdinand and Adelaide Crossman

The Crossman house is a long, low late eighteenth-century structure that still stands near the bottom of a shallow dale in South Sutton in Worcester County. The clear stream just below it likely helped attract the first settlers. Although the house faces south to maximize sunlight, its low setting somewhat darkens it. And four massive hemlock trees that once stood in front no doubt further shadowed the area. As was customary in New England with its

Figure 5. Crossman house. Oil painting, c. 1900. Courtesy of Helen Van Dyke.

severe winters, the barn nestled close by, twenty or so steps from the house. The farm also had a hop house—a tall, barnlike building equipped with a kiln to dry the bitter herbal ingredients so necessary for preserving beer and ale.[1]

By midcentury, this farm where Ferdinand Crossman was raised by his grandparents was large and moderately prosperous. In 1851 its owner, his grandfather Stephen, died a lingering death from "consumption" (tuberculosis), and seventeen-year-old Ferdinand took over. He became part owner in 1854, and full owner in 1856 after his grandmother died.[2] His father, Martin Crossman, had long since remarried and moved to a farm in Vermont. No doubt Ferdinand met young Adelaide Isham during one of his visits there. In any case, "Ferd" and "Adda," as they called one another, married in the spring of 1855. By the time of the war, they had a one-hundred-acre farm valued at over $1,700, two horses, seven cows and calves, and one pig.[3]

The couple's brief diary entries for 1855 and 1857 yield reveal the daily and seasonal farm routine in New England at mid-century. In addition to their farm and household chores, both Ferdinand and Adelaide did extra work to raise cash, partly to pay off debts but also to pay their hired farmhand, William Wright. Like other women who left home to marry men with farms in distant communities, Adelaide found herself relatively socially isolated. Except for rare visits by a younger sister, she was cut off from the female kin who normally would have provided emotional support and an occasional helping hand with children and housekeeping. Thus when Ferdinand went off to war, she was, as she often noted in her diary, "lonely."

Ferdinand's social network was broader and deeper. His uncle Milton lived less than a mile away, and Ferdinand often worked for him. The elder Crossman no doubt in turn loaned his young nephew one of his teams of stout oxen to do spring plowing and winter wood hauling. Ferdinand also occasionally exchanged labor with neighboring farmers.[4] Like many small-town and rural men at the time, Ferdinand did most of the shopping for his household. He even selected and bought kitchen items for his new bride by himself. Moreover, he harvested and sold timber, firewood, and ice—transactions that took him to neighboring towns, and even to the county seat of Worcester. Finally, having grown up in South Sutton, Ferdinand had many friends nearby, including his next-door neighbors Lysander Martin and Chilon Houghton, both of whom also enlisted in Andrew's Sharpshooters in the summer of 1862. The three men often went hunting in the rocky wooded hills, honing skills that later enabled them to qualify as expert riflemen.[5]

FERDINAND

January 1, 1855. Drawing [hauling] ice for Milton [Crossman]. Cash on hand $3.04. Paid postage [for] letter, 5 cts.

January 10. William & I chopped [wood].

January 12–13. Sold Jim Howell 2 oak trees. Chopped . . . Broke my axe.

January 30. Father is not quite as well today. He took cold.

January 31. Consent of Adalad & Parents to our [marriage]. Happiness.

February 15. [Hinesburg, Vermont] Father is much worse. I shall not go home [while] he Lives. He does not have his senses at all. He is going down! Down! Fast.

February 16. Father is dead and he died at 6 o clock this morning.

February 18. Milton came this morning. Father is buried today. Funeral 10 O'clock at House.

February 22. Finished sled & drawed 1 load wood.

February 24. Drawed wood. Sick.

March 6–7. Drawed out wood. Rced letter from Adelaide. Drawed wood.

March 20–21. Drawed out logs. Tried to fix wagon. Recd letter from Dear Adda.

March 22. Drawed logs to mill with Jonases oxen. Wrote Adda.

April 2. Started for Vt. 4 oclock. Arrived in Burlington 7 PM. Mr Isham there after me. Clasped my Dear Adda to my heart.

April 4 A.M. To A[delaide] Isham married By Rev H P Cutting at half past
  seven o'clock.

April 12. Got up at half past 3 oclock. Started for home. Arrive at Uncle
  Miltons at ½ 10 oclock.

April 14. Went to the store. Got a set of cruchery [crockery].

May 3–12. Finished plowing for oats & planted the garden. Sowed oats.
  William Wright harrowed. Sowing & Bushing Hay seed. Planting garden.
  Plowing for potatos.

May 13. A.M., [Sunday] [church] meeting . . .

June 21. Sick as Hell.

June 27–29. Bought wagon off John . . . for $60. Drawed 2 loads coal to
  Whitins.

July 4. Hunting.

ADELAIDE

November 17–29, 1855. William to work. Ferd [went] to mill. I went to Mrs
  C—Mrs Robbins is dead. Verry cold. Ferd making cider. I washed. Ferd
  drawed logs into the yard to here. I ironed. Eve. To the picknick. Snows.
  To Milton's to Thanksgiving.

FERDINAND

January 1, 1857. So. Sutton. The amount of debts outstanding are as follows:
  About one Hundred and Sixty Dollars due Laura Crossman for moneys
  borrowed to pay Debts against the estate which will be due Nov 1861. There
  is ten dollars and interest from Dec 1856 which I borrowed. There is a bill
  due P. F. Johnson, about 25 or 30 dollars. There is an unsettled account
  between I & Johnson, one between VS Head, between AF Goddard. Tim.
  Hewett. Jason. Bacheler. John Robbins & Milton Crossman.

ADELAIDE

January 2–5, 1857. Ferd & Milton drawing out wood . . . I sewing on Ferds
  vest. Baked & mopped . . . I washed & mopped. Ferd to the shop. I work
  on his coat.

January 23. Ferd is to shop. I finished Jess's pants $.40.

January 29. Ferd & Milton drawing wood.

February 9. A.M. Ferd got the pig home. I washed & mopped. Ferd trimmed
  apple trees.

February 24. A.M. Ferd & Daniel shooting to mark. Jane [her younger sister] & I ironed. I baked 4 apple pies.

March 5. A.M. Jane & I ironed. Made soup & baked pies. Ferd to work at hophouse.

March 6. A.M. Daniel & Ferd a hunting.

March 17. I am 20 today . . . I sick. [She was late in her first pregnancy]

June 27. I tried to stand on my feet. Mrs. Thompson [who helped her after she delivered her first child in May] went home.

July 14–16. I walked a line. I had on my dress [for the first time since giving birth].

July 22–24. I went out in to the kitchen. I sat up all day and mended some.

August 9–12. Ferd got in 3 loads of hay. Ferd mowed the peach orchard. P.M. Ferd made . . . hog pen. Raked up hay.

August 27. P.M. paid taxes $6.65 cts.

September 8. Ferd, Jane I & the Babe to Northbridge. Had a good time.

September 12. Ferd cutting Buckwheat for Houghton [a neighboring farmer].

November 19. Verry cold. Ferd making cider. I washed.

November 23–24. I to work on pants . . . I finished pants, $.87. Ferd fixed cellar stairs.

November 27–28. Ferd up in the woods to measure wood. I finished Bick's coate, $2.99.

Moses and Eliza Hill

Eliza Ann Arnold grew up on a large farm owed by her guardians, George and Kezia (Morse) Harding, not far from the village center of East Medway (now Millis), Massachusetts. Eliza and her twin sister, Rosina, were effectively orphaned when their mother, also named Rosina, died of "childbed fever" shortly after their birth in 1825. Their father, Nathan Arnold Sr., decided he could not keep the girls. As one relative wrote of him, "his ruling intention was to do right, Godward and manward," but he did poorly in business because of "shortcomings, which originated . . . in weakness of the flesh." Arnold placed Eliza with the Hardings in Medway.[6] The Hardings had only one child, Maria, of nearly the same age as Eliza, and they likely wanted a companion for their daughter. The two girls became close friends—"sisters"—and Eliza flourished as a beloved member of the Hardings' extensive kinship network. Still, her maternal uncle, the Reverend Adin Ballou, kept a watchful eye over her spiritual growth, and on occasion invited her to stay at Hopedale, the religious commune he founded in the early 1840s. Hopedale would have exposed Eliza to not only the widespread religious

doctrine of "perfectionism," but to the then radical ideas of antislavery, paci-
fism, equality of the sexes, and spiritualism (the belief that the living could
communicate with the dead).

The lean, rough-handed, sandy-haired, and gray-eyed stonecutter Moses
Hill came to court Eliza at the Hardings' home in East Medway in the

Figure 6. Moses Hill, c. 1855. MHS Photo Archives,
Massachusetts Historical Society.

mid-1840s. The two probably met at the town's Congregationalist church, where both were reputed to be good singers. He would find her at home in a spacious two-story, ten-room home on a rise overlooking broad fields of hay, corn, and timothy, and streams and large stands of trees. Fat swine, cows, and chickens crowded the barnyard near the big house. After the couple married in 1846, they lived with the Hardings in what must have been a bustling household. Both the 1850 and 1860 federal censuses list nine people—mostly relatives—living there, including Eliza's apparently hapless and often unemployed older brother, Nathan Arnold Jr.[7]

When Moses was home between stonecutting jobs, he likely helped with his father-in-law's farm work. He also cultivated a large vegetable garden of his own that yielded turnips, potatoes, cabbage, beans, and cucumbers for the table. In his spare time he fished with friends in ponds and the Charles River, or hunted small game in the woods close by. In the evening, he might take out his "fiddle" to entertain the folks at the Harding fireside. And, during quieter moments, he tried his hand at writing poetry. (His sister-in-law Maria once quipped: "Moses, why don't you write poetry for the papers and magazines? I think you would get three dollars a page.")[8] In mid-summer, the women of the household would go "a berrying," harvesting wild fruits that found their way into pies, preserves, and rustic berry wines. And when weather and time permitted, Moses and Eliza took their two children, Lucina ("Sis") and George ("Bub"), to neighboring West Medway to visit their doting widowed grandmother, Persis (Phipps) Hill, and her kin.[9] Thus when Moses went off to war in the fall of 1861, he could at least comfort himself with the thought that Eliza could rely on an extensive and supportive social network.

A handful of letters, many written while Moses was away on stonecutting jobs, reveal small fragments of their prewar lives.

ELIZA ARNOLD

Hopedale, Milford, Mass Dec 16th 1845

Dear friend,
I will improve the stillness of the evening by writing to you. My friends [are] all gone to a [religious] meeting but Luna. I came here on Friday. I arrived here after a ride of two hours that evening. We had a little party and I enjoyed myself very much. Sunday I went to meeting in the afternoon, and in the evening I went to Mr Drapers to sing. On Monday eve I went to a weding to Mr G Reedy. The couple that were married were Mr Grandin of Maine and Miss Leach. They have been staying here about a fortnight. They come up

here to be published here in Milford and have my Uncle [Adin Ballou] marry them because they did not want to be married by a proslavery minister. We passed a very pleasant evening. . . . I suppose by this time you want to have me write about my health which is very good. I have some cold but you know they are common with me. I have not made up my mind when I shall go to Mendon but I do not think I shall before next week. I think I shall come home by the last of next week. I wish you would write to me as soon as you would. Let Father and Mother Harding know how I am for Mother said she should want to hear from me and I told her I would let her know how I was. I have not much more to write and so I must bid you good night by saying,

> I am yours in the bonds of love
> and truth, and hope soon to be more firmly
> united by the bonds of matrimony until death
> shall part us for a short space of time, and
> then to meet in heaven, where we shall
> sing the songs of love, peace, and good will
> to man through the birth and death of our
> Savior.

I must now close for my fingers are tired

> This is from your true and ever faithful and loving friend,

Eliza A. Arnold

Moses Hill to Eliza Arnold, c. 1846

> "Miss Eliza A. Arnold"
> Oft have I met your fond embraces
> With hands in friendship joined;
> Oft has it thrilled my heart with bliss,
> Which cannot be defined.
> Your kindness on my heart I'll write
> Your friendship and your love;
> When I esteem such blessing light,
> Forget my heart to move.
> May friendships harmony and love,
> And every bliss be thine
> That heart can wish or life improve.
> It is the prayer of mine.
> And when at last as soon it must
> Be summoned to the tomb,

O! may we meet the blest
Clad in immortal bloom.[10]

Moses Hill

New Britain [Connecticut], October 17, 1849

Dear Eliza,

I came to New Britain the Day I left you. . . . I am well but have had very bad luck. I came back to Britain at night. Williams [his employer] and his wife boards to Judds. He paid me some money but not all. They could not let me have any more work. They have used me very mean. Monday I went to Collinsville. There is a very large Job and I let myself to cut Stone. By the job I think I can make 2 or 3 Dollars a day [for] about two months. Then I don't know but I shal go to the South as far as Virginia. I have had a great incorage-ment. Mr Prall said he would enshure me two Dollars and a half.

Tuesday. I came from Canton. There is where I am agoing to work. Wednesday. I am a settling up my business here and to night I expect to go to Canton after the Wedding. Mr Judd is agoing to be married to night. He said he would give 5 dollars if you were here. If you was, we should have to stand up. He is agoing to ask about Eighty to the wedding. . . .

I want to hear from you as soon as you get this letter. Direct your letter to Canton. I am agoing to board with the post master. It is about 15 miles from here and about 13 miles from Hartford. I inclose 15 Dollars in this letter for you and I want you to pay Mr. Hall 5 of it and then pay my taxes. I shall have some more soon I expect. I do not owe any one more and I hope I shal get it. I have walked a great meny miles since I came here. You will hear from me again soon. Rite as soon as you get this.

Kiss Sis for me and put your trust in God. That is the way I do. My love to you.

Canton, Sunday November 4, 1849

Dear Wife,

I received your letter last Eve and was very glad to hear that you and Sis was well. I was rather unwell 2 Days last week so I did not work. I had a bad cold settled in my bones but I took a sweat and soon got well again. Now I am well. I have not made so much this last week as I did the week before. The man I work for said he would give me $1.75 to work by the day, and if I cannot make so much by the piece I shall work by the day. I wish you were here to Eat Beefsteake with me and roast Beaf and other living in proportion.

I think you was very prudent in your letter in regard to spending money. I hope you will get what you nead for yourself and Sis too. If you go a visiting I hope you will be very prudent of your health and not get sick. . . .

If I go South I think I shal not want you to make much more clothes for me. If I need any thing it will be 2 shirts and one or two pair of overhals. You can make me two shirts if you have time. I shal not stay with you long when I come home if I go off. I shal stop to Springfield and see if I can let myself. If I do, I shal go to Richmond where Thomas has gone. There is an office in Springfield where they hire stone workmen. If they hire men they pay half of the expenses on. If I can Engage myself for 2 Dollars or $2.50 and half my fare paid, don't you think it will be best for you and me if I should go? He said ordanary men got $2.50 a day in Richmond, but I can feel better after I see some of the Company. If you are very much aposed to my going I shal not go. I think I shal get through in 3 or 4 weeks more here.

I enclose $5 in this letter, and if you go to Fathers you may pay William Clark 5 Dollars and pay Abijah Fales one Dollar. I expect to have more money the 15th day of this month and I shal send home some more. . . . I hope I shall receive another letter from you this week. It is a very great consolation to me to hear from you.

Cordaville, June 24, 1860

Dear Wife,

I don't know but you think it strange I have not wrote you before, but I thought I would not write because I did not know but I should come home today and yesterday I thought I would not come home until next Sunday or the fourth of July. If the men will work the fourth I shal come next Sunday, but if not I shal come the fourth I think. I want to see you & Sis & I want to see Bub and have a good play with him. I hope you are all well. I have erned over ten Dollars this last week besides my board. I have a very hard job here now and I think it will last all the season. I have had only 4 men last week, but I shal have 6 this week. . . . I went down to a mill below here this morning and this afternoon I have been up to the next village with the Agent. And last night and this morning I read the ledger so I have had my mind taken up very well. I don't know as I can write any more to interest you, so now for home.

I want you to get some one to set out them Cabage & turnip plants if they will not do until I come home, if the garden wants howing and the beds thind out if Nathan [Eliza's brother] cannot get home if you think best. I want you or Sis to write as soon as you get this. I want to know how you all do and have been since I left and how you get along for monay. . . .

From your Dearest friend and Father husband, M Hill

LUCINA HILL

[East Medway] Saturday Morn, August 10, 1860

Dear Father,

Mother and Bub went with Aunt Maria to Boston this morning in the seven oclock train. I am glad she is gorn for she has not been to Boston before since Aunt Maria has lived there. I shal have to keep house for Uncle Nathan while mother is at Boston. . . . Grandmother [Harding], Hattie and I went a berrying. I got enough to make some pies and have some berrys and milk. The garden looks nice. I think I shall have a nice time whilst mother is gorn. I suppose that she expects you down Saturday night. I have done all the baking and had good luck. Mother changed your neck hankerchief and got you half of a black silk one. Grandfather has got most done haying. We have had all the cucumbers we wanted to eat off one vine. I don't think of much more to write now. You must let us know how your foot is. Write to us. We send our love. Georgie got your miniture yesterday and red paper. We are all well, and hope this will find you so.

Excuse bad writing. Your affectionate daughter, Lucina

ELIZA HILL

Medway, September 22, 1860

Dear Husband,

You have expected a letter before this but I have had a good deal to do to get Lucina ready to go to Boston. She went Friday in the cars. It rained so hard father did not go. He is agoing next week the fore part. I received the money you sent Wednesday.

I went a barberrying Monday. I got three pecks. I have made the elderberry wine & had two gallons sugar and all. I think it will be nice. It has begun to work [ferment]. Aunt Polly Harding came here last Monday night and staid until Wednesday night. She thought Georgie was real cunning and smart. He is very well now. . . .

There is nothing new here. Georgie says papa all gone. I asked him if he loved me the other day. He said papa, papa all gone.

Your faithful wife EAH

My best love is yours always, EAH

CHAPTER

CAMP BENTON

Generals McClellan and Lander, and the whole war department, were in a tearing hurry to hear our mighty rifles ringing at the front.

—Luke Emerson Bicknell, 1883

"I Am Agoing"

In early September 1861, Andrew's Sharpshooters boarded railroad cars in Boston for their journey south to Washington. They camped briefly on the outskirts of the city, and then marched over thirty miles to Poolesville, Maryland, to join General Charles P. Stone's Corps of Observation. The snipers were, as a private in the Fifteenth Massachusetts Regiment put it, a "great curiosity." He wrote home: "I talked with one of the men a few minits, he told me that he could hit a man every time at half a mile and every other time at the distance of a mile. His rifle weighed 36 lbs."[1]

The sharpshooters were attached to the Twentieth Massachusetts Regiment (called the "Harvard Regiment" for the large number of officers with connections to that university). Their new home would be Camp Benton, Brigadier General Lander's headquarters two miles west of Poolesville and one mile from the Potomac River. Their connection to the Twentieth Massachusetts, however, did not last long. The Twentieth's Colonel Raymond Lee soon requested that the "Andrew Sharpshooters [be] detached from the Twentieth . . . because they would not submit to the discipline insisted on by him. They had enlisted as a separate company and thought they were to be simply sharpshooters, and to be, therefore, exempt from discipline and restraint."[2]

Camp Benton, as one historian notes, "offered a broad, level plain of some four hundred yards of relatively flat land that gradually sloped upward to form two small hills. . . . Behind the hills was Broad Run, a small stream with good water."[3] It was sparsely settled country, with plentiful woods and game, and a fine view of the Blue Ridge Mountains in the distance. Nonetheless, an increasing number of recruits sickened and sometimes died of typhoid, malaria, measles, dysentery, diarrhea, and other nameless "camp diseases" or "camp fevers." To the surprise of many, men from rural areas died at a higher rate than the presumably more sickly men from cities during the "seasoning" process at Camp Benton. Of course, urbanites had had more exposure to contagious diseases and thus had more immunity than those who lived in more isolated settings. Nathan Travis—a farmer—was the first sharpshooter to die in the first month of camp life.[4]

At Camp Benton, too, the Massachusetts men experienced their first contact with slaves and "Secesh"—citizens loyal to the Confederacy.

Moses Hill's letters to his wife, Eliza, and Luke Bicknell's letters to his fiancée, Lucretia, as well as Bicknell's 1883 memoir, detail the men's camp experience and training.

MOSES HILL

Boston, August 22, 1861

Dear Wife,
I have joined the company of Sharp Shooters. My name makes 76. The Company is not organized yet. I should [have] come home last night but the Captain wanted me to be there this morning for the Govener was coming out there to see us shoot. The Company is at Lynnfield. I went out there yesterday and stayed with James [Bickford—his brother-in-law].[5] I am agoing back at 7½ oclock this morning. I shall come home this week, I think. I wish Hiram Kingsbury was there to morrow. I think he would get a chance. It is the best chance he will have. I think I can shoot as well as any of them.

LUKE BICKNELL

Sunday Morning Aug 20 [1861] Letter No. I

Dear Lucretia,
My first letter is to you, of course. I am now in E. Boston at Mothers. Only for today though. I arrived at Boston at 12 o'clock that night after I left you at the depot. Stayed at a hotel overnight and in the morning started for Lynfield where the 19th and 17th regiments were in camp. . . .

I have joined the *Sharp Shooters*. Perhaps you may have heard of them. They expect to receive double the pay that other soldiers do. I happen to be a good shot, so they took me. We use rifles weighing from twenty to forty pounds and expect to leave as soon as our uniforms and arms are ready. I like the company. They are all fine fellows.

Figure 7. Moses Hill, c. 1861. MHS Photo Archives, Massachusetts Historical Society.

I had a chance to go [as] Sargeant of a company in the 19th, but there were too many Irishmen in it to suit me. I think I can do better to go with this company. We shall probably stay at Lynfield this week. This place is only 9 miles from Boston. Everything suits me so far.

It is a beautiful day. I expected last Sunday surely to be with you today. I wish I was at your house now. Yes, I wish I had my arms around you and was kissing you this moment. My visit, short as it was, has shown me what a true hearted girl you are and made me doubly anxious to see you again soon.

I saw you look at me a while as the cars moved away from the depot, as if you thought surely that I certainly should be shot and that you never should see me again, and then before I was out of sight, you turned quickly away. I thought perhaps it was to hide the tears. I am sure that was the case with me. It seemed as if I must jump off the cars and kiss you once more. My heart ached all the way to Boston, and I felt like going back.

I did not know before how hard it would be to part with you. I am glad I have got your picture. It is very natural. . . . I hope this war will soon be through and that I may come out of it safely. . . .

I feel as lonely as can be all the time. I wish I was up to your house. I hope this war will soon be through. I will soon pitch in and kill somebody on my own hook, you see if I don't.

Aug. 31, 1861 In camp at Lynfield

Dearest [Lucretia],

We are off next Tuesday I suppose. I expected we would not go for three weeks yet, and intended to see you again before I left. I meant to come up and stay all next week. I can't now though. . . .

Our pay is double that of other soldiers and we have an easier time, all because we can hit a twenty five cent piece at ¼ mile distance. We have rifles with a telescope on top. They are very heavy, some of them weighing 50–60 pounds and are carried in wagons when we march.

I never saw such a splendid company. All Yankees (with the exception of the writer) smart and intelligent fellows. We choose officers tomorrow . . . and start next day with 123 men. . . .

It seems as if I would give a great deal to just kiss you once.

I must leave off, but I wish I could set up with you tonight.

As long as I am sure of the place in your heart that I now occupy I am as happy as a man can be. . . .

Good bye for a few days.
I am feeling first rate.
Yours through life,
Emerson

LUKE BICKNELL (MEMOIR, PP. 4–5)

We pulled in Sam Gilbrath again as soon as we struck Lynnfield to re-enlist, and also secured a delegation of the old 8th [Massachusetts] men from Lowell.[6] We dwelt upon the extra pay and freedom from guard and drill, and labored so zealously that we soon had two hundred men in camp for the captain to choose from. The captain began to talk of a second company, to be armed with Sharpes Rifles in which [Henry] Martin and I were to hold commissions, and everything was going on swimmingly, when one day I learned that the officers of the 19th Mass., in camp beside us, thought we were being humbugged as to the extra pay.

I started for Boston by the next train to see the Governor about it, Capt. Saunders going with me. We could not see the Governor but the Adjutant General expressed himself as confident that we should get the twenty five dollars per month although he admitted that no positive answer had been received from Washington on that point. The Capt. was fully reassured, but I was not, and determined to clear my skirts with the men before it was too late. So mounting a barrell the next morning I told the men that I was in doubt about the extra pay, but was going to stick by the sharpshooting for the sake of good company and the surety of being constantly kept at the front. Before night so many of the men had left camp that the prospect of a second company had vanished. . . .

Captain Saunders was sore over the results of my speech and very sanguine that everything would all be right as soon as we got under Gen. Landers wing but even he was a little set back when the mustering officer refused to muster us except at regular pay, and would muster only the regular number of lieutenants (two) for the company. But the sweat fairly started from his brow when the Adjutant General introduced Mr. [George C.] Gray of Salem as the gentleman whom Gov. Andrew had selected for his 2nd lieutenant. This forced [Saunders's own picked officers] back into the ranks, for they were all men who had too much pride to leave a company simply because they had been denied a position in it.[7]

MOSES HILL

Lynfield, September 2, 1861

Dear Wife and Family,
I am oblige to inform you that I cannot come home before I go off. I [did] not know as I should go off with the rest of the Company until last night and I was oblige to be here tomorrow morning. We are going with 100 with

telescope Rifles. The rest of the men are going with open Cite Rifles. . . . I
should come home for good if I did not [enlist] in this Company. And the
reason we go, you probably know. It was very sudden to the Company and
the Captain, for we was not ready.

I am well and we live very well. A better Company never went into the
Army. The Smartist & largest lot of men I never saw. We have a good meny
men that weigh over two hundred pounds and some are six to six 3 in. high.
We shall come into Boston Tuesday. I should like to see you, but perhaps it is
best I should not. I should come home if I could, but I feel as if I could not
lose my chance, for if I did, I might be drafted and I might be sorry, for I think
there will be a good meny drafted. I think the Governor is proud of the Company. It is called Andrew's Sharpshooters. He says we can have anything we
want. I expect we shall have Revolvers & Boey Knives. We have one uniform
and we are agoing to have another before we start. . . .

I have been to work today with the Carpenters making gun boxes to carry
our guns in. There has been eight carpenters to work today. They work day
and night so as to have them ready. Oswel [Egbert Oswald] Hixon is agoing
with me. His wife lives in the Willard Clark house [in East Medway]. He is
in camp with me and he is a great deal of company to me. You must go and
see his wife.

I have sent home a note from the Captain. Get your money from the Town
from the time of my enlistment, if you can. If not, I suppose you must send to
the State House and get a stipend from the clerk. My name will be in there.

I think camp life will suit me first rate. I have not been better this summer.
I do not [know] what to [do] about my business at home, but you must tell
Thomas about that Herse I sold for $10.00. He must pay for it, and one half
of that Boat is mine. The stone tools you must lay to one side. They are all in
the shop. Most all the tools and things are mine, some in the shop chamber.

Sis, I want you to be a good girl until I come home again, which I trust
I shal before spring. If any of the Boys want to see the Company, they must
come into Boston Tuesday. I suppose you will not come, for you know my
feelings. You will hear from me again in a few days. I did not expect the Governor would call for us so soon. I shall send you my Degeritipe [daguerreo-
type] in a day or two, perhaps tomorrow.

My love to you, Eliza & Sis [his daughter, Lucina] and Bub [his son,
George] & Mother. I think it all the best I should go now. Love to all.

From your ever Truly Husband, M Hill

LUKE BICKNELL (MEMOIR, P. 5)

On board the train for New York I pushed an acquaintance with a quite-reserved man in spectacles, whom I found to be [George] Whittemore [Jr.], of Gloucester, a graduate of Harvard College, who being debarred from service in other organizations by his defective sight, had sought service in the sharpshooters whose guns were furnished with such powerful aids to vision. I have never met so well and informed a young man as he proved to be and when I told him I had left "Hardi" at home and taken "Blackstone" in my knapsack, it was soon arranged that we should be tent mates.

MOSES HILL

New York, September 4, 1861

Dear Wife,

I received a letter from you Monday. I am well but verry tired for I have not slep much for the last 48 hours. I am on gard at the Barracks. I guarded the men in the cars last night. I did not set down until 3 oclock this morning. I expect we shal start out this afternoon. . . . My love to you all. I do not know what more I can write now.

LUKE BICKNELL (MEMOIR)

When we reached Washington, the captain made a vain attempt to arrange with the war department so that we would have our extra officers and extra pay. Though badly rebuffed he did not yet despair but continued to hope that through the united efforts of Gov. Andrew and General Lander it would soon be brought about.

We were temporarily attached to the 20th Mass Regiment . . . for the purpose of drawing rations, only, as we understood it . . . and ordered with it to Poolesville, Md. to await the arrival of Gen. Lander. The officers of the 20th were untiring in their efforts to bring the regiment to a perfect state of discipline and drill and were no doubt annoyed by the presence of a company who had no daily occupation and in which there had as yet been no attempt to establish discipline. Capt. Saunders had a rooted aversion to all salutes, drills and parades . . . which he regarded as wholly "fuss and feathers" . . . and as for discipline, he was ready to shoot down the first man who disobeyed an order or showed the white feather. Consequently, he turned a deaf ear to the arguments and commands alike of the officers of the 20th. . . . [He] would not willingly see his men obliged to perform duty which he had told them would not be required . . . only at last yielding so far as to say that if any of his men who chose to might drill and stand guard with the 20th. We made some amusing attempts to drill and stand guard with our ponderous arms, and appeared on drill parade each night where we were obliged to stand at "parade rest" all through it; until one night we were surprised to hear an order read—and the order was read at the head of every regiment in the division—speaking of the spirit shown by the sharpshooters in the harshest possible language. We promptly left the parade ground and refused to make any further attempt to drill, parade or stand guard, falling back on the conditions of our enlistment. At this juncture Colonel Lee of the 20th said that the sharpshooters must be left alone until General Lander arrived.[8]

LUKE BICKNELL

Headquarters Andrews Sharpshooters Camp Benton
Sept 21st 1861

Dearest Lucretia,
I am alone tonight in the commisary's tent and have a fine opportunity of writing a letter.

The first thing I am thinking of is how much I love you. The longer I am acquainted with you the more I wish to continue that acquaintance as long as we may live. May we ever be friends and lovers and I ask but little more in life.

Your letters speak your affection for me more plainly than your lips ever did when I was with you and it is in these that I find the greatest proof of your affection and love. . . . You have so far been a true[r] friend to me than any other. You have never played the coquette with me and how can I help loving you.

Everything that will render us both happy I desire. Anything that will tend to separate us I fear. I hope that fate may be kind to me in this.

My happiness will be complete as long as I can be able to gratify your desires.

I cant think of nothing that would be wanting to complete my happiness. . . .

The Gen. has named this place Camp Benton. . . . Last night we was routed in a hurry. I don't know why. Perhaps the Rebels attempted to cross the river. Today, as I was standing by the side of our guns to watch the effect of a shot, which a man was making. The gun burst, slightly injuring the man who was firing. The rifle weighed 52 pounds and the pieces flew in all directions. Many were standing around, but luckily nobody hurt, but the one I spoke of. . . .

Oh, I forgot something up with you that is the best of all. I would like to see you tonight to kiss you and set by your side if your house was my home. I think I should stay in every evening almost.... First let me do my duty and then I will stay at home.

Yours ever, Emerson

MOSES HILL

Camp Benton, Wednesday, September 18, 1861

Dear Loving Wife,

I received a letter from you Sunday and one from Sister Persis, and I was very glad to hear from home and glad to hear that you are all well.... I have not but a very little news to write you today. We have been building a log house for our Captain and Leutenant. If it is a good morning tomorrow morning, I expect to go a fox hunting again. I think we can get one next time. A part of our men [including Luke Bicknell] are still at the river helping Pro[fessor] Low operate his balloon. They go up in it most every day, sometimes two or three times in a day....

I am agoing down to the 20th Rig. to buy me a pen before I write any more.... I have concluded to borrow and not go now. I am all alone now in the tent writing to you, therefore I cannot but help thinking of home and how I would like to be with you and our dear children. What does Bub say to his gold dollar and has Sis got hers? I hope they have. How I would like to see them. I would like to have you send me out a Farmers Almanac by mail. Put it in an envelope. One cent stamp will bring it. Write me all the news you can. And how do you get along? Do you have all the things you need and do you get your money from Capt. Daniels? How much do you get per month? Have you got any provision laid up for winter? And how are you on wood?

Eliza, I think of those things every day and if you are well provided for, I shal feel a great deal better. Eliza, I don't know what I can send you unless I send you fifteen or twenty dollars of money when I get some more. I will send you a gold dollar if you want it.... I must say I do not want to come home and leave the Country in the state it is now in. I should not feel contented at home to stay long until the war is through. That is my feeling now, although as I said before, I would give anything if I could but see you and our dear little children.

Our tent has come and we shal put it up tomorrow if it does not rain. We have very pleasant weather here now. I have got a very good Pr. of boots and I had a tap put on them so they are thick on the bottoms and will keep my feet dry. I think I am very well on it for clothes now. They do not look so well, but they are warm and very comfortable. Hixon just received a box from his wife. She sent him some chicken and pudding and pies. They was all spoilt. A great many of the Company come off the same way, so you are not alone, *Eliza*, but you did not have a Husband that found so much fault with the things that you took so much pains with as to find fault with as H. did. It made me feel bad for his wife. She must took as much paines as you did . . . she sent him a good meny things.

I hear that Gen. Landers is agoing to take us off with him soon South, I guess. I will write again in a few days. A thousand kisses to you and Sis and Bub and may God bless you all.

Camp Benton, September 21, 1861

Dear Wife,

I received your letter the 16th and was glad to hear from you & to hear you was all well. I am very well now. We came into Camp Benton last Sunday. We are all well rested now. The camp is about 35 or 40 miles from Washington. We marched most all last week. We did not think of going so long a distance & started without any provision. Most of the time we had nothing but hard bread and cold water and slept out in the open air on the ground. When we got through with our march we was very weak for the want of food. But now we have plenty of food and feel strong and well except those who are trobled with a diarera.

I could write 24 hours and not write all that would be interesting to you & Sis perhaps, but I will write what perhaps will be most interesting to you. You wrote about having clothes to keep me comftable. I have a plenty; if I had more, it would be burdensome to me. I have 1 Pr draws, 2 Pr woolen shirts, 2 Pr woolen socks, 1 Pr pants, 1 knit fatigue coat, 1 thick black coat, 1 heavy over coat, large coat that I can cover over my head when I sleep at night. 1 India rubber Blanket, 1 heavy woolen blanket. Besides, 1 old under shirt and 1 Pr of woolen & one pr of Cotton socks that I brought with me; 1 fatige cap, 2 good black caps. With my knap sack, haversack & canteen you see it makes me a heavy load. At this moment there is a beautiful Band from Misagan [Michigan] playing. Direct your letter to me Care of Capt. John Saunders, Sharpshooters, Attached to the 20 Mass. Regiment, Vol. Washington D.C. I do this for I may be called off to the River.

We are in camp 2 miles of the River Poetomuck [Potomac] where the rebes want to cross, at least some of them, in the town of Poolsville. Some of our Company went down Tuesday and the rest are a going to relieve them. The pickets are on one side and our troops on the other. They talk to each other. One of the rebel picket said he was hungry and one of the 15th Mass

Boys took him up to his camp and gave him a good meal of victuals, then he went back. He said he would never shoot at one of that Rig. Before I write any more I would say that I am out of money and if you can send me two dollars, I would like it, but do not make your self short. I do not know how I could lived if I had not bought some provision on the Road but I think I shall have more now. I have had to let Hixon have some of my money or I should of had more....

Sunday afternoon. I had to leave letter yesterday. I was called upon to go on gard and my 24 hours was up at 10 o'clock this forenoon. I did not sleep any last night. It was the coldest night we have had this fall. It has been very hot through the day ever since we came to Washington, hoter than it has been any time in Mass. The Company are all together today. *Now I think of it,* I want you to send me a Housewife, that is, something to carry thred & needles Buttons etc., if you can. I nead that more than anything I can think of. I want you to write me soon for I don't know as we shall be with the 20 Rig. much longer. You see I have plenty of clothes, all I can take care of. You must excuse my writing for I have no conveint plase to write on.

A part of the Company have been out practicing with our Rifles two days last week. I believe they give me credit of beating the crowd. We shot one hundred Rods [about 550 yards] and I think I could hit a Turkey twice out of three times. Tell Asahell & William that I have got a good rifle. It weighs about twenty five lbs. and I am well pleased with it. When we marched without our guns, soldiers asked us when we passed them where our guns was & some thought we was prisoners marching with the 20th Rig. But when we march with our guns they say, see that gun, what a gun that fellow has, see that small cannon! At this moment news has come that there was fighting at Chain Bridge near Washington yesterday. There was a fight and the federal loss was not very large but they took a good number of Rebel troops and drove them back but they have rallied again today. *So reported in Camp today.* There is no doubt there will be a great Battle soon and I think the only one that will amount to much. Nobody knows any thing about it. Everything is kept so still, all officers and soldiers are forbid writing . . . that can get into press.

Tell Asahel & William that there is plenty of game here, but we are not allowed to shoot at them. We cannot shoot at targets, only between the hours of 10 to 12 o'clock. If we should hear a gun near the River at any time, the soldiers would be in *arms.* There is Hogs all round the fields and woods here—into our cookery sometimes nights. Tell Bub there is a lot of little niger Boys round here where there is a house, but the houses are very scarce here. The negro Boys bring cakes & pies on the camp ground to sell.

Write me all the news. How is Sis, Crow and the garden? I suppose you will have to get some more wood soon. I want you to make your self comfortable if you can. If I live I think I shall be with you in the spring. . . . There is 3,000 troops on this ground. I think we can raise 12,000–15,000 troops here in one hour time. How are the Rigerments filling up in Mass.? I will leave, for I may want to write a few lines before close this letter.

From your Dearest Husband, M Hill

My love to all. Kiss Bub & Sis & Hattie for me. I think of you a great deal & Bub, I dream of him often. Send me a Boston paper as you can.

LUKE BICKNELL (MEMOIR, P. 7)

As soon as the general arrived we went in camp by ourselves on a hill in rear of his head quarters. . . . We were furnished with twenty light rifles and we soon were as well drilled a company as any in the army. We also practiced continually at target with our heavy rifles, kept a camp guard and a guard at the general's quarters, and picketed a portion of the line at night. We were suddenly transformed into the busiest and best disciplined organization in the division, and got to be known as Lander's Pets.

"All Quiet in Camp"

MOSES HILL

Camp Benton, Frederick County, September 24, 1861

Dear Wife,

I wrote a letter to you last Sunday and asked you to send me two dollars of money, but I do not need it now. If you have not sent it you nead not now for I have sold my wach and got $5.00 for it. It was nothing but a [worry?] to me and I thought I had better sel it. . . . Since I wrote you I have had a turn of Diarear, but I am better now. I felt quite slim [sick] yesterday. I think I shall have a good chance to send a letter to you to day, so I improve my moments.

I have been out yesterday and today to see the men shoot that did not shoot when I shot. General Landers was there to see them shoot and he wanted the Captain to pick out ten of his best shots tomorrow to go to the River to pick off some of the Rebel Oficers and I hope I shal be one of that number. We are going to practice [shooting] one half mile tomorrow. . . .

We took one man near the River. We suppose him to be a spy. He gave signals to the Rebels every night by candles. In his chamber he would lite his lamps and stand before them and give signals across the river.

The officers are very strict with the men here; they are not allowed to drink a drop of spirit or go off the Campground. I feel very well today and I hope you enjoy the same blessing. . . . The Rhode Island 3d Batery are with us and the Mass. 15th, 19th, 20th & 2 Misigan, 1st Minesota and a number within a few miles; the 13th & 2d [Massachusetts] are within 9 miles of here. We like General Landers first rate. . . . I think there will be a battle soon, and if there is, I think it will be a final Battle, but we do not know but very little about it, only we can guess, that is all.

Corn and Potatoes and vegetables are not so forward as it is in Mass. I think they must have planted very late, but the corn is a later kind than our Corn is. We had some baked Beenes for Breakfast and rost Beaf for Dinner, something we have never had in Camp here before. . . . All our men seem very anxious to get a shot at the Rebels.

When I was in Washington City, I went into the Capitol and up on the top of it which is very high. The top is not finished yet. It is a very large building. . . . The Hogs are all round in the streets round the Capitol. When we came through Baltimore we had no trouble. The Captain saw one man in a Chamber that was just a going to throw a junk Bottle at him, but he drawed his sourd and he dare not throw it. Captain said if he had, he should have gone up after him. . . .

Wednesday, 25. I put my letter into the office last night and I took it out this morn to write this, and I received one from Nathan [Eliza's brother] and Sis and was very glad to hear from him and I cannot stop to answer them as I ought. But I will say we have not killed any pickets yet, nor no one else that I know of, for we have not had any chance. But I think some of us will have in a few days. . . . Nathan, in regard to [General] McClellan, I have not seen him as I know of. He keeps everything still. There seems to be a great meny troops all the way up the Potomac. I hope I shall be able to write you some news in a few days. . . .

                                    Camp Benton, September 29, Sunday 1861
Dear Wife,
I wrote to you last Tuesday, I think, and I should of wrote again Thursday but I had some Company and did not have time. It was *Fast Day here.* . . .

Thursday night about 50 of our Company went to the river for fere the Rebels might cross. I was one of that number. We camped on the ground, side of the road. The ground seems very hard here, harder than it is in Medway. I have thought a good meny times I would like such a piece of grounds as Mr. Harding's clover piece. It would seem like a feather bed to what some ground I sleep on. We have straw ticks in our camp to sleep on, but I will go back to the river. We got fairly camped on our blankets and it began to rain. It was all mud & water under us and our Blankets wet through. Some slept all night in that way, but I could not. I sat with my rubber blanket over my head. We see no Rebels, but we had a good view of the Potomac. It rained all day Friday, so we did not go out much, but there was so meny in our camp I could not rite. Nor we could not dry our clothes. We slept in wet blankets Friday night. We did not take cold Saturday. It was pleasant but cold.

I went on gard 9 o'clock yesterday and came off at 10 o'clock today. I would not go into the gard tent for fear I might catch lice, so I laid out. . . . The ground was about the same as [it] is front of the house, only not so smooth. The soil here is red, and when it gets trod down it is very hard, but when it rains it is all mud. I was on gard 2 hours and off four hours. It was so cold I did not sleep much, so I feel some sleepy today, but I feel well. I have been very well a few days past. I think our camp will not have much more gard duty to do. . . .

60 of our men went to the River last night; all was quiet. Nothing but a boat got loose a[nd] floated down. Six shots was fired, but nothing in it. In regard to the war, I sometimes think there will not be much fighting until after Congress meets again. We may, some of our Company, go down and fire on some of the Rebel's pickets and Oficers. I shal go if any of the Company go. We have got 72 Rifles now and six more in Washington. We have not got our pistols yet. I expect they are making them in Mass.

I have bought me a knife. The blade is about 10 inches long. I paid $1.00 for it. I bought it very low, for the man owned it wanted some money. I expect to have a letter from you in a day or two. I like to hear from home, and I expect you like to hear from me. I will write you again in a few days. I do not expect we shall be in the 20 Rigement much longer, for we do not like Colonel Lee. The 19 [Massachusetts] Rig. Band came Friday and the 20th had a Band come this morning. We like General Landers very much.

Pigeons and Turkey Busards are very plenty here. The Busards are most as large as a common Turkey.

There was one death in the [First] Mishegan Rig. a few days ago, *a captain.* That is all the death I have heard of round here. . . .

The men in our tent are now talking about hard Bread. I wish you could see some of it. It takes a long while to soak it in hot Tea or Coffee. I think I must close this letter now and the next one will interest you more. Write me all the news. How is the garden & Crow & Chickens? I want Sis & Hattie & Bub to put in a few lines. Tell Bub to write papa a good long letter. Kiss all for me and love to all the rest and take a large shair yourself.

From your ever Loving Husband, M Hill

Sunday, September 29, 1861

Dear Wife,

Monday. Today was an inspection of arms. Everything is quiet in camp. Some wounded troops came in from Washington. They came up the coast. It seems by some mismanagement some of the Federal troops got to fighting between them selves, thinking they was fighting the Rebels. 9 was killed and a number wounded.

Wednesday [October 2]. Things quiet in Camp. 5 men in our Company went to the River at night. I went with them. We stoped at Edwards Ferry. Every thing was quiet and we went back to camp in the morning. The ferry is about 1½ miles from our camp. We are nearly opiset to Leesburg. The [Chesapeake and Ohio] canal is on this side of the river. It runs from Washington to Harpers Ferry and I do not know how much further.

Thursday [October 3]. We moved our Camp up on a hill near where we was in Camp with the 20 Rig. We are very near to Gen. Lander's quarters. Some of our Company guard his quarters all the time and when you direct another letter, direct it to me, Washington D.C., Care of Capt. John Saunders, General Lander's Brigade.

Friday morning [October 4]. One of our Company died. He was buried this afternoon. He was carried about half mile to be bur[i]ed and they said it was a very solam time. Most every one shed tears and I hope they will remember it. I did not go, for I was on guard that day. This morning the Rebels fired 5 shots from their Batery. Two of their shots stroke not very fer from us. Our troops drawd up their Batery and stild them at once. There was none harmed this side. I do not know whether any Rebels was kild or not.

Saturday [October 5]. We cleaned up our Camp. All quiet.

Sunday [October 6]. I am on guard today. All quiet as yet in Camp. Telegraph Dispach came to Poolsville that Charlestown is taken. We think it is too good to be trew but we hope it is. There is a great meny troops coming from Washington to this ficinity. There must be a good meny thousand troops near here. . . .

Dear Eliza, I am very sorry you have worried about me so much. I hope you will not worry any more, for I will write often. You wanted to know if I was contented here. I must say that I am quite as contented as I expected. I enjoy much better health then I did last year, but I cannot say how long I shal enjoy that blessing. We are on a high point of land and I think it must be healthy. We live very well now. I thought I would have some thing new today. I bought half a pie.

I like all the Company very well, but I should like [it] better if there was not so much swareing in the Camp by some few. . . . Tell Mother I think if

I live I shal see her next spring. I don't know as I want to come home much before, although no one wants to see their family more than I do. . . . I must go on gard again in a few moments. Kiss Bub for me and Sis. Bub must write to papa every time Mother does.

From your Loving Husband, M Hill

LUKE BICKNELL

Camp Benton Oct. 7, 1861

Lucretia,

A heavy thunderstorm is passing over and it would not be strange if a few wet spots should get onto this letter for this tent is crowded with dripping men scarcely leaving me a place to write. . . .

If you was with me, I am sure I would get you to read all my letters to me. I am going to have them all and we will have a nice time some evening when I come home reading them.

The rain drives through the tent and bothers me. Don't you wish you was out here with me, sitting by my side, with the rain sifting through and dripping down. I should be kissing you about this time. I know you would like it first rate, but there isn't hardly room for you on the keg of vinegar which serves me as a seat. I guess I would like you in my lap, throw down my pen, as you said you wished you could, and go on talking.

You can not know how much I love you Cretia. I hope to God that you may never doubt my affection for you. I don't care so much about coming back. I feel as careless about death in the battlefield as I should about taking a drive. I only want you to think more of me than you do any of the rest of the boys and as long as you do, I am well satisfied dead or alive.

I guess it is about time to put in the news. Nothing new. We expected a battle last night, expected a battle today, expect a battle tomorrow or the next day, expect a battle every hour, expect a battle certain within two weeks. We are anxious as can be to have a battle, as soon as possible, as big as possible. Real blood thirsty fellows ain't we, but what is the use of staying here doing nothing.

What you suppose I have done today. Well, I marched the men down to the brook to wash before breakfast. After breakfast run some bullets for my gun, cut some potash, filled my powder flask, cleaned my gun and examined the other side of the Potomac with a telescope to see the rebels. . . . After dinner went out to drill. The orderly drilled the first and I drilled the second platoon. . . .

Went over to the brigade quarter master and found out where we could get a hack saw some fresh beef, which we wanted got him to let us have 130 lbs. . . . asked the orderly to direct men to go down with me and get the beef. He told me to get them myself. Had a funny time to bring it though, for it was hard work getting men to turn out in the rain. Finally got 4, got the meat, got back until after dark. . . .

Wouldn't you like to know what kind of gun I use. It weighs about 25 lbs. Cost $100.00, is one of the best guns in the company if not the best has a long tapering barrel, a brass telescope running the whole length, a very highly finished stock polished and inlaid with silver. The butt is protected by a heavy silver band and the work about the lock is part silver and part of the finest steel. There are but two or three as pretty guns in the company, some more costly, some that carry a ball more true and I think I shall not be apt to throw it away in a hurry. Perhaps you think it strange I say so much about a mere gun, but you don't know how much a soldier thinks of his gun.

I must stop.

Good night. A thousand kisses. Ever yours, Emerson

MOSES HILL

Camp Benton, October 13, 1861

Dear Wife,

Sunday 6th I wrote home, directed my letter to West Medway. I was on guard at night. One of our men was found asleep on guard. The penalty might have been Death with him, but the Captain put him in the guard tent. He was to have nothing but bread and water for one week and was to carry his knapsack 2 hours a day loaded with lead, 40 lbs. There was 13,000 troops in rout from Washington.

Monday [October 14]. Quite Rainy. All quiet in Camp.

Tuesday [October 15]. I was on guard. I received 2 papers from home. I was taken off guard at 11 o'clock at night and our Company was called out in haste to go to the River. They said the Rebels was a crossing. There was confusion in our Camp for a few minutes. 60 men carried small Harpers Ferry Rifles, but I carried my large rifle. I thought if I had got to fight, I wanted my own Rifle. The Captain told us if he ordered us to lay down, he wanted us all to drop at once. We expected a hard fight, but come to get down there, there was no Rebels crossing, so we staid round all night and marched back in the morning. It was 4½ miles down there. We saw 2 or 3 Rebel pickets. I think they was just the right distance for my rifle, but you know they will not allow us to shoot their pickets.

Wednesday [October 16]. Very tired and I did have no sleep the night before. I was very sleepy. We heard some canading [cannonading] but it was not very [near] here.

Thursday [October 17]. All quiet in Camp. I received two papers from home.

Friday [October 18]. On guard at the General's quarters, close in front of his tent. I think Landers is a fine man. I expect he is pointed Major General today.

Saturday [October 18]. All quiet in Camp. Received a letter from Lucina in the evening *and was glad to.*

Sunday [October 19]. I was detailed for guard today, but the Captain said some one else must go, for he wanted me to cut a grave stone for that Mr. [Nathan] Travis that died a short time since. So I went in the woods and found a stone and brought it up to Camp and I have been to work very buisy until most night and I left off work to rite this letter. I have got to letter it on the morning. I have got a very good stone. We have got some more new guns now. We have got about 94 now.

Dear Wife, I am very well and hope you all enjoy the same blessing. . . . I have plenty to eat now. It has been very cold for a day or two here. . . . I suppose I shal get my housewife soon. I would like to come home a week or two, and then I suppose I should want to come back until the war was over. I don't know but we shal go further south soon. It is talked in the Camp that we shal be sent to Misury, but nothing certain yet. I shal write if I do. I want you to write as often as you can. Bub must rite too every time. I was glad to hear from Sis; she must rite often. . . . I cannot see much longer. Excuse my writing, for I have to write on my Knapsack tonight. I want to hear from Mother and all the rest of the folks. My love, dearest, to you and love to all.

Thursday, Camp Benton, October 17, 1861

Dear Wife,

I take pleasure in writing to you if I cannot see you. I have a bad cold today. Otherwise I am very well. I have not lost my apitite. . . .

Tuesday the 15th. I have been to work on that gravestone, yesterday and this afternoon. I have sat it. I have not seen no gravestones in the graveyard here as good as that.

Wednesday. I had a squad of men showing them how to load and shoot their guns and was on water gard too, so it kept me very busy.

Thursday. I have had another squad shooting. I hear some heavy canons this afternoon. I do not know what it means. . . .

We live well now, have plenty to eat, and if I ever come home as well as I am now, I think you will have to cook some extery raitions. If I live, I shal come home next spring or summer, for the Government are a oblige to let all Soldiers have 40 days in a year and pay their expences home and back.

General Landers is agoing to have all of the line of the Baltimore and Ohio R.R. I suppose you have seen it in the papers. And I think he will take this company with him, for it is a favorite Company of his. We may be called out every day, I do not know. He has been to Washington for a number of days and he has not returned yet. We expect him soon. When he comes back I think we can tell better. If he goes into action, you will find at the North that there will be nothing lacking on his part. I expect he is one of the best officers in the whole army. . . .

Friday Morn. [October 18]. Dear Eliza, I think I feel quite as well this morning. I did not receive any letter from you last night. I have not heard any thing more about going off with Gen. Landers, but I expect we shal go. I have heard the climate was not so healthy as it is here, but if I do not enjoy good health, it will not be owing to intemperate habits, for I was not half so temperate in all my habits as I am here. I say this so you need not worry about me in that respect. I know your feelings before I left home.

I have just had to leave off to get my squad of men together to shoot again today. Some of my men can hit the bigness of a cracker most every time 40 rods [220 yards]. I have got to go on gard today. It was very rainy here last night and it is clowdy this morning.

There is an old niger comes into camp to bring corn cakes most every days. He brings them hot and good. He is a slave. He said he had a wife and a number of children and he said there was a man come from Verginia and bought them and carried them off and he said the man was ded and he thought he was now lower than Hell. There is a good meny slaves here although there is not many white inhabitance very near here.

I have not spoke to but one woman since we took dinner in Philadelphia. Then I asked a woman down near the General quarters if she had any cheese to sell. So I don't know what appearance I shal make when I get back to Mass. You must not feel disappointed if I make a very awkward appearance.

Now about our living. Our cook house is about 2 rods [11 yards] square with a pole put up to keep out the men. No covering over it. The way they make coffee and tea, they stick up two crocheted sticks and put a pole on them and hang tin pails on the pole and make a fire under it. They make about 8 pails ful at a time. They boil their beaf in large citles [kettles] but in the same way. As to fire then, we have got a very good oven. We have one Capt. Tent, 1 Leutenant tent, 1 sargant tent, 1 small gard tent, 8 privets tents. The tent where I am is *no. 2*. It is a very poor tent. It is one that got Burned in the rail R.R. near Springfield. When it rains there is a good deal of rain in the tent, but I have got the driest corner. The tent is about as large as our bedroom and we have 11 men to sleep in it and we have to keep our knapsacks and all our things in the camp besides. We all have 1 tin plate, 1 tin diper, 1 spoon & knife & fork. We wash them or our own dishes. In the morning we have coffee or tea, about a pint, and sometimes hard Bread & some times soft Bread, and some times fried Pork & some times boiled beaf. Some times we set down on the ground and some times in the tent. Our food is all saved out for us. We crowd up to the cooking like a lot of Hogs for fear we shal not get our part. At noon we have corn Beaf & some times Beaf stake, bread, and cold water, some times potatoes but sometimes we do not have them for a number of days. And Sunday morning we have bake Beenes, some times we have Homony with a little Molases and water with it, and some times we have donuts and sometimes soop. . . .

Afternoon. I have just sat down to rite again. I have had to attend to the shooting and [was] on gard and now I have got about 3 hours now. I want you to let me know how all the Boys get along and what they are about as soon as you get home. . . . I expect we shall be Paid off before long. We have not been paid off yet. Let me know how you get along for money and how you fare. I have wrote you how I fair. I think we are all getting more use to the Climate then we was. We have not so much Diarear as we did. . . . I suppose you have not forget my House Wife yet. Some of my clothes want mending. Hixon lost his coming on here. *Dear Mother*, do not worry about me. I have plenty of clothes and plenty to eat now. And I hope God will spair us both to see each other again, wich I trust he will.

Love to you. Kiss Sis & Bub for me. I want Sis to write me another letter, and Bub must be sure and write too. My best love to you, dear Eliza. And all, all shair the benefit of this letter. From your Dearest Husband, M Hill

LUKE BICKNELL

Oct. 19th 1861 Camp Benton

My dear Miss Cretia,
Perhaps you do not know how to write love letters as well as other girls. I do not know I am sure, for I never got any letter, love letters, from anyone else. You do pretty well I guess for I never fail to see at once what you mean supposing of course that you mean just what you write. I know however that no

girl could have said more then you did in your last letter to me. If you "love me better than all else on earth," what more can I ask of you. I think you love me too well. . . .

I have to go on guard now, about every other day and stay 24 hours. All I have to do though is tell the Corporal to relieve the guard every two hours. I stay at Gen. Landers head quarters and see to it that a strict guard is kept. I am supposed to be awake at night, but I usually do sleep from ten till one. We watch for signals and whenever a gun is fired I have to turn out and see what the row is about.

I have got an awful cold and feel dull. . . .

I have got a rather easy berth in the company. I happened to suit the Capt. pretty well and he appointed me first a Corporal, then a Sergeant. I have better accommodations, more privileges and less disagreeable work then before. I like the place pretty well. . . .

When I first discovered I was in love with you I had a good mind to clear out and never see you again for I had a notion I would be an old Batch. But for all my strong resolutions I found you kinda, sorta liked me, but I couldn't help pitching in, and am awful glad I did.

Remember I am thinking of you all [the] time now. I didn't know that enjoyment before. You need not ever be afraid of my taking a liking to any other girl, while I live. I won't do it. . . .

"A Crewel Battle"

The Battle of Ball's Bluff on October 21 abruptly ended the sharpshooters' quiet routine of target practice and guard duty. Generals George McClellan and Charles P. Stone mistakenly concluded that the Confederates had vacated Leesburg, leaving only a token force behind. Union troops—including the Fifteenth and Twentieth Massachusetts—crossed the Potomac River on a handful of small boats, and climbed to the top of a high, steep bluff. There they encountered a massive Confederate counterattack. Over nine hundred Union soldiers were lost, some driven over the edge of the bluff to their deaths. Others drowned or were shot as they tried to swim back across the Potomac.

During the Ball's Bluff debacle, Brigadier General Lander was in Washington conferring about his command of a new military district, the Department of Harpers Ferry and Cumberland. When he heard of the disaster, Lander rode all night to reach his men, some of whom were under the command of Brigadier General Willis A. Gorman at Edward's Ferry, several miles south of Ball's Bluff. When Lander arrived, he took command of Andrew's Sharpshooters and helped to successfully repulse a superior Confederate force. A journalist reported: "The enemy's force consisted of one regiment each from Louisiana, Mississippi, and Virginia. The latter attempted to outflank our little force, but the terrible fire from the sharpshooters (a rebel falling at each shot) and the firmness of Co. K [Nineteenth Massachusetts] prevented the execution of their plan. The loss of the enemy was great, while only one of our men was killed."[9] The Edward's Ferry skirmish provided some consolation to the Union army for their loss at Ball's Bluff. One costly casualty at Edward's Ferry, however, was General Lander, who was shot in the lower leg while commanding the sharpshooters' defensive line.[10]

LUKE BICKNELL (MEMOIR, PP. 7–8)

For a number of days before the battles of Balls Bluff and Edwards Ferry our telescopes had revealed the enemy withdrawing from their camps in Port of Leesburg on the opposite side of the river. We supposed they must be concentrating in front of Washington to strike a blow at [General] McClellan, and were very anxious to cross the river and follow them up, that we might be on hand to cooperate with McClellan. A few men under Massachusetts officers crossed the river and reconnoitered around Leesburg coming back with the report that the bulk of the enemy had left, leaving only a small force to hold Leesburg. The pressure to cross was irresistable although we had no better facilities for crossing than a few canal boats. General Lander was away at Baltimore attending to the organization of a force to be thrown into the Shenandoah valley. General Stone had to bear the blame of the crossing [to Ball's Bluff], but I have my doubts whether he ought to have borne the whole blame. We all had the art of war to learn.

Captain Saunders was bound to be in at the fight, and taking all the men who were not on guard he crossed with about seventy at Edwards Ferry, with a portion of Gorman's Brigade. It was my luck to be sergeant of the guard at Landers head quarters, and as the captain dare not take the guard off, he turned a deaf ear to my entreaties to be allowed to accompany the expedition.

MOSES HILL

Camp Benton, Monday, October 21, 1861

Dear Wife,

I sat down in haste to write you a few lines tonight. I don't know how long I can write. The troops made an advance over the river this morning. I had a squad of men this forenoon, and at noon I had to go on gard a few moments after our company was called upon to go over the river [all] but the gards, so I was left at Camp. I thought at the time there would not be much shooting, but I was most sorry I did not go, for I think I could done more then a great many that went. I may be called upon tomorrow. When the Company went off, the Captain said they should be back tonight, but they will not, for they have their blankets and 3 days' rations. . . .

I think there has been a hard fight over the river this afternoon, for there was a continual roar of guns all the time. . . .

I stop in my tent with only one man and I have my large rifle by my side and two loaded Harpers Ferry rifles, so you can judge the position I am in, although I do not realize much danger.

Tuesday Morn. [Oct. 22] We are all safe this morning. 2 of our men came in last night and 3 this morning. It is a very rainy morning here. . . . Now I will write you something that is trew, whatever the papers may say. The troops crossed the river yesterday. All the way up the river at Edwards Ferry, about 2,500 men crossed and our company done all the fighting that was done yesterday. At that point 2 Rigerments stoped near the River & our company was ordered more than a mile off with about 25 Cavalry. They placed themselves near a cornfield, side of a rail fence and about 4 o'clock they saw about 500 Rebels in the woods within shot and some of them come out and as fast as they see them, they nooked them over. How meny Rebels was killed, we cannot tell, but they found 5 this morning ded. Some was bur[i]ed. To speak safe, they killed from 10 to 20 and one Oficer was shot through the head. Old Jenkins said he would shoot him in the head and he did.[11] They drove them off with only 70 men against 500, with no reserve. Was one of the most dangerous and successful fights that ever was in Verginia. *This you may rely upon as true:* there was not one of our men hurt. One of the men that came in last night belongs in my tent said the Rebels could not hit a flock of Barnes. I expect some of our men will come in sick, for it was a cold night, and they had not an over coat nor a blanket to keep them warm and not a mouthful of supper. We could not get it to them. It is gone to them this morning. I should of gone with them this morn, but I had some cold and cough. The men thought I had better not go.

There was a hard Battle up to the next ferry and a good many kild and wounded. There was reinforcements going all night last night. The Rebels will have to move soon out of this quarter, I think. General Landers heard of this battle. He was in Washington and he came here last night . . . full Blooded. I was in his quarters until 11 o'clock last night, and he said he was large and his horse was tall and the Rebels might have him for a target this morning. I have no more paper at this time to write, so I must leave off.

Do not worry about me, for I have many good friends in the Company. I went to bed this morning about 2 o'clock and was up at 5. I have got used to being up nights, so I do not mind it so much. I think this may be interesting to you, more so than the papers.

Love to all. Meny kisses to you and family. Bub must write. M Hill

LUKE BICKNELL (MEMOIR, PP. 7–12)

When General Lander arrived, at midnight, from Baltimore, we had been cut to pieces at Balls Bluff, but at Edward's Ferry the Sharpshooters, and the Boston Tigers of the 19th [Massachusetts] had repulsed the enemy. The general [was] very severe in his condemnation of the movement [at Ball's Bluff] and of the officers who had permitted it, saw no chance for the force across at Edward's Ferry better than death or capture, but after he drank a cup of coffee, and cooled down somewhat, I approached him with the proposition that I take the balance of the company and knapsacks, and provisions, for the men who were over the river, they having left both in camp in their haste to get into the fight.... He finally concluded to let me go, and also to accompany me. ... We found a few who, under the circumstances, were willing to stay and care for the camp on the hill.

I found General Lander pacing the bank of the river and somewhat discouraged about getting us across. Lander had no right to give orders, only to the sharpshooters, as he had [just] been transferred to another department, and all the troops except the sharpshooters turned over to other generals.... [Sam] Gilbrath, who was as handy with the oar as the rifle, borrowed a skiff, and put Gen. Lander across....

On landing we were warmly welcomed by the troops under the bluff, who were ... encouraged by the presence of General Lander.... I found the general already with the company which was strung along a fence against a corn field which extended to the woods that bound the plateau and sheltered the enemy. The Tigers held the fence on another side of the corn field, and the woods running back to Goose Creek were held by another company. Two pieces of artillery were posed in the timber along Goose Creek, to rake the corn field, and the sharpshooters too, if they held their position. At this fence the previous afternoon the sharpshooters had repulsed a regiment; and The Tigers who charged them on the retreat had counted things dead in the corn field and also reported that the whole regiment was loaded down with wounded.

A cold rain came on and by two o'clock we had about given up all hopes of an attack when a whole brigade of the enemy "in column, by regiments" advanced into the corn field, their front diagonal to ours. They commenced firing when the right of their front regiment was within 30 rods [165 yards] of the left of our company and continued to advance firing "by rank." The bullets whistling around our ears was the first intimation we had of their presence, so quiet had been their advance and so thick was the fog and rain. We gave them a volley in return, sighting over the tops of our telescopes, which were useless in such weather, and then began moving along the fence to the right, loading and firing as we went. We were aiming for another fence which ran from this one at right angles back to Goose Creek, thus drawing the enemy into the field . . . where the two pieces of artillery would take them in the flank.

Capt. Saunders and Lieut. [George] Gray were on the right leading the company into its new position, and Gen. Lander, [Henry] Martin and myself, were on the left, having all we could do to force the men to yield an inch of ground, when the general went down. He denied that he was wounded, but as he rose again his weakness was so evident, that we disregarded his command that we leave him, and he limped from the field leaning upon Martin's broad shoulder for support.

The enemy came on as we had planned, and the two guns double shotted with grape and canister played on their flank with fearful effect. The Tigers poured a steady fire into the flanks of the supporting regiments, the sharpshooters played away in fine style from their new position, a perfect shower of shells rose from the opposite banks of the river and fell all over the whole battle field, a long line of our infantry below the bluff was advancing rapidly to our support, when the enemy turned about and retreated in splendid order, considering that they were loaded down with wounded, and pursued with shot and shell as long as they were in flight.

Besides the General, one of the pickets on our left had been wounded, and one killed, but not a hair of a sharpshooters head had been injured, although we were thoroughly surprised to find that we had passed safely through such a storm of bullets. Gen. Lander was enthusiastic in our praise, and sent back word from the ambulance that if he had a regiment of such men he could march through Virginia. . . . We crossed the river that night, were the last to cross, and for a week or two rested on our laurels. We had established our reputation as a fighting company . . . [and] were confident we could do better next time, and were perfectly ready to try it over.

MOSES HILL

Camp Benton, Friday, Oct 25, 1861

Dear Wife,

I feel you are dear to me & Sis & Bub. I am well excepting my cough and cold, and I think that is a little better this morning. I may be called to the River every moment. Six or eight of our men will go and shoot Rebels. I expect to go. I want to go, for I was not in the Battle. I rote you Monday's fight. . . .

Tuesday they had a hard fight, and they had but a little help and they done a great execution. General Landers was shot in the lage, but he is along nicely. One Minisota man was killed & one wounded. When I come home I will tell you all. Landers says if he had 2,000 of sharp shooters, he would march into Richmond in thirty days.

There is nothing but the sharp shooters that can do anything now. I think they have killed nearly one hundred now and not one of them hurt. What I write you, you may depend upon, but do not believe all you see in the paper.

The company all came into camp Thursday morning. They have done most of the fighting at Edwards Ferry as yet. The troops have all come back this side of the river at this point. Up about 4 miles at the other Ferry they had a hard battle Monday, Mass. 15 & 20 & 19, but the 19 was kep back in the island & 1st California. It was a crewel Battle, a great deal worse then the Battle at Bull Run. General [Edward] Baker from Californy was killed. He was shot 5 times before he fel. Gen. [William] Lee was taken priserner of the 20 Mass, and a great part of the officers was killed & wounded. Of the 20th, a great meny of that Rigm. was killed, wounded, and taken priserners & Drounded, what did not swim the river, for all them that did not jump in the River was taken priserners, and I believe the 15th Mass. suffered more then the 20th. It was most crewel Battle & thanks to God that our Company was detached from the 20th Rig. They was ordered no further than the Island about halfway across the River & they was foolish to go any further. All the troops at Edwards Ferry came back this side while the Rebels was asleep. I do not know what this was for, but it is to trick the Rebels somewhere. It may be at Manassas or somewhere, but I do not know. There was a heavy cannonading some ways up the River about 1 oclock this morning. About 75 shells was fired. The Rebels are afraid of our Rifles. General McClellan was here and stoped with Landers Wednesday night & Gen [Nathaniel] Banks was here yesterday.

There is about 12,000 troops between here and the River. The 12th [Massachusetts] Rig. are in about one mile from here. I went to see them yesterday. The first one I saw was Lewis Miller. He said he was never so glad to see

anyone in his life. He is well. Fred Swarman & Gilbert Kingsbury & Charles
Cary & Mr. Prescott—they are all well.... I expect them over to see me soon....

If I ever live to get back to Medway, I will tell some of the Republickans
what I think of them that can come out an help do the fighting as well as not.
The officers are not what they ought to be. I cannot write what I want to now.
I hope I shall some other time.... Write as often as you can. Do not write
more than one letter after you get this, for we may move soon and I think we
shall. Kisses for you. And kiss Bub & Sis for me.

From your Husband, M Hill

(We have not been paid off yet.)

LUKE BICKNELL

Camp Benton Sunday morning Oct. 27, 1861
It is my birthday and I can not refrain from writing a letter to you. It is pleasant cold and clear here this morning. Nearly as cool I think as in your own
mountain home. I wish I could see you and spend the day at your house.
I thought last spring that the War would be through by this time, but now I
should not wonder if it lasted a year longer.

Our company was in a fight the other day and I was lucky enough to be
with them. I remember that I thought of you once during the engagement. It
was not fun by any means, yet there is something grand and beautiful about
a battle, to hear shells rushing over your head, rifles cracking around you and
bullets whistling over head around you and tearing up the ground beneath
your feet and yet snapping your fingers at the rebels and pitching in without
guns. I didn't get hit in this engagement, though I wasn't in any hurry to get
away when the order was given to retreat and I don't think I shall get very
badly hurt in the next battle.

We were attacked by a force 20 times as great as ours and were obliged to
retreat, so I guess I won't brag much this time. The papers praise this company much....

I got in one shot at the rebels at long distance and I hope it killed somebody. At one time I was sighting my rifle over the fence at the color bearers
of the Mississippi Regiment. They saw me and let drive a whole volley, which
whistled over my head and around me, a little too close for comfort. Most of
the boys are squatting down behind the fence and firing through the rails, but
I didn't think of that.

One of our men [Henry Jenkins] was away from us when the fight commenced. He run to the fence from which the rest had retreated, right in
among the rebels. Grabbed his rifle and put his legs for the [rear?]. They

fired as much as 200 shots at him, but didn't hit. He was the oldest man in the company and is sitting by me now writing to one of his old cronies about the fight. It is strange they didn't find any of us Sharpshooters, when they shot other men down right in the midst of our ranks.

The papers say every one of our shots killed one or two of the rebels, but I shouldn't wonder if one or two might have missed.

I write long letters to the Chelsea papers and they send a copy of them to me. . . .

I want to come home when the war is over never to leave you again. . . . I am always thinking of you as the girl I first met in the old red school house and forgetting that you are older, more womanly every day. . . .

I am not as much of a student as I used to be. Not as much of a school master. Not half so sober as I was. . . .

The 19th band is playing beautifully for morning parade. I wish you was here to hear it. . . .

Yours only, L. Emerson Bicknell

LUKE BICKNELL (MEMOIR, PP. 11–12)

The enemy's loss at Edward's Ferry must have been very heavy. . . . One of our men was away from the fence at the time of the attack and the enemy carried away his rifle showing it afterwards to Col. Lee of the 20th [Massachusetts] in Libby Prison [in Richmond], and questioning him as to who carried such rifles, he is said to advise them to send it back or we would surely come and take it from them, and to have received the reply that they had halters ready for us, and that two hundred of their dead at Edward's Ferry bore the mark of the slugs fired from our rifles.

The two battles can be fairly summed up as follows: At Balls Bluff our men were marched out into an open field and held there while they were shot down from the comparative safe shelter of the woods beyond. At Edward's Ferry their men were marched out into the cornfield and were practically held there while we shot them down from the comparatively safe shelter of the corners of a Virginia fence. Both sides got a necessary lesson in the art of modern warfare.

GEORGE WHITTEMORE JR.

Near Edward's Ferry, October 28, 1861

We have seen our first fighting. We went over the river on Monday. The colonel or general commanding showed us the position of the enemy, and told us "to go there and see what we could do." . . . Our company have done all the fighting at this place, with exception of some shells thrown by the artillery. Our men both on Monday and Tuesday were put up close to the enemy, quite unsupported; and this, with their being without food for twenty-four hours and doing nearly all of the fighting, has, I find, gained them some credit with everybody. Even General [Willis] Gorman, who calls [our] guns great humbugs, gives credit to the men.[12]

MOSES HILL

Camp Benton, Sunday Oct 27, 1861

Dear Wife,

. . . I have been in the woods this morning and took my hound dog with me, but I do not like him verry well, but the Captain wants I should keep him a few days longer. I found him in the road yestarday, and the Capt told me to take it, so I did.

It is well for you to caution me in regard to bad habits, but I think it will not do any good, for I have got my mind made up. You rote what you see in the papers about drinking and gambling. There is but very little liquer drunk here in this camp. They are much more temperate than they are in E. Medway, but I think the officers drink some, but not much. There is some gambling done here, not but a very little in this camp. I speak of only of this Brigade.

I don't want you to send me any more blankets or clothes now, for I have got as much as I can convienient carry. It may be if we move to Harpers Ferry or on that R.R. I shal want something more. I hope we shal, for we want to go with General Landers wherever he goes. If the company had not done so well in that Battle, I think they could of got off quite easy. We was told by a captain in the 20 Rigm that 165 men was taken Priseners and kild. The 15 Rigm sufered much more. One company has only 19 privates left. Colonel Lee was taken prisener. I rote you most of the perticlars in my other letter.

I think it has been much colder here than it is in Mass. It is very cold here. When the company was over the river, it was a cold north East storm as cold as we very often have in Mass, and the soldiers had to sleep on the wet cold ground. Some would creap under the fence, some would creap under a stack of wheat, some could not get under any thing. The first night they had no Blankets & over coats. Do the men that have a warm house and soft Bed to sleep in think they can come and help them fight for their country, or will they stay at home and find fault with the Town when they call upon them to help support their poor familys? I hope there is no such men in Medway, but

I feel as though there was too meny of such in Mass. It is so cold & the wind bloes so that it plagues me to write. I hope we shal have a new tent soon, but the men are very well now. My cold I think is a little better to day.

I expect we shal move somewhere this week. Two of our teams has gone to Washington to carry General Landers some of his things. He is getting along as well as could be expected. I expect that Box when the teams come and I hope orders for us to move. The 19 Rigm moved up by the side of our Camp yestarday. Charles Greenwood and his son has just come into this tent. They are all well. Hixon is well. He has not heard from his folks for some time. Have you been to see his wife? He says she is not very well. I think you had better go, if you have not. Let me know how you get along, if you draw your money from the Town and if you have things to make you comfitible.... I was sorry to hear Mother Harding was not well. How is Mr. Harding's health?

From Your ever loving Husband, M Hill

Camp Benton, Wednesday October 30, 1861

Dear Wife,

... I expect our Captain will come to Boston soon. I will let you know when he comes so you can send me any thing you want to then, although I don't know as I really need anything if I get that Box.

I have not much time to write now, for it is most one o'clock and we have an inspection this afternoon. I see that the papers tell a great story about the Battle at Conrad's Ferry [Ball's Bluff]. The Federal troops did not drive the Rebels, but the Rebels kiled and took priseners and drownded a large number. But at Edwards [Ferry] there was only General Landers shot in the calf of his leg, and one Minesoti kiled & one wounded I have riten most of the poticulers about that. I think my cold is a little better. I feel very well now. I think I have not been so well a fall for some time. I wish Sis & Bub was here to crack nuts with me. I should feel hapy. There is a great meny walnuts here. I can go into the woods any time and get a peck of them in a little while. I have a crack most every day and some times two or three times.

There has not been any thing new since I wrote to you. I hope Mass will continue to send our troops, which I believe she is. I understand there is 7 Rigements geting ready to start soon. Some of the Governers aides was here Monday, and they said there was 7 Rigm most ready. I hope they will continue to come. I understand that a man deserted from the Rebbe armey which is now at Poolville wanted to know what kind of Guns we use that made such small holes and could shoot so fer. I have just been talking with the Capt. He says that no doubt we shal go with General Landers wherever he goes. I cannot tell when we shal move, but I expect we shall go soon....

Do you blame me for wanting to hear from you often? And I will try to write to you as often as I can. I wish my dog was at home to play with Bub. He is full of play. *Sis*, you must be a good girl. Mind your mother and take good care of your little Brother. Do so, and I shal always Remember you. I know you will be a good girl. I hope I shal come home in the spring, if not before then. I can talk with you for a week and interest you about the war. Eliza, I have not received any papers since the 10th of the month. Write often, Eliza.

From your loving Husband, M Hill

CHAPTER

WINTER QUARTERS

For then I see the camp-fires blaze,
And sleeping men around,
Who turn their faces toward their homes,
And dream upon the ground.

—J. G. Holland, "The Heart of the War" (1864)

"The One Great Trouble in Our Armey"

During the first year of the war, Union soldiers often wrote home complaining that many officers were incompetent. The army's long and leisurely winter encampment near Washington, D.C., allowed troops to gossip and compare and contrast officers in neighboring units. It was an engrossing subject, for their lives depended on the abilities of those who led them. But, as one historian notes, "Frequently officers had the same amount of military expertise as their men at the beginning of the war—that is to say, none. . . . The Union army had a heavy component of men who tried to learn their jobs out of books." A second lieutenant in the Twentieth Massachusetts wrote that most regiments "were led by inexperienced businessmen and politicians."[1] Although Andrew's Sharpshooters expressed satisfaction with their own officers, visits to friends in other units sometimes prompted sharp criticism and warnings to would-be enlistees back home.

MOSES HILL

Camp Benton, Sunday, November 3, 1861

Dear Wife,

Now I will give you a sketch of the two last days of camp life. We have had the hardest Storm that we have had since we came out here. It commenced raining Friday night. I sleep in the driest corner of the tent, and I was the first one that got up in the morning. It was hard work to get out of the door for the men was packed up at the end that I slept like a lot of Hogs. The rain was beating in all over the tent. Soon after, they all got up and roled up their beds and curled up in as dry places as they could. Through the day we tried to play cards, but it rained in so hard that we could not so we cracked nuts and picked over Beens and spent the day. The cooks could not cook anything through the day, but made some coffee in the morning and at night but we had bread with it. We spread our beds early last night to go to bed but the beds was all wet and our close was wet and damp. I proposed to set up all night, but they said it was no use so we all camped down and covered up with our blankets and when we woke up this morning we was wet with steam. I don't think we have slept so well for a long time. Not one of us took any cold. I think my cold is better then it has been for three weeks. It cleared off in the night and it is quite windy to day. As soon as we get our breakfast, all but two of the men in our tent went into the woods after walnuts. I have taken out the wet beds and cleared out our tent and am drying them. Our tent is very poor. It is full of holes, but I expect we shall have a better one some time.

Can any of the Boys come out here and help me enjoy camp life? I think they would like it much. Those that are not healthy and well, I would advise them to stay at home if they have any homes, but those that are healthy and well, I think it is their duty to inlist if they can do so under *good Oficers*. There is the great trouble in our armey. Our officers are not what they ought to be. If they was all like General *Landers & Capt Saunders the Rebels would* suffer. Everything is quiet in camp since I wrote to you. If it was not so far I would send you home a barrel of walnuts. The Persimons are quite plenty here. They are larger than our plums when ripe. They are very nice. They grow wild in the woods. They are the best now.

There is one thing I would like to write if I have not. That is, the Rebbles are very poorly clothed. They have all kinds of clothing. Some have cotton clothes. Some have to go barefoot. One of the 20th Regm went over to burry their dead after the Battle of Balls Bluff. He said they took off the clothes and shoes of our troops and put them on. One man in that battle got away from the rest, and the Rebels came up to him and he begged for his life. He said he had some small children at home, and praid them to spair his life, but they would not listen to him but run their Barrenets [bayonets] through him. This was privates. The officers will not allow it. I mean the Rebel officers.

I have some good times singing here—we have some beautiful singers in the company. I have not had any papers for a long while. Please send me some and write as often as you can. Sis, you must write & Bub must write every time. I wish I could see you. But I am not homesick.

Kisses to you all. May God Bless you, M Hill

Now I am agoing to take a walk up in the woods with [Corporal James S.] Burbanks from R.I. He belongs to the company.

Camp Benton, November 8, 1861

Dear Wife,

I take time to write a few lines to you this afternoon. I am very well excepting some cold.

Captain Saunders started for Mass. Tuesday morning and James Burbanks from Providence. . . . The Captain went home to recruit some more men. He has got a furlow of 21 days. He is agoing to get up three more companys with Sharps Rifles. He will advertise in the Herald where his office will be and when he will start back again. He does that so his company's friends can send any things to us if they want to, and he will see them on here with them. I don't know but you had better send me my fur that I wear on my neck. You may send me one of your woolen blankets, if you can spare it. I don't know as you can send anything more in the shape of clothing. . . .

There is a good meny in the 2d [Massachusetts] Rig. sick. In your letter you wrote as if I had cotton flannel to wear, but I have 2 woolen shirts & 2 Pr. of draws. The Captain is a going to bring me a Pr. of boots. I think I can get a Pr. of gloves here. We suffer some with cold hands. I was so glad to receive that box, as I should to find dollars at home. I found my socks, and nice ones they was, too & my housewife which was nicer than I expected, and two good silk hankerchiefs & cake & candy which I distributed in the tent, some of it. You cannot think how glad I was to receive those things from home. . . .

There is not been any thing of much importance in camp since I wrote to you. We have built a fireplace in our old tent and run the flue underground outside and built a chimney so we can make a fire and keep more comfortable in cold weather. We can toast bread & we have got a spider [skillet] so we can warm our vitules.

You wrote about Uncle Benom & Amos Morse. I cannot see any chance for Uncle M. now. He can see the Captain. If he is not too old, he can inlist with him. I would not in any other company but his, and I would not advise to enlist in any Infantry company, for the nights are very cold and there is a good deal of night duty to do in all Rig. It is easier for me now, for I am Coperal now and I do not have to stand out on guard, but I have to keep up as much, for I have to put on one releaf once in so often and have charge in my tent. It is gitting late and I have a guard to see today. Sunday I will write you again. I have got another dog. He is a good one. I take all the stray hounds I can get. The Captain took home two with him. . . .

Camp Benton, Sunday, November 10, 1861

Dear Wife & Friends,

I set down this morning to write something and what to write, I hardly know. I know what will interest you, Eliza, and therefore I shall address the first of my letter to you. Dear Eliza, I am very well this morning and I hope you & family enjoy the same blessing. How much I would give if I could but be at home this morning for one hour where I could clasp you, Sis & Bub in my arms, but I feel that I must be contented to be deprived from that privalage. . . .

The Captain is in Boston or at home. He will advertise in the Herald where his office will be and when he will start back. He will take all that his company's friends want to send to them. I was in hopes that we might be paid off so that I could send you home some money, but I don't expect we shal be paid off until the 15th to the 20th. I hope I can be able to send you some before Thanksgiving. I want you to get a Turkey or chickens, such as you prefer. Do not hesitate to enjoy a good Thanksgiving if I am not at home. I shall enjoy myself by thinking you have a good Thanksgiving, but I should not enjoy myself if I thought you would not. I would like to be at home, but it is impossible and I shal be contented here as I am. . . .

I wish to write a few lines in regards to the 2d [Massachusetts] Rig. It is composed of good soldiers, but the officers are a lot of counter-jumpers and Rich mens' sons which are not fit for the office no more than so many children. They drink too much and are so strict with their soldiers, they are no more nor less than brutes. They have made the soldiers carry their Knapsacks so much on double-quick time, that they have breaked from thirty to forty of them. Two of our men went yesterday to see them, but they were glad to get back again. They did not give them anything to eat and they said they was squeased up in their tents like a lot of hogs. They told the company that they went to see, if they would come to our camp, they would give them all they could eat for one week. There was a general order in that rigement read a few nights ago that no one of any other Rig. should stop in their camp overnight and Oficers went round to see if the tents was clear of such as might stop to see their friends. There is some sick with the measles in the Rig.

The one great trouble in our army: We have too many young officers that, if they hear a Ball wistle through the air, they will run if they are not so scared they cannot run. And if ⅔ of the officers in the army was put into the ranks and take out as many privates and make officers of them, they would have a good army. Therefore, I would not encourage any of my friends to join any Rig. until they know what officers they are agoing under. I am satisfied with our Captain and first Leutenant. I think the latter is as good to me as a father could be, and if any that want to enlist as sharpshooters to use Sharps Rifles, I think can have a chance, for our Captain is agoing to Recruit two or three hundred more men to join our company. I would not encourage any of my friends at this season of the year to join any company, but if they are agoing to enlist, enlist under Capt. Saunders.

Camp Benton, November 17, 1861

Dear Wife,

It is so cold in the tent today that it is most impossible to write, for my hands is so cold. It was a very cold, windy day yesterday and it is quite as cold today. My squad went into the woods yesterday and got a load of wood for our tent, but the wind blows through the tent so we cannot keep warm. You might think it strange to have me stand around in the house at home with two coats & an overcoat on besides.

I am on guard today. I think it will be a cold night to be out standing round. I am on the 3d relief today. There is three reliefs; first R goes on at 9 o'clock and off at 11 o'clock and the next goes on the next two hours, and so on, 24 hours. There is 3 coperals, one at each relief. The coperals call their men out in line in time and marches them round the camp and relieves the guard on before him. Sometimes I am on the first & sometimes second and third relief, as it happens to fall on me. After they are all posted, I go to the cook tent and round the camp to see everything is all right and see the guards do their duty, and when my time is up, I go and call up the next coperal and so on through the night. My time comes once in two or three days. I feel very well today, but I have some cough yet. Hixon and I expect to go and see the 2d Rig. tomorrow. . . .

Things do not look so much like fighting here as they did the last time I rote to you. The Rebels over the river fear this company more than they do all the whole of this Brigade. One Prisner at Poolville wanted to know what arms the Northern Army used. He said they would shoot so fer and go through four men and through a rail fence besides. Some of the 15th Rig. went over with a flag of truce. They told them that they would meet them half way, but they did not like them D_____ long gonkins they called us, so one of them told me when they came back. There is a report that the Rebels offer a bounty of $500 a head for us [sharpshooters]. I think it will cost them that before they get meny of us, that is, if they value life anything. I hope we shall not have occasion to shoot any more of them, but if we do, I shal pity the man that comes in good range of my gun. But as I said before, I hope we shall not be obliged to kill any more of them. There is a good meny Secesh here; this county has gone strong Secesh. . . .

May God bless you all and protect you all, M Hill

Let Mother know I have received that box. I think she will feel better. We have not been payed off yet. We may be this week. I hope we shal be so I can send you some home. Enjoy yourself at Thanksgiving. Do not deprive yourself of anything if you can get it. I would like to be at home, but it is impossible, dear Eliza.

LUKE BICKNELL

                                   Camp Benton, Poolsville Nov. 24th 1861

Dearest [Lucretia],

You must know more war news than I do for everything is kept from us. We know that Beaufort, South Carolina was captured by our troops, but since then we know nothing. We have heard heavy firing in the direction of Washington for five days, but what it is we have not heard. Confused rumors reach the camp of first a victory and then a defeat, but nothing reliable. . . .

For aught I know, we shall stay here all winter. Provisions are getting very scarce, especially foraging for the horses and the roads are so bad that the stock of provisions is continually growing less. . . . I hope we get out of this before winter but don't see how. If we were ordered to advance tomorrow our horses would drop down the first day, for they are dying now at the rate of one a day to a regiment. Enough of soldiers.

I feel amazingly contented since you wrote me that you *would marry nobody else.* . . . It took me by surprise. . . .

I would like to be at your house today. We would read a book and walk out and set up too I guess.

You can't imagine what an easy time I am having. When I go to bed nights I am a bit tired and sleep lightly. Never enjoyed myself better in my life.

Much of my happiness is due to you, I suppose. I had ought to train myself to be happy if you should die. But I cannot help it being as it is. *I know I should want to die too.*

You are as very different from what I supposed I should find [in] a woman. They are coquettes mostly. Pretty enough and good enough. But I will be hanged if I care much about them, except for a little fun when I happen to be in their company. But you are the most honest little woman I ever did see. I am precious glad I got acquainted with you. I mean you shall never regret the confidence you have given me. You need never fear that I shall become tired of you. One heart is enough for me. . . .

Yours is the one for me *if you are willing.*

Yours in life in death,
Emerson

Thanksgiving

Whatever the shortcomings of Massachusetts officers, the soldiers did recognize that many of them had money to lavish on their troops for the first Thanksgiving in the field (and on later occasions when army rations ran low). Colonel Charles Devens of the Fifteenth Massachusetts, for example, gave his men fifty dollars to buy food, "and the all-important roast turkey was not wanting." Similarly, Major Henry Abbott of the Twentieth Massachusetts reported: "In our regt. we gave the men a . . . dinner of roast turkey & plum pudding & then most of the company officers gave their men something to drink. We gave our 35 men 5 bottles of whiskey & I am happy that there wasn't the slightest trouble resulted therefrom." And a captain in the Second Massachusetts wrote that his regiment's dinner consisted of "ninety four turkeys, seventy six geese and seventy three chickens, all cooked in the stone ovens which we had built. We also ate plum puddings, apples, nuts, figs, and raisins."[2] Apparently the grandest celebration was among the men of the Nineteenth Massachusetts. Major Abbott wrote that in addition to ample food, "they had a ball to which came a large number of very vulgar & respectable trademen's wives of Baltimore." Two "drinking tents" were connected to a large floored tent for dancing. Some of the officers "got drunk and made fools of themselves and [a] Mass col[onel] was drunk in front of some of his privates, too."[3]

The independent company of Andrew's Sharpshooters, however, experienced a leaner and more sober holiday. Their patron, General Lander, was away recuperating from the wound he had received at Edward's Ferry, and Captain Saunders—a carpenter—likely did not have the means to provide much cheer for his men.

MOSES HILL

Camp Benton, November 26, 1861

Dear Wife,

Hixon and I went to the 2d Rigm. The [Medway] Boys are all very well except one or two from the village. John Swarman has been very sick with the fever but he is better now. . . . Edward Bullen come home with us and staid all night with us. When I say home I mean to our camp. Tuesday we built a cook house with logs and stone, for it was rather cold cooking out doors. We have had one little flurry of snow Sunday night. Last week Tuesday & Wednesday the Rigm was prepairing for Thanksgiving, gitting Turkeys and Geese. I believe the Governor of Mass sent and orderd all of the officers to furnish things for all of the Mass troops that was necessary for their good. The 19 & 20 Rigm had Turkeys and all they could ask for, and the 2 Rigm too,

Figure 8. Eliza (Arnold) Hill and Lucina Maria Hill. Daguerreotype Collection, Massachusetts Historical Society.

but I will tell you how our Company spent the day. We had beaf & hard crakers & coffee for breakfast & hard corn Beaf & hard Bread & water for dinner, and bread and tea or coffee for supper. If we had been paid off we should have bought something better but we had no money to buy with, while all the other troops, Mass troops, had all furnished they needed.

I will give you an idea of the 19th Rigm. Wednesday night, they worked all night a building a large platform for dancing in the afternoon. They sent off and got a lot of women. Some of them came from Baltimore. Two of our teams went and they kild one of our horses. Thursday they put tent cloth over the platform for a cover to keep the cold out at night. They lifted it up very well so it looked well from our camp. Our camp is no more than 20 rods [110 yards] from theirs. Some of the officers came with their nice drest ladys (I think not so respectable), although they appeared very well to see our guns. We had them all spread out on our Boxes. There was a good many from different Rigs to see them. They look well when they are all spread out in line on our gun boxes in the camp street. At night they had dancing, I mean the 19 Rigm. I don't know how long they danced, but I guess most all night. Friday they had a smooth pole raised 25 feet high. I believe it was greased, and if any one could clime it, they was to have $10.00 but no one could clime it, so the one climbed the highest was to have five dollars. The soldiers done all the climbing, then when that was through they had a sack race. They got in sacks hands and all but their heads. Some fell on their fases and some got hurt. One man got hurt so, they had to carry him off. I think that wound up their Thanksgiving.

Now I will tell you how I passed the day. We went out a little while and played Ball, but it was so cold, we gave it up, and then we took out our guns and cleaned them up and spread them out in the street. That was the extent of our amusement.

Friday night we was payed off and Saturday I went to Poolville and got me a nice Pr of Buckskin gloves and a cover to wear on my cap and a cape attached to it that comes down over my neck to keep the rain out of my neck. . . . Did you have a good Thanksgiving? If you did, I am satysfide with mine. If you did not I am not satysfyde with mine for to tell the truth it was a long day with me. I did not write but once last week for I was expecting to be payed off every day. The men in my tent are a going to pay their equal shair and get up a plum pooding. I think we shall not stop here a great while longer. I think I do not get all of your letters. If I do, you do not write as often as I wish you did. Eliza, I like to hear from you as much as you like to here from me. You cannot think how much disappointed I am some nights when the mail comes in to not receive a letter from you. . . .

There has been four or five of us that have had spiritual sittings. [Lieutenant] Wm. Berry, I expect, is a good medium but he has not been in yet. I believe he was the Editor of the Banner of Light [a spiritualist newspaper] until a short time since. . . .

Wednesday. I did not receive any letter from you last night. I was disappointed. It has been rather wet today. Our team has not come to day. No letter from you tonight.

Thursday morning. Our team has come. This morning our Captain did not come, nor did I here any news from Mass. Mr. Berry brought one box of blankets & socks that the Ladies sent from Salem, and some of the company had boxes sent from home. I did not hear much news. The most news I heard was that when General Landers was well he was agoing to move. He got so he walked out two weeks ago and slipped down and put him back again. And he has his choice to go South, East or West, and take our company with him. That is the best news that I have heard of for a week.

We practice shooting most every day now. The company rate me as the third best shot in the company, but I think there are a number of men that can shoot as well as I can. You wrote in one letter about the soldiers gambling and drinking. Since we have got paid off I have seen considerable gambling, but not but a very little drinking in the Company. I have forbid all gambling in my tent but they cheat me some times but I keep them back a good deal. Our Company is composed of Lawyers, school masters, scholars, clerks, Laboring men, black legs [gamblers], machinists, and most everything else. Mr. Berry was the Editor of the Banner of Light. He is another one of our company.

A few moments ago I heard that one Rebble came across the river yesterday and gave himself up as a prisenor and there were two or three more that was afraid for fear they would not be used well, and if the one come across was used well he was to get our troops to fire one musket shot and two pistol shots and I understand they are agoing to do so. . . .

I wish the Captain would come and bring my Boots for my shoes are agiting thin although I have a better chance now since we have built a cook house for I go in there and sit nights when I am on guard duty. They have a kitten in the cook's house, and last night when I put my men on guard, I sat by the fire alone and she came and played with me and it made me think of *home*. I thought then I wished it was Bub instead of the kitten. . . .

Wednesday noon. Dear Eliza, the box has just come, all the things. I believe the Chicken is spoilt and pudding. I have thrown them away. The pies I think are good. I have not tried them yet, but they look good. The Blanket looks well. I think it will do me good in some cold night. My pillow I shall sleep on every night. I would not take anything for it. Is better since it come from you. Mits and socks, I am very much obliged to Mother and Sister. Eliza, I think you was very thoughtful to send me those wristers [fingerless mittens]. The fur & blanket I have hung out to air. The aples and potatoes I think will go well. I have hardly tasted of an aple this fall. They sell small aples for 2 cents apiece. Tell Mother Harding that I am greatfully oblige to her for that Butter. It came nice and good. Tell Ida & Bub that the pipes came safe and sound. I have used one of them and it goes well. You must buy Ida a stick of candy for me. I think Bub will get his pay in this letter. Love to you all, M Hill

LUKE BICKNELL

Poolsville Nov. 30th 1861

Dearest [Lucretia],
Your letter of Thanksgiving Eve was most gladly received. . . .

I remember I did think of you nearly all evening. I can hardly see how you manage to express your ideas so clearly in your letters, your pen is far kinder than your lips. Not that your lips are not very kind, and the sweetest pair of lips I ever saw. . . . Your letters can't be beat. I always keep your letters and read them first thing next morning. Then when I haven't anything to do I read them all over. . . .

Really I should like to see you a few minutes. Guess we would both have a first rate time.

You cannot be more anxious to have the war end than I am, still I don't want it to end until we have whipped the South soundly. . . .

I certainly should like to feel your arms around my neck once more, and receive in person some of those kisses that I know you would give me. There is no need of my saying I should have plenty to give you. I haven't kissed a girl since I saw you.

Ain't you afraid my lips will grow rusty. If there were some good looking girls around camp perhaps I would practice a little, just to keep my hand in, but I will be hanged before I'll kiss a negro wench and that is about all we see here. . . .

The wind shakes the tent [horribly?]. I can't write well as you must see.

I wish I could set up with you tonight. I never feel so happy as when I am setting by you with your head lying on my breast and lips meeting mine.

I am sure that no one can ever fill Cretia's place *by my side.* I wish you were my W___. "There I almost wrote it before I happened to think I promised not to again in my last." You know it is natural for fellows to want to be married to a girl they love and I confess I am like all the rest of the fellows on that point. I hope circumstances will permit it soon. I see no prospect of an engagement here very soon and if there is, I do not think I shall get shot.

I do not think I was born to be shot. Since you show so much anxiety for me to come home I find I want to myself.

The prospect of a married life with you is so very attractive to me that I believe I should like to try it thirty or forty years.

The Creator alone knows the future yet I am very hopeful that everything will be just as I wish it.

Yours truly,
Bicknell

MOSES HILL

Camp Benton, December 1, 1861

Dear Wife,

I would say there is nothing new here in camp but I expect we shall have marching orders soon. If we do not go into action soon I think we shall go into winter quarters. It may seem strange to you and most of people in Mass that we or the army does not go into immediate action and have the thing settled up at once, but the Government is doing as much and going as fast as they can and go safe. They have a large army it is true, and they have a very large army to contend with and the Rebbles are well disciplined soldiers, that is, meny of them, and have the advantage of our army. They are on the defensive, and they do take great advantage of the hills and woods. But if we can get them in an open field fight we can whip them very easy. Our Company fought the . . . Rigement of the Rebble army that is called the Missippi Wild Cats and we could not get them out in fair sailing.

Our Government is doing as fast as they can. Cannon are making and coming most every day and new Rigm are coming, all this strengthening our army very much, and the fleets are doing a great work. And in Western Vergina they are doing good business, and on the Missippi they are getting ready to sweep all before them. And all is working as fast as can be and do it safe.

While the Rebble army are at a stand or nearby so I think, their troops are getting dissatisfied and very poorly clothed, and they cannot get their pay or not but a small part of it. Nathan, I don't believe they can strengthen their army any more, while our army are strengthening every day. Nathan I hope you will not be discouradge, not any one else in Mass, for all is working I think to the best advantage. I want you to write to me again soon. From your Brother, M Hill.

Eliza, I was glad to have three letters from home Thursday night, I guess I was. I was glad to have a letter from Bub. Did he eat a good lot of Turkey and pudding Thanksgiving and pick out the plums? And I was glad to have a letter from Sis. I hope she is a good girl and I wish I could see her too. She must write to me often, *won't you Sis?* It seems as if I think more of you than when I was at home. . . . Eliza, I think I should like to see you and spend the Sabbath with you and my dear children. Would I not be *Happy?* But there is no use in talking for I cannot see none of you at present.

I expect to get that Box this week. Mr. Berry is going to Washington this week. Our Captain got his furlow extended a short time, but I expect him this week. I hope, Eliza, your things will come safe to me. . . . I hope you will have no trouble in getting your money that I sent you.

My tent's crew had their plum pudding this morning for breakfast and there is enough left for Supper. All that we bought, cheese and butter and all, cost $4.90.

I must leave off now to go on guard duty.

Luke Bicknell (memoir, p. 13)

The company built palatial winter quarters, we sergeants even going to the extent of a spacious fire-place in our tent. The paymaster visited us for the first time and laying a pile of gold on one side of his table, and a pile of greenbacks on the other, invited us to take our choice. We knew the [status] of the government, and though nothing was said about paying us twenty five dollars a month, we took the greenbacks instead of the gold.

Winter accommodations for the privates were, according to another member of the company, less "palatial."

George Whittemore Jr.

Camp Benton, November 20, 1861

The principle discomfort here arises from the impossibility of being neat. I was never fastidious, but cannot reconcile myself to the state of things here and to our crowded condition. We have eleven or twelve in tents which were made to hold eight. I shall break off, for the crowd of men and the clatter of voices in this smoky tabernacle of ours seem to make the letter unfit to send to you. . . . I wonder if any of the smoke or other odors goes in the letter to Boston. I believe it can't be helped in the present state of things.[4]

"I Am Very Well Now"

MOSES HILL

Camp Benton, December 3, 1861

Dear Wife,

Our team has gone to Washington today to meet the Captain and get what things there is to come. Two four horse teams has gon after them. It is very cold here. Today is the coldest day we have had. We could see snow on the Blue Ridge Mountains last week. I think I will not finish this letter until the teams come back. I am on guard duty again today. . . .

Wednesday afternoon. I have just been asleep. I received a letter from you dated 17th. I am sorry they do not come more regular.

The 19 Rigm moved today. They went down towards Washington. I believe they have gone to do Picket duty in on the River as near as I can learn. I think we shal move somewhere soon. I expect the Captain back tomorrow night and our teams.

Thursday. The teams has not come yet but our Captain come tonight but the team has not come. He said they was waiting for the baggage to come.

Friday. They may come to night but I think I will not wait so I will finish this letter and write another Sunday. It has been very pleasant yesterday, and today it is very pleasant. The Captain said that General Landers went out Wednesday. He said he carried him down and put him into a carriage and rode out with him. He said the general told him that they had given this Company up to him when he was able to move. I am glad of it if it is so for I think he is a good General.

Eliza, we had a very good pudding last Sunday. It made us two very good meals, but it was not so good as you make. Dear Eliza, I wish I was at home to get some of your good vitules although it may be that the food is as good for our health here but it does not go quite so well. At noon we had split pea soop and dry bread and water. The soop was burnt and I do not like it so I did not eat any and I eat my dry bread with water. Perhaps I would like some of your good meat and potato such as I use to have. One good thing, I enjoy good health. I am very well now. . . .

Tuesday, December 3, 1861

Dear little George,

You have wrote to papa and I think it is time for papa to write to George. I will tell you about little Negro Boys. There was three little negro Boys one day come over here where papa was and they was very black all of them and one had large round black spots on his face and all over his body. Papa pitied the poor little Boy. One day when papa was on guard one little niger Boy come out and brought papa some boiled cabage and give it to papa and papa gave him five cents and he was dredful tickeld with it and he ran home and showed it to his folks. It was when papa was on guard down at the Generals quarters. There is some Niger Boys live close by there. There is lots of little black Boys round here and niger mama come round the camp.

Yesterday the men was chopping in the woods and they found two little flying squerels and they catch them and brought them home and put them in a box and this morning they was both dead. W'ant that too bad? Papa has not got any dogs now. I let them both go and they have not come back, but there is two great dogs here. One is a great black dog, and one is a great yellow dog. The black dog is a good clever dog. Bub, papa will send him home a gold Dollar some time. He must be a good Boy and mind his mama. Papa thinks he will come home and see Bub sometime. Papa hopes he will. Bub must write to papa and tell him how the Crow and pigs and chickens does. There is lots of pigs here. Papa sees lots of pigs in the woods. They go in the woods and eat nuts. Bub, you must write every time when mama does.

This is from your Dear papa, M Hill

Camp Benton, Sunday Dec 8th /61

Dear Wife,

I received a letter from you last night. I am glad to hear that you are all well.... Eliza, I think I dread washing my clothes more than anything else. I washed all my clothes last week. I had a warm day to do it, and washed myself all over too. I get more dirty sleeping with my clothes on nights, although when I am not on guard I take my pants off and sleep with my coat and draws on. I heard some heavy cannonading down the River on the Verginia side yesterday, and last night in the night we heard by very good authority that Genl [George] McCaul [McCall] was fighting and he had took 1,000 Rebels and 600 killed, although it may not be true. But I think there must be some truth in it.

I shall put one dollar in this letter for Bub, and in the next letter I shall send one to Sis. There were only two letters, some for the soldiers in this Company last night, one was for me. There must be more than two hundred back letters for this Company now. They may come all together this week. It is very pleasant here now. I think it is Indian Summer here now....

Wednesday morning. Dear Eliza, I think I shall get all the things you sent me but, the meat will be spoilt, and the pudding. I pray you not to worry about it for anything that I get from you is worth everything to me. I am very sorry to think that you took so much pains to cook and work for me with the pleasure you took in sending me something, and have it spoil. I feel worse on your account then I do for my own, but Eliza do not worry. I am sure I shall get all the things as I said before. If they come today I shall write again tomorrow. I am well. I don't [know] when I have enjoyed better health. That is worth more to you and to me than your chicken is, don't you think so Eliza?

I think that Battle down the River did not amount to much. You wrote in your letter that you was afraid that I should be called off to Kentucky but I think we shall not move any where until Gen. Landers gets better, for he means to keep us if possible.... I hope Lucina will study and learn all she can this winter, for soon she can not have the privalage of schooling and now's the time for her to improve every moment she can.... Do not worry dear Eliza about that box.

LUKE BICKNELL (MEMOIR, P. 13)

Prof. Lowe came on with his balloon "The Intrepid" and forty of the sharp-shooters took charge of and guarded and managed it. Whenever any of our generals wanted to ascend we let it up 600 feet; and were much amused at the wild shots made at it from the opposite side of the river. One day our ground tackle gave way, with Gen. Banks in the basket, but the sharpshooters hung to the rope, although hoisted high into the air, and finally we got a hold upon terra-firma again.

LUKE BICKNELL

Edwards Ferry Camp of Observation Dec 10th 1861
You see I write from another spot now.... Rather uncomfortable now nights. The men are saying every morning "Wish my wife was here to sleep with." I sleep as cold as any of them but don't wish for the lady. Lack of experience perhaps. Don't like the idea of taking a woman to a bed on the ground. Should like to be at home sometimes though....

No one expects this war to last over a year now.... We are in sight of the rebels all the time. But the river is between us all. We shell their camp. But they have not got any guns that will reach us. So we laugh and grow fat.

It is considerable work to attend that [balloon]. We keep him hitched most of the time. It takes 40 men to hold him. We have just been out since I began to write, worked on the old fellow two hours. His name is Intrepid.

We expect the rebels will try to shell us out of this place. But two can play that game. . . .

Absent but anxious to be at home with you, L. Emerson Bicknell

MOSES HILL

Camp Benton, Sunday, December 15, 1861

Dear Wife,

I don't know but you will think that I have almost forgotten you for I have not written to you but once since a week last Friday. But I have not. I waited until Wednesday before the team come with that box. As soon as they come, I wrote, and since [then] I have been up more or les every night since on guard duty. Thursday 40 of our men went to the river to help raise a Balloon and they did not raise it until yesterday. It went up three times and it has been up today. They let it up with a rope and then pull it down again. They do it to see what the rebels are a doing. They cannot see but a few camps. They was afraid the Rebbels was agoing to cross soon or try to. But I guess there is no danger at present.

I sent one gold Dollar to Bub in the letter that I wrote last Wednesday and I shall send one in this for Sis. I don't know as I can send anything else that will be of so much use or do them so much good excepting a Father's love. Dear Eliza, I don't know how I can pay you for that Box. I think a gold dollar will not pay it. Those pies was very nice, you better believe. I think of home when I eat them. I have two left now and some aples. I would not part with my pillow for nothing. I think a great deal of it. I thank Mother & Sister for the presents they sent me. I feel rather tired and sleepy this afternoon for the Captain & Doctor in the 20 Regm & Adjutant & first Leutenant wanted me to go with them this morning after foxes so I went. I have had a good race. I wounded one fox but we did not git him.

I don't know but there will be some movement in the army soon, it seems like it, up tords Harpers Ferry. Banks division is moving up there. . . .

I would like to be at home and hunt foxes. I think I like it better then I do to hunt Rebels. . . . I am very well now and gaining in flesh some. Answer this as soon as you receive it if you can. Eliza, I think I have a good meny friends in the Company and good will of all of the Oficers. That is a great thing in my favor. . . .

My first releaf is off and now I will try to finish my letter. You ask me in your letter how I should like to live out here, if I had the money to buy a plantation, I think, and negroes to do the work. I could live as easy as [if] I was a minister. But this is not the place for you and me to enjoy life with our means. . . .

If any smart man could come out here and follow the Rigements, go from one to another and sell goods, I think they might make money fast. If you can buy some beaf and pork and things that you need this winter perhaps you had better do so. Buy things to make yourself comfitable pray do, and make Sis & Bub so too. I need not say any thing about them for I know they will have everything they need. If you do not have the means let me know. Let me know how you get along drawing money from Captn Daniels. Dear Eliza, write me as often as you can for you don't know how I like to hear from you. . . .

My gun lock is a little out of order. When I get it fixed I will try to make a target and send it home to you. If it is a very still day it will not take a very large piece of paper.

Camp Benton, Monday, December 23, 1861

Dear Wife,

I received a letter from you Saturday night dated Nov. 24th. . . . It is a rainy morning this morning. It is cold frozen rain. . . . I am very well now. My health is as good as I could ask for.

Friday I went a fox hunting again with the Captain. We had two dogs and we started one fox and I shot at him but I did not get him. When we come into camp the officers laught at us some, just as Mr. Harding use to laugh at me when I used to go and not get any. The Captain said he would not give it up. So he wanted to go again yesterday morning. Four of us went out we had six dogs all good hounds they started one and I got a shot at him and kild him ded. The Captain felt better and in a little while the dogs started another and the fox ran within two rods [11 yards] of one man and he shot at him and then he come up to another man, and he shot at him and then he ran up to the Captain and he shot him ded. Then the Captain felt better still and so did I. That wound up the hunting for that time.

Eliza I do not aproove of hunting [on] Sunday but I am glad to get out of camp and it seems good to me to go into the woods. It seems like home, and as long as I keep in with the Captain I can have more privalage, so I think you cannot blame me. Friday the Captain and I was out alone and we sat down and talked about the war. He said there was danger of the Rebels crossing the River here. He said the Rebels was making boats at Leesburg and he said they had about 18 boats out in Goose Creek. He said they could see them when they went up in the Baloon. I cannot think of anything new to write you in regard to the war. I have sent one letter to you with a Dollar in it for

Bub and one letter with a dollar in it for Sis, and if you get them I wish you write and let me know. . . .

I should not wonder if we went out hunting again by tomorrow. I have a great time hunting just now. It takes up my mind a great deal and I get some good meals by so doing. I go in and take breakfast with the Captain. We have Beef stake or something good. Last night we had a good Beef stake. It was a good supper. So you see how I gain it by being a fox hunter.

Yesterday where we got our dogs, it was at a farm house. They gave us a good dinner. We had fresh Pork and sausages. It relished well, I will assure you. I think they are very nice folks and good Union folks to[o]. I will not say anything more in this letter about hunting.

We have got our new tents now. In the last letter I received you wanted to know if you should direct your letters to Co[rporal] Hill but I do not want you to. . . . I would like to have Sis write often. I think it will learn her to write a good deal. Kiss Sis and Bub & Hattie for me lots of times and I will kiss you when I get home enough to make it up.

Camp Benton, Tuesday, December 24, 1861

Dear Daughter,

I was up on guard duty last night and I was rather sleepy today, so I have just had a nap and as I woke I thought of you and I thought I would commence a letter. It is very cold here to day. Last night it was the coldest night I think we have had out here. It was a very rainy day yesterday and it cleared off last night cold.

I want to see you very much. I have not forgot you, for I think of you a great meny times every day. I suppose you go to school every day. I hope you learn all you can now for soon you will be to[o] old to go to school and all you learn now will be a great help to you when you get older. If it had not been so cold I think I should of gone down and seen the Balloon. It is so windy I think it will not go up today. Tomorrow it is Christmas day and I think I shal go and see it. It is a very large one. It carrys up four or five men and it goes up about 1,000 ft. sometimes. The men hold it by a rope and when they have been up long enough they pull them down again. If you was here we would go up in it together. I think we should enjoy it very much. They see a long distance over in the Virginia side.

I cannot say that I like the country here as well as I do in old Mass, but I think some part of Mariland is very pleasant. I wish you could have some of the persimmons. They are a little larger then our plumbs that grow in Mass. When I was out hunting the other day we found them very plenty. We found some small trees that hung very full and we got all we could eat. They are the

best after the frosts comes. There is plenty of walnuts now in the woods. The
Captain and I got more than a peck in a little while the other day. The roads
are very poor out here. They are not better then the cart roads at home. The
houses are not very plenty here. There is nothing but farming here, and every
farmer has a small house, although some have quite a large houses, and all
of them have one or two small houses for their negroes to live in. The Blacks
do all of the work. They do the cooking and washing, so the owners do but
very little work, and the men do all the work out doors. Most of the slaves
fare very well out here. Sundays they have the day to themselves, and they go
round to see their friends. Many have wifes, Husbands, daughters, Brothers,
Fathers, Mothers. Sometimes [they] are owned by different ones, and Sundays they go to see each other. They do not have [to] work very hard.

Lucina, I do not have to work very hard here but being up nights is the
worst, although I do not stand out in the cold as the men do that is walking
their beats, but I am broke of my sleep as much and sometimes more. I do
not have hard work enough to do, I think, for my own good. I wish I was at
home to see you all and hug and kiss you and Bub, but I think it is better for
me to be here to give you better support and to serve my Country. I pray the
National Troble will close soon, then I hope I shal be with you as long as
we live.

Lucina, I want you to write to me often and I will write to you again soon.
Write me all the news you can think of. It is hard writing now, for my hands
are so cold I can hardly hold the pen. I hope it will be warmer tomorrow. I
am very well now. I wrote to your mother yesterday. I expect to get a letter to
night. I hope I shal. Kiss Bub for me and Mother too, and take as meny for
yourself as you are a mind to.

From your afectionate father, Moses Hill

Camp Benton, Friday, December 27, 1861

Dear Wife,
I received a letter from you Tuesday night. . . . I was very [glad] to hear from
you, and to know you was all well. . . .

Christmas day we had two new guns, and the Capn wanted me to try
them, but I could not have time to try only one, and yestarday I tried the
other. They was new guns, and they shot very well. There was not much
doing here Christmas day, but the men had some privalage to go around if
they wanted. I stayed at the camp. I did not feel like going off anywhere. I
have not been to see the Balloon yet. I was going yesterday but I was sleepy,
for I had my own guard duty and duty for one other Corporal, for he was sick

and you see I did not get much sleep the night before. And I sleep so long yesterday that I had no time, and today it is blustering and cold, so I think I will not go today. The Captain and Mr. Berry has gone to Washington this morning. I suppose it will take them two or three days.

Now I think I will write you about something new. Yesterday the men, twenty of them, went to the Ferry and got two small cannons. There is a rifle berel attached to them about three feet long and about the size of a common barrel such as we shoot, and the barrel is screwed into a socket at the breech, and there is a hop[p]er such as our common corn hopers as we shell corn in. They load a little silender [cylinder] with a common cartridge, and drop the silender in the hopper, and there is a crank that carryes the charge in the breech of the barrel, and when the gearing comes round just right, there is a hammer by the force of a spring that strikes the cap and then it goes off. The crank is small, and every time the crank comes round, it shoots, and one man turning the crank, and there is 500 silenders that can be loaded to each cannon, and as fast as you put them in, just so fast they drop out at the under side.[5] It will take six men or about that to tend it. Both cannons are alike. It takes one horse to draw each of them. There is sights on the barrel the same as any rifle, and the Captain says it will shoot 120 times in a minute, but I think it will shoot from 75 to a 100 easy. It will shoot just as fast as you drop the cilenders in that hopper, and they are about 4 in long, and all you have to do is pick them out of a box that they drop into, and put the cartridge in one end and a cap on the other end, and put them in again, and so on. We tried one of them to day, and it shot very well. Gen Stone's this is, or it belongs to his division, and there was two for Gen Banks. I don't know but we shall have to use these two, but if we do, I think we shal have to have more men. They carry a common sized [.58 caliber] minie ball, about the same size as they use in the Enfield rifles. I think twelve men can shoot both of them 12,000 times in an hour. So you see if they work well, they must do great execution. I think I could shoot a single man 40 rods [220 yards] most every time. I can move the Barrel with one hand so as to sight anywhere I choose. I hope I shal not have any thing to do with them, for men that work them must be considerable exposed to the enemy, and if they was not fools, they would take some pains to pick off the men round it. But if one of them is put upon me to shoot, I shal shoot it.

Dear Eliza, it is cold and you must excuse me for not writing any more to day. . . . I feel very well today and I hope you enjoy the same blessing. Kiss Sis & Bub for me. And may God bless you all.

From your Husband, M Hill

Luke Bicknell

Camp Benton December 29th 1861

Dearest Lucretia

You last letter reached me last night. Thank you for the Merry Christmas wish. I wish you a happy New Year. Hope I may see you before it closes. . . .

I am sorry that your dream of seeing me was not a reality. If I *had* been there we would have had a merry time.

I wish I was where I could get you to help me study Latin evenings as I used to. I would learn you to conjugate Amo, I love, in all the moods, tenses, numbers and voices and I would illustrate and explain the subject in a peculiar manner. . . .

I wish I could spend one evening with you. I love you as much and know so well that my love is returned that I long for the day to come when we may once more sit side by side and talk to each other instead of writing. I think war is a "Tremendous Evil" cause we cant take the girls with us. . . .

I used to think love was confined to novels and had existed only in the brains of story writers. But now I know better. I am sure there is one exception. There is no use attempting to write love. I know I couldn't talk to you to suit me if I was with you but if I have my arms around you, you would not doubt I loved you. I dream of you often nights. More often day dreams though. . . .

I expect a successful joyful life. It certainly will be joyful if you share it with me. I enjoy myself more and more in thinking that Cretia Pierce loves me as she does, than I should to have a thousand other friends.

Fine weather. Good health. Excellent spirits. Hope it is the same with you.

Yours ever and only,

L. Emerson Bicknell

CHAPTER

THE WINTER CAMPAIGN

Before we yield the holy trust
Our old forefathers gave,
Or wrong New England's hallowed dust,
Or grant the wrongs ye crave—

We'll print in kindred gore so deep
The shore we love to tread,
That woman's eyes shall fail to weep
O'er man's unnumbered dead.

—Frederick West Lander, "Rhode Island to the South" (1861)

In mid-October 1861, Brigadier General Frederick West Lander assumed command of the newly formed Department of Harpers Ferry and Cumberland in the mountainous northern end of Virginia's Shenandoah Valley. The Baltimore & Ohio Railroad ran roughly 120 miles through this area, but Confederate raids led by General Thomas "Stonewall" Jackson had destroyed tracks, damaged bridges, and severed telegraph communications. Lander proposed an aggressive winter campaign to secure and repair the railroad and to clear the northern end of the valley of enemy troops. His larger strategic goal, though, was to defeat Jackson quickly, destroy Confederate supply lines from the Valley to their forces near Washington, D.C., then launch a two-pronged movement against a presumably weakened enemy. Lander's superior, General George B. McClellan, however, was already planning a massive attack on Richmond. The B&O railroad and upper Valley figured little in his new strategy. Moreover, after the Union debacle at Ball's Bluff, McClellan feared that if Lander were defeated, it might undermine Northern support for the Union cause. Thus McClellan largely limited Lander's actions.[1]

In early January, Andrew's Sharpshooters joined General Lander's forces in Cumberland, Maryland, a major depot of the B&O railroad near the Potomac River. Apparently to minimize costs, McClellan decided to transport the sharpshooters on the Chesapeake & Ohio canal rather than by rail.[2] The result was an agonizingly long journey through ever-thickening ice. After they disembarked at Williamsport, the men faced an exhausting march over the Blue Ridge Mountains to Cumberland.

From early January to mid-March, the sharpshooters saw little fighting. Most of their time was spent in cold and muddy camps, first at Patterson's Creek, then at Paw Paw, both near the Potomac River and the railroad line. Here they served as Lander's "body guards." In mid-February they were involved in a brief attack on a Confederate outpost at Bloomery Gap in western Virginia.

"A Thoroughly Exhausted Set of Men"

Moses Hill

Camp Benton, Wednesday Jan 1st 1862

Dear Wife & Children,

I would like to be at home this morning to wish you a *happy new year,* but as I am not with you I can only wish you with my pen. Therefore I wish you all *a happy new year.* I should of written to you before, but I waited until the Captain come back. He come Monday night. And then I waited until Tuesday to see if I did not receive a letter from you but I did not. I have not received a letter from you since the 24. . . . I suppose there is so much mail matter at Washington that they cannot attend to it all for we have not had but very little mail for a week. It is very pleasant here today. There is a report this morning that we are agoing to move in a day or two somewhere. . . .

Thursday Morning. Last night there was a report that we was agoing to cross the river this morning and they ordered the cooks to cook up two days raishions and the cooks sat up all night and cooked, but we are not agoing to day I think, and I hardly think we shal go across the river for I think we are a going off somewhere else. I expect we are agoing about a hundred miles somewhere and I think it is on the Baltimore and Ohio R.R.

You must excuse my writing today for it is so cold that I can hardly hold my pen. I don't want you to write after you get this until you get another letter from me for I dont know where I shal be. It may be a number of days before I write to you again but I shal write as soon as I have an opitunity. . . . I think we are agoing with Gen. Lander. He is getting better. He is agoing to superseed some one. I hear there is about 7,000 troops where he is a going.

I am agoing to get my clothes ready today and do my mending and be all ready to start tomorrow morning. Eliza, I eat the last of those mince pies about a week ago and I have got one apple left yet. The pies kept very nice. They was the best that anything I have had since I left home. The lock to my gun is not fixed yet. I miss that very much but I think I shal take a new one, but I had rather have my own gun for I am more use to it.

It is a very buisy time here today. I have had to leave this letter twice now & I hope I shal be able to finish it this time. I am very well now and I hope you enjoy the same blessing. I thought that I should be able to come home this winter on a furlow but I don't know as I shal be able now. I feel somewhat disappointed, for if we go off I don't think I can come. I don't want you to worry about me if you do not have a letter from me for some time, for I don't know where I shal be. All the men have come up this fore noon from the Balloon. They are all getting ready to move. We may be here for two or three days longer and we may sleep on Leesburg or somewhere else by tomorrow night. Dear Eliza do not worry about me. I hope I shall live to come home soon and join my family. Kiss Sis and Bub for me, and my love to all. . . .

LUKE BICKNELL

Camp Benton Thursday morning Jan. 2nd [1862]

Dear Cretia,

We are going somewhere, but I don't know where. Shall march tomorrow morning, possibly today. Are getting ready now but haven't the least idea where we shall march to.

Do not worry if you do not hear from me next week. I may be where I have no opportunity to write. . . . I shall be thinking of you though.

I have not time to write more. So I will close by sending my love and a kiss.

Yours most truly,

L. Emerson Bicknell

LUKE BICKNELL (MEMOIR, P. 13)

Gen. Lander had so far recovered as to be at his new head quarters at Cumberland, Md. and on the third day of January, 1862, we left our comfortable quarters at Camp Benton to join the general we loved so well . . . and putting our rifles, rations and knapsacks, aboard a canal boat, [we] manned the drag rope and set off to tow the load 50 miles up the canal to Williamsport.

MOSES HILL

Monocacy, Jan 4th 1862

Dear Wife,

I have just received a letter from you. It was dated Dec 24. I am aboard the canal Boat. I am at this time on gard of the provisions. I am very glad to hear from you. We went on board the boat last night. I slept but very little last night for I was on guard most of the time. Dearest Eliza, do not cortion [caution] me quite so hard, for it almost hurts my feelings. I think too much of you and my Dear Children to forget them. I don't know but I do wrong to write this, but I feel so. I do everything as near right as I can. There is not one in the Company that does as I do in regard to right & wrong. I think a thousand times more of you and my Dear Children than when I was at home. Dear Eliza, do not feel hard tords me, for my whole mind is at home. Eliza, I expect we shall go to Hancock. It is about 80 miles from here. We have some hard country to go through, but dear Eliza, do not worry about me for I do trust in God and I hope he will bring me home safe.

It is hard for the Canell boat for the ice is in some places half an inch thick. Excuse my writing for I have no time to lose. I am well. That is a great blessing to me. I must close soon. Please destroy this letter for my sake. We are in good cannon shot of the Rebls. With a tear in my eye I must Close this letter. . . .

LUKE BICKNELL (MEMOIR, PP. 13–14)

The thin ice with which the canal was covered at the start soon grew thicker and threatened to cut our boat in two, so we put an ice boat ahead. It soon became necessary to keep a detail of men on the ice boat, and as we could not keep the ice cold water out of our boots, it was thought best to keep the same men on all the time, so that the rest of the company might be fit for duty when we arrived. We had on board a keg of New England rum . . . and we tried this on the ice boat until we found out that hot coffee was better. . . . We had thought to make the trip by canal in three, or at most, four days, and had laid in rations accordingly, but were delayed by the ice so much that we had consumed our last morsel of food the morning before we reached Williamsport.

MOSES HILL

Jan 6th 1862

Dear Wife,

I am on the Canall Boat. We stoped at Harpers Ferry last night. I am well now but some tired. I have not slept much since last Thursday. We have got to go about 50 miles more I expect. I have had one letter from you since we have been abord the Boat. It was 10 oclock when I received it and I answered it as soon as I read it. I hardly know what I wrote for I was nervos and tired and sleepy. We have just been fireing at the Rebels and they are a getting out some of our guns to be ready for them. I expect we are going to Hancock. It is very slow gitting along for the ice is in some places 1½ in. thick.

Monday eve 9 oclock. We are all safe and well. We have been through some rough country since we started. The river is not very wide here. I have been most of the time steering the Boat. I try to make myself useful where I can. There is Picket[s] most all the way up the river on the Mariland side.

I shal try to write every chance I can for I know you will want to hear from me often now. When we get at our Journeys end I shal try to get a ferlow to come home. I shal come and see you if I can. It will cost me 13 Dollars and it is worth every thing to me if I could come home [even] if I do not stay more than two or three days.

I know you would like to see me, but not more than I should like to see you and my Dear Sis & Bub. I think there is a convayance from Hancock, but you must not be disappointed if I do not come. I can say one thing: it will not be my fault for I shal try hard enough.

I am now writing on a box of hard crackers. We are about 12 miles from Harpers Ferry. There is some snow where we are now, and it seems colder every day. We could get along much faster if the ice did not trouble us so. I hope I shal be able to give you an acount of the country up the Potomac River sometime. I don't know what to write to interest you, for I have not time nor conveniences. . . . I have destroyed all my letters for I did not want to keep them. I do not mean the Rebels shall read any of my letters, so you see my reason for doing so.

I understand there is troops marching up the river to the same place. I expect General Landers will take command of us when we get there.

I hope Dear Eliza it will not be very long when I shal come home and see you . . . for you do not know how I want to see you. I don't know but I wrote something in my last letter that I had ought not to of written. It is worried me ever since. I am sorry the Crow is stolen. I think it must be very mean and low to do so and I think it well for them that I was not at home. I loaded up two of the new rifles and laid them near the wheel where I was steering, but I did not use them today. I must close this letter and a thousand kisses to you, Dear Eliza, and kiss Sis and Bub for me. And may God bless you my Dear Eliza. M Hill

Luke Bicknell (memoir, pp. 14–17)

We did not reach [Williamsport] till midnight and were able to procure but a scant breakfast. Shouldering our knapsacks and ponderous rifles, we marched on foot without food thirty miles more to Hancock, where we arrived late at night a thoroughly exhausted set of men. It was too late to procure rations that night, and we were too tired to prepare and eat food if we could have got it.

The next day we drew rations, obtained quarters in a barn, built fires in an open lot near by, and spent the day in eating, preparing rations for the remainder of the trip, washing up, and drying our feet and clothing as well as we could by out door fires on a cold, raw, misty day. We reckoned on one good nights rest in the barn, but had been turned in only . . . [to be] routed out by the news that Cumberland was in imminent danger of capture.

The night was very dark . . . cold, raw and misty, while the roads had become softened until the foot sunk to the ankle at every step in a most tenacious bed of mud. But the general who had hurried from Baltimore and crossed the Potomac to stand or fall with us, was now in turn in need of our presence, and we tossed the knapsacks into the teams and shouldering our rifles started off at a long quick step for Cumberland, 41 miles, they told us. . . . We kept it up a mile or two, and then the overtaxed muscles began to give out, and by midnight, when the vanguard halted, it was but a small squad that stood in ranks. Capt. Jack [Saunders] was among the missing and we saw no more of him until the teams brought him to Cumberland a few days later. Poor fellow! He was altogether too fat for such heavy marching. . . .

By morning we had given up all hope of getting the whole company to Cumberland in season to be of any use, and had decided to allow each man to push ahead on his own hook, in hopes to get a few rifles there in season to be of use. . . .

The infantry who had followed from Hancock although fresh for the start, had struggled nearly as bad as the sharpshooters. The road was full of men each of whom was making the best progress possible on his own hook. . . . I was much too exhausted to eat and . . . cold water would not remain on my stomach, but I was no worse off in this respect than many of my companions. We fairly staggered on our way. . . . About five in the afternoon I reached the bridge across the railroad east of Cumberland, and looked down upon the town, leaning on the rail for support. . . .

That night we slept luxuriously on a foot of straw in the pits of the Round House, never minding the engines which were gently backed over us during the night. The next day brought in most of the stragglers, and that night we got aboard the cars and rode to Patterson Creek, Va. jumping off the cars into mud six inches deep.

MOSES HILL

Verginia, Pattersons Crick, Jan 15th 1862

Dear loveing Wife,

I cannot write but a few words for it is so cold. I am writing with my overcoat on and 3 Blankets. As soon as I get where it is warm I can write you more. We arrived in Cumberland Saturday night and we was tired and lame and with blistered feet so we was obliged to stop until Monday. We came out here. We are with Gen. Landers. There is about 8000 troops here. Our troops take Rebels prisenors every day here. We have not had no fight yet. We are all safe and well yet. That is the most I want to write you. I am well and I pray God you enjoy the same blessing. If I live to see the day I start for home it will be the hapyest day I ever saw I think now. But dear Eliza, do not worry about me for I shal try to take care of myself if I can. . . .

We went through Williamsport and Hancock to Cumberland. We marched 39 miles in 24 hours and it was a hard march. We shal not stay here but a short time. I think we shal have fighting to do soon for we are right amongth the Rebels. I expect we shal be paid off again soon. We have not been paid off but once since we have been out here. We are about 8 miles from Cumberland on the Ohio & Baltimore R.R.

Dear Eliza, I will write as often as I can to let you know how & where I am. And as soon as we get to some stoping place where it [is] warm so I can write I will write you a longer letter and I think it may be interesting to you. If I continue here a year and live to get home I can tell you a good history of the army, and I think I can tell my dear Children many a tale that I know it will be interesting to them. It is snowing here and hail for most of the time since we have been here. We have piched our tents but we have not got any fire. I expect we shal have some stoves tonight. I have seen a number of Rebel priseners. They are drest very poorly. . . .

Pattersons Creek, Verginia, Saturday Jan 18th 1862

Dearest Loving Companion and Wife,

... We are at Pattersons Creek about 8 miles from Cumberland in the valley on the north Branch of the Potomack on the B. & O. R.R. It is very rainy here this morning. We got a stove last night but we have no funnel yet so we have to set it half way out of the tent to keep the smoke out but I think it warms the tent a little. I will now give you a little History of our march. ...

We started from Edwards Ferry Saturday morning. We went aboard the Boat Friday night. I believe I wrote that we went aboard Thursday night in one of my letters, but we did not until Friday night. It was cold when we started and quite cold all the way while we was on the Boat. We had horses the first three days to draw the boat, and the second day we had horses to put on an ice boat to brake the ice before the canal Boat. We slept but very little, for everything was damp & wet and we had to keep on the lookout for the Rebles on the opessit side of the River. But the last two days was the worst on the Boat, for the horses gave out and we had only horses enough to draw the icebraker, and some of the men had to take hold of the rope and help them, and the rest of the men had to draw the Canall Boat. But me I steered the Boat most of the time, and when I was not at the helm I was on the look out with the spy glass to see if there was any Rebles near, for we was in some danger all the way. But we saw no Rebles but once. We took out our guns and loaded them but we did not shoot them. The scenery up in the valley I hope I shall live to explain to you. We landed at Williamsport Wednesday night. It is quite a little village about as large as Holliston, I should think. We left the Boat Thursday morning and started for Hancock. It is 26 miles. It was very wet under foot, but for all that we got into Hancock about 10 oclock at night. The men was very tired marching so fer and carrying their luggage. Most of the men was able to get in, however, and we slept in an old Barn on the floor. The floor was hard but we was so tired it seemed good to camp down any-where. We stayed there all the next day cooking up rations. Hancock is near the Potomac river. It is a right smart place, to use the language used here, I think larger than Williamsport.

Friday night about 6 oclock we started from Hancock. There was some snow, just enough to make it wet under foot. There was two other Rig. started with us but we did not keep together. We started for Cumberland, 39 Miles. We marched 13 miles and halted at 2 oclock in the morning and stoped at an old Tavern house but it was not kept as a Tarvern now, and we camped down on the Barroom floor and some went up into an empty room upstairs. Two of us opened a barroom door and I and one other man slept in there on the floor. It was just large enough for us.

We was called very early in the morning and got something to eat and some hot coffee. Then the Capt. called the men out on a line and said he wanted 30 men to go through with him. He knew very well that all of the men could not stand it to go through with their sore feet. I gave out the day before. I had so meny things to carry, but the Captain came to me and put my knapsack on one of the wagons and made me get on too. As it happened, we was up on the top of a mountain and it was down hill for some ways so I rode down the hill and then I got off. I felt some rested and I got along very well as I did not carry my knapsack. I went along and found the Cap. and [he] asked me why I did not ride. I told him I felt able as there was so many worse then I was.

As I said before, he called them up on a line. He said we need not carry our knapsacks, and 33 of us volunteered to go through, for we expected we was wanted at Cumberland. I felt very foot sore but I was the first one to volunteer. We started, 26 miles before us. The Company could not keep together, for some walked faster than others. So we strung along the road the best we could. It was different roads than we have here in old Mass to travel, for one of the mountains was 5 miles over it, and another 3 miles it was all up and down. This was the Blue Ridge.

I got into Cumberland about 6 oclock Saturday night. The rest stoped on the road, but they all come in Sunday morning, of those that volunteered, and the rest of the Company come in Sunday night. When I got in, my feet was blistered, but not so bad as a great many others. I wish you could [have] seen us walk when we come in. It was not a laughing matter, but I think Mother Harding would of pityed us very much and I think she would [have] been very busy in fixing our feet. My feet are most well now. When we come into Cumberland we went into an Engine House. There was some straw brought in and we felt quite comfortable.

Sunday night we had an Invitation to go to Meeting. Most of the men went. I wanted to go but the Orderly wanted 3 privates and one corperel to guard our wagons. No Coperels volunteered, so I went. It was a cold rough night but we got through the night. Sunday morning I must acknolage I felt homesick when I heard the Church Bells ring for Church. It seemed more like home then anything I have seen, but I thought there was no use. Cumberland is the best looking place we have been into out here. It is where so much coal comes from, and the best coal our blacksmiths use in Mass. Coal is worth no more then 50 cts to 1.00 per ton. I think most of the folks are Union there.

Monday morning we put our wagons and all our things aboard the cars and started for Pattersons Creek where we are now. I think we shall not stop here long. We have Rebels all round us. There has been some prisernors taken here since we have been here. I think I have seen 20 prisnors since we came into Cumberland. There is rather busy times here amongth the troops. There was about 2,000 went out last night on an excursion. They went down about 12 miles but they see nothing. They came in about 10 oclock.

There is 18 pieces of Artilery. Ringgolds Cavelry are here. They are very fine horses. I am sorry that there is no Mass troops here. We are in front of General Landers quarters. He stops in a large brick house very near here. The man that ownes it was taken prisenor. That is the only house very near here. It is a very wet place to camp where we are. I cannot advise any of my friends to enlist this winter. If I live to come home, I can tell a hard story and a trew one too. If we had trew and faithful officers in the army I think the war would be nearly closed by this time. . . . Dear Eliza, I don't know as I can come home at present. It will cost me as much again as it would at Poolville or nearly as much. What would I give to see you today and the dear children.

From your ever loving Husband, M Hill

LUKE BICKNELL

Patterson's Creek, Virginia Jan 18th 1862 [to Lucretia] How do you do? If it had not rained today I presume we should have been on the march. But it commenced pouring down nicely early this morning. Everybody goes round with their pants tucked into boots and talks about wet feet. There is no danger of a move until the weather changes. . . .

We are now with Gen. Lander who makes a pet of our Co. and consequently we have nothing to do only when there is a chance for a fight.

Patterson's Creek, from which the place is named joins the Potomac about 40 rods [220 yards] south of our camp. We are right in the fork of the two rivers and only about ten rods [55 yards] into Virginia. . . .

We came down here Monday, pitched our tents about two rods [11 yards] from the railroad and slept in the mud that night. Next day we all put in half a dollar a piece (2.50) and bought a stove of the Ohio Regiment, but there was no pipe. So Martin and myself started out to look for one. We found a piece of cast iron steam pipe long enough and set up our stove. The Capt. sent to Cumberland and drew 9 stoves from Government but they did not come till yesterday, so everybody came into our stove to get warm. Now we have got two stoves.

We have got the worst place in camp I ever was in, a perfect mud hole. But it is a good military position being surrounded on all sides by mountains, excepting where the river and the creek comes through.

I believe I will tell you the names of all the Boys in our tent. 1st the Orderly Sergeant John L. Perley. Dark Complex[ion], Good Looking, 24 years old, Married, Baby. 2nd Sergeant Henry Martin. Dark Complex. Very good looking, always smiling, splendid whiskers, been to sea and married a pretty girl just before he started. These two were out with me before [in the 8th Mass.]. Next Charles M. Ingalls Dark Complex, little gray, very intellectual, large man, good boat business man. Then—Henry Jenkins—The oldest man in the company. The best shot. Has drunk too much liquor in his best days.

You know me. Homely, Red Haired, Fresh Faced and ugly.

We all live together. All married except me. . . .

Sunday evening. But really after all this talk of an advance it is possible that the aspect of affairs may change tomorrow so that we may not move for months, or it is even possible that we may retreat. Uncertainty hangs over everything.

Meanwhile the men wound round with over coats and hands stuck in pockets and pants tucked in boots cursing the weather and especially the mud which is on an average 4 inches deep. We have dug ditches to try to drain the streets of our camp but it is no use. . . . Three days of warm weather has melted the snow upon the mountains, so that the two rivers have overflowed their banks and the water has risen around the knoll on which we are till it is not more than two rods from out tent.

The water is more muddy than any which ever runs in any Windsor road, but we must use it for making tea and coffee. But the boys take it easy and play that what makes the coffee look so is that it has been milked.

All of the troops here are Ohio, Pensylvania, and Virginia Boys except ourselves. Sometimes I allow myself to think for a moment that I should like to be sitting by your side with my arms *round* you. But, Oh Dear. What is the use. It aggravates me awfully to even think of it, when I know it is impossible for me to get there.

You know *Patriotism Duty* and all sorts of things is well enough. But a fellow can't help thinking about the Dear Ones at home. I hope it will not take much longer to save the Union.

There will be a blessed time all round I reckon, when we do get home. One does not know how to value the love of a woman like you till he misses the accustomed kiss and glad welcome every Sunday night.

The Bugle is blowing Roll Call [and] I must stop.

Now good night a thousand kisses

Yours everywhere
L. Emerson Bicknell

"A Very Unhealthy Place"

The sharpshooters quickly realized that disease posed a far greater threat to their well-being than the Confederates. Moses Hill wrote, "I do not dred a Battle so much as I do sickness." Such fears were realistic, as Union army mortality statistics later confirmed: the number of soldiers' deaths from disease in the war was double the number from battle. As one writer put it: "The soldier usually had to drink any water available. . . . Often, water supplies were shared by drinkers, bathers, launderers, cooks, horses, mules, the commissary's cattle, flies, mosquitoes, and other fauna as well as, unwittingly, some protozoa and bacteria coming from skins, nearby latrines, and other obvious sources. . . . [C]amp and field life in many respects microbiologically . . . represented a reversion nearly to the cave-life stage of sanitation."[3]

The major killer diseases during the war were diarrhea and dysentery, typhoid and various other fevers, pneumonia, and malaria. Some men died in camp, some in army hospitals, and many of the roughly quarter million discharged for "disability" later died at home.[4]

However much "seasoning" the sharpshooters underwent during their stay in Camp Benton, clearly their battle against disease would continue unabated. Moreover, as one historian notes, this winter campaign (and the Peninsula Campaign that followed) reveals "a far sicker and demoralized soldier population than often portrayed in the literature," because it "presented a challenging combination of mountainous terrain and variable weather, constant movement, and logistical snafu."[5] By late February 1862 a combination of measles, fevers, and other illnesses had reduced the number of sharpshooters on active duty to forty-three. And by early March two sharpshooters had died, one of them from diphtheria, a contagious disease of the throat, which Luke Bicknell claimed was widespread among the sharpshooters. Moses Hill and others who complained of having a "sore mouth" or "sore throat" may have contracted it. One infected man coughing or sneezing in the close quarters of a stuffy winter tent could have easily infected his tentmates. In any event, many of the company languished in an understaffed and filthy army hospital in nearby Cumberland.[6]

LUKE BICKNELL (MEMOIR, PP. 17–18)

[At Patterson's Creek] . . . we pitched tents, stamping rails and brush into the mud for floors. The sergeants clubbed together and bought a Cone Stove of an Ohio sutter [sutler], which we set up in the tent, and took in as many sick men as the tent would possibly hold.

During the next week the captain procured nine stoves like ours and boards for flooring the tents. Our muddy streets and damp chilly quarters were still an awful contrast to what we had left in Camp Benton, but we had reached our general and believed that a few weeks more would bring on the decision battles which would end the war so our camp with all its discomforts was full of hope and animation.

During the following weeks, rain or snow fell nearly every day. No regular duty was required of us, but there are always odd jobs enough turning up around the head quarters of a department commander to keep a hundred men busy and there was no lack of exercise for those who preferred action to idleness. So it happened that I was brought in contact with the Confederate prisoners and, found them lacking some of the comforts and conveniences which I felt would be worth their weight in gold. . . .

The general had designated us as his "body guard" and was talking of mounting us [i.e., providing the men with horses].

MOSES HILL

Patersons Creek, Verginia Jan 25th / 62

Dear Wife,

I received two letters from you Thursday night and I was glad to hear from you. . . . When I can hear that you are all well, I feel content. It is the most I think of, at home, and I can write that I am well this winter so fer, and I pray to God that I may enjoy good health & streangth that I can do my duty while I am in the army. And how long that will be I cannot tell, but if England does not make war with us, I am certain that the war cannot last very long if we have good success as we have done. . . .

You wrote you worried about me for you was afraid I suffered with cold. You nead not worry about that, for it is not cold here in the tent now, for we have got our stove up in the tent and it is very comfitable now. We put in some straw on the mud, for it is all mud here in the valleys, and then we put in some rails and covered the bottom all over with them and then we put some more straw on them so it . . . is quite dry now and comfortable we think. But you would not think so perhaps. It is about the same as it would be to camp in Mr. Harding's cow yard when it is all mud and water. It is [a] very unhealthy place here. It is clowdy and rainy most all the time [and] the sun has not shown more than one day put it all together since we have been here. It snowd some last night and it is thawing today. Most of us are afraid of fever [and] ague. We expect we shall catch it in February & March but I shal be careful. We have begun to take medisin to prevent it.

We shall have a fight as soon as we can get [a]round or as soon as the going is better. We should [have] had a fight before this time if the going had permited. Last Sunday the water rose in the river and creek I think 20 feet certain. Some think it rose 30 feet. The river is with in 20 rods [110 yards] of us and the creek is as near where it empties into the river. The R.R. is within 4 rods [22 yards] of our camp and the Depot between the river and our camp.

There is but two ways that the Rebels can get in here. They must come on the road or up the RR wich is very narrow passage. There is one Rigem on the Meraland side where you see the dots [on the enclosed sketch] and there is troops camped on the Road where you see the dots. There is excursion partys go down every day. Sometimes there is 4 or 5,000 go at once. They bring in Rebel prisenors most every day. Jackson is the Rebel General that commands the Rebel armey here. He is in Romney now, we expect, with about 17,000 troops. Landers [attacked?] Romney just before we got to Cumberland. I think he done it so that Jackson might come in and now I think he means to take him on all sides. I think there is about 20 or 25,000 troops here, and in Cumberland there is about 15,000 troops here and close by us.

Our Company is looked upon as a company that will do a great execution. I believe the General has sent for our pistols again. He said he would rather give $500 than to have us go without them. He thinks a great deal of us. We are called his Body Guards. All the troops here and in Cumberland think everything of him. The Indiana troops he likes. They are raving for a fight. I think they are as cruel as the Rebels. I will tell you one instance and then you can judge for yourself. They took one Reble prisner. They asked him some questions and he could not give any account of himself and when they came to the RR Bridge as you see on the map . . . they throwd him over into the water and stood with their guns to shoot him if he was likely to get out, and he drownded. That is the dispos[ition] of the western and southern troops in our army.

I expect before I write another letter we shall have a Battle. If we have got to fight, I am as ready Monday as I shal be a week from Monday. I shal try to take care of myself if I can. I hope I shall live to see the war through and to come home to you, dear Eliza and my dear children. I was very glad to have a letter from Lucina and to hear of her studies at school she studied, and I feel that she will be a good girl and a good scholar. . . .

Now I will write a few lines that ought to interest every Union heart in Mass. The Quartermasters and all the officers that furnish Clothing and Provisions are cheating the poor soldiers out of every cent they can. It is nothing but a mere speculation with them. For some Clothing we have had, I think they must of mad[e] 100 per cent. The Quartermaster in this company cheets us out of every cent he can. And in one of the Boston papers I see something said about the 20 [Massachusetts] Rige and especially about the Surgans, the Brigade Doctor [Henry Bryant]. I think he is a good doctor, but he will go off and get drunk and spend the night in that way, but I don't know as he neglects his patients. But as for Doctor Haywood, I do know he has been of[f] and left his hospital when he ought to of been there. I do know he has been out drinking and got so drunk that he could not pass one of my guards with out tumbling down. One man in my tent went to the hospital and the Steward put him to bed. He told him that the Doctor would see him soon. He staid one night and one day and then he told the Steward he could not stay any longer. The Steward told him he could not have his clothes until the doctor ordered him, but he got up and said he would not stay, so he got his clothes and come up to camp. Doctor Haywood was out drinking at that time. I know, for he was within hearing of my voice. Anyhow I heard his voice. That is the way the Mass soldiers have, you may judge, what kind of treatment.

I would write more if I had room. I have just left to go to the D[e]pot to see one excursion come in. They brought in three prisenors and one cavelery horse. It was a very nice horse. I would like to write more about the officers if I had room but I have not. . . .

From your ever loving Husband, M Hill

Vergenia, Pattersons Creek, Feb 1, 1862

Dear Wife,

. . . I am safe and well now. That must give you most satisfaction of anything that I can write. It is so with me when I can open your letters and find you are all well. . . .

It is a very unhealthy place here where we are now for it is so wet and damp. There is not any frost in the ground where we are in camp and it is all mud. We can hardly step out but we go [in] over [our] shoes in mud. We have not been paid off yet but we expect to be every day. We have not been paid but once since we come out here, and then we received $25.13 each. You wanted to know if I had any more pay for doing Corperal duty, but I do not. Corp. do not have any more pay than a private. I am sick of the berth and I told the Captain he must put some one in my place. He has not yet, but I expect he will. I hope he will for I want to get out of it. I don't know how I shal send you more money for I don't know who to trust, and I don't know as I can send it as I did before, and if I cannot I don't know but I shal send it home in a letter $5 at a time if you get all my letters. There is some one coming to

Mass to recrute the Company, for a good many men have gone home sick and got their discharge. A good meny are at the Hospital now.

Eliza, I don't think the war will last a great while longer, for the Reble army are so well hemmed in and we are drawing them up harder and closer every day. I think the Rebel army are left this quarter most of them. I think they are frightened. We have got a good army here. I think there is 25,000 troops here and close by us. I think there is 6 Batterys of artillery here and more close by here. The troops have been coming in from Ohio and 4 more Baterys are coming from Ohio. If they keep coming in there will be a very large forse here soon. We can whip any Rebel army this side of Manassus now I think. [General Nathaniel] Banks ought to do something soon, for he has not made one point yet. His troops are laying at Frederick doing nothing. Our troops here went out this week and brought in about 4,000 bushels of wheat and oats. They bring in prisoners most every day.

I hope we shal all come home this spring and I begin to think we shal. I want you to write as often as you can for I like to hear from you often. . . . Tell William and Asahell that there is lots of game out here, wild Turkey & Deer & Bairs & wild cats &c. . . . We had a good breakfast this morning. We had baked beens. I think I will not write much more now. Kiss Sis and Bub for me and my best love to you and all and

I ever remain your loving Husband, M Hill

Luke Bicknell

Patterson Creek Va Feb. 2nd 1862

Dear Cretia,

It is the first really pleasant day that we have had here.

Sunday, and consequently I suppose, there is a movement of troops, 5000 men leave here today, but this company is not included so I suppose is no great danger of a fight.

Pardon me for not writing to you a week ago but there is not much of interest to put in a letter even now. I hope you have not had the measles at all. . . . One man of this company has been sent to the Hospital with them. I passed safely through them at 15. . . .

Jenkins is writing a letter to one of his old cronies. Perley is peeling an egg which he has succeeded in boiling for dinner. Martin lying flat on his back is reading a paper from home. Ingalls has taken sick and is at the Hospital. Things are strewn around rather loose and thick. A picture of this tent just as it is would sell I think.

There is something in this camp life, a certain freedom from all restraint that is attractive. Still I shall be glad when it is over. Not to speak of the feather bed, pies, cakes and other comforts I expect to find when I come home, for I can do without such things well enough now.

I want to see you. That is enough to make me tired of this. . . .

Moses Hill

Patersons Creek, Virginia, Feb 9, 1862

Dear Wife,

. . . We have been paid off a few moments ago and I can send this to Boston if I get it ready in season. . . . I enclose $10.00 in this and I hope you will get it safe. I want you to write as soon as you do and let me know if you have received it. I am well, that is the best news I can write. I feel first rate, and I hope you are all well. That is the most I think of, and if you get along for things that you need.

I expect we shal move every moment down the R.R. somewhere and I don't know when. There seems to be a general [move] here in the armey. I think there is twenty to thirty thousand troops gone now, and when the General goes we shal go. I think we shal go early in the morning. At any rate, I think we shal see some fighting before we see another Sunday. I wish you would send me some Postage stamps but not meny at a time for it is hard to get them. I have not but one and that I have been keeping for I did not have money to get any, and if I had I don't know as I could get them. . . . Kiss Bub and Sis for me and a thousand for your self.

Patersons Creek, Virginia, Monday Morning, Feb 10th, 1862

Dear Wife,

I received a letter from you last week and was glad to hear that you was all well. I wrote a few lines last night and put in $10.00 in it for you. It will come to you at East Medway by express. I shal have a receipt from him. One of our company are coming to Boston and he is agoing to do the Buisness for me. I want you to write as soon as you get it and let me know. . . .

Dear Eliza, I am well. That is the best news I can write you. We was paid off yesterday. I received $22.50 after paying for some Boots which was $3.50, and I lent a man $2.50 wich I don't expect to get. I had to borrow it before I left Camp Benton and now I have paid it, so I had $20.00 and I think I shal not lend any more money unless I am sure I can get it back again. I expect we shal move today down the R.R. towards Hancock, but I want you to direct your letters the same until I write you different. We had a very cold night last night, I think the coldest night we have had since we have been here. . . .

I think there is a general move here now and I hope something will be done. The troops are going down the R.R. every day. I think there must be 20 to 30,000 troops beside the Cavelery & Artilery. I think we can meet any forse that the Rebels can bring against us this side of Manasas. [General] Banks is down below us and [General William] Rosecrans is up not fer above us, and it looks as if there would be something done soon, for they are getting the worst of it on every point. Most of the troops are gone from here. There has been 3 or 4 trains at work for most [of] a week getting the troops down.

This is a very unhealthy place. I think there is as meny as 2,000 in the hospital at Cumberland. Our company is getting rather small. The man that I send this money by is coming to Mass to recrute the Company. His name is T[homas] H. Heald. He thought he would come out to Medway, but this morning he thought it would take too much time, so he said he would send it by express. I think I will send Sis and Bub each another gold dollar soon. They must be good children wich I trust they are. Sis wrote me a good letter and I hope she will write often. I would like to be at home with you this morning. I pray that the time will soon come when I shal be. I am thankful that I am so well as I [am] now. I was weighed a few days ago and I weighed 153 lbs. What [do] you think of that?

Eliza, I thank God that I am so well. I hope you write often for I like to hear from home so. I would like to kiss my Dear little Bub this moment. Kiss Sis and Bub for me and a thousand for yourself. My love to all. . . .

From your ever Loving Husband, M Hill

LUKE BICKNELL (MEMOIR, P. 18)

. . . We broke camp and moved on by rail to Paw Paw Tunnel about thirty miles from Winchester. We worked night and day for three days building stables, rebuilding the railroad bridge, putting up telegraph, unloading cars and pitching our own tents as we could get a spare moment. Diptheria, the measles, and a species of fever appeared and struck down our worn out company so rapidly that we soon had half the men back at Cumberland, in hospital, with one death in camp before we could remove the sufferer. . . . At what a sacrifice of health and life a winter campaign must be made.

We began to serve heavy rations of quinine and whiskey and men who had promised their mothers never to touch a drop of liquor were forced to take their rations with the rest. . . .

General Lander led a brief attack against the Confederates at Bloomery Gap on February 13–14, 1862. He later exuberantly reported to Major General McClellan: "Had an important forced reconnaissance. . . . Broke up the rebel nest at Bloomery Gap. Ran down and caught 17 commissioned officers, among them colonels, lieutenant-colonels, captains, &c. . . . Engaged them with 400 cavalry. Infantry not near enough to support, and enemy retiring." He added that his men had marched over 32 miles, and that under his direction had built "in 4 hours, in the dead of night, a complete bridge of wagons across the Great Cacapon."

Lander was also able to report that he had accomplished his two major goals: to open the B&O railroad and to clear the Confederates from his territory. He also no doubt felt that he had successfully demonstrated that active winter campaigning was possible. He had, as one writer noted, "smashed and put to flight the rear of Jackson's retreating Confederate column . . . and had shown that he was one of the few Union officers not paralyzed by Jackson's dash." Ominously, Lander finished his report by saying, "If not relieved, must resign. My health is too much broken to do any severe work."[7]

Moses Hill

Paw Paw Tunnel, Verginia, Monday Feb 17th 1862

Dear Wife,
. . . We moved down the R.R. about 20 miles to Paw Paw Tunnel. We are here now. We moved down last Monday in the afternoon [and] we got here at night and we pitched out tents. We slept in the mud, what we did sleep, that was not much.

Tuesday we got some pine and Hemlock boughs, but we could not get but few. So we got along the best we could until Thursday night or just before night. We took down our tents and picked up our things and started for some Rebels up towards Winchester about 14 miles and we had to carry our guns on our shoulders which we found very heavy. We marched about 7 miles over the mountains and we camped about 12 oclock in the woods. The way we done that, we made up some fire and laid down our blankets and stoped about 3 hours. Some slept and some did not. I did not, for when I just in a dro[w]se I was called up to go back and get some gun Boxes, and when I got laid down again we was called up for a start and we made some coffee and started. We went about 1 mile and we came to Great Cacapon river. Our teams did not go any further, and the Cavilry, about 500, forded it and we went across on some wagons with boards laid from one to another, so we got over very well, two Rigm with our company. Then we marched about 5 miles where we expected to find the Rebels, about 800 that was there two days before, but they got wind of our coming and they went back about 1½ miles. Bloomery Gap was the name of the place where they was. When we come in sight of the place, we see the Cavelery going up the road tords Winchester as fast as they could make their horses go. We lernt that they was going to try to cut them off. We went on as fast as we could, but that was not very fast, for we was tired carrying our guns so fer. One of them miles was harder then five in Mass, for it is rough. The Rebels was so far ahead of us that we could not overtake them, but the Cavelery overtook them, and General Lander was at the head of them. He took the first man. That was a Rebel Colonel. We took 54 prisoners and killed about 30 Rebels. We had 2 kiled and two wounded. As fast as the Cavelry took them, we took care of them. We took them down in a house and it made a good housefull. 37 was privats and 17 Commissioned officers. If we could of got in gunshot of them, we could of taken them all, I think, but they went for the woods in a hurry.

We all come back to the house where the prisoners was and about 3 oclock we started back. We had about 7,000 men on the Winchester road a short distance from us, so if we found many Rebels we could fall back on them. We have about 30,000 troops here. We marched back to where we stoped the night before. Our company was all alone that night, and only about 30 of us, for the rest went to camp. It was very cold Friday night. It began to snow before we started from where we took the Rebels and it was so cold we was obliged to go into a barn near by us. So we got through the night, and the next day we started early. It snowed some until noon. It took us until about 8 oclock Saturday night before we got into camp, for the roads was so bad that we had great trouble to get our teams along. When we got in to camp we had to put up our tents again. We made a mistake, for we did not use them at all, our tents I mean. We had ought not to have taken them down, for it snowed while we was gone and the ground was very wet. We did not sleep but very little Saturday night. You may believe we was pretty well used up, and Sunday morning early we was called up to go to Hancock with Gen. Landers to protect him and the train of cars we went in, some baggage cars. About 50 of us went. It was the first time the cars run into Hancock for 7 weeks. The road is open all the way excepting between Hancock & Harpers Ferry. We stoped in Hancock about two hours, and then we started back. We got in to Paw Paw about 7 oclock. We see no Rebels and had no trouble. The distance is 35 miles.

Eliza, this morning I feel some tired and I have some cold and I have a sore mouth. I don't know what it is. More then half the Company have a sore mouth. Since I have commenced writing I have bundled up one man that lay by my side, and he has gone to the hospital to Cumberland. There is a good meny of this Company sick. There is I think over 2,000 sick in the Hospital at Cumberland. There is not so much danger of losing ones life in Battle as there is in camp.

Eliza, I hope this war will not last much longer. We had good news to day from Kantuckey. I hope they will give up soon and I think they will, if England does not encourage them too much. I expect we shal have to take Winchester before we can do much up this way. [General] Jackson has a force there, and I think we shal have to start him soon.

Dear Eliza, do not worry about me, for I tell you just as I am. . . . If you will keep all these letters I will explain them to you when I get home if I ever do. . . . May God bless you and protect you and may I come home to you & My Dear Children soon. M Hill

Luke Bicknell

Paw Paw Virginia Feb 23rd [1862]

Dearest Lucretia,

Two letters from you this week. It almost seemed like seeing you to get a letter only four days old and such a nice, long letter too. . . .

It does seem so strange that you should think so much of certains fellows who are in the army that you cannot enjoy yourself at balls and parties while they are gone. If any of that anxiety is caused by my absence I will do my best to make you enjoy yourself when I get back.

Every letter of yours is so full of loving tender interest for me, that I long to be with you. It shows me what good times I should have. How I wish I could receive those kisses from your lips . . . and I would like to put my arms around you and draw you close to my side once more, and feel that the most precious treasure on earth was within my grasp. Never fear, Cretia, but what your affection is returned with all the sincerity and warmth that you would desire. If I could only see you this evening I think I could convince you of the truth of my assertion.

Ye Gods it makes me feel so restless to *think* of seeing you again. . . .

There I see I have filled two pages and said little. As for now We have done nothing this week. Ingalls is sick and has gone to Cumberland to get better. All the rest of think he pretended sickness to get away from camp. But Perley is really sick. (Perley is the Orderly) He has been threatened with a fever, but is now getting better I think. Jenkins, Martin, and myself are the only healthy individuals in our tent.

One of our rifles accidentally discharged this morning. The ball passing through a tent tearing the trousers of one, cutting a groove on a board on which another was writing and slightly wounding another in the arm. The last was a little scared. It is very pleasant overhead today, though very muddy underfoot. Talk as much as they are a mind to about the sacred soil of Virginia. I for one don't like the style. . . .

A great many of our company are sick. One died a few days ago. Only 40 privates are fit for duty. . . .

LUKE BICKNELL (MEMOIR, PP. 19–20)

During the next two weeks the weather was fine; but the health of the company did not correspond. One morning the general, startled by my report of only 43 men present for duty, told me to offer the men their discharge; but the men, expecting that a general forward movement was in preparation which would win the war with a few weeks fighting, replied that all we wanted was horses to ride, and the general promised to use his best efforts to mount the company.

General Lander had his own plan of advance upon Richmond and was sure of the eager cooperation of Secretary Stanton who had not so much confidence in McClellan's plans and ability. Landers plan was to strike Lee [Jackson], upon the flank at Winchester, so sharp and sudden that his left would be crushed back on his center, in front of McClellan. Then Lander and McClellan would unite in pushing Lee back, and in the capture of the city. . . . Lander had with him, and near at hand, twice the force that history speaks of. He also had perfected maps of every mile of the route we were to follow, and knew the strength and exact position of the enemy around Winchester. I knew all this because I was to ride as his orderly when we moved.

MOSES HILL

Paw paw Tunel, Verginia, Feb 23d, 1862

Dear Wife and Children,

I received a letter from you last night . . . and glad I was to hear from home and my dear family, for my God and family is all that I think of. I am very well. I am better then when I wrote last. I have had a very sore mouth and throat but it is better now. It is a very unhealthy place here at this season of the year.

I think Lucina must of improved very much at school for she wrote me the best letter that she ever wrote before. I could not of believed she wrote so well as she wrote in that letter. I must say it was the best wrote letter that I have received since I left home. . . . Lucina wrote that you had not had a social party or surprise party in East Medway. I suppose the times are so hard that the folks can not afford it. I think if Lucina is 5 feet and 1 inch high, she has grown very fast since I left home. I am glad Mr. Harding has got some cows, for I think he needs some. When I left home I did not know as the old horse would live through another winter. As to Mr. Harding, I think he will be a joking so long as he lives. I am sure that times cannot change him at all.

Dear Eliza, we are not at Romney as you see in the papers and we have not been there and I think we shal not go there. Eliza, we have heard of a great victory the last week [the Battle of Fort Donelson, Tennessee] it makes me think that the war is near at a close. Eliza, I think we shal have but little more fighting to do if any. I expect we shal be at home this spring or summer. We have the rebels in a tight place. They cannot stand it much longer. . . .

Dear Eliza, you wrote that you dreamt that I come home and I did not take any notice of you. Your Dream will never come to pass, for if I come home or live to come home, and do not take notice of you and family, I am mistaken. I think of home as much as you do of me and I think more. Why should I not be out here in Virginia? I think I ought to. I feel sometimes that I am blest while others are taken sick and to think there is only 43 able to do guard duty in our Company. I hope and think we shal leave this place soon. I hope we shal find a more healthy place. I understand there is a great meny in Winchester sick.

There is a scout comes into my tent most every day. He was in here this morning. He lives in Bloomery. It is between here and Winchester. He said he had three sons in the Union armey, and one of his son's wife died, and he was one side of the river and she was the other side. And when she was buried, the nabors buried her, and he did not dare to go to her funeral. Eliza, thank God I am not placed in so bad a position yet, and I hope I shal never be. The old scout has suffered almost everything himself. He has got a daughter. He says she carries letters from one place to another. She caries them, he says, in a poket in her dress behind where no one can see it. Eliza, you do not know what war is, nor anyone in Medway unless they have seen it and been out here, and but very few in [General] Banks Division knows anything about it, for they have not had a chance. They have been kept out in Mariland. Most of them have had an easy chance of it. The Capt told me this morning that General Jackson was leaving Winchester, that is, he heard so he has gone today to find out something about it. I don't know but we shal move somewhere this week.

Eliza, I am glad you have got that money, and I hope it will do you a great deal of good. I buy myself Bread and Cheese and Butter and apples. I eat a good meny aples. Some days I eat 10 cents worth in a day. I get 5 for 10 cents, but they are small. Eliza, I buy them to keep in good health. I do not eat pies and cakes as a great meny do, but I get things as I think will do me good. I cannot live on coffee and hard crackers and beef, so I eat a good meny aples. I think they do me good. I had better do that then be sick. Eliza, if you knew of the state of health in this place you would not blame me. There is no place so sickly in the army as this Division. I mean to preserve my health if it does cost me a dollar once in a while. Eliza, if you was here you would not blame me....

From your ever loving Husband, M Hill

"We Have Had a Meloncolly Time"

On March 2, Andrew's Sharpshooters received the devastating news that General Lander had died. His impatience to return to the field caused him — against his doctor's advice — to cut short his period of recuperation from the leg wound he had received at Edward's Ferry the previous October. The stress and physical demands of command caused his deeply festering wound to flare, and he succumbed to a massive systemic infection at his Paw Paw head-quarters.

A period of confusion for Andrew's Sharpshooters followed, as they were passed from one command to another. First, they marched with Brigadier General James Shields down the Shenandoah Valley to Winchester and Strasburg, where they had several brief clashes with Confederate cavalry led by General Turner Ashby. Then they were briefly claimed by Brigadier General Nathanial Banks. Finally, following a reorganization of the Union army, they found themselves under the command of General John Sedgwick in the Second Corps, Second Division.

MOSES HILL

Paw paw Tunnel, Virginia, March 1, 1862

Dear Wife,

I have just received a letter from you, and was very glad to hear from home. I am going to try to write this before I go to sleep, although we may not sleep much for we are about to march somewhere, I think on to Winchester or down toards Hancock. I expect Banks is or has crossed the river and on a march. I think you can hear of some news of another Battle before another week is gone. I think we shal try to take Winchester. Jackson has been reinforced with 10,000 troops. That is the report.

Eliza, one of our men has died here in camp within 10 minutes or since I have been writing.[8] One died about two weeks ago. We have lost three since we have been in servise. I think there will be more die if they cannot be sent home. The one that died to night came from Shrewsbury. His name was [Edward] Andrews. He was respected very much in the Company.[9]

I have bought me a new cap this week and a new Portfolio to write on and to keep my paper in. . . . I have concluded to stand as Corperel. I expect my commission today, but I shal get it in a day or two. It may be tonight. I am well tonight. I feel very well now. I think I never was so heavy as I am now in my life. I think I am as fat as Lucina is tall. My tent's crew was all weighed before we left Patersons Creek, and we everaged 170 of a pounds on an average. I am the lightest of the lot. Since, there is two more come into the tent. One weighs 195, and the other about 180. Don't you think I have got a large tent's crew?

. . . I could march on to Winchester tomorrow first rate. Eliza, I do not dred a Battle so much as I do sickness. We are troubled with sore throats more then anything. If I had some of Doctor Morse's Medicen I would like it if I could get it. If I was agoing to start from home again I would take a case of medicen with me. But I am very carful what I eat and drink. I buy a good meny things to eat of the different Setelers [suttlers]. Setelers are men that come out here. They have a tent with them, and they make money very fast. Some of them make more then a thousand dollars a month.

Eliza, I want you to write often for I do love to hear from home so much. . . . Dear Eliza, I long for the time to come when I can come home. I think you do not know how much I look for that time. Do not worry about me. . . . Tell Bub to be a good boy and papa will bring him some something when papa comes home. I don't know but we shal start before morning, but I hope we shal not march on Sunday. Give my respects to all my friends. We have had a good deal of extery duty to do. My best love to you and may God bless you & family and keep you safe from sickness and danger. . . .

LUKE BICKNELL

Paw Paw Va March 3 1862

My dear Cretia

Our General died Sunday. Part of the company with the Capt have gone to Washington to carry his remains. Maybe they will get leave to go to Massachusetts with them. At one time it was expected that the whole company would go to Mass. And I had written you to expect me. It was a bitter disappointment to me that the orders were changed.

If the General had not died we should not have been there. The orders were given to march when his sickness stopped the advance. He was, I think, the best

Gen. in the army. Great efforts will be made to get this company discharged
now that Lander is dead. We were his body guard, you know, and indept. organization not attached to any regiment or division. The company was get up
for him and now that he is dead the boys want to go home. There are many
reasons why I should like to be discharged, but I have no hopes of that. . . .

This war will soon be settled I am sure and as I don't see any reasonable
prospect of getting killed in the scrabble I am beginning to think of what I
shall do when I come out. Study Law No. 1 Go West No. 2 Get into practice
No. 3 and then No. 4 may get married.

That is what I suppose I shall do as a matter of necessity. But it would suit
my inclinations better to begin at No. 4. I allow myself to hope that *something*
will turn up in my favor, if I am a good boy. . . .

I sleep all alone in a large tent. It is rather lonesome I wish you were here
of course we would set up and keep a good fire. . . .

Most every one in our company is not very well. Two have died lately but
your humble servant is lucky enough to be in tolerable health. . . .

I can not with truth say that I think of you the whole time yet I think of
you a great deal and you are the source of all my enjoyment and contented-
ness here. . . .

When I think of coming home the first thought is how Cretia will meet
me. And all that can trouble me relates in someway to you.

Here I am and must sleep.

Yours most truly,
Emerson

MOSES HILL

Paw paw Tunnel, March 4th 1862

Dear Wife,

I wrote to you last Saturday night. We have had a meloncolly time since. I
wrote that the General was sick. He died about 5 oclock P.M. He had orders
Friday to be ready for a move as soon as possible, and he went to his desk
about 5 oclock Friday night. He sat and wrote and made his plans until 2
oclock Saturday morning, and then he was persuaded to leave his desk by
his physisions, but he did not go to sleep until 4 oclock Saturday in the afternoon and he slept until 12 oclock Sunday noon, but he did not seem to know
anything. He died about 5 oclock in the afternoon. Eliza, it was a hard blow
for our Company and his death was very deeply felt through the division.

Sunday night our company was ordered to be ready for a start to Mass
with his body. After hearing the officers talk, I thought I was to come home

for a few days. Before I went to sleep I was thinking what a joyful meeting I should have with you & My dear Children. Could I be disappointed? I felt that I could not, but it was about midnight a dispatch came that the Captain might take 12 men, but he took 20. I was not one of that number, but I feel quite contented to stay.

At 12 oclock yesterday all the troops was formed in line between the house he was in and the R.R. There was a prayer, and then his Staff and then 20 men with their Rifles and the rest of the Company followed his corps to the cars. Bands played, minutes Guns was fired, and I must say it was a solum occasion. I don't know as the 20 of our company will go any further then Washington, but I hope they will have a chance to go home for they will be very much disappointed. I hope they can go home and see their familys and friends if I cannot go. But if I live I think I shal have a chance within two months.

I am very well now excepting a little cold. The Rebels have vacuated Winchester. If they had not, they would have been taken or killed before this time. They have gone tords Manassas. We shal go down about 50 miles, I think to Martinsburg. That is on the B&O. R.R. . . . . I think we shal move before the week is out. It may be tomorrow. We are getting the enemy into close quarters and if they are not very foolish, I think they will give up soon. General [James] Shields is going to take Landers place.

General Landers presented a flag to one of his Rigm a few days ago and in his speech he said that if you should live a thousand years, you could not die in a better cause than under the stars and stripes at the present time. He expected to die but he expected to die on the Battlefield. He made his will before he come out here, for he said he was coming out here to die for his Country. Eliza, how meny officers come out here with a will to serve their country as the General did? I believe they are very scarce. If we had more brave officers like him the war would have been closed before this time I think.

Eliza, I hear that everything is very dear at the North, groceries in poticular. I wish you would write about that some time. We have had quite a cold wet time for a few days past but I hope it will be warmer and the ground more settled soon. I wish I had something to send home to Bub but I have not[hing] this morning that I can send in a letter. Tell him I will send him home something soon. You don't know how much I want to see you. Since the General died, I feel that I want to come home, and I pray to God that I may have that privalage soon. If the war should last all summer I think I shal come home on a ferlow, but I don't think it will last very much longer. Kiss Sis & Bub for me, and may God bless you all.

From your best friend & trew love, M Hill

LUKE BICKNELL (*MEMOIR, PP. 20–21*)

Sunday, the 2nd of March 1862 we were to close round [Jackson's] left at Winchester. General Lander had taken the field before he had fully recovered and had not spared himself since. He had refused sick rest since the troops began to arrive, and now it began to be apparent that he must sleep before he could again command himself or his army. His surgeon administered an opiate and I stood guard at his door refusing passage to all except his personal staff while he slept. He slept well. The sun rose high in the heavens and still he slept on; too well to suit the anxious surgeons who crowded his chamber and the impatient legions—who like hounds on a leash—awaited his waking; too well to suit the anxious Secretary of War and all the impatient North. Before night closed down again the Union Army had lost its Stonewall Jackson.

I remained alone in the death chamber all of Sunday night to care for the body and to sort and arrange the generals private correspondence. I read letters from Secretary Stanton and Gen McClellan which showed they ought not to be Secretary of War and Commander in Chief, both at the same time. But Stanton was right in his support of Lander in this respect, that there was no other man so well calculated to push the war as the spirit of the North then demanded as Lander, if, only, flesh and blood could have stood such continuous labor and privation as the execution of his plans called for. History, if correctly written, shows that the enemy withdrew from Winchester on the day of Lander's death, but this does not of itself prove that they were aware of his intention to strike them there on that day. . . .

Gen. Shields succeeded to the command of Lander's division. Captain Saunders with twenty of our company went home with Gen. Lander's body.

Winchester

In late February, Major General Nathaniel Banks received orders from McClellan to cross the Potomac and push General "Stonewall" Jackson's forces farther southwest in the Shenandoah Valley. Andrew's Sharpshooters, under General James Shields, left their camp at Paw Paw on March 10 and arrived in the major Valley town of Winchester on March 14, shortly after Jackson evacuated it. On the 18th, Captain John Saunders and the twenty sharpshooters who had served as Lander's honor guard rejoined the company.

Both Luke Bicknell and Moses Hill recounted their marches and brief clashes with General Turner Ashby's cavalry. On the morning of March 23, one hour before the Battle of Kernstown (just south of Winchester) began,

Figure 9. Figure 9. Andrew's Sharpshooters honor guard for
Brigadier General Frederick West Lander, 1862. *Research Your Civil War Ancestor*,
www.researchonline.net/macw/unit5.htm#.WBoLrPorKUm.

Andrew's Sharpshooters were hustled aboard a train for Washington, D.C. They just missed the chance to participate in their first real battle, and one that ended with a Union victory. As their train started, the men could hear continuous artillery fire in the distance. As Bicknell mused, "We were running away from considerable of a fight."[10]

MOSES HILL

Paw paw Tunnel, March 8th 1862

Dear Wife,

I received a letter from you Thursday night, and was glad to hear from you and from home, and to hear that you are all well. I am quite well this morning. My mouth is a little sore. I think it is Canker, but I am very well. You wrote that Mr. Russell called on you. Eliza, I am sorry he has gone into that Tavern, for it has the name of a not very respectable House. I think you had not better go to see him untill I come home and I will go with you. If I live I shal be at home before a great while. . . . You said Mother wanted to know if I did not want some more socks. You may tell her that I never was so well off for stockins as I am now for a great while. I have, I believe, as meny as 5 good pair of socks, 4 certain. I have got all the clothes I nead now, as much as I could ask for at present.

I expect we move today down tords Martinsburg. I want to go, for I think it is a more healthy place then it is here. They say it is a very pleasant place and the water is good....

General Shields came yesterday. Men that know him say he is a very smart man. Troops have been moveing ever since last Tuesday on the R.R. Cars run day and night. I suppose we shal not go until the General goes, for we shal be nearly the last that goes. I believe I wrote the poticulars of General Landers death in my last letter. I shal send a paper to Bub today. I have sent him one before. I would like to see the little fellow, I can tell you. I shal send you some more money this month, I hope more then I have sent. I think I shal have to send it in letters 5.00 Dollars at a time. All of the [men] want to come home now. Since General Landers is gone and left us, we feel very lonesome now.

Eliza, *I must say our Captain has not a spark of feeling for the Company.* I am sorry to say so, but it is so. Now he is not what he was at Camp Benton. I do not speak for myself, but for Company. Our first Lieutenent [William Gleason] is like a father to us. He is a [w]hole soul man....[11]

There is some snow here off the mountains, and it has been quite cold for a few days past. We have very cold nights here. It freezes quite hard at night and it thaws in the day time. Kis Bub for me, and my love to all my friends and especially to mother....

LUKE BICKNELL

Paw Paw Va March 8th 1862

Dear Cretia,

Still at the same camp you see. No doubt though but this is our last week here.

Most of our troops have already moved to Martinsburg. We wait to bring up the rear with the General in the last train. Our new commander Gen. Shields has arrived. He has the reputation of a smart man and is an old Mexican [War] soldier.

This movement forward to Martinsburg is a bloodless advance the enemy having already evacuated the place.

The rebels have left a small force at Winchester who will probably fall back to Strasburg a very strong position, when we advance. But it is believed by a few that this report is not true and they think the rebels are prepared to resist our advance with a large force which is said to be three miles this side of Winchester.

I should like to be in about one battle a week. A little more fighting and less soldiering would suit me better. Staying in camp is awful *slow*....

By the papers you may have seen that twenty of this company went to Massachusetts with Lander's body. I suppose the reason I did not go was that I have no wife and children at home as some of those who went have. . . .

Everyday I grow more tired of this stupid war. If this is not settled soon I shall be discouraged. [I] do not want to stay out here three years, but things move so terribly slow that I sometimes fear our leaders are holding back as long as possible. I can't for the life of me see why McClellan does not fight on the Potomac. . . .

Yours most truly,
L.E. Bicknell

LUKE BICKNELL (MEMOIR, P. 21)

March 9th what was left of the company in camp loaded our horses and teams on to freight cars and started by rail for Martinsburg. We were switched off 36 hours opposite Hancock and again at Cherry Run. Out of rations for man and beast, the men exposed to a cold rain on platform cars, we abandoned the railroad one morning, and marching twenty miles that day, bivouacked four miles west of Martinsburg on the road to Winchester. We were obliged to subsist man and beast on the country as we marched.

MOSES HILL

Winchester, Va., March 17th 1862

Dear Wife,

I have not received a letter from you since week before last. We started from Paw paw Tunnel a week ago yesterday. We came in this place last Friday night. We was on the road 5 days. It was a hard march and very tiresome too. I got along better then some of the men for I drove a team about 30 miles. We rode within 15 miles of Martinsburg on the cars on the B & O. R.R. We was on the cars three days & three nights. The R.R. was not finished or the track was not all laid, so we marched into Martinsburg and then to Winchester where we are now. I should of wrote as soon as we got here, but we expected the Captain to come all the time, so I waited. He come in last night with the rest of the men from Mass. I would of liked to of been one of the number going home, but not one of their number coming back. When the Captain come, I did not know but we should be ordered home or somewhere else.

I understand that we can go with [General Ambrose] Burnside's expedition. I do not know whether we shal go or not, or what we shal do. I will let you know as soon as I find out. I don't think we shal stay here long, for I cannot see anything to stop here for. There was not any Rebels in Martinsburg, but Jackson had a small armey here when our troops came in here, but he left very soon with out any fireing on either side. Some of his men are within 8 miles of this place and they have had two or three squermishes, and taken some of their men, and some of them come and gave themselves up.

I think the Rebels are going toards Richmond. We are getting them in very close quarters. I think they must give up soon or else be drove into the Gulf of Mexico. General Shields Division is here too; [General] Banks quarters are in Masons house. I mean the Mason that was with Slidell.

I will give you a little Idea of the Inhabitants in Winchester. They thought we was agoing to plunder, kill & destroy everything we come to. Some of the familys left the place, but there could only but few get out before we come in, and they shut themselves up. Soon they began to look out of their windows and now they come doors and some venture out into the streets, now that they have made up their minds that we shall not hurt them. They say that we are not so distructive as the Rebels was. If the Rebels had staid here much longer, they would of destroyed everything. We found some mothers & sisters on the road crying they was afraid we should kill them, two little girls about Sis age in Martinsburg, one was laughing and one was crying. We asked her what she was crying for. She said her Brother was in the Rebel army and she was afraid we would shoot him. That is the feeling. . . .

Eliza I am very well now, and I hope you all enjoy that blessing. Health is everything here in the army. Save all my letters if you can, and if I live to get home I can explain all them to you so it will interest you. I shal try to come home this spring if I can. I think I had ought to have that privalage now. Kiss Sis & Bub for me. My love to you and all my friends. I expect to be paid off this week. The men that went home have been paid off. I long for the day to come when I can start for home to be with my family again. . . .

LUKE BICKNELL

Winchester Va March 17th [1862]

Dearest [Lucretia],

Today I received a most welcome letter from you dated the 9th. I hardly think you imagined how I spent that night. Curled up on a bundle of tent poles underneath a wagon loaded on to an open car. I tried to keep myself from getting wet with the rain that drizzled down.

Succeeded in getting a big cold and a few naps and in the morning waked up at Hancock where we were obliged to wait 36 hours for trains before us to rundown and unload.

Finally we got off again but soon stopped at Cherry Run....

Expected an attack that night. I detailed a heavy guard and about two o'clock lay down on the ground and slept two hours.... No attack that night.

Next day we moved on to the end of the railroad track and worked hard till night unloading our teams and getting ready for a start in the morning.

Detailed a guard, built a fire and slept well. . . . Next day rode a horse twenty miles stopped 21 miles this side of Martinsburg. I rode ahead to get hay and corn for the horses. Stopped at the place where I found it.

It was a fine residence. Rich man. Wife and two pretty daughters well educated and lively, at home. Man gone away.

Two Ohio boys staying beside me.

Three fellows come in and demand liquor and supper. Lady refuses liquor but give supper. After supper the most drunken Irishman caps his loaded gun says he will not go without his canteen full of whiskey. I interfere, tell him to leave. He wont. I lug him out. Ladies run away. I wrest his gun from him (while the Ohio boys hold him) fire it off.

Wrest away his bayonet fix it on the gun and threaten to run it through him if he does not leave instantly. He travels.

Ladies are very much grateful. Show me to bed.... Had a good sleep until late in the morning. Was waked by the man of the house who was profuse in his thanks for our protection of the ladies. Refused all pay for keeping myself and horse and wished me to call again.

Next night we camped at Winchester. I was tired some in the morning.... Here ... I met our Lieut who asked me to give up my horse to the meanest man in the company who played sick on purpose in order to get a ride. I smiled and asked him if he didn't want to ride just as if I liked him terribly but I swore (inside) a little when I saw him ride off as gay as possible while I having ridden hard all the morning. Was a little too sore to walk comfortably.

I got my revenge on him though at night. He wanted help awfully. I had other business and tended to it mighty close. Do you blame me?

Tomorrow this company is ordered to march out and engage the enemy. I have no fear of the result. Our guns are terribly sure in the cool steady hands of our boys. I do so long to finish up this business and get home.

Our boys got back last night from attending Gen. Lander's funeral in Mass. I should not have had time to have come up to Windsor so I am glad I did not go to Mass.

You flatter me when you call me noble and good but I must say that the knowledge that you think so gives me a great deal of pleasure and makes me resolve not to disaffirm your opinion.

If it were not for you I fear I might have been very different from what I am now.

Above all things I would like to stand well in your estimation. I am glad that I do. Time only increases my regard for you. I could not bear to lose you now....

My health is not so good just now as it would be perhaps if I had not a cold, but then it is generally good enough. And as to the danger, "What is to be will be," I suppose. At any rate it is a most noble death to die for one's country. A man who would stay at home for fear of being shot would not be a fit companion for you and I am sure you would not smile on him....

LUKE BICKNELL (MEMOIR, PP. 25–27)

Capt. Saunders and the men who had been home rejoined us at Winchester, and the 18th of March General Shields started down the valley, the sharp-shooters leading the column. We left our knapsacks and blankets in camp and struck Ashby's Cavalry posed on a hill west of a village about six miles from Winchester. The captain with the main body took possession of a line of fence just outside of the village and sent me around with ten men to steal up to the cavalry and pick off Ashby. I was discovered as soon as I left the village, and advanced under a warm fire to a barn yard within thirty rods [165 yards] of the enemy before we could obtain a rest for our heavy rifles; when the cavalry bolted without waiting for a shot. When the captain came up the hill enraged at the failure of his plans, and the escape of Ashby, he pulled out his revolver to shoot me, but was prevented from exacting his purpose, if he really intended it, by the interception of the burly form of Cyrus K. Hatch, till his anger had cooled somewhat.[12]

The captain added more men to my squad and started us off at the double quick with orders to bring down Ashby if we had to chase him clear to Richmond. . . . They bolted again and we pursued, until late in the afternoon we struck them for a third time, heavily reinforced, dismounted, and posted behind a Virginia fence which extended both sides of the road to the woods. . . . I had somewhere [between] fifteen to twenty men, and taking a fence in their front on the left side of the road, kept up an exchange of shots for half an hour; their bullets lodging in the fence corners and ours crashing right through with deadly effect . . . just as I was sending two men around through the woods to put in a flanking fire the whole expedition came in sight, over a hill, in our rear, when the cavalry in our front fled, leaving their dead and wounded on the field.

Further on the enemy burned a bridge and checked the advance of our expedition. The Sharpshooters who had halted at the farm where we had last fought were ordered forward to dislodge the enemy from the opposite bank but darkness prevented our [accomplishing] it. . . .

After an excellent breakfast the next morning the captain re-iterated his orders to me with regard to Ashby, and taking a few picked men I pushed ahead until about 10 o'clock A.M. We stood behind a fence on the brow of a hill which fronts Fisher's Hill. We were within the enemy's lines, but concealed. The road to our left was filled with their cavalry and the woods to our right with their infantry. Finally Ashby rode part way down Fisher's Hill and halted in the road with his glass to his eye. It was a long shot—but the best chance we were likely to have. We fired together and his horse fell dead under him, and, ere we could reload, rode off up the hill, apparently unharmed. . . .

The enemy retreated to Fisher's Hill as Gen. Shields pushed forward. . . . A cold rain set in and the sharpshooters, being without blankets retreated to the town of Strasburg. Here I secured quarters for the night, for twenty men, in the house of a citizen, and paid him fifty cents a head for a ham and egg breakfast the next morning. . . . We marched back with the rest of the expedition and the next day, floored our tents from a pile of lumber near by.

About sunset the next afternoon, March 22nd, cavalry appeared on a hill south of the town and commenced throwing shells towards the town. We turned out and formed a line of battle south of the town. After Gen. Shields had been struck with a piece of shell, our cavalry drove the enemy off. As late as ten o'clock the next morning it was supposed that Ashby's Cavalry was the only force near the town.

MOSES HILL

Winchester, March 19th 1862

Dear Eliza & Wife,

I have just got into camp tonight. When I first came in I thought I was too tired to write, but I thought I must write, for we have got to go to Washington tomorrow. We were sent for Monday but General Shields said we must go with him 3 days. He Telegraph to Washington that he would be responsible. I expect we are agoing into [General Irvin] McDowell's Division. We started with General Shields Division Tuesday morning tords Strasburg. Most of the Division went another road from us. We found some Rebels Cavelery, Colonel Ashby's men. Two N.Y. Companies and our company went ahead. We drove them, but we drove them too fast, for when the rest of the Division came out on to the road that we was on, the Rebels had been past about 10 minutes. So we lost them that time. That was in Middletown. The Rebs went down below that town and crossed over a river Bridge and then they Burnt it. We first saw them in Newtown. When they crossed the River they formed a line of Battle and they gave us a few Shells from their cannon, but did not do any hurt.

It was night. We retreated a little, and camped all night. The next morning we put chace to them again. Our company was close behind them. Then we drove them through Strasburg, and then they halted on a hill and showed fight. They had three cannon planted before we got there. So we had to wait until our cannon come up. We fired 18 shots at them all at once, and they scattered very quick. We drove them about 4 miles further and then we left them. And we went back to Strasburg and stoped over night, and then we started for Winchester this morning, except one Brigade that was left to guard the place and R.R. that goes to Manassas. We had 20 miles to walk back to Winchester and we are all very tired. We drove the Rebels about 15 miles.

Eliza, I am well. I found a letter here when I got back to camp. I found a great present in it. I found Bub's picture. It is everything to me. I shall kiss it every time I get a chance. Eliza, I don't want you to write again until you hear from me. I shall write as soon as I can. Save all these letters so I can explain them to you when I come home if I live to come home. Eliza, our company do more work then any Mass Rigm. that I know of. I am afraid the Mass troops have sufferd some on the Burnside expidition. All Banks troops have done is to brush their clothes and black their Boots, but we don't get any time for that. But we do not complain. Dear Eliza, excuse me to night for I am tired. When I took my pen I did not know as I should write so much as I have. May God bless you and protect you and keep you safe, M Hill

LUKE BICKNELL

Winchester Va March 22nd 1862

Dearest Lucretia,

We leave at 8 o'clock in the morning for Harpers Ferry. From there we expect to go to Washington and there to join McDowell's column beyond Manassas. . . .

Last Tuesday Gen. Shields made a reconnaissance toward Strasburg. We met the enemy about six miles out of camp and drove them till night when they burned a bridge which stopped our advance till morning.

The next day we were after them early and found them posted on a hill beyond Strasburg. Our company led the column and were almost constantly skirmishing with their rear guard. I was rather in advance of most of the men and they thought I was taken prisoner twice. The second day the rebels surrounded a few of us who were skirmishing on a hill about two miles ahead of our line of battle. But Searg. Martin coming up just then with a few men routed the cavalry in our rear, when we fell back by order of the Gen.

For a little time the mountain seemed to be alive with bullets and bursting shells but they didn't know exactly where we were and so did us no harm. They came within a few inches of me a number of times. I think I must have killed some of them. I hope so at least.

When you see a fellow get off his horse and resting his gun upon a fence take deliberate aim and send a ball plung[ing] right into the fence beside you. Why you are apt to try to hit him in return.

At one time during the fight I fought a duel with a rebel in this way for half an hour. At last I saw no more of him. I am afraid his friends will never hear from him either.

Another time I thought I had got a tiptop position where I was well concealed. So I began firing at some rebels on a distant hill. It turned out that I was right in the midst of their concealed forces and before I had time to load, the balls began to kick up dust around me, but I got out of it all right.

To night I was writing a letter to you (it was about 5 o'clock) when we heard a big cannonading commence and soon the whole division was on the move. The rebels were almost in our midst with their cannon all planted on a little hill shelling away at us in fine style.

As soon as our artillery got em to the ground we cleaned them out soon enough, but one of their shells bursting under one of their guns dismantled it and wounded Gen. Shields (broke his arm). Another shot killed a man and a horse. Our shells did not, as we can learn, injure them.

Our cavalry is in pursuit but has not yet returned. This company went out but the rebs were off before we got there. It was Ashby's cavalry and was a brilliant dash. I do not see why they were not discovered before they came so near. . . .

LUKE BICKNELL (MEMOIR, PP. 27–29)

An order had been received at headquarters some days before, for the sharpshooters to join McClellan's forces on the Peninsula, but Gen. Shields had been trying to get the order countermanded, so we did not know of the matter. At last when the telegraph brought premonitory orders for our instant obedience, we were given but a few moments to hurry aboard the special train that stood ready to convey us to Harper's Ferry. Gen. Banks in command of the department, went down on the train with us, and we sharpshooters understood that he proposed to use his influence with the war department to retain us in his command.

We steamed out of the station at 10 A.M. and soon learned by the heavy and continuous reports of artillery, back at Winchester, that we were running away from considerable of a fight. Gen. Banks left the train and started to intercept and turn back a division, on its march to Harper's Ferry. Arrived at Harper's Ferry, the captain, desiring to keep his finger on his company at a moment's notice, marched us to an unoccupied house, built against the cliff, and put a guard at the door. We tore up the floor, built a bridge to the cliff in the rear, and telling the guard to fire his rifle in case we were wanted, scampered off all over town. We visited the Engine House, Jefferson Rock, the ruined Armory; bought all the cakes and pies in town, and notwithstanding our chagrin at being kept out of the battle of Winchester, managed to make it a day to be remembered . .

[In Washington] I visited friends in the 10th and 15th Mass, looked over the Smithsonian Institute, White House and Capitol, and at night returned to camp to find the boys packed up, and no chance for supper then. I went back to the Soldiers Retreat near the depot and while eating was informed by an Aid[e] at the table, that our company had been attached to [John] Sedgwick's division, 2nd corps. . . .

CHAPTER

THE PENINSULA CAMPAIGN

Early in the war the enemy learned to know and dread us, till the name of the
Andrew's Sharpshooters was as familiar a sound inside Lee's lines as was Ashbys
Cavalry inside our own.

—Luke Emerson Bicknell, 1883

By March 1862, Major General George B. McClellan was ready to unleash
a massive assault on Richmond. His enormous Army of the Potomac—more
than a hundred thousand volunteers—had drilled for months near Washington. His men were eager to escape the tedium of camp life to fight what many
believed would be the war's decisive battle.

McClellan's plan was ambitious and daring. He would first move his
army by boat down the Potomac River to Fortress Monroe at the end of
the peninsula formed by the James and York Rivers. Then he would march
northwest sixty miles, seize the Confederate capital, and break the back of
the rebellion in one bold stroke. As the army marched, navy gunboats would
protect the movement of supplies up the rivers and keep lines of communication open.

The Peninsula Campaign became an embarrassing debacle for the Union.
Heavy rains turned roads to quagmires and streams into torrents, impeding
the movement of men, artillery, and supplies. Faulty intelligence reports persuaded McClellan that he was facing formidable opposition and had to move
with the utmost caution. On reaching the enemy's fortifications at Yorktown,
he settled his army into a siege that dragged on until May 3, when the enemy
quickly and secretly fell back toward Richmond.

Figure 10. *The Army of the Potomac—A Sharp-Shooter on Picket Duty.* From *Harper's Weekly,*
November 15, 1862. Smithsonian American Art Museum, The Ray Austrian Collection,
Gift of Caryl A. Austrian and James A. Austrian.

After enduring the winter campaign in northern Virginia, Andrew's Sharp-shooters traveled to Washington in March to join McClellan's expeditionary force. After a few days in the city, they boarded one of a vast fleet of ships leaving Alexandria bound for Fortress Monroe. They were now under the command of Brigadier General John Sedgwick, a Connecticut-born West Point graduate and career military officer who headed the Second Division of Edwin "Bull" Sumner's Second Corps. A brave yet unassuming and kindly officer in his late forties, Sedgwick was affectionately nicknamed "Uncle John" by his men. "Soldiers," his biographer writes, "responded to his open nature, modesty, and blunt, straightforward manner."[1] Andrew's Sharpshooters, however, expressed more ambivalence. As Luke Bicknell remarked, "General Sedgwick was both a soldier and a gentleman, but he could not control his instinctive aversion to sharpshooting and sharpshooters." Shortly after they arrived on the peninsula, Sedgwick attached the sharpshooter company to Brigadier General Willis A. Gorman's First Brigade. Gorman's evident hostility toward them was a serious blow to the company's morale.[2] Moreover, by early June the wagons assigned to move the sharpshooters' equipment had broken down. Since they were neither repaired nor replaced, the men had to carry their heavy rifles constantly.

Despite the difficulties they encountered, Andrew's Sharpshooters (along with some of Berdan's Sharpshooters) successfully met the new challenges of siege warfare. Yorktown marked their true baptism as snipers. Previously they had participated only in small actions—at Edward's Ferry, at Bloomery Gap, and against Ashby's cavalry in the Shenandoah Valley. At Yorktown, however, the demand for their lethal skills was relentless. They had to silence Confederate batteries, pick off officers, and provide protection for work parties constructing entrenchments.

"Cool Blooded Sharpshooting"

LUKE BICKNELL (MEMOIR, PP. 29–30)

As I was leading the company on the sidewalk down to the boat [in Alexandria], with the captain at my side, we passed the camp of a regiment where liquor reigned supreme.[3] A drunken soldier cocked his gun and threw himself before us, pressing his bayonet so hard against my breast that I was thrown back on the man behind me. Quick as thought the captains sword sprung from its scabbard and sunk down through cap and skull; the man sinking to the ground without a groan and, luckily, without discharging his rifle or attracting the attention of his comrades. Next morning papers gave the dead soldiers name and regiment and we were somewhat startled during the afternoon to find that the regiment was to go on the same boat with us. We kept our own counsel however and with the exception of [Oscar] Clement, who was knocked overboard on the trip and then pulled in at the cabin windows, we avoided all difficulty with the still drunken men.

We threw our provisions overboard while crossing Chesapeake Bay, on account of rough weather, arriving after a passage of three days and four nights, at Fortress Monroe, very empty.

While the rest unloaded I found head quarters five miles inland, and brought back orders to march up, and that rations should be issued to us the next day. I remained to guard company property piled on the wharf which the teams could not carry, and was very glad to accept an invitation to supper from the fort. The fort guard also looked out for our property at night giving me needed rest. The next day April 1st I joined the company and settled down to regular duty and rations again.

MOSES HILL

Washington, March 26, 1862

Dear Wife,

I am in Washington. I am well except some cold and tired. Last time I wrote to you I was in Winchester. I had just got back from Strasburg. I forgot I had received a letter from Sis, and it was a very good one.

We had a fight the night before we started. We killed 19 Rebels & lost one man and two wounded. One of them was General Shields. We drove the Rebs about 3 miles and went back to camp. We started about 9 oclock the next morning and another Battle [Kernstown] commenced about 10 oclock, which I suppose you have seen in the papers. We stoped in Harpers Ferry Sunday night. Monday night we was in the Cars, and they was so cold and full that we could not sleep. We came to Baltimore and then to Washington, and I expect we are going in General [Irvin] McDowell's Division. We shal start tomorrow from this place. I shal try to finish this letter tomorrow morning.

Thursday. I did not finish this letter today, for I was in hopes I could get a furlow and come home, but we was ordered at once to bord a boat to go some where. We had no time but to go at once to the boat. Then I was very unfortunate, for I had a good meny things to carry. So Hixon said he would carry my Carpetbag as he had some things in it, and he took it with him. I did not see him again until we got to the Boat. When I found him, he had been drinking some and had lost it. My fur Collar was in it and my housewife the other things I did not care so much for. My housewife I thought the most of. The Boat did not start until the next morning. I woke him up early to go and find it, but he could not find it. When we came to the Boat I found we was going to Fortress Monroe. We are aboard the South America. I have a stateroom and a very good place to sleep. The N.Y. 42 rigement is with us.

Friday. We have not got but a short distance yet.

Saturday. We have got down near the bay. We do not run the Boat nights. I have seen more Ducks to day then I ever see before, I think.

Sunday. We started early this morning. It snowed quite hard last night, and it is clowdy this morning. I am thankful I have not lost Bub's picture. I have just been looking at it. I sleep with it under my head every night. Sunday night we arrived in the harbor at Fortress Monroe. We found a large fleet and we come very near running into the Monitor. You would not think it is a boat. It is very short, and it is not more then 18 inches out of [the] water. I hope I can give you a discryption of it some other time.

Monday morning. We went ashore. I still hope I can get a furlow. I saw some very large guns here, one Floyd gun, 15 inch, and one Union gun, 12 inch. The Floyd gun carries a ball that weighs 434 lbs. We started from the fort this afternoon for Hampton. We passed the Town that the Rebels burn. I think it must of been a very pretty place once, most all brick buildings, and camped about 4 miles from the fort.

Tuesday morning. I am very well now. I don't know as I can get a furlow, for the Captain don't seem wiling to have me leave. I think he might help me to [get] a furlow if he was a mind to. I am waiting to see if our first Lieutenant can get a Furlow. He is trying very hard. I have been expecting I could come with him if he comes.

Eliza, you may direct your letter to Fort Monroe care of Captain John Saunders, Andrews Sharpshooters, General McDowell Division. If Lieutenant [William] Gleason comes, I shal send you 15.00, but if he does not I shal enclose 5.00. I dare not send any more at once. I do not expect to stop here but a few days, you may depend on that. There will be something done soon. The troops are coming in here all the time. I cannot find any account of the number here, but I think it must be over a 100,000.

Eliza, I think if this company helps take Richmond and all the other principle places in V.A., we shal do our part. We have done more then our part now. We have been from the Right to the Left wing of the army, and if they have another hard job in Western V.A., we suppose we shal have to go back.

I am sick of it. I want to come home, I assure you. But here we are, although I think the war will not last much longer. The Lieutenant has just informed me that he cannot get a furlow, so we cannot either of us come home now. So I will enclose $5.00. I suppose you are worrying about me, for you have not heard from me for some time. I shal send it the next mail that goes out. May God bless you all and protect you.

From your Trew and dearest Friend and Husband, M Hill

EGBERT OSWALD HIXON

Mon. [March] 31 Weather cloudy. Steamer Monitor close by: looks like an old raft with a kettle on top. Got unloaded about 2 o'clock P.M. Marched out to Hampton by the fortress. Hampton was burnt last year by the Rebs. . . .

Tues. [April] 1 Quite warm, peach trees in blossom. . . . Our Capt. Is mad with the whole com[pany]. Going on in his military[?]. . . . Earful.

Wed. 2 Cold weather. Looks like a storm. The capt. put us through a knapsack drill 2 ½ hrs. We are in a flat level country.

Figure 11. Egbert Oswald Hixon, n.d. Courtesy of John Robinson.

LUKE BICKNELL (*MEMOIR, P. 30*)

We arrived before the line of fortifications at Yorktown the afternoon of the 5th [April] the march having been without incident except a few minutes shelling at Little Bethel. The sharpshooters pitched tents beside a house said to have been occupied during the Revolutionary War as British head quarters.

It stood near the enemy's works at Winns Mill and was now occupied by Gen. [Willis] Gorman to whose brigade we had been assigned.

The sharpshooters' first fight of the campaign occurred on April 7. They— along with the Nineteenth and Twentieth Massachusetts regiments—moved close to the Confederate fortifications on a reconnaissance mission. When enemy artillery opened fire, the riflemen were ordered to silence the guns. A soldier in the Twentieth Massachusetts later recalled, "A detachment of sharpshooters was sent forward, and soon the firing of the rebel artillery slackened very much."[4] A later regimental history elaborated:

The Andrew Sharpshooters came up and advanced to the edge of the woods. . . . Taking a position behind a fence they fired at the men in the enemy's works, then dodged back into the ravine to reload. The enemy at once sent back a volley of musket balls which went buzzing harmlessly overhead. The sharpshooters crept up again and gave them another shot, receiving the same attention as at first, accompanied by an unearthly yelling and howling from behind the "Johnnies'" breastworks. . . . The enemy tried canister, and finding that those did no damage, fired solid 32 pound shot, all going overhead and far to the rear. Then they tried a shell which fell nearer; another burst directly overhead and the next burst directly in front, sending the pieces with full force among the men but doing no harm.[5]

MOSES HILL

Yorktown Va Apl 13, 1862

Dear Wife,
I received a letter from you last night, and was glad to hear from you, for I have not heard from you since I was in Winchester. . . . You may direct your letters to Washington DC Care of Capt John Saunders, for I don't know what division we are in. We are not with McDowell as we expected. I think we are anywhere & everywhere. We are now within good cannon shot of the Rebel in Yorktown, not more than ¾ of a mile off from there.

The last time I wrote to you I was in Hampton near Fortris Monroe. The next morning after I sent that letter to you, we started and came up through Bethel and within 3 miles of this place. We arrived there a week ago last night. We had no tents, so we had to sleep on the ground and in the open air Saturday & Sunday night. I think our army then was nearly 100,000 but we was not all together.

We found there was something in Yorktown that we could not run over. Last Monday our company with 2 other Rige. went to guard the Enginears so that they could find out some of the best places to attack and to plant Batterys whenever they attacked the fortifications. We was received with good reception and shell and balls aplenty. One of the Nineteenth Mass Rigem. was killed and some wounded. I was within 15 rods [about 83 yards] of their breastwork, I think, at one time, and the balls came by my head a little closer then I wanted them to. I should not of gone, but our Captain orderd us up and swore because we did not go. There was some trees and a fence between us, so none of us got hurt. After we found out what we wanted we started to the camp again. There come up a cold north East storm and it rained very hard. We had about 5 miles to go, and we got to camp about 9 oclock at night. I hardly ever see such a rainy night as it was, no tents to go in, not but a very little to eat. We made up a fire and sat up all night with our rubber blankets over our heads. We made some coffee and we had a very little hard bread for breakfast the next morning, and we lived through the day, for the men, most of them, went into the woods and put up brush and got along.

Hixon and I found Charles Greenwood [of Medway]. He drives a team, so we got into his wagon and slep very well. The storm lasted 3 days. You have seen the account of it in the paper I suppose. We are within ¾ of a mile of the Rebel battery. We have been here two nights, and I suppose we shal stay here until McClellan makes an attack. I see him most every day. There is woods all round us. We are in an open lot, one Brigade, but we have troops on our right and left close by. I suppose as soon as the General can get his cannon along, we shal make an attack.

The Rebels fortification is about 7 miles long, well fortified, so you may judge what this army has got to do. It seems to me if we whip them out here, the fighting in Va will be nearly done. I dred it, for I know there must be a great loss of life on both sides. Our company will commence on whatever point we may attack. I think we shal spread out to pick off the Gunners so our own batterys may get their position.

I pray to God that we may all live to come home to Mass, but I think it is almost impossible, for there is a great meny Mass troops here. I saw William Daniels at Fortress Monroe. He is well. He is out here somewhere. General McClellan & staff is passing me now. Troops are coming in all the time. I think there must be nearly 200,000. I suppose before you hear from me again, the Battle will be decided. We put all confidence in the General.

Lucina wanted to know if the snow was all gone here. There is no snow here. Two weeks ago the Peach trees was in Blossom at Fortress Monroe. Peach trees are very plenty here.

Dear wife, write as soon as you get this. I am writing this letter under an apple tree. If I live I think I shal come home soon if we take this place. I think we shal go to Richmond. If we can take this place, we can go to Richmond very easy. Eliza, I am glad that you have got that money I sent you. If I ever come home, I shal know how to appreceate home more than I ever did before. Men living in Mass don't know what home is. Eliza, do not worry about me for I am very well now. I have seen the time that if I could go to your swill pail, I could make out a good meal. We do not have half enough to eat now, for they cannot get it along fast enough, the roads are so poor. I will write again as soon as I can. Kiss Sis and Bub for me, and may God bless you and protect you. . . .

EGBERT OSWALD HIXON

Mon. [April] 7 Weather cool & chilly. Getting ready to start. 9 miles to the rebel camp. Most out with the Brigade reconnoitering: one man killed in the 19th & 3 or 4 wounded. Came back & sit up all night in the rain, the most miserable night I ever [saw] Rain/cold N.E. storm . . . no rations no nothing. Got some meat for dinner, the first we have had for a week. The men are building camps in the wood. Rain rain rain, cold as thunder.

Wed. 9 Staid in Greenwood wagon. Slept well. The storm continues. All mud. Fair rations but not enough. . . .

Fri. 11 Beautiful cool morn. . . . Getting ready to move, don't know where. Went out about 8 [?] miles, we are now with Gorman Brig. & formed a line of battle. The rebel camp is about ½ mile off.

GEORGE WHITTEMORE JR.

Near Yorktown, April 9, 1862

On Monday [April 7] our company was not called into play until late in the afternoon, when we came in front of the Rebel batteries in two squads, supported by two regiments. Only our squad fired, and that with only thirty or forty shots; but the Rebels answered with volleys that would have cut us up if we had not been protected by a small knoll, and received some credit for coolness, but it was the coolness of perfect safety. Some doubts arose in my mind when the first shell came. It burst over my head so near that I felt the hot air on my face and the presence of the gas in my ears, and it scattered the branches all around me; but I thought it would not happen twice in succession, and stayed where I was. The Colonel, having found out what he wished to, retired, and we with him. It was growing dark, began to rain hard, and the roads, under the tramp of so many men, were mere sloughs. We had the choice to lie down in the mud or sit up all night about the fire. I chose the latter, and with a rubber blanket and a good fire was pretty comfortable.[6]

LUKE BICKNELL

Camp near Yorktown, Va April 13th [1862]

Dearest [Lucretia],

... We are laying today within 300 rods [a little more than nine-tenths of a mile] of the rebel fortifications. Yesterday I was so close to them that a man came out and asked me if I would come over. I didn't see the point and said nary a word, but immediately departed.

Last Monday we had a little fight in which they killed one of our men and we expect they lost more.

Some time this next week the greatest battle of the war is expected to come off. The rebels are strongly fortified for 5 miles with a great force behind the entrenchments. We have also a great force in front of their works. Your brother's regiment is in Gen. Porter's division on the right. The 15th Mass. is behind us not more than half a mile. I shall see the [Windsor] Boys after I finish this.

Our company occupies the advance position and will probably see a little of the fun....

So you will teach this summer. I will be at home before you are through. The greatest hardship I see here is that I can't see you. One hour in your company and I should forget that I had been to war at all. There will be an additional pleasure in meeting you, now that we both know that we entertain an affection for each other which time will not change. No thought gives me near so much pleasure as that I shall soon see you again.

This next battle must have a bad effect upon the rebels if we whip them....

Splendid weather here today. The troops lay out in the open air at night without fires. This all well enough if it does not rain.

I have got an abominable cold and sore throat otherwise well as usual....

Immediately after the battle I will write you if I come out safe.

I wish you was here to day. I would take you to where you could see the rebels and our forces laying opposite each other, just out of musket range. You would hear the pickets firing occasionally. Now and then a cannon, and from one side Hail Columbia and the other Dixie....

Sedgwick's Second Division camped near the center of the Union line at York-town, near the Warwick River. Andrew's Sharpshooters pitched tents near the Moore House, where in 1781 the terms of surrender of the British army were negotiated. Captain John Saunders and other officers used the house as headquarters for a time. A caption to a photograph of the house stated:

Much frequented was it by the sharpshooters, the orchard beyond offering fair opportunities to advance to the front unobserved. Stealing amongst the trees, purple with the bloom of the peach, the riflemen would proceed, at the first glimpse of dawn, while yet the mist hung in the air, to take a position they would not dare to leave till night extended her friendly cover. With their heavy, telescope-sighted rifles, they made deadly work among the gunners upon the fortifications, the sturdy company of Massachusetts riflemen, called the Andrews Sharpshooters, proving themselves much superior to the squirrel-shooters of Mississippi, who were driven to the exercise of great caution in their endeavors to retaliate upon the working parties.[7]

GEORGE WHITTEMORE JR.

Camp near Yorktown, April 13, 1862

Dear Father:

I have received ten letters during the week. I cannot tell you how precious they are to me. . . . I wonder if I shall ever see you all again. I have very little fear of being killed, a great deal more of being sick; but I have not felt as though I were to die yet in either way. We are encamped, if the term may be used,—for we have no tents, and are sheltering ourselves in the cellar and out-buildings of a little farm-house, while the brigade are out in the fields and woods. Yesterday I spent the day with a dozen of our men in the outskirts of the woods, within two hundred yards of the works. We lay concealed and very quiet, so as not to draw their fire; our orders being not to fire, unless they opened with cannon upon our troops elsewhere, in which case we were to shoot the gunners. As they did not fire excepting once, when they did no harm, we did not. The day was beautiful, the woods warm and pleasant, and I could not help enjoying it. How different the woods seem from what they have in former seasons. Now the sun shines as warm as ever, the tops of the pine-trees whisper in the wind, and the dry leaves and pine needles are as luxurious to lie on; but grape-shot and shells may at any moment come cutting everything to pieces. We don't sit in a social circle as in our picnics at home, but each one take a tree to himself; and, instead of wandering round in pleasant meditations, we creep on our hands and knees, and talk in whispers.[8]

Both Luke Bicknell and Moses Hill complained that the press often confused Andrew's Sharpshooters with Berdan's Sharpshooters at Yorktown, with the

latter receiving credit for the Massachusetts snipers' exploits. A member of
the Second Company Massachusetts Sharpshooters wrote home:

All the exploits of the sharp-shooters, have been almost universally attrib-
uted to Berdan's regiment. This is both unjust and untrue, for by far more
execution and real work has been done by the two Massachusetts companies,
the Andrew sharp-shooters, Capt. Jacob [*sic*] Saunders, and the second company sharp-shooters, Twenty-second regiment, Capt. Wentworth, than by
the whole of Berdan's regiment. I do not wish to be understood as detracting
in the least from that regiment; but I do say, that our Massachusetts companies have the best rifles, weighing from twenty-five to fifty pounds each, and
have done the most work. We only wish that we should have credit where
credit is due, and that our companies should not be confounded with the
Berdans.[9]

On April 16, General McClellan ordered the first—and only—attack of the
Yorktown campaign against what he deemed to be a weak spot in the enemy's
defenses just behind the Warwick River at Dam No. 1. But rather than com-
mitting sufficient troops to break through the Rebel line, he sent a small
force with instructions to merely stop the Confederates' efforts to fortify the
area. Too few troops plus tentative leadership led to a quick and costly defeat
for the attackers.[10] Sharpshooter Sergeant Henry Martin was badly wounded
during the action.

Luke Bicknell (*memoir, pp. 30–31*)

We were soon set at work upon the enemy's front. Lieut. Gleason had bid us
good bye at Fortress Monroe and Mr. [William] Berry had been commissioned in his place, but from one and another cause, the captain, [Henry]
Martin and myself were the only available men to take charge of the men
under fire. The captain and Martin attended to the forts to the right and left,
and did great execution amongst the enemys gunners, their exploits being
chronicled and illustrated from week to week by the New York papers, and as
a matter of course loyally credited to Berdans sharpshooters from New York
state. I was left to prowl along the Warwick river, in the mile or two of woods
between, with somedays ten, and on others forty or fifty men, to shoot down
men with shovels in their hands as well as those who carried guns. Charged
to prevent their strengthening their fortifications and to obtain all possible
information of their positions and strength.

EGBERT OSWALD HIXON

Tues. [April] 15 Morning warm with a little rain. . . . We go out in sight of the
rebs camp in squads to watch them. They have sent a balloon up twice. We
are going to shoot at it if it comes within range.

Wed. 16 Morn warm. One year ago today I was in Faneuil Hall, Boston. The
whole com. are out & the batteries are fast, they keep it up good. 5 P.M.
sergeant [Henry Martin] just got wounded in the thigh, pretty bad.

LUKE BICKNELL (MEMOIR, PP. 31–33)

I soon ascertained that the current opinion as to the strength of the enemy
was wrong, that the woods in my front were full of men and artillery, though
the river was fordable in many places, and the first line of breastworks on
its opposite banks were slight. My opinion was not backed up by my men
however. They did not pass along the whole front each day as I did, and then,
they got to perfectly hate their murderous work and to share in the sentiment then quite popular that sharpshooting was out of the pale of honorable
warfare. I had sent many of our best men back to the hospital wounded in my
efforts to penetrate the mystery of the opposite woods. . . . The pressure for
an assault was tremendous and I stood alone in my advice that the assaulting
column consist of at least ten thousand men, and be pushed vigorously ahead
till the woods beyond were cleared of the enemy.

An assault was finally made with three thousand men at Dam No. 1. They
easily carried the first line of works and halted, but were soon driven back
by overwhelming masses of the enemy who emerged with batteries from the
woods in their front. When they recrossed the river many were drowned,
the enemy having flooded it from a dam above. The sharpshooters under
Martin advanced and poured in a rapid fire at a point where their breastworks
came close to the river, and did not fall back till their works fairly bristled
with reinforcements, and the water was rising rapidly around us. Then, carrying Martin who had fallen by my side and who urged us to leave him and
seek our own safety, we fell back out of range.

For a day or two after the assault we laid in camp and had time to wash
and change our clothing and write letters home for the first time since striking the peninsula . . . [John] Perley being sick and Martin wounded I now
had to act as orderly and occasionally relieved the captain on the right where
some twenty of our men kept the forts, 1200 yards distant, silent. One day a
union general and his staff rode up and indulged in so much ridicule of our

fire being effective at that distance that I ordered the men to cease firing. Immediately the gunners, in the fort opposite, sprang to a gun and burst a shell over the mounted group in my rear. It proved an effective argument, and the general was man enough to admit his error before he rode away.

EGBERT OSWALD HIXON

Thurs. 17 Morn warm. . . . The batteries have been playing all night. Just got our pistols. . . Start out, all day our boys are shooting the rebs. . . .
Fri. 18 Morn. Two alarms last night, heavy fireing for a few minutes. Don't know certain what it amounted to. Warm muggy weather with ticks aplenty.

GEORGE WHITTEMORE JR.

Camp Near Yorktown, April 21, 1862

Quarter of a mile from the Rebels' first battery is a rising ground, where the ruins of a fine house stand. There is little left but three large chimneys and the brick foundations of the house. These ruins have been the scene of the sharpshooters' operations for a few days past, and I have been mostly there. So little shooting has been going on, that we have been able to make our arrangements almost as we pleased, and we established ourselves in a style of luxurious comfort quite unknown to privates. From the furniture lying around, two men took bureaus and set them up by a chimney to rest their guns on. Another found a thick tree that divided about five feet from the ground. He cut out the notch large enough for his gun, and put up a seat behind it, where he spied around very much at his ease. I took a position at the side of a chimney, with a black walnut table in front, the leaf hanging down and making a tolerable protection from bullets, &c., at this distance; and to cover my head I set up two or three timbers, charred rafters, &c., the ends slanting up over my head, leaving a narrow port-hole for the gun. It happened to do me service. Toward night our batteries, stationed very near the chimneys, threw some shells into the works, while we kept our guns leveled at their embrasures. At last, after our cannon had sprinkled their shot and shell in various parts of the fort, an iron howitzer, on the battery nearest and just opposite to us, which not a man had approached all day, now, touched off by an unseen hand, threw a charge of grape or canister at us. It struck the ground a few yards before us, and scattered. Some of the balls struck my table, knocked down one timber from before it, and scattered the nails, charcoal, &c., over the table. One ball glanced and struck a tub behind me. My companion behind the chimney wanted to know if I was "hit." He seemed to think a ball that that struck behind me must have gone through me. This iron howitzer is the one the negroes fired when the place became too hot for the chivalry.[11]

MOSES HILL

Yorktown, V.A. Apl 20th 1862

Dear Wife,

. . . I expected we should have a battle before this time, but we have not yet, but we have been out most every day last week shooting Rebels off their fortifications. I have not been out much for I have not been very well, but I feel better now. I was not out yesterday. We have had two men wounded last week one in the hip and one in the thigh but I think not serious. I think our Company have killed 75 to a 100 last week. In our whole army here perhaps we have lost 100 and perhaps more. I don't know exact the number.

We have had very pleasant weather last week until last night. It rained some and it was very wet today. We have just been called out on account of an alarm, and we was called out last night. The pickets was firing. There is firing all the time. We do not go out today, it being Sunday, and our Boys are glad for they have been out every day last week. This is not a very pleasant place, I can tell you, for the two armeys are close together and we do not know when we are safe. I hope it will be over soon. I think it will be a hard Battle. I hope it will not last as long as it did when Cornwallis surrendered. I sleep in an old celler under an old house [where] Clinton's head quarters was, and I enclose a piece of moss that I got off the roof, and a little shell that I found on the beach at Fortris Monroe. That is for Sis & Bub.

I think that when this Battle is through, if we are successful, that we shal not have but very little more fighting in V.A. and I expect there will be a good meny troops discharged, and I think we shal stand a good chance to come home to Mass. I expect that General McClellan is getting heavy guns up here. I expect he will take the fortification by Bombarding it. It is a very strong [one] to take. The soldiers seem to be in good spirits and ready to do their part.

I want you to write often. You have a better chance to write then I have, for I do not have much time. . . .

There is some small baterys fireing night and day and to tell the truth I am sick of the noys. It is quite cold and stormy here today, but when the sun is out it is quite warm and cold nights, but I expect it will be very hot here in the summer. We are very glad to hear the victorys that we have, in Island No 10, and Pitsfield Landing [the Battle of Shiloh], two great victorys.

Eliza, I want you to see to our garden this spring for your own good if not for mine, but I hope I shal receive some benefit of it, and I hope to live to come home and have some good of it. I want you to have as much planted as we usualy do. You will have to get some one to plant it for you. Plant it the same as I do, that is, if you think best. If I come home I think I shall be hungry, but I have more to eat now then I did.

Our Company have got, all of them, a Revolver, Colts large Army size. We got them last week. Our company have done service enough, I think, to have the State and Government give us our arms. We are doing a great deal here. One of the Rebels fortifications, our company kept two guns still so they could not load them. If a man come up to load, he had a ball through him before he could do anything, so the Rebs whipped up a Niger Gunner to load, and he threwed his arms up and fell, so they left it. There is a swarm of Rebles in their entrenchments. They have got so they dare not raise their whole body in sight but only show they head, and if they see the flash of our guns they can git them down out of sight, but if they show any of their breast they cannot dodge the balls. If the Rebels get hold of any of our Company, I do not think they will give us any quarter, but every soldier say they will fight for us until the last moment. We have protected them when they was building their breast works and protected our Bateryes, and I am confident that before they take us there will be a hard battle. You don't know how much the soldiers think of us, and well they may.

Our Company are getting [tired] of the war and want to get home except the officers. They get more pay then they can get at home, so they do not care so much as the soldiers. This is a curious company for we have not got but one officer in the company, that is Captain. There is no other one that has a commission. We had first and second Lieutenant & Orderly Sargent, but the first and second Lieutenant has got their discharge and the Orderly [Luke Bicknell] acts as Lieutenant now, so you see he has no commission for that office. And by some neglect of the Captain, the Sargeants & Corperals have not had their Certificate. So you can see we have but one officer. I think it is not generally known. I can explain to you if I live to get home. I would like to see you & Sis & Bub today. I think of you all the time. I cannot help it.

The apple trees are in blossom here now. Peach are very plenty here and they look beautiful. . . . I hope we shal be successful in this Battle. If we are, I think we shal not have much more fighting in Va at present. . . .

LUKE BICKNELL (MEMOIR, PP. 32–33)

I found my position as orderly no sinecure. The men sincerely regretted having been beguiled into service in the sharpshooters. The continuous and dangerous service, the sentiment against sharpshooting, the broken promises as to extra pay, the report that we were outlawed by the Confederacy, added to the effect of the terrible marching of the winter before, had broken the health and spirits of the men; and they rendered in camp a sullen and tardy obedience to the orders of the non-commissioned officers.

LUKE BICKNELL

Head Quarters April 20th 1862

Dear Lucretia,

We are still in front of Yorktown and the great battle is still to come off. Whether this is likely to happen the present week, or not for a month, I am unable to conclude from present appearances.

For the last four days our boys have been out scouting around the rebel fortification front of our lines picking off every man that showed his head over the breastworks.

Two of our men have been wounded. Henry Martin our Orderly was shot through the thigh. Another man who had just come out to join the company was shot in the hip. In return for this we have shot, it is thought, nearly 100 men. . . .

The rebels come out of their fort this morning and attempted to strike one of our batterys but was driven back. Night before last and last night all the troops were turned out by picket firing.

I thought I would send you a small bunch of flowers today but it rained so that they are all wet.

Cherry and peach trees are in blossom and plenty of wildflowers cover the ground. As there begins to be some prospect of the war soon closing I think more of you. Sometimes when bullets are flying around me I dread to think of the danger I am in. I do want to come home safe and see you and I think I shall.

My Captain says there is no danger of Bick being shot. In fact I do seem to have extraordinary luck in getting out of tight scrapes.

Time will not let me make this a long letter. . . .

We are so busy fighting you must excuse short letters, and poorly written letters. . . .

I must bring this letter to a close. I have so much writing to do now that I have a clerk part of the time. He does writing for the company though. . . .

EGBERT OSWALD HIXON

Sun. [April] 20 Morn raining. It rained all day & all night.

Mon. 21 Cool morn but inclement. A squad gone to the rebs batteries. Not much fireing. Stormed hard all day. Dull & dreary enough.

Tue. 22 . . . Went out near the Rebs works. Mel [David M.] Littlefield got shot in the leg not very bad.[12]

Wed. 23 Beautiful morn. One squad went out this morn. I did not go till after dinner. Relieved those that were out.

Thurs. 24 Morn inclement. Went out in the woods. Capt. Bartlett of the 20th Mass got wounded in the knee. Brought him to our surgeon & cut his leg off.

LUKE BICKNELL

Camp Winfield Scott near Yorktown
Saturday Eve April 26 1862

Dearest [Lucretia],

. . . I will tell you what we have done each day this week.

Monday it rained and we staid in camp. Tuesday it rained in the forenoon, but in the afternoon I took twenty five men and had a fine time picking off rebels in the woods. We got behind stumps, trees and old logs and whenever a rebel showed his head fired at him. At dusk we returned all safe. The next day I took twenty men to the same place and blazed away at the rebels all the forenoon had good luck and came back for dinner all safe.

I had the luck to hit one rebel myself.

On the afternoon I took ten men to the same place again. As soon as we opened fire one of our men was hit. I sent him to the rear and soon found the rebels had got a new position which so completely commanded ours that they would do us more harm than we could them.

Very soon the Gen. learning of the new position of the rebels ordered us to fall back.

Next day Thursday we did nothing. Friday ditto. Today we took out forty men. It began to rain. I sent twenty of them to annoy the rebels on the left and waited to see what would turn up.

It began to rain torrents and the order came to fall back.

You see that I have used the first person very freely in my account.

It happened so this week that when the boys were in the field there was no other man there to direct their movements.

So you must excuse me for egotism.

One Lieut has resigned another is sick. The Orderly Searg is wounded, another Searg is sick, another is a coward and so it happens that besides the Captain there is only the Searg to take charge of men.

Next week it is intended that this company shall annoy the rebels as much as possible. Some of us will get hit but your humble servant hopes and expects to get through safe.

During the last week, I have had bullets plunked into trees all around me. One struck just side of my foot. Another covered me with dirt from a rotten log behind which I was laying and over which I had just fired.

Two balls came both sides of my head at the same time both so close that I felt the wind of the balls on my cheeks.

There wasn't any use of dodging that time. One picket fired at me and sent a bullet whizzing over my head, while at the same time a buck shot struck at my feet in a good line only one was too high and the other a little too low.

I rested over a stump and taking a good sight as possible did my best to drop that man.

Every day we have hair breadth escapes and have got used to it now that we think a miss is as good as a mile.

If the rebels make a fight at Yorktown I think it will nearly, if not quite, end the war.

This chap intends to take very good care that he does not expose his precious carcase unnecessarily and hopes he won't have to meet the rebels again. They shoot too careless to make it entirely safe when they are around.

... I never loved you as completely as I do now. If anything should happen that I should have to come home on a furlough I shouldn't feel so very bad I believe. Though I wouldn't come home without a cause still, I should enjoy it very much to be there.

I cannot write in a letter as I would talk if I was beside you. Perhaps I shall never sit there again but the thought gives me pain.

I can not bear the thought so I will not dwell on it. I hope for the best. . . .

Out here away from all my friends I often think that if it were not for you I should not care much if I had to die.

I like my Mother, Father, sister and all relations pretty well, I suppose. But then I don't know why it is but it is true that whenever I think of happiness you are the only person I am thinking about.

How will it suit Cretia is the only question I ask. If I could be sure that after this war was over I could always have you near me happy and contented I should be suited.

I wish it was our wedding night. I hope that time will soon come round. God knows though and determining to do my best to hasten it.

I will wait (im)patiently for the happy day.

I would like to see you for a few minutes this evening. I wouldn't care if I did have to come back.

There would be some satisfaction in putting my arms around your neck and giving you one kiss.

I know I shoudn't think of anything else for a month.

MOSES HILL

Yorktown, Va Apl 28th 1862

Dear Wife,

I received a letter from you yesterday and I should of wrote yesterday, but I could not for I was called out all day. But your letter was brought down to me, and I was very glad to hear from home. Today I expect to be in camp all day. . . .

Dear Eliza, as to being homesick, I keep up as good courage as I can. I am glad to hear that Mother Hill is well. I would like [to] see her very much and I hope I shal live to come home and see her soon. If you choose you can copy this letter and send to Uncle Phipps.

You spoke of Mr. Blodget. I can say I do not shoot Rebels for money or by the head. I shal not nor I have not shot anyone unless it is agoing to do some good for the Country. I have had balls come around me very close when I did not return a shot, for as to slawtering men when it does no good, I cannot do. When we fight for a victory, then is my time if any. Some take pride in going out and shoot a man from the Rebel breastwork when it does no good at all, but I cannot slawter in that way nor I will not.

Three of our men have got wounded since we have been here. All of them have been wounded in the hip & thigh, all on the right hip. Captain Bartlett, [William Francis Bartlett] acting as Lieutenant Colonel in the 20 Mass Rigm was wounded in the leg and he was brought in to the old house where we are. I spoke of this old house in my last letter. It was the Clinton's head quarters. The Doctors took Bartlett's leg off. Our wounded are getting along very well. I think they will all live. It has been quite cold and stormy for a number of days past, but it looks more like breaking away this morning.

Dear Eliza, you write cheering to me in regard to being home sick, but I must say I am sick of the war and want to come home. Yestarday was Sunday, and a part of the company was down near the pickets in the woods. We lay there as reserve. Some of our Company was swearing and some was gambleing. Do you blame me? We are quartered near the 15 Mass Rigm, and the Chaplain sent to our Captain and told him he wished he would not alow so much profane language in his company, and the reply was that his men was good fighters and he did not want to learn them any new tricks. Do you blame me Eliza? Last night our Captain had two or three oficers in the house with him. I sleep in the cellar under his room. I woke up in the night by the fireing of cannon & musketery, and they was drinking their whiskey and I think quite merry. *Do you blame me Eliza?* When I see sergents so drunk that they can hardly set on their horse, *do you blame* me Eliza? And when I see Generals with too much whisky in their brain to conduct a Brigade or a Division, *do you blame me Eliza?*

I believe we have some good Generals & Oficers and I believe General McClellan is one & I believe he would not alow all that is going on if he knew it. There is too much life at stake here. I should not notice it so much if we was fer from an enemy in camp. But we are close under the enemy guns and an attack may be expected at almost any moment. Rebel deserters come over most every day. I believe 72 come over yesterday and 6 last night. So it is most every day.

Our Company have great praise here in Sedgwicks & [William F.] Smiths Division. We are now in Sedgwick's Division. We can hold positions where Berdans Sharpshooters have been drove out. They cannot begin to compare with this Company as to close shooting, but it seems they get all the praise in the NY papers. They belong to [Fitz John] Porter's Division, and two companys have been detailed to go up to Smith's Division near us or within a mile of us, but they say they would rather we would of stayed, or part of our Company.

Some of our men was up there yesterday, but General Sedgwick sent for them to come back. He don't want us to go out of his Division any more. I think if the Rebels stand a fight here it may be a hard Battle but I think General McClellan means to do the fighting mostly by sieging. You may think in Mass that he gets along very slow, but it is not so. There is not a moment lost. The men work all night, some of them throwing up earth works, which they cannot always do in the daytime. The General is getting the siege guns & mortars along as fast as possible. There has been a great deal of work done here since we have been here.

The Rebels the other day had a rifle pit outside of their breastworks, and 2 companys of the First Mass Rigm volunteered to drive them out the other morning, and the Chelsea Company went at them and the other followed them with their shovels. They got almost to them before the Rebels see them. They took 16 prisoners and killed a number in the pit and the other Company came up and buried them up and filled up the pit. Our loss was 6 kiled and a number wounded. I don't know the exact number. There is more or less wounded on both sides most every day, I believe. I don't know when the Battle will come off but I hope the General will get all things ready so as to commence soon. I understand that he means to fire 1,000 shells a minute. The shot and shell weigh from 10 lbs to about 400 lbs. So you may judge it will be a hot place for the Rebels. I think if the Rebels do not attak us until we get all ready, they must leave or surrender.

Dear Eliza, I am very well today. I am better than I was a few days ago.... I hope we may get through with this Battle soon, for we have to carry our ammunition in our pockets ever since we have been here. What would you think if I should go to bed at home with my clothes all on & my pockets full of amminision and gun & pistol close to my head and sleep, as the old saying is, with one eye open all night? And sometimes alarm is given and all rush out in a line and a rower of musketery is heard, perhaps dark and rainy. That is the position we are in all the time. And may God speed the time when I can be at home with you & my dear children unmolested. And may God watch over you and protect you from all danger & sickness that might befall you.

From your ever loving Husband, M Hill

Eliza, I do not want any Officer to get hold of this letter until the war is over....

LUKE BICKNELL (MEMOIR, PP. 33–34)

The only ringing laugh I had heard for many weeks from my comrades arose one night as it was related how that [George] Whittemore, when the bullets fell like hail, had obeyed the order "to cover" by stepping behind a tree as thick as his arm and continuing his fire from it although there were plenty of sizeable trees near at hand. Whittemore either had perfect self control or else he forgot his own danger in a fight, and though he hated cool blooded sharpshooting, and I have known him to spare many a man entirely, and fire to wound only as a rule while we prowled along the Warwick river; whenever we got into anything like a square, open, stand up fight he entered it with a charming disregard of personal consequences.

Egbert Oswald Hixon

Sat. [April] 26 Rained all night & rained all day. Went out & stayed almost
   all day in the rain. Went to camp about 3 o'clock, on guard.
Sun. 27 Cold nasty weather, wet all day. ½ of the army goes out every day &
   the other half stay in.
Mon. 28 . . . Went out with a squad but did not do anything. A Lieut. In the
   15th got shot in the leg by a shell they say badly.
Wed. 30 Wet stormy. Infirmary [officers?] have taken our house [for a] hospital. Moved our tents.
Sat. [May] 3 . . . got to stay here, all day I expect. Dull enough. Looks like
   rain. Start out till sundown. Disagreeable place. Don't like it. Heavy fireing
   all night.

Moses Hill

Yorktown VA May 3d 1862

Dear Wife,
. . . I was out on duty, but I did not shoot. We was in the Batterys. We had
orders not to shoot unless the Rebels fired at our Batterys. They did not fire
so we did not. I was very glad to hear from home. . . . I am very well now. We
have but a very few sick in our Company now. The three that was wounded
are getting along very well. . . .

I am in camp today and I expect to go out tomorrow. So I thought I would
write today, for I don't know when I can write if I do not write today, for we
may have a Battle Monday. I think the General is most ready now. You may
think the armey gets along very slow, but we have had a great deal to do. The
troops work night and day. When there is a fortification or breastwork to
build in sight of the Rebels Baterys our troops have to do it nights, so they
work all night as well as day. But there is one good thing for us, this Company, that is we do not have to work nights. But we are called up nights when
there is an alarm given. That is quite often.

Eliza, we hear of glorius victorys in the papers, and I hope the time will
soon come when we shal not be oblige to win another victory. I get a paper as
often as I can. They come into camp every night. I have to pay 10 cents for all
the papers except the Baltimore Clipper that is very small, and I have to pay 5
cents for that. It is only one half of a paper and small at that. We have to pay
three times what a thing is worth here if we buy anything.

I hope this Battle will be the last that we shal have to fight. I am sick of it,
but I think that if we are successful here it will do a great deal in closing up

the war in Virginia. Eliza, we have good water here. That is a great thing for us. We have good Boiling Springs to dip our water out of. I am drying my clothes today. I washed day before yesterday and did not get them dry. I was out yesterday so I have to dry them today. Eliza, you do not know how much I think of home, you and the children. It seems as if the summer could not pass off without my seeing home. Tell Asahell Lovell that I would like to go a fishing with him this spring but I cannot. I would like to go down on the River bank where all is still and when I should not be oblige to look on all sides to see if some Rifle or a musket was pointing at me, or to listen to hear if there was a shell coming over my head so that I could drop on the ground before it bursts, or to lay myself down at night to sleep where I know I should not be attacked before morning. Tell Asahel he don't know what a diference there is between a quiet home and a life that I now live, but I think it cannot last much longer. I can go out but a few rods and see hundreds of Rebels any time on and around their fortifications.

I lay under an old fence and fired at them about ⅔ of a mile the other day. I had been there not very long before there was some shots fired close to me from some other direction, although they did not come nearer than ten feet from me. You might ask why we could not see all their movements. It is because there is so much woods and swamps in front of their fortifications.

There is cannonading now within ¼ of a mile of us. I stop my pen to listen to hear where the shells burst. It takes 5 to 8 seconds to reach their destination, from our Batterys I mean. Then I hear a Rebel shell coming into our Baterys, so I listen to hear that burst and feel as if it has wounded or killed some of our men, wich it does more or less most every day. So it is the whole length of the line. But next week I expect to hear at least 1,000 shells in a minute from our Guns. I think then it will be a hot place for the Rebels. Our Gun Boats can shell the village in Yorktown now. The Rebels Burst their largest Gun yesterday morning that was ranged to sweep the River.

Eliza, write often and I pray that I may soon come home safe and be with you. May God bless you and protect you & children.

From your ever loving Husband, M Hill

Do not forget to kiss Sis and Bub for me. I hope I can do it myself soon.

For reasons that are far from clear, relations between Captain John Saunders and a significant number of his men seem to have become strained by the spring of 1862. As Moses Hill remarked in March, "our Captain has not a spark of feeling for the Company." Moreover, Hill hinted that at Yorktown, the captain was drinking heavily. Egbert Hixon's remarks suggested that Saunders had become more authoritarian and punitive. Luke Bicknell suggested that the strain of the constant demand for the snipers' service, plus the broken promises left the men sullen. Captain Saunders chose to—or perhaps was forced to—increase discipline among the men, as Bicknell's account reveals.[13]

LUKE BICKNELL (MEMOIR, P. 34)

A skilled optician and machinist was borne on our roll, as artificer, who at enlistment had not only been promised extra pay but also, that keeping the guns in order, was all the duty which would be required of him. One day Capt. Saunders ordered me to include him in the detail for the front [at Yorktown]. The artificer refused to go and demanded a court martial . . . [and when] I remonstrated with the Captain, he said "he had no option in the matter, that I must go to the general commanding the division if I would avoid my duty of punishing the man as directed." . . . I carried his demand to Gen. [John] Sedgwick who commanded the division. He rated me soundly for bringing such a demand to him while we were engaged in a campaign. . . . After he had abused me to his heart's content, [he] sent me back to tell Capt. Saunders that "if he could not make his men obey orders . . . to take a four foot stick and thrash them till they would," and ordered that the artificer be punished until he would do duty in the ranks. Capt. Saunders then ordered that the man be tied up to a tree and kept on bread and water under guard until he gave in.

I pleaded with the man in vain and finally tied him up as directed, making a long comfortable loop in which he promised to keep his hand. . . . I detailed friends of his on guard over him, who I knew would privately give him rest and food at night . . . all might have ended well in time if some traitor had not watched at night and discovered that the man was taken down and allowed to sleep and eat while a comrade took his place at the tree till near daylight. So I had to tie up the guard to another tree and put men on guard who were not in sympathy with the artificer. . . . When I went to tie up the guard, he having sworn that he would not be tied up alive, sprang for me as I approached him with the rope. But the Captain, who, unbeknownst to me had followed me, struck over my shoulder, a blow that felled the guard like an ox. The man struck down was one of the bravest men that stood in ranks during the whole conflict; and never seemed to bear me malice on account of the affair. . . .

Some thought the artificer had no more right to refuse duty in the ranks than the rest of us. Some blamed the General, some the Captain, and some blamed me for not refusing to tie the man up at all. Others thought I had shown too much sympathy with the man. . . . A cold rain came on and the artificer finally gave in more dead than alive but as we supported him to his tent he vowed that Capt. Saunders should die for this.[14]

"Who Would Not Be a Soldier?"

The Confederates secretly evacuated Yorktown during the night of May 3. They left behind many "torpedoes"—concealed land mines—an act that shocked many Union soldiers. As one soldier explained, "The rebels had buried shells all about where our troops had to pass."[15] Most expected a rapid march on Richmond and a quick end to the war. But General McClellan's pursuit was slow and cautious. After pushing Confederate defenders out of Williamsburg (May 5), defeating them at Hanover Court House (May 27), McClellan's men fought them to a bloody draw at Fair Oaks (May 31). One fateful casualty of that fight was Confederate General Joseph E. Johnston, who was badly wounded by an artillery shell. He was soon replaced by Robert E. Lee. After the battle, McClellan hesitated. Instead of pushing onward, he set his men to building defensive entrenchments. Some Union troops camped so close to Richmond that they could see its church steeples.

Meanwhile, when the officers of the Fifteenth Massachusetts detailed Andrew's Sharpshooters to draw water and haul wood, some of the riflemen nearly revolted.

Anonymous Private, Second Company Massachusetts Sharpshooters

May 4th [We] were informed by the guard that the enemy had evacuated Yorktown during the night but before leaving [our] entrenchments two companies were ordered out and deployed and marched to their works, on the ramparts of which the *Stars & Stripes* were unfurled at half past six o'clock A.M. amid the deafening cheers of the regiment. Then the remainder of the Reg't was marched out in closed column by companies and marched towards Yorktown.

When we had got about half the distance between our works and those of the rebels, an "infernal machine" in the ground exploded as Co. G was passing over it, severely wounding five of them but killing no one. It was afterwards learned that the field in front of their works was full of them, so continued as to explode by the pressure of ones foot but fortunately we encountered no more of them til we got inside the fort and then explosions were frequent. We marched into the town carefully avoiding all suspicious looking places in the surface of the ground. Halted in one of the principal streets and were ordered to rest in place but most of the companies roamed at large in quest of trophies till it was ascertained nearly as possible that torpedoes were placed in all parts of the town. . . . Then it was that guards were stationed to keep the men from moving about. While the cavalry were passing through the fort to pursue the enemy another of those "machines" exploded killing two horses and wounding the riders. A short time afterwards, one of the Telegraph Boys while in the performance of his duty stepped on one of them and was injured so badly that death is inevitable.[16]

EGBERT OSWALD HIXON

Sun. [May] 4 Weather fine . . . 8 o'clock, the rebs have left & gone & our forces are after them. Went into a secesh house to get some plunder.

Mon. 5 Morn. rainy. Slept in a secesh tent. It rained all day in torrents & till 12 o'clock at night. The secesh left lots of torpedoes in their works & blew up some of our men, a d—d cowardly act.

Tues. 6 Getting ready to move. Don't know where. Went on board steamer Eagle about 8 o'clock P.M. Slept on deck first rate. The moon shone bright. It was a beautiful night.

Wed. 7 Morn. started about sunrise up the York river; went very slowly. Went up to West Point and unloaded. [General William B.] Franklin's Division has been fighting the Rebs all day, good many killed & wounded.

Thurs. 8 Morn. Weather fine, going to be hot in camp out in an open plain, no trees no shade. Troops marched all day & night.

Fri. 9. Morn. Cool last night. Going to be a hot day. We moved about 2 miles. . . . It was a beautiful evening. The sun shone bright & the bands played. Who would not be a soldier?

LUKE BICKNELL (MEMOIR, PP. 35–36)

After a day or two at West Point we marched seven miles up the Pamunkey River and camped. While here we were required to furnish a daily detail to bring wood and water for brigade head quarters. Three months before we were the proud favorites of the commander of a department, and now we were ordered to perform the scullion duties for a mere brigadier, was the way the men felt about it. It was generally understood throughout the whole division that this order was intended to show the sharpshooters, once and for all, that they like all other soldiers must stand ready to perform any duties required of them notwithstanding their peculiar armament and the promises made to them at enlistment. . . . The men felt it as an intended insult and would not answer to my detail.

The Captain soon learned that the crisis had come; that his company would be broken up and distributed amongst other regiments; the commissioned officers dishonorably discharged . . . or that he must, at once, reduce the company to the state of discipline which prevailed around us, instant and unquestioning obedience to all orders, in camp, as well as in battle. There must be no more falling back on the conditions of our enlistment.

He called me into his tent, explained the situation and promised to back me to the best of his ability if I would undertake to keep the company together. He finished by saying that unless I could and would enforce obedience, I could take my place in the ranks and he would put another man in my place. I, in turn, explained the situation to the men. More than half told me to stick; that if there was no possibility of the conditions of their enlistment being fulfilled, they preferred to serve on in the Sharpshooters. So I told the Captain I would try to make the next morning's detail serve. . . .

I was obliged to drive men into the wood and water detail at the muzzle of a revolver. . . . The detail was to be called before light. Before I went to sleep I knew that one man on it had sworn he would not stir a step and that some had promised to stand by him. Next morning, when Corporal Gilbreth reported that one man refused to get out of his blankets, I cocked my revolver and followed him to where the man lay. My first grab stripped him of his blankets, my second tore off his shirt front and brought him to his feet, revolver in hand. I pressed the muzzle of mine against his temple and said "Mine is cocked—drop yours, and march into those ranks." A dozen men rose out of the mist around us, revolver in hand, but I did not hear the click of a single lock, for as they rose I said, "If one of you cocks your revolver, I pull this trigger." The man was brave, but he was not a fool, and had not come out to die for such a cause. I was, however, greatly relieved when he, at last, dropped his revolver and took his place in the detail, for I had no ambition for such death as must have instantly followed his.

This ended what might have been a mutiny in camp. . . . They made all the resistance that brave men could make and not throw away their lives; but what was the use—a regiment which showed its sympathy too plainly was kept standing at shoulder arms in the hot sun two hours—they saw the utter uselessness of the struggle, and gave in. They did not blame me, and when I offered to step back into the ranks they would not hear of it. From that time forward no orderly in the division had less difficulty with his company.[17]

MOSES HILL

Opiset West Point on Sunday May 11, 1862

Dear Wife,

I have not heard from home since a week ago last Friday. I am well and safe as yet. I suppose you have worried about me some since I wrote or since you have heard from me. . . .

Eliza, the prospect of things have changed some since I wrote. Sunday morning I went with a part of the Company to protect the Baterys as usual, but we found the enemy fortifications was vacuated. We went on to them and moved down tords the River. We went about 3 miles Sunday and camped over night. We found the Rebels has left their tents, Flour & Meal & Bacon & Pork and cooking things, so we lived well that day. We found lard and a Keg of molasses. We made flippers [pancakes] and fried donuts & made Puddings until we had our fill.

Monday we moved to Yorktown near the river where the Rebels had their strongest fortifications. They left their large Guns &ct as you have seen in the papers no doubt. I see a good meny of the Torpedoes that they laid for us, but I was sure not to go very close to them. I see one go off and it blowed one man most all to peaces. We stoped here Monday night and we found it a very rainy night too.

Tuesday we went aboard of a Boat for West Point. The Boat did not start until Wednesday morning early. One Division went the day before. If you remember, I wrote that I was in Sedgwick Division. A part of the armey went by land and you have no doubt read of the fighting they had at Williamsburg. Some of the Mass troops suffered very much. We landed at West Point a little before noon Wednesday. There was a fight up in the woods close by us which the Division that came ahead of us was engaged. We was orded ashore as soon as possible. We all went ashore in small Boats. They was Pontoon Boats. But by the time we got ashore the fight had stoped. When we was coming ashore the Rebels shells burst near us but the first Mass Batery was play into them all the time, and the Gun Boats brought their Guns to bear and they done a great exicution and it drove them back very quick. Our killed and wounded I think must have been as meny as two or three hundred. Some of the Rebels after wounding our men cut their throats when they called for quarter and ground their faces all up with the brich of their guns.[18]

There was a good meny Negroes in Rebel armey here, and some of them are as bad as the whites and some of them are better marksman than the whites are. There was a whole Brigade of Blacks in the engagement that I last spoke of. Our troops do not have so much sympathy for the Blacks as they did.[19]

Where we went ashore was nearly opiset of West Point in a large open field and a very pleasant place. Wednesday night it was very quiet all night. Thursday. The troops continue to come in.

Friday. It is very quiet here. In the afternoon we had orders to be ready to move. We packed up and soon we was all on a march. Franklins Division went ahead of us. We moved about 3 miles and we camped near the River within a few rods in a very pleasant place.

Saturday. All is very quiet here, and in the afternoon our teams came in from Yorktown. They came along with the land army. They said they see a great meny Guns, horses, mules &c that the Rebels left on the road. I think most of the Rebel armey came up near the James River. I expect we was hurried up here to keep them off from the R.R. that runs from Richmond to West Point. The whole of the Rebel armey seem to be in a rather bad position. They are discouraged and demoralized I think. I expect they will make one more stand near Richmond if they can get there. We keep on their right flank so I think they cannot do McDowell much harm.

Sunday. I expect we shall move today or tomorrow up further tords Richmond. Franklins Division is moveing now, and there is about 1,000 Cavelery near where I am writing that are getting ready to move in a few moments. I went down to the river yesterday to see if I could ketch some fish but the tide was going out and I lost my line so I gave it up. Fish are plenty here.

Eliza, I feel very hard tords Henry Wilson [a U.S. Senator from Massachusetts] and others when they are doing all they can to injure McClellan. I think if he had took Yorktown by a charge of Bayonets and lost 25,000 men, which he probibly would have done if he had taken it that way, he would have been thought more of by a good meny such as Wilson. It would have been a great victory then. I wish such men would come and charge on some of the Rebels brestworks and see how they like it. It does make no odds whether [he] is a Democrat or Whig or republican. Any man that tryes to inger McClellan cannot have one vote from any man that now is in McClellans armey. That is what I think and that is my feelings now. I believe every man in the armey sets their life by him. They have all confidence in him. He tryes to do his fighting so as to save life all he can. I mean the lives of his own armey. If you could see the works he has done since he has been here to Yorktown, you would not of believed it. Some days he is in his saddle all day and he is from one end of his armey to the other all the time. We are now within about 30 miles of Richmond, I mean to where we are, but some are a great deal nearer then that. I don't think this Division will go so soon as I wrote in the fore part of my letter. We may not for 2 & 3 days.

Eliza, I was much disappointed a few [moments] ago for the mail come and no letter from you. Others direct their letters the same as you do. . . . Eliza, I feel that I shal come home soon now if we are successful in taking Richmond, wich I have all the Confidence we shal be, for I believe the General is more than a match for the Rebel armey. . . . We have cheering news from all parts most every day. It was reported yesterday in camp that the Merrimac was taken and if that be trew we are safe in Verginia, I believe, for we can go up the James River with our Gun boats and I expect they are up there now. You cannot think what a help them Gunboats are. Them 100 lbs shell makes havocking work with an enemy.

I must close soon. . . . It is quite warm here. I have been through some pieces of clover that was a foot high. There is nothing planted here by the people for they have left their homes. . . .

Our troops are all determined to bring this war to a close soon. I believe the armey are in good health now. I think our Company was never better. . . . Do not worry about me Eliza. When I can see the day that I start for home it will be the happiest day I ever see, I believe. Love to you.

EGBERT OSWALD HIXON

Sat. [May] 17 Morn. The sun rose beautiful, the bands are playing. Nothing new. The roads are in such a state that it is almost impossible to move. Nothing to do. Good many of the boys are sick.

Sun. 18 Morn. Got orders to move. Started about 7—hot marching. Came about 9 miles & camped in a wheat field. Got our tents so we have good quarters. Hot muggy weather. Don't know how long we shall stop here.

Mon. 19 Morn warm & sultry. Had a beautiful job today, was detailed to lug water for the cook, had to tote it about ¼ of a mile up a steep slippery bank, don't like it. Had several showers.

MOSES HILL

Near Kent Court House, Va May 19th 1862

Dear Wife,

. . . I have not been very well for a week past but I feel a little better yesterday & today. I expect to receive a letter from you to day. *I hope I shall.*

Monday May 12th. All quiet [and] we have had no orders to move yet. Troops continue to come in.

Tuesday 13th. All quiet in camp to day. I feel a little better then I did yesterday. I had a diarear yesterday.

Wednesday 14th. All quiet in camp to day.

Thursday 15th. Packed up our things early in the morning and moved tords Cumberland. We moved about 8 miles and camped in the woods. It has rained very hard all day, no tents to sleep in tonight.

Friday 16th. It did not rain much last night. It is quite pleasant today. Stoped here all day.

Saturday 17th. Quite pleasant all day. Stoped here all day. I do not feel quite so well today. It is very warm today.

Sunday 18th. Packed up and moved about 3 miles near [New] Kent Court House where we are today. I feel some better today.

Monday 19th. We had orders to be ready to move at a moments notice. It begins to rain and I think we shal not go today but we may have orders to move before night. I feel some better today.

Eliza, I think we have got the Rebel armey in rather close quarters and it seems to me that they cannot stand out much longer. They are trying to make another stand about 8 miles this side of Richmond. There may be a hard Battle, but it seems to me that they will not stand a hard fight for they seem to be discouraged. I think they had rather break up and go to their homes. If McDowell gets down there in season I think they must give up. Our troops are moveing up all the time. This Division is not in the advance now. We are on the reserve. As fast as troops move that are ahead of us we move up. We are within about 22 miles of Richmond now. We shal come up to the enimy soon if we keep moveing. I expect we move about 5 miles next time, and the advance troops must be in sight of the enemy or nearly so. I don't care how quick we attack them for I want to see the way clere to Richmond. The troops are all very anxious to close this thing up and go home. I hope we shall here cheering news from [General Henry W.] Halleck again soon.

Eliza, I don't know as I can give you much news of the Rebel armey or of our armey for I [have] no doubt you see all in the papers and perhaps more than I can write. I think our troops enjoy very good health considering the weather and hardship. It is very warm here most of the time. Water is very good in most places we have found. I think if we stay here much longer we shal have Cherrys & Peaches plenty but Peach trees are not so plenty here as they was down near Fortress Monroe. I have not had a paper for a week and I went out and bought one a few moments ago. It was the N.Y. Hearald. I paid 15 cts for it. I see no victory from Hallock yet. Papers come into camp every day, but they are so dear that I cannot afoard to buy them very often.

Eliza, I think there will be some change in the course of things before two weeks more pass over our heads. I have been thinking how I should like to come home before the 4th of July and I cannot give it up yet.... I think of you

& children all the time when I am awake, and if I could get up some morning knowing that we was coming home to Mass it would be the happiest morning that I ever saw. But I have made up my mind to wait patiently for that day. I am willing to stay here to see the end of the fighting in V.A. and then I want to come home the next moment.

I hope you are all well. I expect we shal move from here tomorrow morning. The mail goes out in a few moments and I must close. Do not forget to write often and Sis must write too, and *little Bub*, if only he makes a mark on a peace of paper I like to see it. My love to you all and may God bless you and protect you.

From your ever lover Husband, Moses Hill

Kiss Sis & Bub for me. Plant a good lot of Garden sauce this Spring, and I hope I shal be spaired to come home and help you eat it. I think it would tast better then hard bread & coffee & salt beaf. I have not had a potato for 3 months. I think if I could come home and eat good vituels with you I should feel better than I do now. . . .

LUKE BICKNELL

15 Miles from Richmond [May 1862]

Dear Lucretia,

The present is the worst possible time to form an opinion about the war.

Whether it shall close this summer or next spring depends on whether the rebels are captured or allowed to retreat from Richmond.

They have so large an army that we can not do with them just as we would like to.

Ever since the evacuation of Yorktown the service to which this company belongs has been held in reserve. It is quite likely I have seen my last fight although it is possible we may be engaged if there is a great battle. . . . We are all very anxious to see the result of matters around Richmond. If we gain a great victory and disperse or capture the army opposed to us then we can go home.

I tell you we are all anxious enough to finish the war.

I had the misfortune to lose my knapsack at Yorktown. All I care about is that your picture was in it at the time.

I should have thought the thief might have had politeness enough to have returned the pictures. He must have known whose it was for the articles were marked with my name. Your letters (the only ones I keep) were in the breast pocket (of my shirt) and they were saved. I used to carry your miniature there till I found that the features were being spoilt by perspiration. I hope I may soon see the original of the picture. I am sure that I shall begin to enjoy myself fifty percent better from that time. All the desires I used to have before my acquaintance with you have been absorbed by my love for you and if our plans should fail of realization I am sure that nothing else would ever after satisfy me. I didn't suppose that any one would become so dear to me. I wouldn't for the world give you up now.

One kiss from you is more pleasure to me than a thousand years with another woman. I hope I shall even have an opportunity to take one from your lips. I want to be alone with you once more to draw you close to me and press my lips to yours. I want to look into your eyes as I set by your side and read the love that no language can tell.

I can not tell whether I am more anxious to be at home or whether I am more contented to stay here on account of the good understanding there is between us. Perhaps both. I am certain that I wish to see you as soon as possible and when I get to W I think I will manage to see you as often and stay as long as used to. Oh for one more evening with you!

. . . If we have a fight in which I am . . . engaged I will write you immediately after is over. . . .

MOSES HILL

14 Miles from Richmond, Va May 26, 1862

Dear Mother,

I received a letter from you today, and I was very glad to hear from you, and I am very glad to hear that you have enjoyed so good health this Spring and winter. Dear Mother, how glad I would be to come home and see you, and I hope I shall have a chance soon. Some times it looks rather dark and as if the war might last for some time yet, and sometimes it looks as if it might close soon. I suppose you have seen all my letters that I have sent Eliza so I will not write many poticulers but I can say that I have seen some hard times, at least I should think so if I was at home.

I am now within 14 miles of Richmond and we have been expecting to march for the last 3 hours. I expect there will be a battle here soon. It may come off tomorrow. It begins to rain this afternoon, so I don't think there will be a Battle today. I have not been in a hard Battle, for the Reble armey have not stood a Battle at any time we have tried to engage them. Mother, I am sick of fighting and shooting our Brother man and I hope they will not try to hold out much longer but give it up, which I think they will have to do some time. There is a report today that Banks has had a fight and been drove back but it may not be true. If it is true I suppose John and Albert has seen a little of it. I hope it is not so, for they don't know what fighting is and I hope they never will. I have seen enough of it and I hope I shal not see any more but I expect to see a hard Battle before this week is out. Our Company has seen something in western V.A. and since we have been here we have seen more and it is not very agreeable.

Dear Mother, I do not see such times as I use to when I could go to the old cupboard and eat of your cooking and eat my fill of boiled vitils and custards, pie and everything that was good. I cannot have that now. I must eat hard corned Beaf that you would not think of eating and hard bread. Some of it is so hard that hot coffee will not soak it, but it is the best that we can get unless we buy it ourselves. I do buy a good deal and I should buy more if it was not so dear. We have coffee. It is sweetened, but no milk. That is out of the question. If we could have some potatoes it would be a great rariety. Dear Mother, I hope I shal live to come home and eat one good meal with you. How I would enjoy it. And I hope that time will come soon. I feel that I shal come home before a great while.

Mother, I am not so well as I was last Spring. I think the climate does not agree with me so well. It is quite warm here and cool nights and a very heavy dew. I would be glad to have my sister to write to me often. I would like to know where to direct a letter to Aaron [his brother]. If I did I would write to him. I have not had any letter from him. I am glad to hear he has got work, and I am glad he did not come out here in the armey.

Mother, you must take care of your health and I hope God will presure you and protect you and all my Brothers & Sisters. And I hope the time will soon come when I shall come home and see you all. Love to you all.

From your never forgetful Son, Moses Hill

Egbert Oswald Hixon

Mon. [May] 26 . . . All the troops have got orders to be in reddiness to march, without blankets & with 60 rounds of cartridges.

Wed. 28 Morn started about 4 o'clock & moved about 4 miles to the right & laid in the woods all day. We had no blankets & I caught cold & was about sick all day.

Thurs. 29 morn I shook with the cold but the sun came up & I got warm. Lots of news of rumors about our army. We started back to camp about 5 o'clock. I felt weak & tired but we got some whiskey.

Fri. 30 . . . We are having a thunder shower, they [have] just as smart thunder & lightening south as we do north.

Moses Hill

14 Miles from Richmond, May 30th /62

Dear Wife,

...Tuesday we stoped in camp all day. Wednesday we packed up and marched and camped near Bottoms Bridge. Very hot day. 3 men died on the road. I think the General that was in command was to blame to hurry the men up so fast. I received a letter from you when we got there.

Thursday. Stoped all day. Had a heavy shower and hail. The hail stones was the largest that I ever saw. We are near the Railroad.

Friday. Packed up again and moved about 4 miles at the Right, but not any nearer to Richmond. We went into camp here.

Saturday. All quiet in camp last night.

Sunday. Not very well today. Quite pleasant. I went out to the 34 NY Rig. near night to hear a religious survice.

Monday. I received a letter from Mother. I answered it today.

Tuesday. Heard cannonading on the Right in Porters Division. At night General Porter reported to of taken 3,000 prisenors and kild & drounded meny. We was held in readiness all night. We slep but very little. We expected to reinforce Porter.

Wednesday Morning. As soon as it was light, the whole Division marched. We went off in such a hurry some of the men could not stop to get their Breakfast but put their rations in their haversacks. We marched without any blankets so we could go quick and be ready to fight if we was wanted and we stoped after marching about 3 or 4 miles and stoped in the woods and stayed there all day and night. We did not sleep much. I did not sleep any, but sat up by a little fire for I thought if I laid down I should catch cold. You see, there is very heavy dews here.

Thursday. In the morning the Rebel prisoners passed by, a large number of them. Some of them told our Boys that they was glad they was taken and they wished they had more of their men with them. Eliza, this Division is held in reserve to go anywhere they are wanted the most, so we was called out to cover General Porter. He wanted to Distroy two Bridges that lead up tords Jacksons armey. It cuts off all comunutacion. They cannot reinforse the Rebel armey from that quarter. I suppose you will see it in the papers. That perhaps will explain better then I can.

McClellan expected they would come down on Porter with a heavy forse to drive him off, and if they did, we should have been engaged and there would have been a hard fight no doubt. After Porter had done all he wanted we marched back to camp again, and now we are ready for another start.

Eliza, I am sorry Banks has got drove back [in the Shenandoah Valley] but it may be a good thing. I dont consider it more then a Skermish, but I suppose the folks will make a large Battle out of it. It does not begin to be so much of a Battle as Porter had, but I think it happened in the right time to call out volenteers, and I think it will hasten to close the war very much. I received a letter from you & Sis today and was glad to hear from home and would been glad too if had you wrote more.

Friday morning. I feel a little better this morning. . . . Sis wanted to know what that ring was made of. It was made of laurel root that we got in Western Va.[20] I will send you another one that I finished yesterday, a Black one that is not made of wood. I have made a larger one out of the same root that I sent to you. I make them with my knife. . . .

Eliza, I hope I shal not be obliged to go any further than Richmond if I have to get there. I think this war must close sometime and I pray to God that may be tomorrow. . . . I will try to keep up good cheer a little longer. I gues I should like to be at your table and eat with you for a week, and I think I should feel a great deal better. . . .

Fair Oaks

As the Union army approached Richmond, General McClellan divided it, placing part of it—including John Sedgwick's Second Division—north of the Chickahominy River, and part of it south. Confederate General Joseph E. Johnston recognized the opportunity presented by a divided enemy army. Johnston was further emboldened by a terrific storm that flooded the Chickahominy. He believed that McClellan would be unable to supply or reinforce his troops if he attacked one of the wings. On May 30, Johnston threw the bulk of his army against McClellan's forces south of the river. Fortunately for the Federals, the complexity of the Confederate plan, plus major failures of communication among Confederate officers, spared them the full brunt of the attack. Even so, by midday on May 31, Union defenses south of the river neared collapse.

General McClellan ordered Edwin Sumner's Second Corps to cross the surging Chickahominy. John Sedgwick's Second Division reached the so-called Grapevine bridge over the swollen river first. Even though the bridge was beginning to disintegrate, the men crossed. Brigadier General Willis Gorman's troops—including Andrew's Sharpshooters—were the first over: "Men went in up to their waists; horses floundered and fell down. Three pieces only of the leading one of our four batteries could be dragged through in time to assist in resisting the first attack that awaited us."[21] Then after slogging several miles through swamp and roads knee-deep in mud, Gorman's Brigade formed on the left of the division's line in a field. Within a half hour, Confederate infantry came swarming out of the woods at them.

The timely arrival of Sedgwick's troops, plus artillery under Lieutenant Edmund Kirby, turned the tide of battle. In his memoir, Luke Bicknell claimed that the Andrew's Sharpshooters helped defend Kirby's battery, which was the focus of repeated Confederate assaults. He said the men used their new Colt revolvers in the close fighting, and—along with two infantry regiments—successfully repulsed the attacks, which at times got as close as twenty yards from the battery and threatened to overrun it. At one point a Confederate officer even managed to place his hand on an artillery piece and claim it before he was killed.[22] Bicknell's—and other sharpshooters'—letters, however, indicate that they did view some of the fighting, but had no active part in it. The second day, June 1, Gorman's Brigade saw little action, since the fighting shifted to the left of Sedgwick's division. Ultimately, the Confederates withdrew.

Andrew's Sharpshooters experienced their first major battle at Fair Oaks. And since they had to camp for several days amidst the carnage of the battlefield, they also received their first vivid impressions of the human cost of war. A New Jersey private described the scene: "The dead rebs were still laying where they fell on the second day after the battle, and presented a horrible sight. They had swelled to double their natural size, and as a consequence their clothing had burst, thus exposing their bodies to the sun, and turning them black as ink. . . . They were now so far decomposed and made such a horrible stench, that it was as much as we could do to get them under cover."[23]

EGBERT OSWALD HIXON

Sat. 31 Cloudy. Got a letter from home & wrote one. Heard heavy firing towards R[ichmond]. Our Div. moved out about 2 o'clock, had a forced march 4 or 5 miles. Had a big fight with the rebs. Never saw such fighting before.

LUKE BICKNELL (MEMOIR, PP. 36–37)

While our division was crossing a bridge over the Chicahominy, the afternoon of May 31st, to go into the battle of Fair Oaks, the further end of the bridge rose and floated off before us. When the front rank reached the break, quickly gave the order "forward," and the men, who had swung up their cartridge boxes as they marched, stepped off, without a halt, into water breast high, and, with many a slip and tumble and rescue, the division reached the opposite shore in time to save the day.

The sharpshooters were put in the rear of a section of Kirby's Battery, with orders to advance with revolvers and retake the guns if they should be captured. The enemy made three desperate charges through the woods at the corner of which the two guns stood . . . but it mattered not who led against the murderous fire of Gormans Brigade and Kirbys battery that night. We had no chance to retreat from the overwhelming force thrown against us except into the swift and deep river at our back. Each time as the yelling mass neared the two guns—and once I saw them lay their hands upon them—the sharpshooters rose to their feet and bent forward for the spring with revolvers cocked and muscles strained to their utmost tension, and, each time, as they recoiled in disorder we sunk down again upon the ground trembling in every limb from the relaxation of the terrible strain.

GEORGE WHITTEMORE JR.

Fair Oaks, June 19, 1862

Our quiet life ended with May. On the 31st, we set out from the camp two miles the other side of the Chickahominy, crossed the river and swamp in water up to our knees, and stumbled on the enemy. Before a line of battle was fairly formed, the firing began, and our company, who have no place in a line of bayonets, and in the hurry of the moment had been assigned no station, was ordered to lie down. The shower of bullets fired over the head of the line fell all about us, but only one of our men was hit. The fight here on Saturday night lasted not over an hour, but it was well after dark before it was decided. While it lasted it was furious, not broken for an instant, and at times swelling into a louder roar, like gusts of wind in a storm, as the Rebels charged up to one or another part of our line. The battle of Sunday was in the woods, and hidden from our view; but we saw the regiments as they filed in, saw the smoke, and the wounded and the prisoners as they were brought out. Our division was not engaged, occupying the battlefield of the day before.[24]

EGBERT OSWALD HIXON

Sun. [June] 1 Laid out all night. It rained this morn. The rebs opened the ball. The battle lasted about 4 hours. A great many were killed on both sides. Camped out in the woods. Had 2 alarms but slept pretty well.

LUKE BICKNELL (*MEMOIR, PP. 37–38*)

The next day we occupied a fence where we could have done good execution if the battle had been fought on that part of our line, but it was fought in a swamp near by and we did not get a chance to fire a shot. Line after line moved down into the swamp until it seemed as if there could be no reserve left. For three hours the deafening roar of musketry continued until the living fought behind breastworks constructed of the piled dead. At last the Irish Brigade [Sixty-Ninth New York Infantry] charged with a fierce yell, which sweeping on through the swamp in place of the noise of firing, told those the conflict had ended in our favor. A report was current the next day that Irishmen fighting on the other side broke and fled before the green flag of our Irish Brigade.

We bivouacked, in the blood stained woods through which the enemy had charged the night before, amongst their dead who lay thicker than the trees. Perhaps it was a week, part of the time rainy, before we got tents and blankets, and we shivered through the nights as best we could.

EGBERT OSWALD HIXON

Mon. [June] 2 Warm this morn. They are burying the dead; it is an awful sight. They say the Rebs are leaving Richmond but I don't believe it. Laid around all day. The Rebs fired 2 or 3 shells just at our right. Had an awful thunder shower in the night. It rained hard.

Tues. 3 The sun rose beautiful but it going to be hot. We expect to be attacked every minute. Let them come, they will find us all ready, I guess. They are burying the dead. The rebs left lots of their dead & wounded on the field. It is hot & the bodies scent bad.

LUKE BICKNELL

Fair Oaks Va June 7th 62

Dear Cretia,

Knowing that you must have heard of the late battle on the Peninsula I have been very anxious to write and assure you of the safety of your Brother, all of the Windsor Boys and myself, but the want of all materials to compose a letter except lead pencil has prevented me for a week.

To day some of our knapsacks came in one of the teams and I have borrowed paper, envelope and stamp and gone at it.

I will not attempt to describe the battle, the papers have done that, but will simply mention that this company took no part in the engagement further than to lay flat on their faces behind a bridge where most of the bullets passed over our heads. We were in the rear of the 15th Regiment which was in the front and the thickest of the fight. Only one of our men was wounded and that only slightly in the head when he bobbed his head up to take a look. This was Saturday night. Sunday a most desperate battle was fought in which we also took no part and didn't even have bullets come near us. . . .

It is the first pleasant day we have had since the battle. It has been all wet, cold, most miserable weather to stay out of doors without blankets, overcoats or tents or even without scarcely anything to eat.

It is a little the roughest I have ever experienced and has seemed worse to me that I have been about sick for two weeks.

But it is all right if Richmond is taken soon. . . .

No room now to indulge in fine sentences. I hope I may ever hold the same place in your regards as I do now. Believe me yours only and truly

L. Emerson Bicknell

MOSES HILL

Front of Richmond, June 10th 1862

Dear Wife,

. . . I will commence the 31st day as I wrote to you the 30th.

Saturday. We heard guns about 4 miles from us before noon and our Division was called out about 1 oclock. We started and went across Chickhomney River. We was forsed through as fast as we could go when we crossed the River. Some places we waded out to our knees in water. We got on to the Battlefield just in time to save the Battle, for if we was 30 minutes later I think our men would have been taken and cut to pieces. The Rebels was trying to take Rickets [Kirby's] Batery. They made a charge and was forsed back. They fought untill dark then was drove back a little. Our troops lay on the Field where they left off the fighting.

One of our men in our company was slitly wounded in the head. I went back to a house that our men used for a hospital with him, and we staid in the front yard all night for we could not get into the house, for there was so meny that was worse off than he was. The Surgents was cutting off legs and armes, and dressing wounds all night. The groans was terable. I did not sleep that night.

Sunday morning early I started for the Battlefield again. The Rebels commenced the Battle again about 9 oclock. They had been reinforced. They commenced on the left of the R.R., a different position than the day before. Our company was up on the Right in case of an attack, but they did not attack that place all day, so we was not in the fight at all Sunday although the fight was in range of our guns, but we could not fire for our troops was between the enemy and us. They was in the woods or near the edge. Our troops went in Regm after Regement and for the time I think it was the hardest Battle on record and the last that engaged them was Mass. Irish Brigade and then such a volley I never heard, and they charged Bayonets on them and drove them. They retreated back the best they could. I think it was after 11 oclock when the fireing ceased. Our reinforsements was coming in all the time.

The dead and wounded lay one [on] top of another when the Battle was through. The ded lay on all sides of us where they was killed the day before. Along the fences they lay, some with their faces up and some with their faces down and in all shapes. It was a horable sight and I hope I never shal have an occasion to see it again. I think the number of killed and wounded was more then the paper gave. I think the Rebel loss was very heavy. We stood all day here and at night we moved about 20 rods [110 yards] in the edge of a piece of woods up to the right. We had nothing but our Ruber blankets. The 15th Mass was close by us. I did not sleep much.

Monday. Our troops formed a line and put up some breastworks to protect them if attacked but we was not. The dead was about all buried today. Our armey did not bring many shovels with them, so it took some time. There was 688 wounded that lay by the side of the fence in 5 rods [less than 30 yards] of us. Their wounds was drest, but there was so meny that they could not take care of them all very quick. There was one on each side of where I slep that day dead within a few feet of me. They scented very bad. The maggots was on them, but they buried them as fast as they could.

Tuesday. We had a heavy shower last night. I think I never see it rain much harder, but it is pleasant this morning. We some expected to be attacked to day but had only some slight skirmishes. The dead are all buried to day that they can find and the wounded carried off. The wounded that I spoke of was carried off today. They was wounded Saturday. They belonged to Georgia, Alabama, North Carolina. I went and talked with them. They said they wanted to get home. The ground was so wet that it was very uncomftible for them. I pitied them from the bottom of my heart. The ground was most all coverd with water. One of them asked me for my pipe, and I gave it to him to smoke. I asked them if they wanted anything to eat. They said they did not. They said our troops took as good care of them as they could. I did not sleep much last night for it was so wet.

Wednesday. It rained all night and it raines this morning. The way I slept last night, I got two rails and laid one end up on a log and the other on the ground and I slop on them with my Ruber blanket over me. Nothing of a great importance happened to day. I have altered my location a litle. I have put up some Sticks and put up my blanket a little from the ground and stuck up some brush at the sides and laid in 3 pieces of rails and slep on them. It was very comftible. Once I should think it rather hard if I had to sleep on rails to keep out of the water, but I find no fault here. Our teams cannot get along with our tents & woolen blankets & Knapsacks. All the clothes we have here is our pants, shirts, Coats & Ruber blanket.

Thursday. Troops come in & we have good news from Halleck & [Major General John] Fremont & Banks. Nothing more of great importance.

Friday & Saturday. All very quiet.

Sunday. Our men went out with the pickets and was drove in. We expected an attack. There was a line of Battle drawn up but there was no attack.

Monday. Our tents & Blankets have all come. We moved a little way near General Gormans head quarters to the Right, not more then ¼ of a mile, and put up our tents. A lot of our troops was out in front of the line cutting down a lot of trees and timber so our artillery can have a better chance and the Rebels shelled them. I don't know whether they hurt anyone or not. Some of their shells burst over near where [we] are.

Tuesday. Quite rainy this morning.

Eliza, I don't know but we shal have another Battle, but I hope we shal not have another hard one. I have seen enough of it. If we are successful and get to Richmond, I shal not go any further unless I am better, although I feel better today then I have for a number of days. If you see anybody that complains of hardship, tell them to come into this armey and they will begin to find out what it is.

Lucina, I sent you another ring. It is made of root. It is a root that we got in Western Va. I have made another of Sweetbrier root....

I like to have a ring or a pipe in my pocket so that when I think of home it will take up my mind. Some days I can set and whittle most all day. It takes up my mind. Lucina, I have made me a pipe out of the same stuff that I made your ring of.

LUKE BICKNELL (MEMOIR, PP. 38–41)

After the battle small details from the sharpshooters were in demand to accompany reconnoitering expeditions. The enemys pickets had learned to distinguish and dread the crack of our heavy rifles and it made but little difference whether we fired from a rest or at hap-hazard; they dusted [fled] just the same, and if no one was hurt they reached their reserves all the quicker; but this I take from hearsay, for my illness and my duties as orderly kept me in camp.

We finally got our tents and a supply of blankets, and my health improving, a grand reconnoissance, by the sharpshooters alone, was determined on. The object of the move was to see about advancing the picket line about a mile forward, on the right of the 2nd corps. I had full command, and must have been seen by the enemy from the moment we passed beyond our pickets. The enemys pickets retired so swiftly and secretly before us that we did not see a single foe until I had crossed a creek in our front on the stringers of a bridge and penetrated a wheat field to a log house, where I obtained a splendid view of the enemys fortifications and the spires of Richmond beyond. . . .

Bridges were laid at frequent intervals across the creek and we all supposed that we were to advance upon Richmond through the wheat field. I never heard any reason given why we did not do so, except the strength of the works on the other side, and that I do not think a good reason, from what I saw of them.

There was not at this time a single well man in the company. Our severe winter marches and labors in Western Virginia, had well prepared us to break down under our severe duties and heavy loading and exposure, on the Peninsula. But the men who would go out of the service through the door of a hospital, as long as they could stagger to their feet alone, had been pretty effectually weeded out, at Paw Paw Tunnell. We were so confident of the speedy capture of Richmond, and so anxious to take part in it, that when the paymaster came down, most of us decided to wait until Richmond was taken, and he came down again for our pay.

LUKE BICKNELL

Camp News Fair Oaks Va June 16th [1862]

My dear Miss Pierce,

This Monday finds me camped not far from the place called Fair Oaks. I am not in very good health, but aint dead yet by a great deal although for the last three weeks I have felt more miserable than I ever did at home.

But aside from myself and about twenty thousand others who do not feel right smart, things are going tip top. Our breastworks and batteries are creeping right up to the rebels. Very soon our big guns will be right under their noses where they must fight or skiddadle. I expect to wake up some morning to find the rebels missing. . . .

Yesterday morning we were up at half past two eat breakfast and marched to the outpost picket, as soon as light came we saw the enemy pickets. They came out after a while and waved newspapers signifying their desire to exchange. One man went out, met them half way and changed papers, talked a little while and came back.

We made an agreement with them not to shoot pickets, so both parties showed themselves without fear of bullets.

About noon we were startled by sharp musketry on the left about a quarter of a mile distance.

It proved to be nothing but a skirmish and will not extend to us. I presume it would seem queer to you to see Secesh and Union good friends with each other one hour and shooting each other the next, but such is the way we do it.

We are on duty now almost every day. . . .

It is a fine cool morning here. By the way that affairs move here I conclude I shall not be at home before your school is through. Would it not be curious if the whole three years should pass away in the state of expectation of soon going home.

God grant it may not be so. There is nothing pleasant in a soldiers life. I am willing to see the play out, but hope they hurry up the end.

I am going to just make a guess that we shall have Richmond by July 4th, but not before unless the rebs skidaddle. . . .

Write often will you not. Make them as long as you have time and paper. Remember that my heart is wholly yours.

L.E. Bicknell

EGBERT OSWALD HIXON

Fri. [June] 20 Morn—nice pleasant weather. We expected to have a good
    fight today but did not. Dont feel very well. . . .
Sat. 21 morn. Fair & warm. Feel about sick. . . .
Sun. 22 Morn warm. Been out helping cover up the graves. They were not
    properly buried. Lots of alarms last night. Did not sleep much. Very quiet
    all day. Hot weather, the ground is getting dry.

MOSES HILL

Near Richmond, June 19th 1862

Dear Wife,

. . . Eliza, I am not very well. I was quite sick yesterday. I had cramp in my stomach & Bowels but I feel better to day, although I am rather weak. I have had a diarear for some time. I got something of the Doctor yesterday that I think has stoped it.

There has not been any thing of importance since I wrote to you. We think it very quiet here when there is not more then two or three killed on picket. Last night we expected there would be an attack this morning but there was not. A lot of Rebels came into the woods where our pickets was last night, and then moved back expecting our troops would follow them but they fel back and the Bateryes opened fire on them and I understand this morning the Rebels killed & wounded was several hundred. Our loss was 7 kiled and but few wounded.

I don't think there will be any engagement today but I don't know. I hope this Battle will be ended soon. I am sure I shal not go any further then Richmond. I think the Company will be discharged then, for the wagons are broke and run down. I mean the gunn wagons, and the Harneses, and the guns are out of order or a good meny of them are, and a good meny of the Company are sick, not fit for duty. The Government will not be to an expense to recrute the Company again. So when this Battle is through I think you will see this company coming home.

Eliza the water is very poor here. We had beautiful water at Yorktown. That is everything in the army.

The mail has come in and I received a letter from you and a hankerchiefe in it, and another Package from Doc Morse with Medicen in it. It came just in time for I wanted some of it. He has sent me a good lot and I think it will do me some good. And I was glad to have a letter from home for it is a long while since I have received a letter from you. You wanted to know if I wanted any Tea. I can get it here. Yesterday a man in my tent got as much as ½ lb and he gave me half of it. You wanted to know if I was in that Battle. I have wrote you all the poticulars since then in a letter.

Eliza, I think there will be a Battle here soon. It may come off before you receive this. I have had a bad Dierhera for a number of days past, and if I am not better than I am now, I think I shal not be engaged in it but I think I feel a little better to day than I have for 2 or 3 days. Now that I have got some Medicine, I think I can cure myself. . . .

I suppose the things have come up in garden. Write me how they look. I wish I was at home to go into the garden and work some. I suppose Sis does some work in the garden. Tell Bub he must be papa's farmer Boy when papa is gone. I rosted me a potato at noon and I have got another one for tonight. It was very good. Kiss Sis & Bub for me. Love to all.

Egbert Oswald Hixon

Thurs. 26 Warm. They talk of having a battle—heavy firing on our right. Towards night it was terrific, they say our folks got the best of them.

Moses Hill

Fair Oaks, Wednesday June 25th 1862

Dear Wife,

... Eliza, I am some better then I was last week. I feel a great deal stronger. I have not much news to write about the war for it has been very quiet most of the time. Saturday there was a good deal of picket fireing and there has been yesterday and today. This afternoon there been more canonading on our side than there has been any day yet, but I don't know what it will amount to. The last time I wrote to you I expected there would be a battle before this time for I expected the Rebels would attack us. They may now any day. I should not be disappointed. I think I will not finish this letter today for I cannot send it until tomorrow so I will finish it in the morning.

Thursday Morning. It is very pleasant. There was a good deal of picket fireing last night we was called up a number of times. I did not sleep but very little, but I feel quite smart this morning. I am in hopes I shal receive a letter from you to day. Some of our Pickets advanced a little yesterday. There was, I believe, about 50 of the Mass 19 Regm killed & wounded yesterday. I think some of our troops will advance a little to day. I understand the Picket fireing did not amount to much last night. Our men was cutting down trees all night along the line.... We have one man in our Company that is sick and I expect he will not live untill night.

Eliza, I think there must be a Battle here soon for I think our Right & Left wing will advance and that no doubt will bring on an ingagement. We are in the center and I expect we shal hold this point while the Right & left advance. There is a good meny of our troops gets killed & wounded most every day.

Eliza, how is Mr Hardings health this summer & Mother Harding's? Are they well? How does the fruit look? Will there be meny apples, and how is the garden getting along? I suppose the things have all come up before now. Sis, how did you & your Grandmother make it a fishing? When you wrote you thought you would go in a day or two. I wish I was at home to go fishing with you. How I would like a good mess of pouts [freshwater codfish], don't you think I should. I hope I shal have that privelage before long. If we are successful here, I am quite sure I shall. How is Mr Hardings Grass look this summer and his corn and cranburyes &c.?

I should of asked for a furlow a few days ago if I thought it would of done any good, but they will not give any furlows untill we get to Richmond if we ever do get there wich I hope we shall soon. I expect we have got a large armey here now. There is a good meny troops that has not crossed the Chickhomony yet. [Brigadier General George A.] McCalls Division is over there held as a resurve, and I expect more of McDowells troops are, or coming.

...I had a piece of [cheese?] for my Breakfast yesterday morning and I shal buy some more in a day or two. I bought me lemon and a piece of cheese yesterday so I lived quite well. I cannot drink coffee and I have had Tea. I make it myself in my dipper. Eliza, I have given up the Idea of coming home the 4th of July now but I hope I shall come home before the month is out, the month of July I mean....

Kiss Sis & Bub for me. Tell Sis to catch one good meal of fish and eat them for me. I think Bub can go a fishing with you. I think he can catch fish. Go to the Store and buy him a good line & hook if he has none. Get him a lite pole and try him. I gues he can catch fish. Sis, if you have not a good line & hooks get them. You cannot fish with a poor hook and line.

LUKE BICKNELL

Camp at Fair Oaks Va June 27th 1862 In camp Friday P.M.
Dearest Cretia,
There is considerable fighting along the line today. At this point the firing has been confined to artillery. Yesterday afternoon the rebels undertook to turn our right flank. The firing was very rapid and heavy till about nine in the evening when it was announced that we had repulsed an overwhelming force of the enemy with tremendous slaughter.

The reports of cannon were so frequent that at times they formed one continuous roar. Early this morning the contest was renewed and continued till about nine in the forenoon. We seem to have got the best of it. About now the rebels commenced to throw shells into this camp. Our artillirests promptly answered them and for two hours there was a tremendous snapping and cracking around here.

Finally the rebels dried up and we let them alone. At the same time there was rapid cannonading just to the right of us which still keeps up the rate of about twenty discharges a minute.

Down to the right and a little to the rear of us there is a dull heavy roar which one not used to war would take it to be distant thunder. We know it to be a fierce fight going on. The rebels are trying to do their best, but no one here fears for the result.

We are well pleased to have them attack us. If they keep still in Richmond about a week longer we will pitch in and lick them.

The troops on our left made an advance last Tuesday. The rebels disputed every foot of ground for a while but at last fled in a panic and our troops hold now a position two miles nearer Richmond.

Two weeks of good weather will I think finish up this little affair of Richmond.

Enough of war.

Your kind letter of the 18th reached me today and was more than usually welcome as I had not had one from you for some time.

If it is possible I will be at your house and go strawberrying with you on the 4th of July. . . .

My health is better now than it has been for a month. I have just had to lay the letter by and go out to the breastwork. The rebels opened on us (and there they are again) with muskets. Our artillery drove them back with a few shots. The whole occupied about half an hour. A few bullets whistled high over our heads as we marched out but it was soon over. The little flurry which caused me to put in the parenthesis did not last but a few minutes. We did not fall in.

There is a pretty good prospect of an engagement this evening.

Really I cannot see what cause you call yourself dull. Your letters are far from dull to me.

They are the most interesting and the most sensible I get. Perhaps there is not as much nonsense and froth, so often mistaken for wit and brilliancy, as most girls would write.

But there is a genuine good humor, a fund of real thoughts, and a quick, easy self possession in your style which I do not find in any other letters I receive. . . .

It is very pleasant weather here, a little too hot and a trifle too damp nights for a New Englander. I do not like the climate at all, nor the people nor the country around here, nor the business we are in, yet I am not very mad about any of these things.

I didn't expect to like them, but thought I could stand the pressure till the war was over and I guess I can do so. . . .

I wish I could talk to you two hours. Write me often. Tell me all the news and ever remember that time nor absence can not change my affection for you. I would like to see you occasionally to prevent your fearing that I might be growing cold. I know such thoughts are natural during the absence of one we love. . . .

"Retreet"

After the battle of Fair Oaks, McClellan's failure to follow up his successes allowed the Confederates time to reinforce. Led by their new and very aggressive general, Robert E. Lee (Johnston was wounded when a fragment of shell hit him in the shoulder), the outnumbered Confederates boldly seized the initiative and began to attack the Union forces. After the first two of the Seven Days Battles in late June, McClellan feared that his army might be overwhelmed. The sudden and unexpected appearance of General Thomas "Stonewall" Jackson's Shenandoah troops southeast of Richmond further alarmed him. By June 27, one historian writes, "the commanding general of this magnificent army was paralyzed by fear, delusion, and exhaustion."[25] On June 28—in the face of inferior numbers—McClellan decided to retreat.

The Union army struggled day and night through swamps and sweltering heat, fighting more battles at Fraser's Farm, Savage's Station, and Malvern Hill on their retreat, until they reached Harrison's Landing, its new base on the James River. One private remarked, "I am sick tired and disgusted and how I ever got through the retreat is more than I can account for, in addition to all our other troubles, the last day of the rout we had a drenching rain which made the roads knee deep with tenacious mud, and it was as much as I could do to pull one foot out after the other."[26]

At Harrison's Landing, the exhausted army suffered from intense heat, mud, and swarms of insects until it retreated to Washington in late August. One soldier wrote, "Everyone and everything were crowded together, the water was bad and the sanitation worse, and plagues of flies drove men and animals to distraction. The list of the sick lengthened, especially those with dysentery."[27] Moses Hill and other Andrew's Sharpshooters contracted this debilitating disease. A regimental surgeon lamented, "Men are rotting with scurvy and have been for months, no vegetables." He added that some days the temperature reached "102 in the shade."[28] Andrew's Sharpshooters' misery was compounded by a lack of tents, new clothing, and boots. Moreover, a long delay in pay meant the men could not supplement their painfully meager diet by purchasing food from "suttlers"—private food vendors who followed the army.

EGBERT OSWALD HIXON

Sat. [June] 28 Morn. Started out at sunrise, terrible fighting on our right. They say that the rebs have got the best of it. 6 o'clock P.M. We have got orders to start towards James River.

Sun. 29 Looks very much like a big retreat. Started about 10, came 3 miles &
   camped out. Had a big battle.
Mon. 30 Fighting & retreating. The rebs don't come out but stick to the woods.
Tues. [July] 1 Moved again and had another fight ... moved again in the night.

LUKE BICKNELL (MEMOIR, PP. 41–43)

On the retreat, our teams were fully loaded, for such roads, by one sick man
who died on the retreat, and the indispensible part of the company property;
leaving us to carry our knapsacks as well as the heavy rifles and revolvers. As
I have already said, there was not a well man in the company, and this terrible
load seemed as if it would crush us to the ground even as we started. The first
nights march comes up in my memory as a fevered dream, and I do not suppose I was in my right mind much of the time. I think I urged my comrades
to go back with me and fight it out at the breastworks we had left, and that I
tried to slip from the ranks and steal back alone, and that Capt. Saunders was
ever at my side restraining me and coaxing me along.

   I do not seem to have come out all right until we faced about and stood in
the line [of] reserves about noon next day at Savage Station. When the shot
and shell began to plow our ranks, the cloud over my memories of the past
lifts, and I see again the burning of the vast pile of stores we had accumulated
there.... The stubborn fight continued till the stars came out. We moved but
once. When it seemed as if the enemy would succeed in driving our infantry
from the woods at our left, we threw ourselves behind some stumps on which
we could rest our rifles, ready to receive them as they came on.

   Again, the night march to White Oak Swamp is a blank to me, and so the
next day, until the battle [of Glendale; also called the Battle of Fraser's Farm]
opened. During this battle we stood in the center of the field around which
the fearful struggle went on, our rifles being entirely useless in such a hand to
hand fight in the woods.

   Of the march to Malvern Hill the following night, I recollect, only, of being
often led back to the ranks by comrades.... When we finally approached a
creek, my thirst was so maddening, that I filled my mouth with the mud beneath our feet, ere I could get to the water.

   We saw the whole battle of Malvern Hill, standing at ease behind a fence
near the heavy artillery, where we could have done good service if the enemy
had broken through our lines, and charged on the artillery....

   On the night march from Malvern Hill to Harrison's Landing, our Captain,
realizing the exhausted condition of his men, who were fairly staggering under
their great burden, said that he would shoot any man who should abandon

his knapsack on the route. While the company was at "halt" beside the road, I left it . . . to walk along . . . to learn the fate of friends. I finally sat down beside the road to wait for the Sharpshooters to come along. When they appeared, Capt. Saunders marched at their head, lugging my knapsack, as he supposed, in his hand. . . .

Those who have blamed us for not pursuing the defeated enemy from Malvern Hills do not seem to take into account that man is a creature who must eat and sleep. Many, like myself, started on the retreat fitter subjects for the hospital than the march. When we finally arrived at Harrison's Landing, I had been without food for three days, and now, I sank down with but one thought, and that, to sleep. So, thousands sank around me.[29]

EGBERT OSWALD HIXON

Wed. [July] 2 Morn: begun to rain about daylight & rained all day & all night. We all got wet through. Nothing to eat. Mud knee deep. All in a heap. (Want to go home.)

Thurs. 3 Rain not over with. We are all down by the James river. I never saw such mud. Our com. got quarters in a barnyard. Nothing to eat but hard bread. Everything looks dark.

Fri. 4 Independence day. It is a lovely day. We started & marched about 2 miles through the mud back from the river & camped. Salute was fired & Gen. McClellan was cheered by the troops. We got some pork & that was all the Fourth we had.

MOSES HILL

Harrisons Landing, July 5, 1862

Dear Wife,

I received a letter from you last night and one from Persis too and was very glad to hear from her [per]haps more so at this present time. I am glad to hear you are all well, but I am sorry to hear that Maria's child is ded, for she must miss it very much. Eliza, I suppose you are anxious to hear from me, but I am safe and very well, better than I have been for some time, but it is a wonder, for you don't know what hardship I have been through since I wrote to you.

Saturday June 28th we had a fight on the line at the right of us. Little we supported one Battery. They did not come in shot of us. I left my Over Coat.

Sunday. I did not sleep any last night. We stoped here [Savage Station] all day. The Rebels come on to us in the afternoon and we had a Battle. We kept the Rebels back. Was thousands of Dollars worth of provisions at the depot. At dark we retreated back, and we marched all night until day light and I slept about one hour. It rested me very much.

Monday. We started again and marched a little way and halted. The Rebels came on and another Battle comenced. It was a hard battle, too, near White Oak Swamp. I suppose you have seen the account in the papers. I gave out about noon, for I was rather weak and it was so hot. I went back in the rear and I had to throw away my Knapsack & Blankets and all that I had. I went back about 2 miles and stoped all night.

Tuesday. I could hardly go, for I had no blankets to sleep on and I did not sleep much so I started along and went about 3 miles and laid down. There was another hard battle today.

Wednesday. I got up about 1 oclock and started for the landing, and in the morning it began to rain and it rained very hard all day. There was no fighting today to amount to much. Most of the baggage wagons came in before night and most of the troops. I did not find our Company so I sat up by a fire all night.

Thursday. In the morning I went to our Company. There was an old shed by the side of a barn yard. It was in a very good place. I slept some through the day and slep quite well all night. Most of our Company come in and most all of the troops.

Friday. It does not seem much like the Fourth of July. The Rebels have retreeted back and we moved back about 1½ miles where we are today. Eliza, I don't know what this armey will do but I suppose we shal stop here until we get recruited up more and move again. You don't know what we have sufard on this Retreet. I have no pen and ink or paper so you mus excuse my writing. I will try to write again soon. I know you will be glad to hear that I am safe and well. Write often, dear Eliza, and may God bless you and protect you.

Your ever loving friend, M Hill

I think the Government will furnish us with blankets & Knapsackets again soon. Kiss dear Sis and Bub for me I have wrote this in a hurry for I did not have much time. Love to all.

Luke Bicknell

Harrisons Landings Va July 6th 1862

My Dearest Lucretia,
A letter from you today was truly welcome. Today is the first opportunity I have had to write since we commenced the retreat from Fair Oaks.

This retreat is a bad business for our army. I wish the authorities had re-inforced McClellan so that it need not have been necessary. I can not but see that it will add another year to the war.

I saw a great amount of desperate and bloody fighting during the retreat being in the Corps which covered the retreat of the Union forces.

Our company was not however at any time engaged.

There was no opportunity to use such guns as ours. . . .

Do not worry on my account. If I am lucky enough to get off safe I wont care. The climate does not agree with me very well, but I shall get used to it pretty soon.

We are now camped about a mile from the river on the banks of a creek. A fine place to rest and clean up. How long we shall stay here is more than any one can tell. A few days I hope at least.

How I should like to drop in and see your school. I think I should be pleased with the teacher. I would like to take some evening lessons in private.

It is almost too bad to talk about those things now that the time is likely to be so long before I shall see you. I am not so tired of war as I am tired of being away from Windsor.

If we could only go home occasionally as the rebel soldiers do it would be fun.

You need not expect it though. It is no use to talk about furloughs. I hope someday when the war is at an end I shall come home safe and sound and then we will have many fine times together.

I know I shall prize home and your society more than if I had not been thus separated from you.

Your letters are really most precious to me. The day that sees us united will make me the happiest of mortals. A new and great happiness which I know will continue till death parts us.

It is dark. Many kisses. . . .

EGBERT OSWALD HIXON

Tues. [July] 8 Morn hot & sultry. . . . Might[y] hot. The sweat runs off from me lying in the shade. . . .

Wed. 9 Another hot day. It is getting dry & dusty. Our com. is doing nothing. . . .

Fri. 11 Morn—rains hard. Dull enough. Went up to the 18th Reg. Jon Daniels, he is going home soon. Wish I was. It rained all day, nothing new.

Moses Hill

Near Harisons Landing, Va Sunday [July] 13th 1862

Dear Wife,

I received a letter from you last Thursday. I wrote to you a week ago yesterday and I should of written before, but I had nothing to write with for as I wrote to you, I had to leave everything that I had on the road for it was so hot and I was so much beat out that I could not carry anything but my Gun and pistol & my haversack and canteen. You see, it would not do to leave them. I had tea enough & sugar that I got [at] Savage Station. They gave it away. I had hard bread enough to last me 2 days and then I had to beg where I could find any, so I got along.

You wrote that you did not understand why we had to fall back. It was because the Rebels had so much larger forse then we had and they could flank our right wing and it was the only thing McClellan could do, and it was the graitest thing that was ever done, I think, to save so much stuff, wagons &c. We retreated nights and had to fight day times but kept the wagons in the rear all the time. The enemy was defeeted or got the worst of it every day. Their loss was very heavy. (I cannot explain it all to you, but if I ever live to come home I will try to.)

I think there must have been a great many sick & wounded limping and working themselves along the best way they could. It was a horable sight to see them exert every nurve and strive for life. I am glad you did not see them. Horses would run over them and nock them down. They had to creep, crawl, any way to get along, but we are in a very safe place now I think.

Eliza, I am glad that the Presedent has called for more troops. It ought to been done before. If it had been done when we was at Yorktown, we might have been in Richmond before this time. I think it was as much as we could do to hold the place at Fair Oaks as long as we did. The troops are all tired out, Rigements cut up and a great meny sick. Some of the Regm cannot muster 200 available men. Some can muster 300, and some can muster 5 but I guess not meny can muster 600. So you see how this armey stands.

Eliza, I am quite smart today. For 2 or 3 days I have not been very well, for I have had a diarea, but it is better today. I have lost the Doctors Medisen with my other things and if it is not too much troble I would like some more Diarear and Fever Medison. And Eliza, if it is not to much troble you may send me out a box by Adams Express. It comes close to me now. I cannot send you any money now, for I have not been paid off since I sent you home some when we was in Hampton the first of April. I would like some tea and a

Box of Mustard and a little tobacco and one of my fish lines & hooks ... some needles & Thread and pins & paper & invelopes. I cannot get tea here nor a good meny things that I would like. You may put in a paper of ginger too if you can. Eliza, you must make up a Small box and have it nailed up tight for if you don't it will get broke. Do not put in any heavy things for the express bill will be too high.

Eliza, it is hot weather here and I am some weak & worn down and I hanker after a good many things that I would like that I cannot get.... I cannot get potatoes & pickles, meal, Flour nor any such things. If I could have a crust of brown bread ... it would taste good. The Oficers can get potatoes, ham or anything they want, but the privates cannot get them. Oficers can send to the Comersarys and get things cheap, but they will not sell any thing to the privates, and if we want any cheese we have to go to the Suttlers and get a piece of cheese or ginger cakes or a lemon. Cheese, we have to pay about 75 cts per lb and other things in proportion.

Yesterday I went to the 16 and 11 [Massachusetts] Regm and see a lot of men that I knew. I saw little Joseph Richardson. He is sick in the hospital, but he don't want to let his folks know it. I think he will be up soon. . . .

Eliza, they say nothing lost without some gain and after I throwed my things away, the next day I found a pair of good congress shoes and a set of Dentist tools to pull teeth with, 3 kinds of instramints to pull teeth, and other tools with them. I suppose they are worth $20.00 and I expect the Bands are coming home and I am going to try to send them to you by William Daniels or somebody else, and if I do I want you to scour them up, and oil them a little, and keep them dry. I found them near the Battlefield. If you have not the money, I don't [want] you to send me anything, but I expect we shal be paid off this week and if we are I shal send you home some as soon as I get it. You must send the box as soon as you can. If you do send one, I want it to be a small one. Oh if I could be at home with you again how happy I should be. God bless you. . . .

LUKE BICKNELL (MEMOIR, PP. 43–44)

[Sergeant Henry] Martin, who was wounded in the assault at Yorktown, reported for duty soon after we reached Harrisons Landing, relieving me of the duties of orderly. With nothing to do, I soon recovered my health and spirits. Not so however with the men who had been with the company from the start at Lynfield. With a few exceptions they succumbed to the hardships and depressing influences of the situation. We were now obliged to send our sick to the hospital, as we were without tents for three weeks, during which time it often rained. This exposure and the bad drinking water took the men down very fast. We had lost prestige in our division by being obliged to stand idle, on account of our heavy rifles, in all the battles of the retreat. Our requisitions for clothing were unheeded, until we were much the raggedest company in the army.

Here and elsewhere Bicknell exaggerated the degree to which the rifles hindered the men during the battles of the Seven Days. For example, General Gorman's brigade (to which Andrew's Sharpshooters were attached) missed the hardest part of the fighting at the battles of Savage Station and Glendale. At the Battle of Malvern Hill, Andrew's Sharpshooters—along with most of the rest of John Sedgwick's division—remained in reserve and were never sent to the front. The sharpshooters thus missed most of the major fighting simply because of the disposition of their brigade and division in the various battles, and not because of the "uselessness" of their rifles.

According to his own account, Bicknell convinced his superiors to take away the target rifles and replace them with lighter rifles more suitable for skirmishing. Since Bicknell was, as he once put it, "fond of action," he likely preferred skirmishing to the more isolated, stationary, and less "glorious" role of sniping. In any event, he was involved in getting the company equipped with Sharps Rifles. He seems to have kept his role in the matter secret.[30]

MOSES HILL

Harrison Bar, Va July 16th 1862

Dear Wife,

I wrote home to you last Sunday about sending out a box to me and if you have not sent it you may Direct it to Me, Andrews Sharpshooters 15th Mass Regm, Gormans Brigade, Sedgwicks Division, Armey of the Potomac, and I think it will come safe. . . .

The weather is very warm here, so much so that we do [not] move round much in the middle of the day. There is a good meny sick in the armey here. I am better now than I was and I hope you are all well at home. I think of you all the time. There is not moments in a day but I think of home.

We have not got our blankets yet. There was some come yesterday, but they was damaged so much that they was good for nothing. I think we shal get them soon. . . . The bands are going to have their discharge, and so William Daniels is coming home and he is going to bring that case of instruments that

I found and I want you to skour the rust off of them and keep them dry until I come home, if I ever do, wich I pray I may some time. There is nothing more that I can send now. If I had not lost my Knapsack and things, I should of sent home more things. We have not been paid off yet, but I think we shal be soon. I have borrowed some money so I have got along very well.

All has been quiet here in Camp since we have been here. This armey is fortifying some for fear of an attack. . . . Eliza, if I was out of the armey, I would like to stop here a little while and peddle out things to the Soldiers that comes up on the Boat. I could make a $1,000 Dollars in a little while, I think. I want you to write me how the Medway volenteers get along. I understand Medway has got to raise 37 more men and I want you to let me know who is a coming. I am sorry to have any more men come out here to suffer, but if this war is ever put down there has got to be a good meny more and I hope 300,000 will do it. I hope they will come soon and help close it up, for I have seen enough of soldiers life, and better it will be for the country.

I want you to write me all the news. How is the crops going to be, Potatoes & corn? Has Sis eat a good mess of [fish] for me yet and has Bub caught any fish this summer? Hug & kiss them both for me.

Eliza, I see by the papers how well the soldiers are used, but they are not used so well as the papers represent. I will tell you one instance and that is not uncommon. Within a few steps of my tent the other day a [fatigue] party was detailed to go out to work & one of the privates was sick, but the doctor would not excuse him from duty and the Oficers would not. He was forsed out. He went and he died about 12 oclock that night. That is the way. They can sleep out in the rain without blankets sick or well (unless they are so sick that they have to go to the Hospital), it is all the same, they are all cared for. Heard an Oficer say the other night that their men wanted to go home, and he swore that a good many had never ought to go home. *That is the way*, but it is not the way for me to live and I pray that God may spare me to come home to you safe, wich I trust he will and I pray the time may not be not very fer distant. . . .

EGBERT OSWALD HIXON

Fri. [July] 18 It is a cold dreary morn. I went up to the Mozart Reg. [40th New York Infantry] yesterday & saw my cousin Wm Adams die. Went up again at 4 o'clock for his funeral. It seemed all wrong. He was a fine fellow—but so it goes.[31]

Sat. 19 . . . Nothing to do but loaf around. A good many of our boys are sick

& everywhere around the hospitals we can see the dead laid out almost every morn.

Mon. 21–22 ... We have got some tents again. Looks more like a camp. ... It seems lonesome since W. died.

Thurs. 24 ... Doing nothing. No clothes, laying around lonesome as the devil in a crowd.

Sat. 26 Nothing to do & nobody to help me. Warm weather. ... Had a letter from my wife last eve. Wish I could see her but I don't think I shall at present.

LUKE BICKNELL

Camp near Harrisons Landing James River Va July 26th

Dear Lucretia,

It is a beautiful day. We have got tents and have a dry sandy camp ground in the woods which we keep very neat and clean.

I have excellent quarters now. The Orderly Perley has come back and I am relieved from performing his duty which for the last three months I have attended to.

We have formed a mess the four of us, one does the cooking and the other three pay the bills.

Today for dinner we had what we call duff pudding. It is very much like suet pudding at home and is very nice with such lemon sauce, as our cook fixed up today. We had fritters this morning and shall have doughnuts tonight.

We are going to have soft bread too.

Do you not wish you was a soldier.

With nothing of account to do, good quarters and good living you will not be surprised that I am picking up flesh quite fast.

Now if I can only get letters from home to make me feel contented. ...

Next week will be the last week of your school. How I would like to take you home after it is over. In fact I would like to drive out with you any where. I have not forgotten Sunday nights yet. There is an unsatisfied spot in my heart growing larger and larger each day which would be removed in a moment by one kiss from your lips.

I long to see you if it is only for an hour. My love for you has become part of my nature and when ever my thoughts turn homeward, I wish I was with you.

I am anxious for this war to be over so that I may realize what a joy it is to be always with a dear friend. ...

Moses Hill

Harison Bar, Va July 27th 1862

Dear Wife,

. . . Dear Eliza, you wanted to know how I got along and how I did. I will
not deceive you and I will tell you. When I wrote to you after we halted here
[I said] that I was a good deal better. And I was for a little while, but it did
not last long. I have been quite unwell long back. I have had a bad Diarear
for some time & I am very weak some days, and then other days I am a little
better. I am some better today. I have walked as much as 2 miles. I have seen
the time that I could not walk a ½ mile. I am going to try to keep round until
colder weather, and then I hope I shal be better. I was weighed the other day
and I weighed 126 lbs. I think likely I shal not [be] more then 120 lbs soon if
I keep on. I am run down. Our guns are too heavy to carry this hot weather,
but Eliza, do not worry about me, for I think I shal get along. We have had
some flour for 2 days past and I think that helps me some. We draw ½ ration
of flour now instead of all hard bread. I think it would make you laugh to see
us cook it. Every man had his ration dealt out to him, and we do our own
cooking. I have mixed some flour with water, got a spider, and greesed the
bottom over to keep them from burning, and made some thin flippers as we
call them, and when I have any molasses to eat on them, they taste good I can
tell you. When we get paid off I shal buy some things to cook with.

You wanted to know what I thought of McClellan, if he was to blame.
You wrote that some blamed him and some did not. I shall answer you just
as I feel and think. I think that if he was not formerly a Democrat, and I
think he is now, he would not of been blamed by the party that blames him
now. If the Black Republickans had let McClellan alone and shoulderd their
muskets and done their duty, the war would have been nearer to a close then
what it is now. I think and know McClellan has done the only best way that
he could of done. If he has done wrong, why does the armey think so much
of him? They are ready to fight night & day for him or do anything that
they can do. He cannot pass our lines, but every man that has strength will
cheer him no mater how often he passes. Eliza, I am just as much Union
now as I ever was, but I like to see justice. You may ask where is the blame.
Is General [Irvin] McDowell to blame? Now I think you have it. I think
McDowell had more to do with this retreet than the north think for, or some
of them at least. Why was McDowell to blame? Because I believe he might
of stoped Jackson from coming down upon our right wing. I think Jackson
might have been taken & his whole armey. I will explain this in my next letter,

so I think you will be satisfied. I have it from honest men that was eye witness to Jacksons escape.

Eliza, if the Oficers under McClellan was what they ought to be, I think it would improve this armey very much. The Colonel of the Mozarts Regm [40th New York Infantry] was taken off the battlefield Drunk and he went to N.Y. and now I understand he is coming out as Brigadier General. And so it goes. And the Colonel of the 4th Ohio is drunk all the time. And so it goes. But as I have told you before, the privates are of no account. I will tell you how we think the men rank. Oficers first, Nigers 2d, horses 3d, Mules & privates are about the same 4th and last. I don't know but you will think this is a funny letter, but there is more truth than you think for.

Eliza, I have just had some fried donuts for Supper and they was good. I want you to write often. Hixons wife writes to him twice a week. I like to hear from home often.

I hope the Govener will call us home but I don't know as he will. I would like to come home. I think I could recrute some. It would take me some time to get strong and well again. I pray that I may come home soon. There is no place like home when a man does not feel well. I pity the men that are coming out here. Amos Morse had better of stayed at home if he knew what he has to go through. I think he would if he has to go through what I have. I think it is a chance if he ever sees his family again. Don't worry about me Eliza. God Bless you all.

From your loving Husband, M Hill

I guess when Amos has to live on hard bread and salt horse as we call it & side Bacon & coffee, and gets coverd with body lice, he will wish himself at home this hot weather. Kiss Sis & Bub for me. Look out for the Garden. I think of that a great deal. Raise what you can, for it will be a great [help] to you if not to me.

EGBERT OSWALD HIXON

Tues. 29 Morn warm. No news. Doing nothing as usual. I get awful lazy every day. The flies are so thick that it is impossible to read or sleep in the day time.

Sat. [August] 2nd is my birthday. Hot weather all the time nothing new. It is about the same thing over and over every day. Our com is talking about taking some other gun.

Sun. 3 What it will amount to I don't know. I hope we shant make any movement until cooler weather. They say we have got to take sharpe[s] rifles.

Mon. 4 . . . Gen. Gorman inspected our guns yesterday & told us there was
   no right for us to get out of the service.
Wed. 6 . . . We have rations of flour now & we are cooking most of the time.

LUKE BICKNELL

Harrisons Landing [July 1862]

[Dear Lucretia,]
A dozen kisses till the war is over. I hope the war may end soon and that
circumstances may favor a wedding soon after.

But I suppose that I cannot hurry the course of events. . . .

Tomorrow is Sunday and I shall surely think of you and of the setting up
room.

I can remember every article in that room and just how it looks, the old
lounge which would creak so, the table covered with books, and the rocking
chair, which held two so well, but I can't remember how you looked.

I wish I could close my eyes and see you in my minds eye. I should jump
to kiss you I know.

I used to sit and look at you then and wonder why you loved me and wonder how long it would last.

I supposed you would get tired of me and then it would end, as courtships
are apt to.

I used to hope it would not though and that was all I dared do. But I have
got to be a little bolder now. I dare to hope and even to expect . . .

Yours ever

L. Emerson Bicknell

It's a mile from this place to the James River, but a brook runs by our camp
which serves us for washing purposes. . . .

All the water of brooks and rivers here is muddy as it can be. Interesting
aint it when a fellow wants to wash his shirt.

This company camps by itself on a bend of land, the brook running around
three sides, just large enough to hold the Sharpshooters.

Those of our sick boys who were not too low when we came here are getting better. Some are very low.

We play cards, chequers, dominoes and back gammon. Sing songs and see
who can jump the furtherest evenings.

Chat about the friends at home or write letters to them and so pass away
the time.

The mail comes every day now. You ought to see the boys gather round
when the letters are given out. . . .

LUKE BICKNELL (MEMOIR, P. 44)

I finally drew up a petition, setting forth the circumstances of our enlistment, the condition to which the company had been reduced by the privations and hardships we had undergone, the proved uselessness of our guns in ordinary battles, and asking that the company be discharged. I carried it to General McClellan, who received me with that invariable courtesy, to all.... He read my petition carefully, and asked me many questions ... and then, pleasantly asked me how he could consistently endorse the petition for discharge, while he was urgently calling for reinforcements.

He promised however that we should never again be asked to carry those guns again on the march.... He also assured me that our lack of clothing must be from the neglect of our own officers, who knew not of the petition which nearly every enlisted man had signed....[32]

LUKE BICKNELL

Harrisons Landing Va Aug. 7th 1862

My dear Lucretia,
Your letter of the 3rd came in last nights pack, and made a happy fellow for a while.

My health is improving fast. I am quite well now. It is still dry, hot pleasant weather.

We are all in high spirits today for the last nights paper brought the news of the determination of the Government to put 600,000 more men into the field by drafting if they wont volunteer.

Hurrah for the draft! Hurrah for a short war!

I am almost a mind to cry Hurrah for old Abe, who has at last waked up to the actual needs of the case....

Our guns are to be changed soon. We shall be the left flank of the 15th [Massachusetts] reg.

We are to be armed with Sharps Rifles. I am very much pleased with the change. In fact I brought it about myself by sending a petition to Gov. Andrew and Gen. McClellan.

My love to all friends ... Remember my heart is entirely yours and—will be....

Moses Hill

Harisons Landing, Aug 7th 1862

Dear Wife,

I received a letter from you last night . . . and a lot of medisin from Doc Morse. . . . I have been expecting to hear from you since I heard that you sent that Box. . . . I have not got that Box yet, but I expect we shal get our Boxes soon, for there is a good meny in this company that have got Boxes on the way and expect them every day. . . .

I have nothing new from the Armey to write. The first day of August about 1 oclock in the morning the Rebels brought up a Battery in front of Harrisons Landing and commenced shelling, but our guns and a few shots from the Gun Boats stoped them so they did not [do] much damage.

Last Sunday this Brigade was called upon to march at 6 oclock with two days raitions and I believe two other Divisions went too. There was a small forse of Rebels near Malvern Hill. It is out tords White Oak Swamp. Our troops took some prisenors. I understand they drawed out a large forse from Richmond which I suppose they wanted to draw the troops from [Union General John] Pope.

Eliza, it is very hot here, and the flies are very troublesome. I never see flies half as thick before. I was glad to receive that picture from you last night. I think it looks natural if you look as you did when I last see you. It is almost a year now since I left home. It seems a long while. I hope I shall not stay out here much longer, since the last call for 600,000 more troops. It is what they ought to of done last spring, and the war would have been closed now. I think the last Call will make some of the Boys squarm at home. I hope they will have good Oficers and Doctors that have got some souls. We have but few in the Armey.

If we could have a good hospital to go to and have some females to take care of them as they do in some places, it would be much better. The ladies have done a great deal for this war or for the sick. They have sent them clothes and a lot of eatables, preserves and fruit &c, wines and everything that would make them comfortable. But Eliza, all of the nice stuff that is sent by the ladyes that the sick want, they do not get. The Oficers & Doctors get it. I would venture to say that they get $9/10$ of it. You may think it is a hard story, but it is too true. I hope that the ladyes will not send out anything from Mass that the Oficers & Doctors can get into their mouths unless they know where it is going.[33]

Eliza, Direct your letters the same that you did before. I am not very well.

I am not able to go on a march now, but I hope I shal be better when it is cooler weather. I would give anything if I was at home. . . .

Eliza, may God bless you and preserve you and children.

Your Husband, M Hill

Sis must write often & *Bub too.* Would I like to hug him once. . . .

We have not been paid off yet. I hope we shal be soon. All the Regm have been paid off since we have, and most of them twice. I am very glad that Deacon Mitchel is not going [to war] and Plimpton too. I do not like to have men come out here to sufer, although I think they can stand it better than we can for we have got so broke down. I expect something will be done with this Company and I don't know what. I wish I had that box. I want to see what you sent. I think the Doctor was very good. I think some of that whiskey would do me good. I need something to strengthen me. I have not had anything of the kind since we have been here. How is the garden? Save a good lot of Pickels for me, for I have not had one in [the] armey yet. We have a few onions once in a while.

Eliza, write often. I am very sorry you do not write oftener. Hixon has a letter about twice a week. I hope now you have got home you will write often. Some nights I am greatly disappointed when I find there is none for me. Kiss Sis & Bub. Tell Sis that paper come safe. If I was at home, money would not hire me to inlist again. . . .

EGBERT OSWALD HIXON

Fri. [August] 8 Very hot & dry. The roads are terrible dusty. There is talk of our moving soon. They are carrying off the sick down to the river.

Mon. 11 Morn—had a little rain last night & the air feels better. The troops are getting ready to move. I don't know whether our com is going to move or not.

LUKE BICKNELL (MEMOIR, PP. 44–45)

. . . we learned that we were to be armed with Sharpes Breech Loading Rifles. The majority of the men, having got their minds bent on discharge, were not satisfied with McClellan's decision, and sent a letter to Gov. Andrew, of which they had such great hopes that they continued to talk mainly of enlisting again in the navy and cavalry. Part would go with me in the cavalry, and part would follow [Henry] Martin, who had been a sailor in the navy; but no one thought of footing it any more.

Capt. Saunders had not been taken in to our confidence, and when he did learn of what had been done, took it very cooly until he learned that Sergt. [Charles] Ingalls was one of the signers....

Ingalls was too sick to leave his tent unattended, but would not go to hospital, and pluckily held on to his duties as commissary, by my insistance, until the Captain ordered me peremptorily to relieve him and send him to hospital. This broke Ingalls down badly, and, in a few days, I got a message from the hospital to come that day if I would see him alive.

MOSES HILL

Harisons Landing, Va Aug 14th 1862

Dear Wife,

I received a letter from you last night and was glad to hear from home.... I have received some Medison from Doctor Morse, and a letter since with some Postage Stamps in it. I have not got that Box yet but I hope I shal get it soon. There was a lot of Boxes come to the landing last week. But we have been expecting to Skedadle again, so they was not given out or unloaded. A good part of the troops if not all have been under marching orders since Monday night. Their Knapsacks & tents was sent to the landing, but I have heard they was coming back. *I don't know but I think* we was going to reinforse General Pope, but as he held his ground we may not go.

Eliza, some of our Guns have been taken from us and I expect we shal have to take Sharps Rifles. The Company feel rather bad about it, but they will press us into anything or do what they please with us and we are not allowed to say a word. There was 13 of our rifles saved out and mine was with them, but I don't know whether I shal be allowed to use it or not.

All of this Division excepting our Company went to Malvern Hill and had a little skirmish and took some Prisenors. They was gone three nights & two days and they came in again. Everything is all quiet here now. We have not been paid off yet, but I still live in hopes. I think you had beter not send me any money, for I think we shal be paid off before it could get here. We do not draw much rations now on account of a move, and out of money, and it is rather tough. You may send me a towel for I wash me a good deal and my towel is all worn up. I have used one of them that William gave me ever since I left home. The other good one I left on the last retreet. Send it in a paper by mail. Send a small one. We have plenty of soap. I must always wash me all over as much as 3 times a week.

I received your Picture and I think it looks very naturel, or as you looked when I left home. I think I should remember how you all looked if I was off for a long while. I like to take your picture out and look at it. I think of you a great deal and the children too. You wrote that the Boys wanted to know what to inlist in if they was oblige to come out or was drafted. As to that I think they cannot choose their position, but if they can I would say to Asahel to go with a Battery. I should if I was in his place with a wife at home, & if I was not married and had no family, I would enlist in the navy. The navy is the least danger and you are better fed & clothed but you may have to be some considerable longer from home. I will say to all do not take but a few things with you, 1 coat, 1 cap, 1 Pr shoes, 2 shirts, 2 Pr socks, 2 towels, (thread & needles & sisors), comb, Portfolyo Paper, ink, pens pencil & a Memorandom Book is all you want. Do not take anything more. Government will furnish you with clothing. Be sure to get dark colored shirts. If you have to buy them get woolen. The armey now is furnished with white cotton & wool and they are durty all the time. Be sure not to take a lot of stuff from home thinking you might want them. Eliza, write often as you can & may God bless you all. M Hill

. . . Eliza, I am not very well but I am no worse. I feel a little better today. I will write again as soon as I get that Box. How is the garden? I hope and pray I may get some of it this time. I hope I may come home before it is all gone.

LUCINA HILL

East Medway, Aug 13th [1862]

Dear Father

Mother received a letter from you dated Aug 7th & I received one from you dated Aug 8th. I will write you oftener than I have so far. I am very glad you enjoyed the mustard. I could not send more very well, but you will have enough when you get mothers box, I guess, for she said she sent a paper of it. I wished she had shipped the box here for then I might have sent something. Mother said she did not have time to get the pipe which I wished her to send to you, but very likely you can get one there. But I suppose it would seem better to think some of us sent it to you. I was glad you ans. my letter so soon, but I will be up with you for I received your letter tonight & shall send this in tomorrows mail. Mother thought I had better wait & send you a paper in a day or two instead of having them all at one time. Would you not like a story paper to read & thus make the time pass more pleasantly? If I find a good story I will send it to you.

I guess Hyram Kingsburry will enlist by next week. Ellen don't want to have him go & she said she should follow him everywhere he went to be shure he did not go off. I commenced sewing straw yesterday for the first time this season. The vines in our garden are not as good as usual, but the other vegitabels are doing nicely. Mother wrote to you last Sunday. One of the Bullard boys are going to war. We hope they will not have to draft in this town & I guess they will not. I was sorry to hear you were not well. We hope Dr Morses medicine will do you good. Those three Stamps he sent you were some mother gave him to send but he forgot to send them in with the medicine. Change is dredful scarce now. Every one is pleased enough to get postage stamps now. In Boston mother said they would not change a bill unless what was bought amounted to more than 50 cents. My hens lay quite well now for them. We sell a doz[en] about every week. There are going to be a lot of fall apples, Porters in particular.

I think I will send something in most all my letters & if you do not want it there are enough that will & I guess you can find a place for anything that will be small enough to put in an envelope with a letter. Grandfather has got some pretty good oats. They say they are all crakeled, ready for gathering. All his English hay is in the barn & one of the meadows. The others, they will go in too soon I suppose. There will not be as many cranberrys this year as last. & now good by. With much love & well wishes forever,

Your daughter, Lucina Hill

I wish there was such a thing as sending a cucumber in a letter. I guess you would find more than one in this if I could. Georgie has been a berrying to day with the rest & picked ½ a pint. After I had read your letter to him, I had to tell about the [army] mules and how they kicked like fury.

On August 16, Andrew's Sharpshooters, along with the last of the troops at Harrison's Landing, began a march of about sixty miles to Newport News, passing through Williamsburg and Yorktown on their way. The men had had virtually no fresh fruit or vegetables for months. During the march, they stripped farms of crops, even though they were not yet ripe. "We are half starved for something besides Hard Tack & S[alt] Horse," one Fifteenth Massachusetts infantryman remarked.[34] A New York regimental surgeon worried that the men would become ill from their foraging. Instead, some diseases "disappeared as if by magic on the march to Yorktown in August when the men ate greedily the green field corn and unripe apples, both previously thought harmful."[35] After arriving in Newport News on August 22, many bathed and hunted for oysters.

During this transitional time Egbert Oswald Hixon disappeared and was presumed to have deserted. Moses Hill continued to be seriously ill, and Luke Bicknell struggled to help his fellow sharpshooters.

LUKE BICKNELL (MEMOIR, PP. 46–47)

When we started from Harrison's Landing to march to Fortress Monroe, we put the Captain and Lieut. Berry, the guns, revolvers, and everything but our knapsacks, haversacks and canteens, aboard of teams, for McClellan did not forget his promise. Martin was designated acting lieutenant, which brought me as orderly again. When we first started on this five days march it did not seem possible that we could stand it to march five miles to save our lives, but we picked up on the green corn, unripe fruit, unlucky swine and poultry, that fell in our way, as wonderfully it did all the rest of the army; arriving at Hampton Roads in prime condition for a grand assault on the oyster beds of that vicinity....

On this march, I fixed the clothing business. We were called on about five one afternoon for a detail for grand guard. The corps had halted and bivouacked for the night, which promised to be cool. I selected the very men whose ragged, hatless, shoeless condition least fitted them for the required duty, and marched them up in front of Gen. Gormans tent at an early hour. The chosen squad had got themselves up splendidly for the occasion. One with barely the rim of a hat and one shoe, one coatless, one with but one leg to his pants, others without shoes, and one, whose promotion I immediately resolved on, marched stoutly at the head of the squad without a sign of any pants.

I had about half the brigade at my heels, as I halted, and, with my squad, saluted the general. He made a tremendous effort to blow me up, but broke down in the middle of it, and sent me back for a more fitly clothed detail. During the next days march we came upon clothing wagons, halted beside the road, and were told to help ourselves without the formality of a requisition.

MOSES HILL

Newport News, Va Aug 23d, 1862

Dear Wife,

I received a letter from you last night and was glad to hear from home. I suppose you have seen in the papers of our retreet. We was orded out in line to start last week Friday. We was all ready to start at 2 oclock but we did not start that day, so we slept in line all night. We started Saturday morning and marched 4 or 5 miles and camped for the night. There was so meny teams and troops that we had to move slow. We started Sunday morning and marched about 10 miles and camped near Chickhomeny River down near

James River. Monday we marched across the Pontoon Bridge. The Gun Boats was up there to protect us but had no troble. After we got across we stoped on the bank of the River until all the troops and teames was across. Then we marched tords Yorktown. We marched about three miles and stoped over night. Tuesday we started and marched through Williamsburg and camped about 4 miles beyond. Williamsburg is quite a large place, much larger than a mile through the place.

Wednesday we started and marched within a mile of Yorktown and camped. I went in the York River and had a good wash, and I got some clams or Cohogs and cooked them. They was good. Thursday we marched through Yorktown, and I saw the spot where Cornwallis delivered up his sword. I will explain when I come home if ever I do. We marched to Bethel and camped. Friday we marched to Newport News where we are today.

When we first come in I received a letter from Sis and a paper, and at night I received a letter from you. Eliza, I am very tired. It seemed as if I could not of got here. I think I am a little better then I was when we started. I hankerd after some green stuff, so I eat most everything I could find. We was short of provisions, had nothing but hard bread & coffee untill we got to Yorktown, and then we [had] a little side bacon. We lived mostly on roast corn that we got out of the corn fields. We took all the corn on the road, but it was most too green to rost. I eat green apples, green peaches, green tomatoes, Elder Berrys, Sasfras leaves, green pears, raw green squash, and most everything I could get. We are in a good place now, and if I had any money I could get along very well, but I hope we shal be paid off soon. I dont expect we shal stop here long. We shal go aboard the Transports and go somewhere. Direct your letters to Washington the same you did, only put on the 15 Mass Regm.

I have not got that Box yet but I hope I shal soon. We have had something good this morning. We have had half of a pickle. It is the first we have had since we have been in the service. That does not corispond with the paper talk, does it? Eliza, forward me a towel if you please for I have not a piece larger than my two hands left of mine. I think a great deal of washing. I hope we shal draw some clothes soon, for we nead them. The Government owes us them. My cap is most all to pieces, my pants is all out in the seat, my shirt is dirty and no other one to put on, but I can wash that and dry it in a little while. The Andrews Sharpshooters are not what they are cracked up to be. Our Oficers don't care. . . .

Eliza Hill

East Medway, Aug 31, 1862

Dear Husband,

I sent you a letter Thursday morning with a gold dollar in it, and Friday I sent you a towel. I hope you will get them safe. There are a great many rumors about the rebels coming on and attacking our men, and getting between Gen. Pope and Washington, but last night it looked a little more favorable. I expect they have destroyed a good deal of property and taken some prisoners, but we cannot get anything official, so we do not know what to believe.

I suppose you would like to know how old Medway gets along about raising her two quota of men. I believe there are a few lacking on the first quota for three years, but the last for nine months are all filled up so there will not have to be much of a draft if any. Tomorrow is the day that they commence drafting where the quotas are not filled up.

Have you got your box yet? I am afraid your things will be spoiled, but send home for what you want and we will send another. James Fales has enlisted in the nine months men. William and Sewel Clark, young Addison Richardson, Mr Cliffordson, Lewis Wheeler, Augustus Phitts, Henry Daniels of Rockville, another of William Daniels sons, and a good many others that I do not think of now. I expect Mr Mitchell will go yet. He has been twice to be examined, and is going again to Dr Munroe Tuesday. He wants to go very much.

William Daniels called here Thursday. He did not bring that box. He said he packed it with some others things of his that did not come at the time he did, but he expects them and when he gets them he will bring them down to me. He says he is very lonesome. I heard he told his son that has just enlisted, if he would stay at home he would go in his place. I do not know whether it is so or not. I think he looks rather thin.

We are well. I must tell you about George going a fishing last Tuesday night. He wanted a pole so I fixed him a little light one, and sat him down on the bank. He would not let his line be in the water long, but he pulled it out once and there was a great perch on the hook. It was a very large one. He teases to go most every day. I have been twice this summer. It is very healthy this season thus far. Mr Micah Lovell died last Wednesday morning. He was 82 years old. Elizabeth sent back that two dollars by Lucina and she told her to send it to her father. So if you need it, you send for it, and I will send you another gold dollar, for I suppose a bank bill would have to be discounted out there.

I hope you are better now you have got out of those swamps. Does not Dr Morses medicine help you? Those stamps he sent you were some I gave him to put in with his medicine. I put in some in that box, and paper, and envelopes. I hope you will get it now. It is nearly time to get ready to meeting. I go to Mr [Reverend Jacob] Roberts once in a while. I went last Sunday. In the afternoon he had a very good sermon. It was about trusting in God, and you know that subject would suit me. I did not like his morning discourse so well but I leave out what I do not like and except the good. I do not like to stay at home all the time.

We have just heard that William Daniels has gone back to Washington after his son that was wounded. He has had to have his arm taken off. He started for him yesterday. Much love to you with my prayers.
Dear Father,

I have returned from West Medway as I suppose you will see. Aunt Persis & Aunt Sarah will send you a box. I guess they spoak of it when I was up there. I will write again about the middle of the week. Do you think your Company will be disbanded? I hope it will. Have you got your gun yet, or have they taken it from you? I will write more next time. Grandmother Hill is in Foxboro. I cant write more this time. Good By with much love, Lucina

Two of John Clarks sons have gone and one of Elbridges and Warren Clark and one of Lewis Fishers sons and Robert Morse.

From your Eliza A. Hill
May God watch over you and care for you always.

CHAPTER

ANTIETAM

The fern on the hill-sides was splashed with blood,
And down in the corn, where the poppies grew,
Were redder stains than the poppies knew,
And crimson-dyed was the river's flood.

—Nathaniel Graham Shepherd, "Roll Call" (December 1862)

At Harrison's Landing in July 1862, Andrew's Sharpshooters were formally attached to the Fifteenth Massachusetts Infantry. It was, as one historian noted, "an event which would have tragic results" at the Battle of Antietam two months later.[1] Historians have long believed that Andrew's Sharpshooters carried their heavy, telescoped target rifles into that battle, and that they suffered severe casualties in part because, as one writer observes, "rapid loading and quick shooting with them was out of the question." After seeing how useless their old weapons were, the story goes, the snipers finally acknowledged the superiority of Sharps rifles as well as the skirmishing tactics that went with them—and eagerly adopted both.[2]

The snipers told a different tale. They reported that the change of weapons actually took place before the Antietam fight. While still at Harrison's Landing, both companies of Massachusetts sharpshooters learned that they had to give up their target rifles and take Sharps breech-loaders instead. In July the Second Company protested vigorously, followed by Andrew's Sharpshooters in late August. The men expressed virtually unanimous opposition to the new weapons. Many asked to be discharged, while some talked of transferring to other units.[3] Both companies refused to take the new rifles. Only when threatened with arrest, court-martial, imprisonment, and—in the case of the

Second Company—possible execution, did they relent. Thus when Andrew's Sharpshooters marched into battle at Antietam, they carried the same rifles as Berdan's Sharpshooters.[4]

The Massachusetts sharpshooters' rebellion dramatically underscores the men's involvement in their role as an elite body of snipers. Only Luke Bicknell expressed relief at no longer having to carry the heavy target rifles, and looked forward to the more exciting—and dangerous—"action" of skirmishing.

"Our Guns Have Been Taken from Us"

During the last of the Seven Days Battles at Malvern Hill on July 1, some of the men in the Second Company Massachusetts Sharpshooters lost their knapsacks containing rifle equipage; they had left them behind the lines before going into battle, and another unit stole them. Without the bullet molds they needed to produce their ammunition, their rifles would be virtually useless until the equipment was replaced. The regiment's colonel soon decided to replace the target rifles with Sharps; a regimental historian later wrote that "this was done because fixed ammunition for this arm was always on hand in the ordnance train, and could be served easily and quickly. It was also decided that a lighter arm would be better for the health of the men, as they could drill with it, carry it on marches, and so keep in better physical condition."[5]

One detail is missing from the account by the Second Company sharp-shooter quoted below: During their brigade commander's tirade over their refusal to accept the new rifles, they were surrounded by armed guards, whom, he suggested, he might "even order . . . to shoot them."[6]

ANONYMOUS PRIVATE, SECOND COMPANY
MASSACHUSETTS SHARPSHOOTERS

Monday [July] 14th. [1862] The Co. was thrown into a high state of excitement by hearing that Lieut. [Charles D.] Stiles had (by order) sent in a requisition for Sharps breech loading rifles, which the men loudly protested against taking. There has been nothing talked of but the hated rifles. The conversation extended far into the evening. We have carried the old rifles so long that we have become attached to them and to part with them would be like parting from a tried and valuable friend. We have resolved to try all the means in our power to prevent such a disaster befalling us.

Tuesday July 15th It is now since the 28th of Feb. since we have been paid and we are sadly in need of pocket change to furnish ourselves with a few small articles the Government does not provide. . . .

July 28th This has been a day of events to the 2nd Co. Mass Sharp-shooters. . . . The paymaster made his appearance among us this forenoon and paid us for only two months when we expected pay for the last four but we were thankful for a part. . . . But [our] spirits were soon dampened by receiving information that the Sharps Rifles had come into camp. We were soon after ordered to "fall in" with rifles and equipments. Were marched up to the Q[uartermaster's] Dept and ordered to lay down our rifles. The equipments of the Sharps rifle was first offered us. Only *one* of the company seemed inclined to take them and he threw them down when he found that he was alone. After a consultation with the Col. [Charles E. Griswold] we were ordered to quarters. Got our suppers and were ordered to fall in with arms & equipments again. The Col. addressed us for a few moments, then he *kindly* gave us five minutes to lay down our arms and accept Sharps rifles. Only three complied with the *gentle request*. Those we think disgraced themselves and the company they belong to. The five minutes passed, then the Col. called for the objections that the men had to taking other arms. After hearing them, we were dismissed and we thought the matter settled for the present, but shortly afterwards Col. [James] Barnes commanding the Brigade in the absence of Genl [John Henry] Martindale came down and ordered us into lines. He addressed us at some length accusing us of being in a state of mutiny and being in rebellion towards our officers and being a disgrace to ourselves and to the state we came from, using the most *opprobrious* epithets towards us, to all of which we listened very respectfully, knowing full well that we were innocent of all the charges brought against us. To close up the matter, we were all put under arrest with the pleasant intelligence that we were not to be released except by Court martial. We all were quite willing to comply with these terms, but Col Barnes did not seem quite satisfied with the way the matter was left, so he made another proposition which was: all those who were willing to obey all lawful orders of their officers step six paces forward. As we have always obeyed such orders and always intend to, there was no other way for us to do but comply with this last request which released us from arrest and ended the matter for the night, but not very satisfactorily to us, as we were anxious to receive the punishment that was threatened with, which was to be sent to [Dry] Tortugas or the Rip Raps [prisons].[7]

Tuesday July 29th Contrary to our expectations, we have not been further importuned in the matter of Sharps Rifles. Nothing has occurred to disturb the quietness of the camp. . . .

Wednesday July 30 The detested Sharps Rifles were again given or offered to the company with the equipments. They were taken very unwillingly and under protest by the entire company with one exception: The two [sergeants] that superintended the distribution of them appeared to do it with evident satisfaction. Had just time enough to get some of the rust off the guns when we were ordered to "fall in" with arms and equipments for company drill. This may be all very fine amusement for these *petty officers* that are now in authority over us. There seems to be a disposition to tyranize over us. Our only consolation is that their authority over us cannot always last....

Friday Aug 1st Our company began to practise the bayonet exercise with the new rifles this afternoon. They made rather slow progress in the first lesson—"none are so dull as those who won't learn." It appears that we are gradually being brought down to infantry tactics altho' we had the promise that our duty would be no different than it was before taking these new arms.[8]

In his 1883 memoir, Luke Bicknell—in what was likely an embellishment—claimed he met with General George McClellan at Harrison's Landing in August 1862. As we saw in chapter 5, he wrote that the general promised him "that we should never be asked to carry those guns [target rifles] again on the march." At the time, Luke confided to his fiancée, Lucretia, that he single-handedly persuaded McClellan to provide Sharps rifles to his company. But he said nothing about actually meeting the general, only that he had sent a "petition" to him. Captain Saunders and the other officers were unaware of his negotiations with McClellan, and when Saunders found out, he was furious, but Luke said, "had very little to say about the matter."[9]

Bicknell suggested that Captain John Saunders and First Lieutenant William Berry either could not or would not adapt to the change to Sharps rifles and skirmishing tactics. Luke noted their "incapacity . . . to handle the company in action in its new character." The entire company, he said, was thus "left . . . almost entirely in my hands." From the start Luke had aspired to become a lieutenant, and now with the dramatic change in weapons and tactics, he quickly succeeded. Meanwhile, Saunders and Berry soon began the process of resigning from the army, possibly in part because the company had lost its independent status.[10]

Luke's account of the Andrew's Sharpshooters' rebellion over the change in weapons was brief. He did make one point clear, however: the men had to be forced to take the new Sharps rifles at the point of guns and swords. Even so, he later said in his memoir that "our new rifles rested so lightly on the shoulder that we marched gaily on towards Antietam." Most of his comrades likely did not share that sentiment. In fact, after the fall of 1862, on the rare occasions when the men had a chance to use the old target rifles, they eagerly abandoned their Sharps breech-loaders—and the skirmishing that came with them.

LUKE BICKNELL (MEMOIR, P. 47)

In a few days [after his petitioning General McClellan at Harrison's Landing] we learned that we were to be armed with Sharpes Breech loading Rifles. . . . We saw no more of our telescopic rifles and revolvers. After arriving at Alexandria, the men formally invited me to lead them in refusing to take Sharps Rifles, or even to serve longer, except upon the conditions of our enlistment—twenty five dollars a month—no guard duty—guns to be carried on the march. I politely declined to end my life as the leader of a mutiny. . . . The men retired, and, first passing a resolution that I was all right, agreed to stand by each other in refusing to touch the new rifles. Their ground for calling my action all right, was that on account of Martin's sickness, I had been designated acting lieutenant.

A few days after, we were marched into a short cross street, in front of a long, low brick building, in Alexandria or Georgetown, and, while the cannonniers stood with lighted matches beside their guns, at one end of the street, and a company of cavalry with drawn sabers stood ready to cut off our retreat from the other end, we were forced to take the Sharpes Rifles. . . . Captain Saunders passed out the rifles, one at a time, from the scarcely opened door, and I passed them to the company. Corporal [Samuel] Gilbreth . . . [,] who rowed General Lander across the Potomac [at the battle at Edward's Ferry in 1861], standing at the head . . . [,] was allowed to make a neat manly protest for himself, and for the whole company, but it was several days before we were allowed ammunition for our new rifles.[11]

"The Hell of Antietam"

From August 25, when Major General John Sedgwick's Second Division left Harrison's Landing, until the Battle of Antietam on September 17, the Fifteenth Massachusetts and Andrew's Sharpshooters were almost constantly in motion. Sedgwick wrote his sister in late August, "The men are tired and to some degree dispirited, but a few day's rest will bring them up." They never did get their rest. On August 30, they rushed to Centreville to help cover the retreat of Major General John Pope's new Army of Virginia, which had just been badly outfought at the Second Battle of Bull Run. Sedgwick boasted that "in thirty-six hours we made fifty miles, and after a rest of a few hours twenty five miles more."[12] Not long after returning to camp just outside of Washington, Sedgwick's men had to march again, this time to help halt a Confederate advance into Maryland. On September 5, as the Fifteenth Massachusetts marched towards Rockville, Maryland, one private noted sadly, "We took the same road that I made my first march on last year from Washington to Poolesville. Who can foresee the fortunes of a War."[13] During that same march, sharpshooter Moses Hill collapsed and was sent to a hospital in Washington.

LUKE BICKNELL (MEMOIR, PP. 48–49)

At last being furnished with ammunition, Capt. Saunders leading us, we marched with our corps, towards the firing, on that most disastrous day of the 2nd battle of Bull Run. Our progress was slow, for not only was there an unusual ignorance of plan and detail amongst us, but our feet were shackled by lack of confidence in the new favorite of the government [General John Pope]. He had shown his ignorance of the power and ability of the foe, so plainly, by his sneers at strong positions, lines of retreat and bases of supplies, that we felt it a useless waste of effort to hurry to his assistance.[14]

Finally the sharpshooters got tired of so much standing in ranks, and began to straggle ahead. By two P.M. we were all collected, in the shade, beside the road, at least a mile ahead of our corps, and as near the fighting line as it was safe to rest. We could not see the fight in progress beyond the intervening woods in which we rested, but our trained ears finally told us that our whole line was rapidly giving ground. In a few moments a carriage came dashing along the road from the front. Gen. [Irvin] McDowell, recognizing Capt. Saunders, jumped out, and urged him to deploy the sharpshooters across an open field nearby, and try to check his men, who were close behind him. McDowell drove on, to hurry up the 2nd corps. I deployed the sharpshooters as requested; but you might as well have thought to stop Niagara with a shingle, as to stay the torrent that rolled over us and on to Washington. We detained a few men however, and were the first to listen to the story of a Union general's [McDowell's] betrayal of his own men on the field of battle.[15]

When our corps came along we fell in and went forward with it to check the enemys advance. We also went with our division to Chantilly, and got badly scattered, in the darkness, by a charge from our own cavalry, who mistook us for the enemy. We stood, with our division, as rear guard, at Fairfax; and, being the last men to leave the ground, as we fell back, left the tail end of our company in the hands of the enemys cavalry. We marched on, day after day, in our new characters, as part of the 15th Mass Reg.

LUKE BICKNELL

Sept 5 1862

Dear Lucretia,
From the 15th last month to the 5th of this I have been too busy, too tired or too something else to write letters to any body. . . .

I dropped you a note at Newport News. After we left here we went to Alexandria by steamship, then marched to Bull Run and then skedaddled back to Maryland shore. We are now camped near Chain Bridge.

I don't know the name of the town. We got here the afternoon of the 3rd.

The hardships of the march to Bull run and back exceeded anything experienced here before. I came out of it tip top, but I carried no weight.

We are off in a hurry. No one knows where except the General. . . .

MOSES HILL

Washington, DC Harwoods [Harewood] Hospital,
Ward H, Sept 18th 1862

Dear Wife,
I have received two letters from you since I wrote. I received $1.00 in one. I was quite unwell then, and when the troops went to Rockville, M.D. I could not go any ferther and I come back to Georgetown, and was ordered to go to the Medical Director and he sent me to where I am. It is a very pleasant place but it is not home when one is sick. I think I shall get my discharge soon and come home. I am going to try for it, for I cannot get well here. I have been paid off. I have plenty of money. I can get fruit and all such things, all I need. Eliza, I should of written before but I have been so unwell that I did [not] feel as I could. I think I have worried about you as much as you have about me, for I knew that you did not know what had become of me.

I am run down and want a good nursing. I ought to be at home. Some days I am better and then I am worse, but if I take good care of myself I think I shall get a little stronger. If you write to me Direct your letter to Me, Washington DC, Harwoods Hospital Ward H, tent No. 11. The letter is the number of our ward and our tent is No. 11. We are about 1½ miles from the Capital.

Dear Eliza do not worry about me for I shal try to get along. I will write again soon. You must excuse me for I am very tired.

My love to all and lots of kisses. I hope you will not worry so much about me now, for it is better for me to be here than with the Regm, in the hospital.

From your dear loving Husband, M Hill

[p.s.] There is about 3,500 in this camp in the Hospital. There will be a good meny discharged soon and I am agoing to try to be one.

LUKE BICKNELL

Sept 7 1862

Dearest Lucretia,

Written on a cartridge box under a log.

We are at Rockville, Md. The enemy are at Poolsville 18 miles distant.

Whether a battle is likely to be fought or not is not known. Every one seems to be about as willing to fight as not. I would rather like to have a battle.

Our company has got very light pretty guns, Sharps Rifles loading at the breech, and capable of firing 8 shots a minute. . . .

I suppose you have heard all about our grand skedaddle from the second Bull Run. I was in it. Marched clear out to Centerville and then back again with the shells of the rebel artillery flying after us and bursting in splendid style right over our heads. I have begun to have a great deal better opinion of these rebels, since they have licked us so often.

When we marched up to the front we passed more than 50,000 stragglers skedaddling for Washington each one saying that his own regiment was all cut up.

Half of our own company dropped behind so that I reported only 20 men present when we got up to the front.

You must not put any confidence in dreams when I appear cold to you. I love you dearly and always shall. I hope I may be at home soon.

Till I do come trust me for that. I only hope I may be fortunate enough to always retain your affections. Every thing else is secondary to that.

Yours ever, Bicknell

At a halt a mile west of the city of Frederick Maryland
6 o'clock P.M. Sept 13th 1862

Dear Lucretia,

We are driving the rebels out of Maryland. Last night they occupied the town. Today they are off and over the mountains where there is a steady cannonading going on which has continued all day. We have halted and appearances indicate that we shall stay all night.

I have eat supper spread out my blanket and laid myself flat to write to you. It has been pretty hard marching that we have had lately, but I am tough as a ———.

Not much fighting now a days. I saw a little at Centerville two weeks ago none since, but lots of slogging it from ten to twenty miles a day. . . . I like to be doing something if it is nothing but marching around. It keeps a man alive. Some of the men growl awfully about the marching. It plays out a great number.

By the way a good part of us out here begin to think we shall never whip the South. We know that once or twice we have been whipped ourselves.

If the war is managed right however we may lick them yet. . . .

You must be teaching now again. I had rather be out here just now than at home even though I can not see you. I feel as if I was the right man in the right place here and I shouldn't at home.

Night has come. My chum is calling me to put up our tent.

You happened to say in one of your letters that you dreamed of me as cold towards you. . . .

You must never forget that I am completely in love with you that I am only happy in feeling that my passion is reciprocated.

Never fear of my getting cold. It is impossible. It is the chief joy of my life that I have gained your love. Now it shall be my chief object to keep it if I can. I really wish I could see you to night. I should like to talk with you.

After the Second Battle of Bull Run, General Robert E. Lee and his army marched into western Maryland. The Union army pursued and by September 15 had pushed the Confederates back through several strategically important mountain passes. Lee's army next consolidated near the town of Sharpsburg, Maryland. Major General John Sedgwick's Second Division (part of General Edwin Sumner's Second Corps) missed the mountain fighting, and arrived on the east side of Antietam Creek on the 15th. Late on the 16th, Union Major General Joseph Hooker's First Corps crossed the creek and prepared for an assault on the Confederate left the following morning. That evening, General Sedgwick's men—including the Fifteenth Massachusetts Regiment and Andrew's Sharpshooters—received eighty rounds of ammunition apiece. They and the rest of Sumner's Second Corps were ordered to support General Hooker the following morning.[16]

On September 17, General Sumner led three divisions in column formation forward across Antietam Creek. Sumner hoped to provide support to the First and Twelfth Corps, whose men had been badly mauled in a fight just east of the West Woods. He also hoped that his men might smash the presumably weakened Confederate forces in those woods and turn their left flank. At the East Woods, Sumner regrouped his men into three long, parallel battle lines facing west. Sedgwick's division led the way, marching through a stretch of pasture littered with dead and wounded and into the now empty West Woods. Sumner had not sent out skirmishers to determine the enemy's position and strength. Neither did he position any men to face the left to fend off any flank attack on that end of his line. Partly because of the terrain, General Sumner did not know that substantial Confederate reinforcements were arriving behind the West Woods and to the left of his line. Neither could he know that enemy reinforcements would also soon arrive to harry the right of the Union line. He did not know that Confederate batteries had been shifted to a concealed position on a ridge with good range of the open areas near the West Woods. Finally, none of the officers realized that the Thirty-Fourth New York Regiment at the far left of Gorman's line had not heard an order to shift the whole line to the right. Instead, the Thirty-Fourth drifted away to the left, leaving a dangerous gap in the Union lines.[17]

General Willis A. Gorman's brigade was on the far left of the battle line. The seasoned veterans of the Fifteenth Massachusetts and Andrew's Sharpshooters were most vulnerable of all, since they anchored the end of the line. The Battle of Antietam would witness Andrew's Sharpshooters' "first and last use as traditional infantry."[18] Colonel Francis Winthrop Palfrey of the Twentieth Massachusetts (writing two decades later in the *Campaigns of the Civil War* series), Private Roland E. Bowen of the Fifteenth, and Luke Bicknell described the advance of Sedgwick's men.

ROLAND BOWEN

Between 8 and 9 oc [on the morning of the 17th] Sumner's Corps was ordered up.... We [Sedgwick's division] soon crossed the Antietam, the water being nearly 2 feet deep. After crossing we stoped to ring out our stockings. We then proceeded around the hills so as not to be discovered by the Enemy, and then alternately through wood and field. Soon our approach was discovered by the Enemy and they commenced to shell us with a vengeance. The Shell burst thick and fast over and around us ... but we pressed steadily on. Soon we came to a large open field planted with corn ... and it seemed as if the ground was almost covered with dead and wounded.[19]

LUKE BICKNELL (*MEMOIR, PP. 50–51*)

At the battle of Antietam, Capt. Saunders led his company as far as across Antietam Creek, on the forenoon of Sept. 17th, and then both he and Lieut.

[William] Berry requested me to take charge of the company; for they had learned at Fairfax that I did not feel at liberty to give even a necessary order in their presence. They told me that they had both resigned, and that commissions were now on the way from Massachusetts, for men who were competent to handle the company in action, but that they could not bear to see the company go into this tremendous battle without them. So I gave them a few simple instructions as to how they could assist me as we moved forward in line of battle and led the company forward into the line at the proper moment.

Our division, Sedgwicks, moved into line at quick step, while solid shot plowed our ranks like hail, until we had reached the historic corn field, already once won and lost. We halted here to dress the line. Sergeants were ordered two paces to the rear to shoot down any man who should falter or turn to look at a wounded comrade.

Then the long line, of which our division was but part, swept on at a double quick over the mingled dead amidst a shower of shot and shell. When we were half way across the field the order came down from mouth to mouth from the right "right oblique." Fatal order! The 34th New York at our left could not obey it. They were cut in two by a road fenced on both sides; and down this road a battery was dashing lashing their maddened horses to a run—else the noble brutes would not have trod upon the dead with which the road was choked—with guns and caissons bounding over the dead and swaying from side to side, and cannoniers desperately clinging on for very life. So a gap was made in our charging line and the 34th thrown into disorder by its attempts to obey the order.

Keeping closed up to the 15th on our right the sharpshooters swept on, the left now of the right division of the broken line, through the corn field and up a wooded slope, where the enemys dead with saber bayonets crossed in confusion lay so thick upon the ground as to check our progress, over a fence and part way down the opposite slope driving the enemy before us until we stood in the "Hell of Antietam" and the order came down from the right, "halt—right dress." Fatal order, again!

COLONEL FRANCIS WINTHROP PALFREY

The corn was very high and very strong. There was a short halt while a fence which formed the eastern boundary of the cornfield was thrown down. Then the column marched straight forward, through the corn, and into the open ground beyond. Few troops were in sight. So far as the men of Sedgwick's division could see, they were to have the fighting all to themselves. . . . So far as they could see, their advance, at least from the [Hagerstown] pike, was made all alone. . . .

Sedgwick's division emerged from the cornfield into the ground near the pike, and swept steadily forward. There were no fences at the part of the pike where they crossed it to delay them. Their march was rapid, and nearly directly west. There was very little distance between the lines. . . . Not a regiment was in column—there was absolutely no preparation for facing to the right or left in case either of their exposed flanks should be attacked. The total disregard of all ordinary military precaution in their swift and solitary advance was so manifest that it was observed and criticized as the devoted band moved on. . . . [T]he division entered the West Woods, . . . and it moved safely through them to their western edge. There there was a fence, and, bordering it on the outside, a common wood road. . . . In these [West] woods, and especially to the left of the ground over which Sedgwick passed, there were many inequalities of surface, and many ledges of limestone which cropped out, and thus excellent cover was afforded to troops on the left of the Federals. . . .

Sumner had marched his second division into an ambush. There were some ten Confederate brigades on his front and flank and working rapidly round the rear of his three brigades. The result was not doubtful. His fine division, containing such sterling regiments as the First Minnesota and the Fifteenth, Nineteenth, and Twentieth Massachusetts, was at the mercy of their enemy. The fire came upon them from front and flank and presently from the rear. Change of front was impossible. . . . In less time than it takes to tell it, the ground was strewn with the bodies of the dead and wounded, while the unwounded were moving rapidly off to the north. . . . Nearly two thousand men were disabled in a moment.[20]

Luke Bicknell (*memoir, p. 51*)

I could not see clearly for the smoke which filled the woods, but made out, while the "right dress" was in progress, a stone wall about twenty rods [110 yards] in our front, and masses of the enemy in motion behind it. The darkness and smoke increased till, with a deafening roar, a broad sheet of flame leaped forth from over the stone wall, the Hell of Antietam was for an instant lit up by its infernal fires, revealing a triple line of Jackson's veterans standing up with guns still pointing at us; and three out of four of our line down.

Unharmed by this terrible volley, except a scratch on my leg, I snatched a rifle from the ground and fired. Before I could reload my arm fell useless at my side, and then a ball crashed through my hip and I went down. . . . I began,

with my unhurt arm and leg, to draw myself towards a tree behind which one
of the Sharpshooters knelt.

He was a praying man, and I imagined him in ill-timed devotion, but
found that he had knelt to get below the smoke and had laid his cartridges
beside him for convenience. He continued to coolly load and fire, until his
pile of cartridges was exhausted. . . .

I thought to get a drink from [Marcus] Parmenter's canteen. . . . I drew
myself to [his] dead body and tried to drink from his canteen, when a bullet
crashed through it and into my chest, and I sank down discouraged.[21]

Bicknell's friend George Whittemore Jr. fell too. His death was described in
a short biography published after the war:

Whilst asleep in a barn, on one occasion, with men of his own and other
companies, Whittemore's rifle was stolen from him. This happened a few
days before the battle of Antietam; and at the commencement of that engagement he was unarmed, and at liberty to be a non-combatant. He was urged,
if not actually ordered, to remain in the rear. This he could not do. He went
cooly toward the front, looking for a weapon. An officer saw him take a gun
from a fallen soldier and calmly load and fire until he was hit and instantly
killed. This occurred in the woods adjoining the corn-field where Sedgwick's
division met with its heavy losses. The next day, when the ground came into
possession of the Federal Army, his body was carefully and tenderly buried
by his comrades, with a headboard inscribed, "Sergeant Whittemore."[22]

The Fifteenth Massachusetts also took "friendly fire" from Union Brigadier
General Napoleon J. T. Dana's troops just to their rear. Colonel Ezra A.
Carman of the Thirteenth New Jersey Infantry recalled: "[Dana] permitted
the 59th New York, 20th Massachusetts, and 19th Massachusetts to go forward
and halt in the rear of Gorman, and very soon the 59th New York closed up
on and began firing through the left wing of the 15th Massachusetts upon the
enemy in front. By this fire, many of the Massachusetts men were killed and
wounded, and the most strenuous exertions were of no avail either in stopping this murderous fire or in causing the second line to move to the front."[23]

LUKE BICKNELL (MEMOIR, PP. 51–52)

Our line of supports came as far as the fence behind and began to fire amongst
us. I motioned them to fire higher but they soon drew back out of sight. . . .
[George] Whittemore lay dead upon the field. I had tried to keep him out of

the battle because the lock to his gun was broken, but he had answered that he could soon take the rifle of a wounded comrade. . . .

Thirty out of forty five of the sharpshooters had gone down on my left; four hundred and fifty out of six hundred of the 15th Mass had fallen on my right; and still the enemy poured in a steady fire upon the line of dead and wounded. They afterwards explained to me that they thought we were "playing possum"; and no wonder that they did, for such terrible execution by a single volley was unprecedented.

Soon they returned the charge, passing over me in column brigade front. I begged for water. From the first line I got an inquiry if I had got enough of the war now; from the second no reply, and as the last and third passed over me, a soldier dropped behind a moment and held his canteen to my lips. This did not prevent my calling upon the stragglers, for water, for I was losing blood fast. Finally one man undertook to bayonet me, to cure my thirst he said, but was prevented by his general who came riding up at just the right moment.

The column which had passed over me met with a terrible reception in the corn field, and were driven back to the fence, pursued by a vigorous shelling, most of which bursting in the woods where I lay, finished the career of many a wounded comrade. I was struck three times and each time it seemed as if the piece of shell had gone clear through me and buried itself in the ground; but I was in fact only sorely bruised.

Capt. Saunders and Lieut. Berry, and Whittemore lay amongst the dead; but Capt. Saunders had not fallen by the enemys fire, but by a shot from the artificer who had been tied to a tree at Yorktown, and who himself fell dead the next instant. . . . A wounded comrade, who went down soon after we halted, told me that the man who was tied up at Yorktown, stepped out and fired at the Captain as he stooped over to pick a cap out of his box. . . . In that leaden storm no man can certainly tell whose bullet pierced the Captain's heart and whose the assassin's brain.[24]

Luke Bicknell was wounded early in the fight at the West Woods. His comrades fought on doggedly until ordered to retreat. Brigadier General Willis Gorman later reported: "The coolness and desperation with which the brigade fought could not be surpassed, and perhaps never was on this continent. Captain Saunders' company of sharpshooters, attached to the Fifteenth Massachusetts volunteers, together with the left wing of that regiment, silenced one of the enemy's batteries and kept it so, and for ten minutes fought the enemy in large numbers at a range of 15 to 20 yards, each party sheltering themselves behind fences, large rocks, and straw stacks."[25]

Hospital

Luke Bicknell's account of a conversation with General Thomas "Stonewall" Jackson and his staff in the following passage is likely not true, especially given that he did not mention such a remarkable meeting to his fiancée in his letters.

LUKE BICKNELL (MEMOIR, PP. 52–55)

After the shelling ceased, the enemys ambulance corps came in, and two of the men serving in it were of those I had interceded for at Patterson Creek the winter before. They carried me from the field and around behind a straw stack. Stonewall Jackson and staff rode up, and the surgeon, dismounting, examined my wound and gave me brandy.

They questioned me, and when I assured them from actual knowledge that McClellan was in command of our army, it came out that they had not believed all they had seen in the newspapers and learned from prisoners that they had not believed that he would again take command after being so abused [after the failure of the Peninsula Campaign], and had suspected that the rank and file of the army, as well as the public were being deceived by our government. But they knew what historians seem to have missed to this date, that an actual count of nearly all the troops engaged on our side had been made the day before.

When they found that I had talked with Gen. McClellan the night before, and also that I knew the result of the count, but would only answer that they would find before it was over that we had enough men to whip them, they tried to surprise the information from me by saying that they knew already how many we had; that we had at least 120,000 and that they with not a man over 100,000 were whipping us along the whole line. But the plan failed to work, though I had drank very freely of the brandy as urged to by the surgeon.

They said however that they would see to it that I didn't lead the sharp-shooters any more during the war, that they should start me for Richmond in an ambulance at once where I would remain a prisoner, if I lived through the war. The surgeon and the men who had carried me from the field talked with Jackson apart, and then the surgeon told me that a guard of cavalry would be sent with me to Richmond, that I should be taken to a private house there and given the best of care, and that if I chose to give my parole not to leave the city, it would be accepted, but no exchange. They surprised me by telling me of my petition for my company's discharge, and of how we were forced to take Sharps Rifles, and jocosely said that they thought it their right to hold on to men who had asked to be discharged from our army. I wondered if they had spies in our army, until I remembered the sharpshooters they had taken at Fairfax [after the Second Battle of Bull Run].

The surgeon had just mounted to order up an ambulance, when the shelling was fiercely renewed and one, bursting in front of his horse, caused the animal to rear and fall over on his rider, who was taken up dead. A sharp firing broke out on the front line and Jackson and staff rode rapidly away. One of the men who had brought me off was killed by a solid shot, but the other came round at frequent intervals and did everything possible for my comfort. I lay stupid except when aroused and the last I remember is being told that they were about to retreat and given my choice to be left or taken.

This must have been the night of the day after I was wounded. Some time the next day the surgeon of the 20th Mass dug me out of the straw stack. Stakes had been set against the stack, and the straw pulled down till I was well sheltered and concealed. A canteen of water, a full haversack of provisions and a loaded revolver were laid beside me. My watch and pocket book, with money all right, had been placed on the blanket under me. This was hardly the programe of stringing up sharpshooters to the nearest tree.

[David M.] Littlefield who had got a bullet through one leg at Yorktown, lay close beside me with a bullet through both legs this time. He had fallen at the first volley, and from him I had the story of the captains death.[26] We were both carried to Hoffmans barn in one ambulance, and laid side by side on straw in the barn-yard. Mr. Ladd of the 15th Mass Reg., a fellow townsman of mine who was detailed as a nurse at the barn, in a few days got us both inside; and used to go an hour before daylight to a distant farm house to procure bread and milk for us. His son James, who had lost an arm in the battle, but didn't seem to mind it much, also looked out for our welfare.

I cannot resist the temptation to tell how the elder Ladd came to be so providentially on hand to look out for me, after he found I was in the barn yard. Having stood it as long as he could with his son serving in the 15th Reg., he had finally enlisted and joined the regiment the day before the battle of Antietam. He was delighted to think that he could stand by his son's side in the coming battle. Very naturally, the son was anxious to keep his father out of danger, as the father was to be where he could care for his son. The son got me to arrange with the officers of the 15th that, at the last moment, his father should be left behind on guard over the regimental property. And when the demand for nurses became great he was of course forced in the ambulance corps, where he proved so good a nurse that he had great difficulty in ever getting back to his old regiment.

[Henry] Martin, who was too sick to go into the battle, took command of the fifteen sharpshooters left, and also visited the wounded men in the hospital before the army left the vicinity. A recruit who had joined us the night before the battle, and who got mad as a rail when I filled his cartridge box with cartridges which would not fit the rifle he had brought, also came round to tell me it was all right. That as soon as he had fired the two in his pocket which did fit, there were plenty of Sharpes Rifles to be had for the picking up, if he had not at that moment got a bullet through his right lung which knocked him flat.

The Battle of Antietam witnessed the highest number of casualties—over 23,000—of any single day of battle in the entire war. John Sedgwick's division lost 2,200 men, and Sedgwick himself was carried off the field with three wounds. The Fifteenth Massachusetts lost more than half of its men—344 killed, wounded, or missing, more than any other Union regiment. Andrew's Sharpshooters also sustained heavy losses: nine killed (including their captain and a first lieutenant), at least seventeen wounded (one of whom was Luke Bicknell), six deserted, two missing, and one captured. More than half of their effective strength was destroyed that day.[27]

LUKE BICKNELL

Not far from Sharpsburg Maryland Sept 22 1862

Dearest,
At the late action near this place I received a wound in the side and am now off duty on account of it....

It was a severe action attended with heavy loss. I think the hardest fight of the war. The 15th Mass. suffered severely. It went in with about five hundred men and can not muster now two hundred men.

My company was badly cut up. Lost and killed and wounded about thirty out of a party of forty five, who went in.

The Captain, 1st Lieut and six men were killed. Seargent Littlefield, who was out with me in the three months campaign [in the 8th Massachusetts] lies beside me with a severe wound in the leg.

We shall be chums in this business.

He has been wounded once and tells me he thinks I will not be fit for duty for three months. I am looking forward to a gay time at home.

The bullet knocked me flatter than a flounder at first and I haven't got so as to walk yet.

Then our men retreated and the rebels rushed up over me and your humble servant found himself a prisoner. Two days after, the rebels left the ground and our folks came and picked us up.

The rebels treated me well, helped me to a stack of straw gave me water and apples and talked as good natured as you please.

I shall be all right again in a little while and shall probably see you before long. . . .

United States Hospital, Frederick, Md. Oct 4th 1862

Dear Lucretia,

I will try to answer your two last letters now. I cannot write much at a time nor very well.

My wound is doing well. I can walk a little now, not much though. I shall be well in two months I think. We came to this place yesterday. Rode twenty two miles. It was rather rough but we have much better quarters here.

We laid in a barn there. Now we have excellent tents and good beds. It would please me very much if I could get leave to go home as soon as I am able and stay till I get well but I suppose by what I hear that it is impossible. . . .

And I believe I remember that something hit me on the hip and something dropped about that time about my size as near as I can recollect, and I haven't felt well since not all over. My wound in the hip is not at all dangerous.

A bullet cut my throat a little bit; just about half the bigness of the bullet was taken out of the flesh. That is well now.

A bullet tore my coat sleeve and just down below on my arm. Another went through my pants and just touched my leg, so that it itched badly for a week.

A piece of shell hit me on the right arm and made it black and blue. Another piece took me in the side and took the breath out of me for a moment, but I got out of it I notice. I thought though for a while that it was an awful close squeak. There I guess I have said about enough about that. . . .

If the war is to continue till the South is whipped it will last a great while yet. I am well satisfied that they have a larger and more effective army than our own at the present time.

If our people had drafted promptly on the first day of September all the men needed, put them in camp, drilled them two months and then brought them into the field we might have stood some show of whipping them this year.

The people at home act like cowards. They prate about poor Generals . . . when the fact is, that our Generals haven't had half enough men to work with. Let them enlist and stay out here a few months and they would know then what fools they are making of themselves. But what is the use of talking. I get mad about it sometimes to think that we should try to whip the South with such a small force. But I comfort myself with the thought that it is only for three years.

If it was not for the pain it would be gay laying around in the Hospital.

I wish I had your picture. . . .

I must close now with much, very much love and many good wishes. May I have a chance to see you soon. I have nothing else to do and am thinking of you nearly all the time. . . .

Luke Bicknell (memoir, pp. 55–56)

In time I was able to be moved to Frederick, Md. We were quartered in tents some distance from the town. We had the best of surgical treatment but the Germanic system of diet which was adopted did not satisfy the cravings of our American stomachs. In our tent, it was a month before we were furnished with knives, forks or spoons, though we had soup served every day. Like all men weakened by long confinement to a bed of pain we craved delicacies. Some longed for one thing and some for another. Bread and milk was my weakness, and as I had money left I bought milk of a farmer near by and learned to eat bread and milk with a pocket knife.

One man in our tent craved chicken. He had lost an arm near the shoulder, but the stump was doing well. He had money and could have procured his chicken if he would have used it, but he felt that it was the duty of the government to furnish what he needed. When the surgeon told him plainly that he could not have it furnished, he turned his face away with a moan which never ceased day or night until he had moaned his life away.

After an abcess formed upon my hip and the fractured bone was taken out I soon got able to bear the weight of my clothes and finally would walk without help. I longed to be home during my convalesance, but applied in vain for a furlough.

Luke Bicknell

United States General Hospital Camp A
Frederick Maryland October 16th 1862

Dearest Lucretia,

It is just four weeks today since the battle of Antietam. I am good for two more months I guess. My wound has not yet begun to heal but still it is doing well.

I have got to be quite lazy lately, lay abed all day. Eat my meals in bed and am writing in bed. It is the fashion here. I can stand up and walk some. I go two or three rods [11–16 yards] each day lately. . . .

It isn't very hard work that I am doing now but it is awful tedious. People bring us tracts and testaments to read. One more sensible man brought playing cards. Magazines are scarce and in great demand. Letters from home are the most interesting and also the scarce article at present. . . .

I have leisure now to think of home and loved ones. Many times I have pictured my glad meeting with you when the war shall be over. I can see you coming forward as you used to and can almost feel the warm touch of your lips. It is hard for me to give up hopes of a speedy conclusion to the war. I hope almost against reason I may see you before the three years are over.

We came very near being taken prisoner by Stuarts Cavalry when they made their late raid around our army. They came within five miles, but were so closely pursued by our troops that they had not time to enter Frederick. . . .

Please excuse poor writing

Believe me always the same

Yours only,

L. Emerson Bicknell

Shortly after the battle, Eliza Hill received a letter from Moses, sent from Harewood Hospital in Washington. She and her daughter, Lucina, wrote him several times, but he was too ill to reply.

LUCINA HILL

Monday, East Medway, Sept. 22d [1862]

Dear Father,

We received your letter tonight with the greatest pleasure imaginable, for we have been worried indeed about you. Do pray try to get your discharge. Mother did not write last Sunday for she did not know where to direct and was not certain you would get it anyway. We are glad you have got as far as Washington tords home. We hope and pray our wishes will be gratified & that you may be at home with us once more, never to leave it I hope. I shall send this letter of yours up to Grandmother Hill. I shall carry ours and my letter up to the office tonight I guess. The folks have been worried about you very much up to West Medway.

James Fisher and Adison Richardsons little child died last week and were burryed today. They both had the diptherea. Charlie Howe has gone to war—went off this morning. Grandfather [Harding] has not got a hired man now and I guess he will not have one this fall. A great many have gone off to war from Medway. I have been down to Readville once & when they get their uniforms I shall go again.

I cant write much of a letter, not that very good. I am so impatient to have you get it. The folks are well. Willie Arnold has been in camp two weeks. His mother feels very bad about his going for he is so young. We have been a bar-berrying last week and got a bushel. Grandmother [Harding] got a bushel also. Mother has made some splendid nice slippers for you. Now if you could only get them it would be a comfort to us. . . .

ELIZA HILL

East Medway Sept 28. (62)

Dear Husband,

Last Monday night I received a letter from you for the first time for nearly four weeks saying you was in the hospital sick. We had heard that you was there, but did not know in what one you was in. In your letter you did not write what ailed you, and I want you to write all the particulars about your-self. Have you a cough or a low fever, we are all very anxious to know.

I think you will have to call yourself luckey for once in being sick so as not to be in those battles week before last, for the 15th rigm. and the Sharpshoot-ers suffered badly. I know it is selfish to say so, but I cannot help it. Your Capt was killed and Lieut. Berry also of the Sharpshooters. I see Thomas Munyans name amongst the wounded in the shoulder. Albert Fales was wounded again, in the hand this time, but he is in hopes he shall not have to lose his hand. He is in Philadelphia in the hospital. Henry Ward was wounded in the shoulder. He has not been out there only four weeks. He and Amos Morse are in the 35 [Massachusetts] rig. And they have not heard from Amos at all since the battle. Fred Swarman has had one of his legs taken off below the knee, and he is coming home as soon as he is able to come. He will be discharged. Lewis Miller was wounded at the Bull Run battle in the leg. He has since lost his leg and is not expected to live. His mother has gone on there to take care of him and his Uncle from Providence. Dr Miller is in there with him. We have not heard how many more from the 2nd rig have been wounded. This is the third time that Albert has been wounded.

I hope you can get a furlough to come home. All the Fales think that it would be better for you to get a furlough at first and then be discharged. I hope you can come same rate or other, and if you get discharged, you will not have to think that you have got to go back again. Do what you think is right about it. All the reason that they think it better for a furlough is because you would be drawing your pay just the same as so would mine from the town [the town provided support for soldiers' dependents], but I will not be selfish myself. I hope you can come any way.

We have formed a Soldiers Aid Society. Both Societys have come together and work for the relief of the sick and wounded soldiers in the Hospitals. We are going to meet once a fortnight and oftener if needed. The people are working all over the State. We sent out one box with over one hundred dollars about six weeks ago, and shall have another one ready this week. The Society have chosen your humble servant for their President, Mr Frank Lovell, Treasurer and some directors. Mrs. Roberts comes and is very much interested. We are making shirts and drawers, slippers, and anything that will be needed by the sick.

At the time of the Bull Run battle, news came last Saturday night and it was mentioned in meeting Sunday how much things were needed for the wounded, and a great many churches were turned into a working room immeaditely. Express wagons were running back and forth, and Sunday night they had 11 car loads on their way to Washington. I suppose you have not heard from your box, and if you cannot come home, just write what things you need to make you comfortable, for your sisters want to join with me in sending you some things. So send for anything that you want, for it will be a pleasure to send any thing to you. We are all well. George teases for his father every day. I have made you some slippers. I wish I could send them to you. I send you my best love, and my prayers you have every day.

East Medway, Oct. 5, 1862

Dear Husband,

I have not received any letters from you all this long fortnight. I feel very anxious about you. If you are not able to write yourself, do get some one to write for you. Mother Hill and your sisters are as worried as I am. We want to know just how you are, what ails you. I want to have you come home for me to take care of, if it is possible.

There is a great deal of sickness in the place. It is the putrid sore throat, the same that Uncle Isiah Morses children died with. Last Sunday night Robert Morses little child died with it. Tuesday night his wife died and Friday night he died. The whole family are gone in one week.

Adison Richardson has buried two children with it. Dr. Jones was the attending physician. Dr. Gale has several patients, but they are getting better.

We are all very well. Georgie has been very well all the summer. It has been very warm but rather stormy this last week. Amos Morses wife has heard from him this week. He has been in two battles. He says he never wants to be in another. Lewis Miller is dead. His folks received a message yesterday. Albert Fales wants to come home on a furlough, but cannot get one. His hand is very painful. He is in Philadelphia in a hospital.

Do you not want to have me send something? I do hope you can come home. Do write as often as once a week for I feel so worried about you. If you cannot, get some one to write for you. I do not know what is to be done with your company, whether it is to have a new Capt. or be disbanded.

I think of you, and pray for you, daily and hourly. But let us in all our troubles and trials put our trust in our Heavenly Father, for we know he doeth all things well. Lucina will finish this letter. I wish I could come on and see you if you cannot come home. I want to see [you] so much. I send you my best love and wishes, with many kisses. . . .

LUCINA HILL

Dear Father,

I will end or to finish mothers letter. How are you now? Write or have some one write just how you are. I so [w]ish I could see you. Have you tried to get a furlough, or discharge? We expect a letter every night lately. Bub has not received one in a fortnight. Do you have good care in the hospital? Georgie asks for father about every day. It is growing colder now. The folks are all well here. . . .

Have you proper food there? Frank Browns babie has been sick but it is better now. I expect Louisa Forster will keep our school this winter. I like her very much. Grandmother sais "Give my good wishes and love to him and tell him I hope he will come home" and this is what we all hope. . . .

Excuse my writing. The ladies have a soldiers meeting every week. Mother for a wonder was chosen president. I can't think of more.

Good bye from your loving daughter, Lucina

GEORGE RICHARDSON

Washington House [Washington, D.C.] Oct. 10, 1862

Mrs. Hill,

I arrived here Wednesday night, and yesterday morning found Moses and I set about getting his papers for discharge immediately. There is a great deal of machinery to work but I am in hopes I shall get the discharge to-night. I shall then get his pay as soon as possible.

We hope to start for home Saturday night but may not be able to. At all events we shall come soon as we can get away. Mr. Hill says he is feeling better than he has done. I think the prospect of going home has cheered him up.

Yrs respectfully, Geo. L. Richardson

CHAPTER

FREDERICKSBURG

The land is red with judgments. Who
Stands guiltless forth?

—John Greenleaf Whittier, "Anniversary Poem" (1863)

Along the Rappahannock

The Army of the Potomac remained near Sharpsburg and Harper's Ferry until late October 1862, then moved to Warrenton, Virginia. In mid-November it shifted to the Rappahannock River, just across from Fredericksburg. Led by their new captain, William Plumer, Andrew's Sharpshooters participated in the battle of Fredericksburg on December 13, 1863, but were not part of the suicidal Union assaults on the well-fortified heights behind the city.[1] Captain Plumer, grandson of a New Hampshire governor and a graduate of Harvard Law School, submitted a brief report on Andrew's Sharpshooters' part in the fight:[2]

REPORT OF CAPTAIN WILLIAM PLUMER

The company was detached from the Fifteenth Regiment December 11, and ordered to the front, to protect the engineer corps in laying the pontoon bridge. This service they attended to. On the passage of the river they accompanied the Fifteenth, and encamped with them at night.

Next morning, at 4 o'clock, [the sharpshooters were] ordered to the extreme front on picket duty. The company was again detached from the Fifteenth about 11 o'clock, and ordered on special duty, as sharpshooters, to pick off the enemy's artillerists, and kept up so continued and effective a fire on the enemy as to engage nearly the entire attention of one of his batteries during the afternoon. At night were ordered on picket duty again.

Next morning (Sunday), our ammunition being almost exhausted, were relieved from duty by General [Alfred] Sully.

Monday morning, having replenished ammunition, a detachment of the company under my command was posted in front of the Gordon House [in downtown Fredericksburg, near the Rappahannock River], to support the Rhode Island battery, and remained there until evening. Not being able, after repeated inquiries, to find General Sully, I reported to General [Andrew A.] Humphreys as ready for any duty required, and was requested by him, unless otherwise ordered, to report at the Gordon house again the next morning. At 12 o'clock received orders to cross the river. Did so, and returned immediately to the former camp of the company.

Every member of the company present and fit for duty faithfully did his duty, especially Sgt. [Oscar H.] Clements, acting as orderly. Robert Wilson was slightly wounded by a shell. James N. Archer is reported as missing. The above is all the loss the company suffered.[3]

Luke Bicknell briefly returned to the Andrew's Sharpshooters in December at their encampment near Falmouth, opposite Fredericksburg, but he had to undergo further surgery on his shattered hip, and returned to Massachusetts to recover.

LUKE BICKNELL (MEMOIR, PP. 58–62)

At the provost marshals office I learned that I should find a fight in progress when I reached the front. I finally reached Falmouth on the evening of Dec. 12th. Here I learned that the sharpshooters had been engaged in protecting the engineers while laying the pontoon bridge the day before, and were now across the river in Fredericksburg with the 15th Reg. Also that we had a new captain who had brought out forty recruits.

All the tents around the stations being overcrowded, I was quietly taking up quarters for the night in one of a pile of coffins, near by, when the owner of the pile appeared and objected, offering me lodgings in his own tent which I felt obliged to accept. I was grateful for the coffee and hard tack he furnished, but, as to the lodgings, I wished he had let me alone; his tent was so crowded and my hip was so sensitive to every movement.

The next morning I surprised my comrades by appearing amongst them and reporting for duty to the officer in charge of the 15th Mass. Now said they we know there is going to be a fight today; for they had been saying to each other the day before that it would not amount to much of a row as long as I was safe in hospital. Before I had scarcely greeted each old comrade they sent Jonah out of camp by written order, directing me to, at once, proceed to the camp they had left and take charge of it.

Recrossing the river I sought the porch of a house which overlooked the City and heights to be assaulted. Here I saw each assault and repulse and wondered in which line of living or dead the sharpshooters lay. I afterwards found out that they were deployed from the Gordon House to the Cemetery, firing at the gunners on the heights, losing only two men, both slightly wounded.

After our army had recrossed the river, men from our company who went over to bury our dead told how that Confederate generals came down from the heights and talked with them of the foolish waste of life, and their astonishment to see line after line dashed so recklessly against their impregnable front, claiming to have refrained from firing on our army after the assaults, and to have allowed it to recross the river from motives of humanity and hope that now the foolish attempt to crush the Confederacy would be abandoned. In this connection I may as well mention that I afterwards had it from the best possible authority that President Lincoln sent peremptory orders to Gen. [Ambrose] Burnside to carry the heights—*by assault* [Bicknell was wrong on this point]. And that Lincoln was forced to this by public sentiment which demanded a more heroic, direct, aggressive policy at the front. The successive charges, by men who fully realized the impregnable character of the position, will ever stand unquestioned amongst the most heroic acts of men.

After the battle I obtained leave of absence, and only stopping on the way at Washington to have more bone taken from my hip, and to report my doings to the hospital I had left, was soon seated at my grandmothers table in Massachusetts. There never was a cook quite equal to my grandmother....

At first I enjoyed myself chatting with old friends and acquaintances as well as I had anticipated, but soon became sensitive to the unjust criticism on the conduct of the war.... At last, I had heard enough about our having been worsted in every battle and the great superiority of the Confederate generals, and longed to be with my brave comrades who were filled with faith in themselves and their leaders, and in the final triumph of the right.

I had promised the men to call on Gov. Andrew before I returned and see if anything could be done about the extra pay. The extra pay question was summarily disposed of by the govenor. At first he did not remember that anything had ever been said about the matter at our enlistment, but on being reminded by the Adjutant General of his telegram to Col. Dalton the July before we enlisted, he dismissed the subject by the conclusion that he had done all he could about the matter. He plainly showed his annoyance and asked to see my leave of absence.

As soon as he had examined my leave of absence I told him that I thought he had done wrong in giving a civilian [William Plumer] a command over a man of Lieut. [Henry] Martins experience in the service. The govenor justified the act by the forty recruits thus obtained. I improved the opportunity to denounce the means resorted to by the State to fill her quota, the formation of new regiments officered by civilians, the payment of high bounty regardless of the character or fitness of the men, the cowardly fear of the draft, and above all the sending out of civilians to command veterans, as unworthy of the people and govenor of a state which claimed to be foremost in devotion to the cause of human liberty.

When I had finished the bearing of the proud man before me was changed, and he sadly replied that he often wished he was but a private in the ranks at the front. That here he was not free to do what he felt was best and right but must in all be but the servant of the people, and do the best he could to help on victory; working in their way and by their methods. He assured me that he was glad that I had spoken so freely; and made me sit down and tell him just how others in the army felt about these matters. . . .

I spent the night with Lieut. Martin, Newburyport, who was at home on leave of absence, and, on my way to the army, met and made the acquaintance of our new captain who was returning from a two months leave of absence. I soon saw that we should not fraternize well.

After the defeat at Fredericksburg, the demoralized Army of the Potomac languished in miserable winter quarters across the river from the city. Newly appointed Major General Joseph Hooker replaced the unpopular Burnside and reorganized and resupplied the Army of the Potomac. The Fifteenth Massachusetts and Andrew's Sharpshooters went to the Second Corps, in the First Brigade of the Second Division. On April 3, General John Gibbon, a graduate of West Point and "a fine soldier of unquestioned courage," with more than twenty years' military experience, assumed command of the division.[4]

Luke Bicknell returned to his company in March and briefly expressed disappointment over William Plumer's appointment as captain. It seems that Bicknell had hoped that he—or at least his good friend, Henry Martin— might get the position. Unfortunately, there are virtually no sources to shed light on the evident factionalism in the company, though a few tantalizing hints do exist. They suggest that the conflict between Luke and Plumer was primarily over which role—sniping or skirmishing—the sharpshooters should play. Captain Plumer seems to have favored sniping with telescopic target rifles. First, even though he was to lead a company of skirmishers armed with Sharps rifles, the captain chose to pose with a telescopic target rifle for his first formal portrait in uniform.[5] Moreover, at least three of the new recruits he brought with him to Virginia had trained with target rifles. Third, in April or May 1863 Luke claimed that he was ordered by General Gibbon to train the new recruits in the fine art of skirmishing, and remarked that Captain Plumer was largely "ignored at headquarters." But it appears that the captain must have conferred with General Gibbon on the sharpshooters' role, for Ferdinand Crossman happily reported to his wife that Plumer was ordered "to not ever take his men in front skirmishing." Instead, the men would operate "under cover where they could harass the Enemy's Gunners, Officers & of course we are willing" (see Crossman's letter of 26 May). Bicknell never mentioned the change. Finally, in late May the sharpshooters were allowed to vote for their new first lieutenant. Bicknell ran and was beaten soundly. It likely was at least in part a vote against skirmishing.

The conflict over sniping versus skirmishing persisted. For example, it appears that the company split in two during the second day of the Battle of Gettysburg—Bicknell leading a group of skirmishers with Sharps rifles in one direction and Captain Plumer leading a second group armed with target rifles (and possibly a few Sharps rifles as well) in another (see chapter 8). Had Bicknell and Plumer somehow resolved their conflict with an informal division of labor, one leading skirmishers, the other pure snipers? At this point, we can only speculate as to whether—and to what extent—Andrew's Sharpshooters evolved over time into such a hybrid organization.

The surviving letters of Ferdinand J. F. Crossman—recruited by Captain Plumer along with Crossman's Sutton friends Lysander Martin and Chilon Houghton—also begin in April 1863.

FERDINAND CROSSMAN

Camp near Falmouth, Va Apr 5 [1863]

Dear Adda,

Yours of March 31st I received just as I left camp for picket. It was delayed on account of the severe storm we have had here & I will answer a few lines as I almost must mail this.

I am still here & well as usual. And you do not know how glad I am to hear you and the Dear Children are still well. I have wrot 4 times before since the

18th of March. Have you recd them? There is no news to write this time, if I had time. This is mearly to let you know I am still well &c &c. Capt. Plumer came back last Night. Lysander [Martin] is on picket duty today. I saw him when he came out to relieve me. He is well, only a bad cold.

I want you to send me a *plaster* to put on my back. Doctor says I had better have one and the Government does not furnish anything of the kind. I also want some more postage stamps. . . .

The [comb?] came safe & I am much obliged. I also want ½ yard of silk ribbon like that on my memorandum book. I do not know what you think of my sending for so much, but I cannot get anything here. I have not been paid off yet. But shall soon. . . .

Picket Post Rappahannoc River, Va Apr 9 [18]63

Dear Adda,

Your letter of Apr 2d was received last night but I did not have time to write Today. I am on Picket as you will see by the date of this. It is quite pleasant but will bee cold tonight. I shall go to the Front or out posts from 2 PM until 6 PM & then in reserve No. 1 until sunrise when I shall come to the front until relieved at 10 PM.

I received the BOX yesterday PM & everything was all right & safe. It came through verry quick. . . . We have a great many Pickets out lately. Where we had 250 men on a time, we now have over 800, which make us do duty nearly every other day, but this is the last time I shall come out here on Picket, if nothing new happens, as we shall leave this Regt & go to Berdans Sharp-shooters the last of this week or fore part of next.

The Boots are just the kind I wanted & fit me, also the Hat, only it is a better one than I deserve and all the other things are verry acceptable indeed. I fried 3 of the Sausages & have them for dinner today, also a cup of Tea & some cake, cheese & Butter. It looks the most like Home of anything I have seen since I came out here.

My old Boots I can weare more yet when the ground is dry, but the last time I was on Picket I wet my feet & have a cold but the Doctor thought I was playing it [feigning sickness] & would not excuse me. The Sargent would, but I told him I would come as the day was fine & the more I go on Picket the sooner I should apply for my discharge. I hope you have send that plaster I wrote for as I want it verry much.

But after we get out of this d—d Regt we shall not have to go on Picket only once a month unless there is some new arrangements. . . . If I can get a Reb paper I will send it to you. . . .

The [farm] lot I want broke, it *is* the one I seeded down 8 years ago where we used to shoot. Have the stoneheaps drawd off before it is plowed & put in a hole near the lower end of the stone Brook where the wheels cut in so bad & it will help make a road to the lot. I have sent some grafts home & shall send some more, also a rose Bush in this.

There was a Grand Review yesterday of this whole army by the President, but I did not feel well & did not see him. I have got over running to see *great men* & i[t] does not pay in the army. Lysander has a bad cold. I have not been on Picket since the 5 of April, 4 days. Albert was out the 6th & again yesterday, only 2 days, so you see we have an easier time than the rest of the Regt.

There is no news to write, but you must write as often as usuall, at least let me know you are well. Have those Photographs taken the first opportunity. I have not been payed a cent yet, but shall be soon. As it is time to go to the Front, I will close. Love to all as usual. . . .

Camp near Falmouth, Va Apr 13 1863

Dear Adda,

Yours of Apr 5 was received just after I came in from Picket & as I had just wrote to you. I have waited until today thinking we should change our position & go to Col. Berdans, but I see no prospect of it at present. We are having some trouble here with the officers of the 15th Regt. Col. [George H.] Ward has applied to Gen Hooker for the company to fill up his [15th] Regt. If his request is granted, we shall be put in the small companies of the Regt to equalise them. We shall have some fuss before we go in as infantry & take a Springfield musket. . . .

We have had some verry pleasant weather for a few days. Yesterday (Sunday) I went out north to see the country & get my dinner. It is the first time I have sat down at a table since I was at Home. I had a boiled dish, part Beef, cabbage, potatoes & the folks are verry old, between 70 & 80, verry neat. I go to see them once or twice a week. I have given them several pounds of coffee as I get more than I use. I should like to send it Home. We now have 5 or 6 lbs on hand. . . . I get a letter most every day from some where, night before last from Oliver & the night before from you. Daniel was well the other day but a little scart about the conscript act. . . . Lysander has not changed his shirt since he left the camp & how long he had worn it before I do not know. It is *verry clean,* but how many *louse* there is in it, I do not know. It costs 8 cts to get a shirt washed.

My clothes are all good except the lineing of my coat is worn out in 2 or 3 places where my pistol & knife comes. My old pants have not a hole in them yet. Lsys[ander] has drawn a new pair and worn a hole through the seat. I do not set down enough for that. My old boots I wear in dry weather & dress up Sundays & Inspection days. . . . We talk of having a Dance or Prayer meeting & shall get Mayers to preach.

Ever your Husband, Ferdinand

"We Are Where We Belong"

On April 17, 1863, not long after Luke Bicknell met with the Second Division commander, General John Gibbon, Andrew's Sharpshooters once again became an independent company.[6] Their spirits were further lifted when at least a dozen of their old target rifles were returned to them. One of the rifles likely was Moses Hill's. (When the old weapons were taken from the men at the end of the Peninsula Campaign, Hill said his rifle was one of thirteen held in reserve.) Until August (when they were attached to the Twentieth Massachusetts Infantry) they once again enjoyed the support and protection of a high-ranking officer. General Gibbon—like Frederick West Lander earlier—designated Andrew's Sharpshooters as his "body guards."

LUKE BICKNELL (MEMOIR, PP. 62–63)

About two weeks after my return Gen. Gibbon who was in command of our division, 2nd Div. 2nd corps sent for me and questioned me until he had learned the history of the sharpshooters. . . . He had received letters from Massachusetts, which covered the points of my interview with the govenor, and was determined that while under his command there should be no just cause of complaint by the company. He required me to suggest measures to him which would in my opinion render the company most effective as a distinct branch of the service, as sharpshooters.

The result of this interview was that the company was detached from the 15th Mass and ordered to camp by itself near division head quarters. We made reports, took orders, and drew rations direct from the division head quarters. Any one who wanted our services must go to division head quarters, be he colonel or brigadier. Thus we again occupied the same position in the army that Gen. Lander assigned to us at Camp Benton.

It was generally expected that our new captain [William Plumer] would soon see the propriety of resigning a position whose duties he could not properly fulfill, and consequently he was to a certain extent ignored at head quarters, and I was ordered to personally superintend the fitting of the company for its special work. The weather being favorable, I soon had the recruits well drilled in target firing while advancing and retreating as skirmishers as well as while lying flat. I also drilled them many days in the art of springing to cover, until they would all sink out of sight, in a moment, where you would not think it possible to conceal a man at all.

Gen. Gibbon also had ten of the lightest of the old rifles brought down from Washington and carried in his own teams, to be used whenever the occasion called for it, and I drilled the men in the use of them, also. Like a regiment, we had dress parade, inspection and a guard around camp. All worked lovely, except that the captain's superior rank, and my practical knowledge and experience, unfitted us for our respective duties towards each other, and so we, mostly, omitted them.

FERDINAND CROSSMAN

Camp near Head Quarters 2d division 2d army corps,
Near Falmouth Va Apr 19 [1863]

Dear Wife,

I have received your letters of the 8th 12th & 14th also 2 papers, plaster, pencil & all since I wrote to you, but the uncertainty of our next camp and the moveing is my excuse. The next day after I wrote last, I went on Picket & that day we had marching orders with 3 days rations of meat, Bread, coffee & Sugar in our Haversacks & 5 days more Bread, coffee, Sugar & salt in our Knapsack & to send to Head Quarters all our extra blankets etc & be ready to march at 6 AM the next morning. 5 days rations of meat was going on the hoof. But the rain again prevented & when we shall start no one knows, perhaps tomorrow & perhaps not in 2 months. But We the Sharpshooters are . . . clear of the 15 regt and *all* Infantry. Our division General, Gen. Gibbon sent an order for us to report for special duty at his Head Quarters & day before Yesterday we packed up & moved here. We have a splendid camp where the Davis Hospital was & yesterday the Gen. gave an order for a pair of the best Horses & a wagon that could bee found. So now we have a good team, no picket duty or guard, except on our own Quarters, which takes 4 privates and a Corporal. So you see we are where we belong. The Capt's Pass is good everywhere only to the Creek & [Lysander] & I expect a pass from the Generall to go there today so this will be short but I will write again tomorrow if we go today. . . .

My back I think is better than it was a few days ago. I shall throw away some of my things when we march & carry as little load as possible, but 8 days rations & 60 rounds ammunition makes a good load itself.

Col. Berdans Sharpshooters are in the 5th army corps near Stonemans but we shall stay in this division & corps. . . . While I have been writing the above, several have applied for passes as we cannot get one, so when I want to go away I shall do as I used to: make my own. I shall go and try to get a rose bush today to send to you. So no more at present. Give my respect to all. . . .

Head Quarters 2d Div 2d Corps Near Falmouth, Va Apr 21st [1863]
Dear Adda,
It is a verry cold wet day & we have no fire, so I cannot write much but I send one sheet of my Diary & will send more soon. I thought it would be interesting to you and the children if I did not ever get home. But I intend to come, you know, but the fortunes of war are uncertain. But we shall not have to go in line of Battle now as infantry, so there is more hopes of us. There is no news to write, only I went to White Oak Church last Sunday instead of after your rose bush. . . . I am well as usual, weigh 172 lbs without an over coat. My coat you made me is so tight it cuts under my arms so I shall have to throw it away, I am afraid. . . .

Camp near Head Quarters 2nd Div 2nd Corps Falmouth, Va Apr 24th [18]63
Dear Adda,
Yours of the 19th was received last night & I hasten to reply. I am verry sorry your Cough & Cold still hang on but hope to hear you are better verry soon. I am as well as usual. It is verry unpleasant weather here now as it has stormed for 2 or 3 days & is quite cold. Our house is not so large as the old one, as we have our shelter tents & no fire. So we have to lay abed when it rains. Lysander is on guard to day & I am laying down writing this. We were payed off yesterday & I have 70 or 75 dollars to send you, but shall not send by mail at present as there is a great deal mail robbing *just after the pay master has been around*. Last week there was *One hundred & Thirty Thousand dollars* stolen from the mail between here & Washington in small sums that soldiers had sent Home. I think I shall go to [Aquia Creek?] & send by Express if there is an office there. If not I shall wait a week or 2 untill the excitement is over before I send by mail. . . . I want you to get Photographs . . . of Yourself & the children taken, a Doz of each. Have the Children taken together & Yours in 2 positions, one sitting & the other standing & send me one of the best.

There is no new signs of our moving at present. In fact the army cannot move now until the mud dries up which will take severall days. . . .

It rains like the Harry and spatters through the cloth. There is a squad out shooting at a target in the rain. I escaped by shutting up the tent & going to bed. . . .

I have a song & music I picked up on the Battlefield at Freder[icksburg] which I will send home soon. I thought part of it was gone until today. Please take it to *Flora* & have her play & sing it & tell me if it is a good one. The Box was *Not* opened & every thing was all right. I eat the last of the Butter & cheese yesterday. . . .

Love to all & Kisses.

Ever your Husband Ferd

"We Did Considerable Execution"

By late April, the Army of the Potomac under Major General Joseph Hooker was once again preparing to strike the Confederates across the Rappahannock.

FERDINAND CROSSMAN

Head Quarters 2nd Div 2nd Army Corps, Falmouth, Va April 28th [18]63

Dear Adda,

Yours of April 22nd was received yesterday. I was verry glad to hear your cold & cough was better. I went to the Creek yesterday, and sent you $75.00 Dollars by Express. . . . Write as soon as you get this so I shall know if you have got it. I have nothing to write as the [Captain] wants me & I am on Duty today. I shall write again tomorrow or next day. All the army is in motion except this Division & we expect to move every hour. . . .

Head Quarters 2nd Div 2nd Corps, Near Falmouth, Va Apr 30 [1863]

Dear Adda,

I intended to write so as to send it in todays mail, but I had so much to do that I culd not. We have made a *large* change in our house since I wrot befor. We now have a Wall Tent which one of the regiment left when they moved & have it fixed up nice with table stand, bunks & a floor. There is 4 of us in it, the 2 Bancrofts & Lys[ander] & I, but we have got to leave it tomorrow morning at daylight to join the rest of our corps (the order sais) which is somewhere between here and Kelleys Ford. You will know the result before you get this.

There has been a great deal of moveing back and forth for the last few days. Old Hooker is playing them a game that they do not know. Yesterday morning, 4 32 lbs cannon went up to the Right toards Banks Ford, and last night about 11 Oclock they went back to the Left with 10 to 12 Horses on each. Where the main part of the army will cross, whether on the Left or the Right, no one here can tell, but we suppose they will cross both ways. Some of our Boys have been up on the hill back of camp & could see the flash of cannon on the left 4 or 5 miles below Fredericksburg & the report is that the Rebs are whipped there. If so, their cake is dough. . . .

Where or when I shall write to you again I cannot tell, perhaps tomorrow or next day and perhaps—but do not worry as it will do no good. I think we have the best chance to keep out of the thickest of the fight, although we shall have to do some skirmishing and engage the Rebs at long range, and if they keep the rotten [sharps guns?] away from me; I do not care for them. I shall write as often as I can . . . but they will be short, just to let you know where I am & you must write often too. . . . Dear Adda Kiss the Dear children, *Georgie* and *Adda* for me once more, and receive the Love & Kisses of your Husband, Ferdinand

In the Battle of Chancellorsville, twenty miles west of Fredericksburg (April 30 to May 6, 1863), Andrew's Sharpshooters once again saw limited action. General John Gibbon's Second Division remained in reserve in and near the city. After the Union defeat, the sharpshooters served as part of the rear guard for units retreating across the pontoon bridges over the Rappahannock.[7] Captain Plumer (writing here in the third person) submitted a brief report.

REPORT OF CAPTAIN WILLIAM PLUMER

[Capt. Plumer reports that he] received orders to march at 12 o'clock on the night of the 2d instant, and at 12:30 P.M. were *en route* for the Lacy house, where he was ordered to report. At 11 A.M. crossed the river as ordered, and soon went to the front, where they deployed as skirmishers, and advanced about 2 miles, but without meeting any body of the enemy. Sent in 3 prisoners; were ordered back to Fredericksburg, and subsequently to the Lacy house, where they arrived about dark and encamped.

That the next day (the 4th), about 11 A.M., they were ordered to cross the river and report to Colonel [Norman J.] Hall, who ordered them to the front to protect our pickets, who had been much annoyed by the enemy's sharpshooters, posted in rifle-pits, &c.; that the enemy's fire was soon silenced, with considerable loss to him. At dark, the company again crossed the river, and encamped in rear of the Lacy house, where it still remains.

That he is happy to be able to add that his command suffered no loss, not a man being killed or wounded. He is also happy to bear testimony to the good conduct of his men, who well upheld their former good reputation.[8]

Luke Bicknell, Captain Plumer's competitor for the leadership and loyalty of the company, left a more detailed account of Andrew's Sharpshooters' actions.

LUKE BICKNELL (MEMOIR, PP. 63–65)

At the battle of Chancellorsville we joined in the assault which resulted in the capture of Marye's Heights back of Fredericksburg. My diary reads as follows: "Lacy House, May 5, 8 P.M. It rains torrents. At midnight of the 2nd, we left camp and marched to the Lacy house. At day break of the 3rd our division laid pontoon bridges and crossed with out the expected resistance, the 6th corps, across below the city, having cleared the enemy from the opposite bank, for us. At 1 pm, our division charged Marye's Heights in front, the 6th corps charging them from the left at the same time. The heights were carried after a sharp struggle.

As the enemy fled, in the direction of Chancellorsville, a battery with infantry supports, halted and began to shell our lines, reforming on the heights. I deployed the sharpshooters and routed and chased the battery and supports about three miles back to the woods: the battery halting and shelling us several times during its retreat. We did considerable execution without losing a man ourselves. At dark our division fell back to the city and the sharpshooters were ordered back to the Lacy House.

On the morning of the 4th the enemy reoccupied Marye's Heights without opposition and their sharpshooters soon began to annoy our division in the city. I was ordered to cross the river with the company and to report to Colonel Hall in the Cemetery back of the city. The colonel ordered me to occupy some buildings across the street south of the cemetery, so that his men would not be annoyed by the return fire we should draw. When I reached the street I found that it was continuously swept by a fire which made the surface fairly boil, and the air, as blue as twilight. Nine out of ten would have fallen in crossing the street; so I commenced drilling holes through the brick wall of the cemetery. Firing from the top of the wall was out of the question until we had the enemy quieted down, for a ramrod held above the wall was hit again and again, and a hat pushed up was riddled in a moment.

Before we had perforated the wall an aide brought me a preemptory order to cross the street. I declined to obey unless he would lead the way. As this looked like instant death he concluded to go back and report. Before he had returned we had perforated the wall and reduced their fire on the cemetery to an occasional shot. We could not however from our position stop the fire which rendered the street impassable, so the aide said stay where we were.

We held the enemy as we had them till dark, excepting that when they left their trenches during the afternoon to assist in the attack on the 6th corps in their rear, they suffered fearfully from our fire delivered rapidly from the top of the wall; their dead were literally piled in heaps. At dark we retired to the Lacy House, having suffered no loss.

Early this morning [May 5] our division evacuated the city and took up the bridges, the enemy then taking quiet possession of the opposite shore. It has rained hard for the last five hours. The floor of the room in which I am writing is covered to the depth of an inch with blood and water; the room having been used for amputating. May 6th, 9 A.M. I have just learned from President Lincoln's private secretary, who is down here, that we have been badly defeated at Chancellorsville. The whole army has recrossed the Rappahannock."

FERDINAND CROSSMAN

Lacy House, Va May 9th [18]63

Dear Adda,

. . . I am verry glad to hear you are all well at Home. Tell the Children to be good at school as well as at Home & learn all they can before I get back.

We have been supporting a battery here since we crossed back from F[redericksburg] but our teams have come down to camp & expect to move back to our old camp as the Division Head Qu[ar]ters are moveing back. I have got to go to get my meat.

2 O'clock P.M. We have been staying in the Lacy House since I wrote, but shall occupy our tent tomorrow if it does not storm and we do not move. It has rained since Tuesday nearly all the time until to day & now it is verry pleasant. . . . We are having verry good times here, all things considered— nothing to do, only lay around & Keep our guns in order "in case of an attackt." Some one stole our wall tent which we left at Division H. Q. before Lys[ander] & I went after it, but we captured a good . . . wedge tent which I should like to send home for You & I to eat our Dinner in in warm weather. . . .

The 6th Army Corp I hear has lost a large number in wounded. The [?] Brigade were in that corps & they say the 2nd & 6th were badly cut up. A flag of Truce came across yesterday & wanted Gen Hooker to send over & get our wounded & this morning 4 pontoon Boats were launched but the [carter?] is not ready yet but will be in an hour or 2. In all probability some of our acquaintances are among the wounded. I shall look for them when they cross. The [6th?] was nearly all wounded & verry few Killed, but here one man is as likely to be killed as another & all are in the same danger, but I have escaped 3 times & think I am good for the rest. What has been accomplished by the last move no one here knows as we have no papers yet & you hear more reliable news than we do here.

I must close soon. Write often & I shall doe the same. I am obliged for the stamps. The ambulance train is coming in after the wounded....

LUKE BICKNELL (MEMOIR, PP. 65–66)

Being in Richmond in 1869, I was complimented by ex-confederate soldiers on the drill and marksmanship shown by the sharpshooters at the battle of Chancellorsville. At the time of the action Colonel Hall, instead of being offended at my exercise of discretion, formally thanked me for the services rendered during the day.

While the storm continued and we were still in the Lacy House I found an officer of a Massachusetts regiment laying up stairs so low from loss of blood that a fire in the room was necessary to preserve his life. No wood was to be had, so I tore off the rich foreign wood which lined the amputating room to start a fire for him. While I was kindling it, the sharpshooters started a fire for themselves in the amputating room. Mrs. [John] Harris of Pennsylvania had her sanitary head quarters at the Lacy House, and was much horrified at the desecration of the mansion. She was a rare woman; the longer she lectured me the more I loved the old lady; but I kept up the fire in the sick room all the same; and we got nicely acquainted before the storm was over.[9]

I presume that it was by Mrs. Harris' request that after, we went into tents back of the Lacy House. I was ordered to see that no disturbance took place around the house which might annoy the ladies of the sanitary commission. It was a lovely place to lounge. A magnificent lawn shaded by huge sycamores stretches far towards the river in front, and finally drops in successive terraces to the river bank. Sitting upon the balcony the city of Fredericksburg with its tier upon tier of overshadowing hills is spread like a picture before you.

FERDINAND CROSSMAN

Lacy House, May 11th [18]63

Dear Adda,

... You will see by this that we are still here supporting the Battery. It is as warm as July now, but cold nights. The Flag of Truce is still crossing the river bringing wounded, but I have not heard of any from Vermont yet. . . . I heard yesterday that the 2nd [Vermont] loss in Killed Wounded & missing [is] 103. I should have gone to see the Regt today but it is so hot I cannot go.

My side is better & I am all right. The Chain was at Jonas' Barn not to the Waterman place—who lives there now. You can *swap* the Horse off if you please. Lysand & others are well. I cannot think of any thing to write, only I am alive & well. I shall write again soon. . . .

May 15th 9 PM, Head Quarters 2nd div 2nd Corps

Dear Adda,

Soon after I closed the first of this letter we had orders to strike our tents & pack up everything & be ready to march to our old camp at noon & here we are. My tent did not get here until almost night, but we put it up in 5 minutes & then commenced to gather timber to raise it up with as everything we left here 2 weeks ago is stolen, but we now have more things. . . . We backed ⅓ a mile and are now waiting for daylight to commence our operations again.

I think the prospect is: we shall stay here several *weeks*, but may move before morning . . . you cannot always tell, you know. Lys[ander] is asleep. Mrs Bancroft are out some where, but will be in soon so I must close. . . .

May 17th 1863, Head Quarters 2nd Div 2nd Corps

Dear Adda,

As Lysander is writing home to day, I will send a few lines to let you know I am still well. It has been quite warm today but is cooler just now. . . . I have not received any letters since I've come back to this camp, but shall look for one from you tomorrow.

We have got a very good house built. Lys & I sleep in the lower story & the Bancrofts in the second. The walls are not verry tight, but just right for the kind of weather we are having here now, as there is a free circulation of air in the lower story.

I intend to go visit the 6 army corps the first cool day & then I can tell you who was killed or wounded from Vt (if any) that we know. Do you have any letters from Vt ? . . .

Near Head Quarters 2nd Div 2nd Corps, Opposite Falmouth, Va May 20, [1863]

Dear Adda,

Yours of the 24 was received last night & finds me better than when I wrote you last. I am rejoiced to hear you and the children are well.

We moved our camp about ½ a mile yesterday toards the railroad & now are between the Generals Quarters and the Enemy & opposite Falmouth. We are the Gen's Body Guard, so we move when he does. Our camp is on a hill & a verry pleasant location, quite cool as we have a good breeze here. There is a Division review & I will close for the present as there is [so] much drumming, I cant write.

I expected to get a furlough next fall until yesterday, but Gen Hooker has stoped them again, so I shall not come home until my time is out unless something new turns up. Our time will be out in 15 months from the 3d of June.... It will be the 3d of September, 1864.

I too Dreamed of Home & loved ones there last night, but found myself opposite Falmouth this morning, all safe. You can Guess a part of the Dream I shant tell. I am verry much obliged for the gossip of the Neighborhood which you wrote to me. I am afraid [D?] is getting Demoralized. But Scandal will float you know, and so will any *light* matter. In your next, please give me more of the particulars in relation to the *war Widdows*. But their time is short. They must hurry up, as the 9 *months Men's* time will be out the middle of July. And then Oh!—I suppose L[?] W.—takes care of E. A.— during S's absence. You will be about the only Widdow after the 9 month men get home & if you cannot get along you know what to do. I shall not worry a mite.

There is no news to write that I think of. They say the rebs are making a demonstration at the fords, but probably only to cover some other movements, although we are liable to move any hour. We may stay here all summer.... Lys[ander] also sends the same to the same & you. As it is mail time I must close by Wishing you well & please receive the Love of Ever your Husband, Ferdinand[10]

LUKE BICKNELL (MEMOIR, PP. 67–68)

It becoming apparent that the army was to remain inactive for a while we removed our camp to near division head quarters and resumed our drill and target practice. Lieut. Martin, who had remained absent on leave, sent in his resignation at this time. The captain ordered an election to fill the vacancy and a majority of the men expressed a preference for Mr. [Oscar H.] Clement, the orderly sergeant, for 1st Lieut. Of course, I refused to take part in so un-military a transaction and expected no attention would be shown to the affair, but it would have hurt me to thus learn that the men were averse to my promotion if they had not immediately told me that the majority of the new men felt that I was inclined to seek opportunities for putting the company into action and, also, inclined to take great risks in a fight.[11]

There was no denying the charge, for though up to this time, except at the battle of Antietam, we had not had a man killed in action, I had brought in more wounded men, and got out of more tight scrapes, than any other man who had been trusted to lead. And while the captain hesitated on Marye's Heights after two men had been struck down in the regiment to our left, I had taken the company out of his hands and chased off the battery, without having received an order. They were not old enough soldiers to understand, if told, that it was far safer to deploy and advance on the battery than to stand and take it where we were; so I turned away with the retort that the best way to have avoided danger was to have staid at home.

Ferdinand Crossman

Near Head Quarters 2nd Div 2nd Corps Falmouth, Va, May 26 1863
Dear Adda,
Your letter of the 21st was received last night & finds me better than when I wrote you last, although I have not been reported for duty yet but shall report myself tomorrow. The Doctor lanced the sore Saturday. He called it an abcess. . . . It continues to discharge, but does not smell as bad as the one [D?] had. I was sorry to hear Adda had been sick, but I hope it will not bee anything serious. I think she must have gone out in the sun without her bonnet or hat, and that caused the blindness. They must bee verry careful about exposing their Heads bare to the sun. It has been verry *hot* here until yesterday. Now we are having a cold storm without rain.

We had 14 Telescopic Rifles come here last night from Washington. They are same that belong'd to the old company. We expect some sport, so 27 have applied for them, and they have got to shoot for them, but I suppose this does not interest you. Gen Gibbons sent an order to Capt Plumer to *not ever* take his men in *front skirmishing,* but put them under cover where they could harass the Enemye's Gunners, Officers & *of course we are willing.*

You say trees are in blossom. Peaches here are as large as your thumb, apples &c. L[ysander] is well, sends respecs. Give mine to all. Kiss the children for me. Tell them to be good. And receive the Love & best wishes of Ferdinand.

Deep Run

In the first week of June, Major General Joseph Hooker ordered part of the 6th Corps across the Rappahannock to test the Confederate defenses around

Fredericksburg. Andrew's Sharpshooters accompanied them to suppress Confederate sharpshooter fire at Deep Run, a stream that coursed through a steep ravine and into the Rappahannock a mile and a half south of the city. On June 9, according to a historian of the Massachusetts regiments, "Captain Plumer with ten men went to the scene. The following day Lieutenant Bicknell with a larger force went over, and after a day or two of sharp practice forced the Confederates to ask for a cessation of picket firing."[12] Private Roland Bowen of the Fifteenth Massachusetts made note of the sniper war at Deep Run: "It is quite common for me to say All quiet on the banks of the Rappahannock. I shall have to change this so as to read, There is a cursed guerilla fight going on on the opposite bank below the city continually. Our men being in possession of said bank. . . . Our pickets were thrown out [a] considerable distance toward the range of hills wich they held and continue to hold, since wich time the sharp Shooters continue from morning until night, each and every day to blast away at each other at every conceivable opportunity."[13]

The sharpshooters' engagement at Deep Run was brief but costly: the company was badly shaken by the loss of one of its most popular members, Lysander Martin of Sutton.

FERDINAND CROSSMAN

Camp near 2nd Div 2nd Corps, June 5th 1863

Dear Adda,

Yours of the 31st May came to hand last night, but I did not get back from . . . Church until late, so I could not write until this morning. I am well at present, as are all our friends here. I saw Miron Palmer . . . & several others yesterday. They are all well except the youngest, Tiley. A shell burst so near his head at Fredericksburg, that it made him Deaf. The next younger was wounded in the leg, as was also Oscar Palmer. They are in the Hospital at Burlington Vt. I also saw Eli Osburn. He is well & I guess he might as well be in the army as anywhere. I rather think he is a *miserable cuss* at best. He was so engaged playing Bluff [a card game], he did not get up while I staid. He lost about 12 dollars while I was there [in] about an hour. You will please not tell any one in Vt what I tell you about him. . . .

I sent you $20 yesterday by Express. Lysander sent $22 in the same package, making $42. You will have to receipt for all of it. . . .

There is no news to write, only a small part of the army has & are now moveing up to the Right. . . .

June 9th we were ordered to send ten men to Deep Run. It is a deep ravine with very precipitous banks, just below the city on the Fredericksburg side. [Brigadier General Albion P.] Howe's division of the 6th corps was over the river south of the run. Being annoyed by sharpshooters they sent up to the 2nd corps to borrow us.

The captain went down with the men and got at work about noon, firing from the breastworks which the division had thrown up on the south side of the run for its own protection. He returned at 12 p.m. with five men, having left the other five at the breastworks and sent me down with sixteen men to continue operations. The captain had sprained his ankle, or knee, badly, in fact it proved a permanent injury. He had not silenced the enemy and in fact the return fire had been worse for the division than what they had before. He had not however fired without effect on the enemy who were protected by a fringe of timber on their side of the ravine.

The next day, I accomplished no more than the captain had the day before, and saw that we never should while we let them hold their side of the ravine. I found out during the day that we had at last met our counterparts in drill, discipline, and skill, and that they outnumbered us five to one. After their withdrawal at nightfall, and the posting of their pickets a few rods back from the ravine I set to work with details from the 6th corps to construct three rifle pits upon their edge of the ravine. This we did by filling sand bags from the loose dirt in the ravine, being careful not to make the slightest noise.

By steady, persistent effort we finished them in season for the 21 sharp-shooters to get into them, and mask their fronts with green twigs before day-light. As soon as it was light enough to enable us to fire with effect we opened fire and routed the picket line along our front and out of a clump of trees to our left. Soon after this we picked off a mounted officer at long range with one of the old [target] rifles.

Finally our real antagonists appeared. A long skirmish line, about two hundred strong, advanced through the wheat field in our front to drive us out of our pits. We drove them to cover in the wheat field in our front, but, on the left, they gained the clump of trees, and silenced our left pit which was a few feet from the edge of the run. . . . We did not like the looks of the cap we raised to test their skill and they showed us that they could hit a ramrod, too. . . .

I was in this left pit and had to jump out and roll to the bottom of the ravine to get clear. I spoiled my uniform and scratched myself badly in my hurried descent, but lost no time in posting two men from the next pit where they could command the clump of trees and let our silenced pit, full of men, get to work again. . . . Then I found a place on the edge of the run, where, by enlarging a hole between two trees that had grown together, a man could fire through safely, and with effect, if he had a comrade with him to watch his flank. . . . I ordered [Lysander] Martin and [Ferdinand] Crossman, the two men I had called, back to the center pit whence I had taken them, for I did not like their position as a permanent one, but they begged so hard to stay where they were a little longer that I yielded while I made a visit to the center and right.[14]

Martin and Crossman were beyond the rifle pits, hiding behind fallen trees, and, according to one historian, "were firing through small apertures, and took turns in watching the firing of the enemy." A contemporary newspaper report notes that Martin "was armed with a telescopic rifle," and Crossman probably was as well.[15]

Luke Bicknell (memoir, p. 70)

Coming back to the point where I had left the two men I found Crossman with a finger split open by a bullet. He had been firing through a hole in a tree; and the bullet had come along the rifle barrel, split open his finger and passed through his hat as he was taking sight. I told Martin to go to the pit, now, but he begged so hard for one shot more, to avenge his friend's injury . . . for they were messmates and old friends . . . and both men were so sure that it was only a chance shot, that I yielded against my better judgement and allowed him to go up the bank again. He fired his shot and then tumbled down the bank, falling at our feet mortally wounded.

Martin was "wounded by a ball which entered his cheek, knocking out several teeth, and came out at the back of his neck." The sharpshooters exploded in grief and fury.[16]

Luke Bicknell (memoir, p. 70)

[He was] shot through the neck. Some of men in the pit near by came down, and as we washed the blood out of his mouth, and saw that his wound was mortal, we spoke of it as so, thinking him unconscious . . . when he looked up and said "never mind lieutenant, I have wiped out a score of them today."

As the news of Martins fatal hurt spread along our line, the pits began to fairly blaze, and the men exposed themselves recklessly to do all the damage possible to the foe, for Martin was a general favorite.

In a letter to a friend, Private Roland E. Bowen of the Fifteenth Massachusetts recalled the deeds of sharpshooter David Temple, a thirty-five-year-old butcher from Marlboro, and one of the company's original "old gunners":

"Old Dave"

David Temple, a member of the Andrew Sharp Shooters and more commonly known as 'old dave,' is called the best shot in the Company. [He] is a reckless old Cuss and cares nothing for any body. He had been detailed in the Commisary Department for sometime past. Yesterday he volunteered to go over as he says "And kill a few God damned Johnnys in revenge for the death. . . ." So down he goes with two more men, gets the most advanced position he can find and proceeds to give them Hell. He bangs away all day. Both men that go with him get badly wounded. He r[e]turns at night unhurt himself and glorifying over the *fact* that he has caused 20 of the damned Skunks of Hell to have a reckoning with their Eternal Creator. It is my opinion that he can beat Theede Barton [possibly a fellow soldier] in the way of Profanity.[17]

Luke Bicknell (MEMOIR, PP. 70–71)

At this juncture, David Temple, who was serving as brigade butcher appeared on the scene. I don't know, to this day, how he happened to be at Deep Run that day. Hatless, coatless, bare armed, rifle in hand, he asked to be shown the place where Martin fell. Barely stepping behind the tree to load, each time, he stood out in plain sight as he fired, until he had used up a full box of cartridges, when he descended and grimly said as he strode away that he had doubled Martins score. Those who knew how sure he was of a bird on the wing did not much doubt the truth of his statement.

Soon after a flag of truce was sent over by the enemy who proposed a mutual withdrawal of sharpshooters. Gen. Howe agreed to this, and ordered us, at 11 A.M. to abandon our pits and hold ourselves in readiness to answer his further demands.

The captain relieved me at noon next day, and I found the whole company in camp at the end of the pontoon bridge in rear of Howes division. I was very glad of the chance to rest and sleep, for I had not slept for three nights.

Before I was wounded at Antietam I could sleep as soundly, at night, in the midst of a battle as if I were amidst the most peaceful scene. Now a long period of quiet and rest must intervene between each period of excitement and fatigue, and subsequent sleep. Another curious effect of the wound was that I could no longer dodge a bullet, as before, because quite a perceptible interval of time elapsed between the command of my will and the resultant action of my muscles. Both of these effects have proved life long.

Such a period of rest as I needed was not on the programme, for we started at II P.M. that night, on a series of marches which led us finally to the battle-field of Gettysburg.

CHAPTER

GETTYSBURG AND BEYOND

I wondered if this scene were present in the mind of God when he created man.
The dim planets above and all pulseless voiceless nature beneath seemed to unite
with the dead in silent protest; but reason answered, Yes!

—Luke Emerson Bicknell, Gettysburg

After decisive victories at Fredericksburg and Chancellorsville, General Robert
E. Lee invaded Maryland and Pennsylvania. The Confederates hoped to seize
desperately needed supplies, and to demoralize war-weary Northerners and
possibly persuade them to abandon their war effort. Lee's Army of Northern
Virginia marched north and east in early June 1863, the first units splashing
across the Potomac on the 15th. The Army of the Potomac caught up with the
Confederate army near Gettysburg weeks later, just in time to divert an attack
on the Pennsylvania state capital at Harrisburg.[1]

Andrew's Sharpshooters—along with the Second and Sixth Army Corps—
made up the rear guard of the Pennsylvania-bound Union army. The
sharpshooters left Fredericksburg on June 14 and did not enter the fight at
Gettysburg until July 2, the second day of the three-day battle. Lieutenant
Luke Emerson Bicknell's memoir provides most of the surviving details of
Andrew's Sharpshooters' part in the contest.[2] Bicknell was still suffering from
the wounds he had received at Antietam, and Captain William Plumer was
still badly hobbled by the injury he had sustained at Deep Run.

The March

FERDINAND CROSSMAN

Wolf Run Shoals Va June 17 [1863]

Dear Adda

I take this first opportunity I have had since I wrote to Mr Sibley to let you know I am still well. We left Fredericksburg 3 days ago & since then have been on the march, but where we shall stay no one knows now although you will hear before this reaches you.

My finger is getting along first rate. It has not hinderd my keeping up with the 6th Corps Head Quarter teams. How long we shall stay with them I do not know, but I think not but a few days longer.

Lysander [Martin] I have not seen since I wrote to Sibley the morning after he was wounded. They sent him to [Potomac?] Creek Hospital & before we got there on the march they had sent him to Washington so I did not see him. The Surgeon says he will bee well in a few weeks.

I shall send home my hat the first opportunity so you can see how near they came to my head, but they say a miss is as good as a mile. But I had rather have a miss.... When we come to a stop I will give you the particulars of the skirmish & the march but at this time there is no chance to write more or send what I have written....

LUKE BICKNELL (MEMOIR, PP. 71–75)

We marched with the 6th corps until the 17th, not knowing the position of our own [Second] corps. The captain rode nearly all the time, but I determined to keep on foot and with the company as long as possible. My hip and back, for the bullet which smashed my hip, also clipped the back bone as it came out, gave me no rest, day or night. The pain was most tedious when I stopped to rest, and motion, at first, was a relief.

We got out of rations while we were with the 6th corps, and when I asked them for food, Gen. [John] Sedgwick gruffly told me that it was as much as he could do to provide for his own corps, and that we ought to have gone to our own corps before we left the Rappahannock. The 6th corps was at a halt at this time and by dint of much inquiry I found out that the 2nd was supposed to be not far ahead. We did not know what had become of our captain, so I led the company on, thinking it would soon go hard with some farmers stores.

Before we were out of sight of Sedgwicks quarters the men overturned a sutters [sutlers] wagon and filled their haversacks, Sergt. [Samuel] Gilbrath, leading the men in the raid. There was so much riding to and fro and falling in of regiments, before we moved on, that I ordered the men to load, fix bayonets and bring their cartridge boxes to the front. Then I marched on, while aids sped in all directions, ahead of us, and the regiments which had fallen in, stacked arms and broke ranks, like magic. Cartridge boxes, to the front, meant business!

An aid [i.e., aide] galloped furiously ahead of us as we approached the woods which bounded the field where the corps lay, and, a little further on, he stood beside the road with half a dozen men, and soft bread enough for a regiment. The aid urged us to take our fill, saying the whole affair was inexplicable, and much to be regretted, and that our corps was probably but a few miles ahead. General Sedgwick was both a soldier and a gentleman, but he could not control his instinctive aversion to sharpshooting and sharpshooters. When I learned how he finally met his death I ceased to wonder at this.[3]

We found our corps the same day [June 17] at Wolf Run Shoals and marched on with it, through Fairfax, to Centerville. Our division left Centerville, at noon, June 20th, and arrived at Thoroughfare Gap at midnight of the same day. The sharpshooters reported the next morning to General [Joshua T.] Owens, who was across the creek, on the enemy's side, with a small force. He was expecting a cavalry charge up a road which runs near the stream, and wished me to check them as they came on.

I unslung knapsacks and went down the road, a mile, intending to make a running fight of it back through the woods between the road and stream. A cold rain storm setting in, at noon I sent the company back for dinner and their knapsacks, except four men, who staid with me and eat bread and milk at a farm house.

During the afternoon our cavalry scouts reported the enemy advancing, and we went forward again. The enemy settled down and pitched tents on the other side of the woods, so I took supper at the farm house, and ordered breakfast, for four, next morning. We spent the night shivering beside a wall, and, the next morning, I invited three of Gen. Owens' officers to go out to my hotel to breakfast. It was half a mile beyond our picket line, to be sure, but our cavalry videtted [posted ahead as sentries] were out a full mile beyond that, and I was so accustomed to life outside the picket lines that I did not dream of any impropriety in the act. Gen. Owens, however, lectured my companions so severely when we got back, that I countermanded our order for dinner, and settled down to army rations, myself.

We left the Gap the morning of the 25th, the enemy shelling the division, meantime, from their side of the stream, as long as we were in sight. Then they crossed over, and followed on, keeping up a running fight with our rear guard, all day. Except the cavalry, the Sharpshooters were the rear of the rear guard; and the captain, being unable to get a lift as usual, was forced to limp along at the head of his company. We took it easy, for the captains sake, and to avoid the dust, keeping just ahead of the cavalry.

About five P.M. the company was strung along, in a go as you please order, for a quarter of a mile. I was marching at the rear, and finding it pretty close work to keep up, on account of the pain in my hip and back, when the cavalry dashed by us saying that the enemy had come out from a side road and cut them in two and were now chasing them up close. There being a growth of shrub oak one side of the road, I sung out to the sharpshooters to spring into it, and when the cavalry came along, each one select his man, and secure a horse. The rear of the company heard me, and obeyed, but the captain, as the cavalry gave him the situation, sung out, "double quick," and the front of the company heard and followed him.

We waited for the enemys cavalry to ride up and give us their horses, until I feared we should find them in front, and our retreat cut off. Then we hurried ahead and joined the rear guard in camp, after dark, but the captain and his end of the company were missing, so I reported them, absent without leave, being too tired to go to head quarters and explain.

The next day [June 26] we marched in the middle of a regiment; and I thought best to visit head quarters and explain matters that night. My contraband [his African American servant], with all my blankets and rations, was lost with the captain, but, as it happened, many of my warmest friends were in the squad I had left so I suffered no inconvenience on that account.

We marched on with our division, crossing the Potomac at Edwards Ferry, and catching a sight, in the distance, of the chimneys of our old quarters, at Camp Benton, still standing. The captain and his squad rejoined us at Frederick Md. having made a detour through Washington.

My old uniform had suffered so at Deep Run, and I suffered so much while marching hot days, in winter clothing, that I improved the opportunity to go into the city and procure a lighter outfit. I paid out my last cent for it, and then recollected that I had no shoulder straps suitable for such a light coat as I procured. The dealer persuaded me to be content with a strip of gilt braid on each shoulder, saying that he had fixed lots of them so that morning. The only objection to the arrangement was, that as fashions were in the army then, it made me appear as a staff officer, in search of a horse.

On getting back to the company, I found that they had left with the 2nd corps, on a forced march to Uniontown, my contraband alone remaining. Leaving him to follow with blankets and rations as best he could, I pushed on, and overtook the company during the afternoon. That night, at the end of their thirty two, and my thirty six, miles tramp, I sunk down so utterly exhausted that I was unconscious of the care of comrades who made me comfortable for the night.

July 1–2

The Second Corps, under the temporary command of General John Gibbon, arrived late the first day of the battle and settled near Little Round Top, at the south end of the battlefield. Their stay there was brief. Early on July 2, Gibbon's men—including Andrew's Sharpshooters—moved to Cemetery Ridge, roughly in the center of the Union line. Many of the troops sheltered behind a long stone wall that ran part of the length of the line. The far right of the Second Corps line was anchored by Brigadier General Alexander Hays's Third Division.[4]

Bicknell briefly noted Andrew's Sharpshooters' involvement in the fight for the William Bliss barn, a sturdy brick structure in the no-man's-land between the Union and Confederate lines. The fight for the barn was, as one historian puts it, "a protracted skirmish that rose to the level of a small fight within the larger Battle of Gettysburg." Possession of the barn passed back and forth several times until General Hays ordered it burned down.[5]

LUKE BICKNELL (MEMOIR, PP. 75–77)

The next day [June 30] we rested and drew rations. The next, July 1st, the first day of the battle of Gettysburg, I led the company all day, towards the battle field. Many strong men who carried all a soldiers panoply grew suddenly black in the face and fell from the ranks as we hurried on. I had discarded scabbard, pistol, canteen, haversack, all that weighed an ounce; even photographs and last letters from home; and carried only my naked sword. At last the sweet music of sharp cannonading in our immediate front drew a spontaneous cheer from our weary column and, at 9 P.M. I led the sharpshooters into the Peach Orchard in front of Round Top.

Pain, excitement and lack of blankets, made sleep an impossibility; so I rested till chilled, then walked and rested, alternately, till morning. I was profoundly grateful that I had been able to reach the scene; it having been for some time, in fact ever since leaving the Rappahannock, my whole ambition to lead the sharpshooters in one more great battle, and then resign. At light [July 2] we joined our [Second] division which had bivouacked south of the Cemetery on the east side of the Taneytown road.

Here I found my servant who had come up with the wagons during the night. After a hasty breakfast—I had not eaten for 24 hours—I told Gen. Gibbon, who was in command of our division that day, of my physical condition, and my desire to find a location where we could do well in the coming contest, which I expected to be my last battle. The general sent an aid[e] with me to mark the position I should choose, and requested me not to move from it, except at my own discretion, or at his orders.

I selected a position behind a low stone wall, part way down the west slope of Cemetery ridge. Zeiglers Grove and the Cemetery were to my right. The Emmittsburg road wound along at the foot of the slope in my front. An elevation of the ridge, and, further on, Round Top to my left. An apple orchard extended up over the ridge and nearly down to the Taneytown road in my rear. All that I had learned of the art of war convinced me that I had pitched upon the spot that we must hold, and they must take, to win or lose the contest. I knew that the orchard, and ridge, behind us would draw the fire of the enemys artillery over our heads; and that they would be unable to do much damage at the wall I had chosen. So much for looking idly on at Malvern Hills, and Savage Station [during the Seven Days Battles in the Peninsula Campaign].

The enemy occupied beyond the Emmittsburg road in our front with infantry and artillery. We did not break the peace until the 2nd corps moved into position on the ridge, to my left, when I sent five men forward with their skirmishers, to gain a brick barn across the road. The men gained the barn and, from it, harassed the enemys gunners. . . .

Captain William Plumer did not submit a report following the Battle of Gettysburg, and Luke Bicknell's squad engaged as skirmishers, so we know very little about the activities of the company's fourteen or more snipers armed with target rifles. Captain Richard S. Thompson of the nearby Twelfth New Jersey Regiment observed Union snipers firing on the Bliss barn. He assumed the marksmen were Berdan's Sharpshooters. But undoubtedly they were target riflemen from Andrew's Sharpshooters.[6] Captain Thompson recalled:

The enemy's skirmish line was advanced so that this barn was used as a reserve post for their skirmishers. It was also occupied by sharpshooters who, from two openings in the second story of the structure, annoyed our main line and made themselves particularly disagreeable when any mounted officers came within range of their rifles.

During the 2d of July, a detachment of Berdan's sharpshooters, using very heavy, long-range telescopic rifles, with a sort of tripod rest, were placed on our main line with instructions to stop the annoyance. The method adopted was somewhat peculiar. The enemy's sharpshooters soon discovered, not only that we were using rifles that had sufficient range, but also that they were being used with remarkable precision. With a field glass it was easy to observe the effect of this rifle practice. Several men were seen to fall at the openings in the barn, and the enemy's sharpshooters became more and more cautious. At the flash of a rifle on our line they would instantly disappear, and upon the ball passing through the opening as instantly reappear, ready to try a shot or fall back again if a second rifle flashed on our line. To meet these tactics, new methods were adopted by the telescopic riflemen; they formed themselves into squads or partnerships of three, and when the three were ready with correct aim, number one would fire; the enemy would instantly retire from the two openings; then counting "one, two, three," the remaining two partners would fire simultaneously, each at this appointed opening; the ball from number one passing through the opening, the enemy immediately reappeared, too late to see the flash of the second rifles, yet in time to receive their bullets. Alas! how little we thought human life was the stake for which the game was being played.[7]

Captain Benjamin W. Thompson of the 111th New York Infantry also observed a likely member of Andrew's Sharpshooters in front of General Hays' line on July 2.[8]

At sunrise we were marched to our place in line, just in rear of the brow of Cemetery Hill. . . . An incident occurred here which gave me a new idea of the range of the telescope rifle. . . . A sharpshooter had made his burrow behind a stump in front of our regimental line and a few of us who had ventured over there began to question him about his—to me—novel arm. Said he—"Put your field glasses to your eyes—Yes—do you see that single horseman just coming out of the woods which covers the enemy? Well, keep your eyes on him."

He discharged his piece and in a moment that horseman, so far away that we could hardly distinguish him with the naked eye, dropped from his steed with a Yankee bullet in his body.[9]

"The Volley They Gave Us at Antietam
Has Been Returned"

On the third and final day of fighting, Andrew's Sharpshooters split into two groups. One—twenty skirmishers armed with Sharps rifles and led by Lieutenant Bicknell—fought in Ziegler's Grove, roughly eight hundred yards to the right of the center of the Union line. Captain William Plumer led the rest of the company, including the snipers with target rifles, away from the stone wall near Emmitsburg Road to a new position facing the town of Gettysburg. In a letter after the war, Bicknell wrote: "Capt. Plummer took the balance of the company and distributed it in the Cemetery and, I think, also in the grove to my right and around a battery in or near the Taneytown road. He held this position all day. Whether the Sharpshooters held the whole line from the Cemetery to the west end of the grove alone all day in conjunction with the battery [Woodruff's Battery I] spoken of or whether Capt. Plummer, on my right, was mixed in with an infantry line I do not know." Plumer's men were actually detailed to suppress Confederate rifle fire coming from houses at the edge of Gettysburg.[10]

LUKE BICKNELL (MEMOIR, PP. 78–80)

The next morning our Captain who had been in ambulance appeared at the wall and assumed command of the company. I told him of Gen. Gibbons orders, but when in about an hour after the general commanding the right of the 2nd corps [Brigadier General Alexander Hays, Second Corps, Third Division] appeared and politely requested that the sharpshooters would occupy the grove to our right and relieve his men from a most annoying fire from rifle pits in his front, the captain ordered me to take twenty men and go with the general. I remonstrated and quoted Gen. Gibbons order, in vain. He allowed me to pick my twenty men and of course I took Sergt. [Samuel] Gilbreth and a good many of my especial favorites along.[11]

Our line had been entirely driven from the grove. I entered it by a ravine back of the ridge and we worked our way forward from rock to rock and tree to tree until we had fought our way through the grove [Ziegler's Grove] and looked down into the rifle pits, and Gettysburg, behind them. We finally occupied a knoll to the right of the ravine, and the ridge to its left, as well as the ravine. I found we could hold it as well as a brigade of infantry, even better, but we could not hope to do more than hold the enemy down in their pits, for they were evidently our old antagonists at Deep Run.

By the time that we had gained all we could hope to. I was so exhausted that I lay down beside a rock in the ravine where I could see most of the men at their stations. I noticed that [Sanford K.] Fuller, close to me, exposed his ankle, as he knelt, and cautioned him about it. He did not heed the caution, in fact rather resented my well meant advice; and received a shot through the ankle, in a few minutes, from which he afterwards died.[12] It was close work, and the men who held the pits hour after hour got in their work at a terrible sacrifice of life. The heavy dead line of infantry in our front showed that our line had not been driven back into, and out of the grove, without a most gallant resistance. About noon I saw the aid[e] Gen. Gibbon had sent with me the day before leading the rest of the sharpshooters towards the Cemetery, which lay across the Taneytown road to my right.

When the artillery duel which preceded the grand charge [Pickett's Charge] was fairly opened, both sides seemed to consider sharpshooting as too insignificant to be continued in the presence of the greater work of death, and the ravine where I was gradually filled with men who sought its seeming shelter. Its security was only seeming, as every moment proved, but still they

Figure 12. Luke Emerson Bicknell. c. 1863.
Courtesy of Evangeline (Bicknell) Dollemore.

came, and threw themselves face downwards and covered their ears, to shut out horrible sights and sounds.

Two of our cassions just back of the grove exploded in quick succession; there was no break in the continuous roar, and shower of shot and shell around me; the ground reeled and trembled so that men staggered as they walked. I reclined on the sward beside my rock, as calm as if the air was only filled with falling blossoms. This was what I had marched on many a weary day and night to find, and I was, simply, supremely content to be here, at last.

Mid-afternoon on July 3, toward the end of the massive Confederate barrage, Brigadier General Alexander Hays appeared in Ziegler's Grove and began organizing the troops scattered there to meet the coming assault. Luke Bicknell's description of Hays is probably not exaggerated. The general was intense and flamboyant: "a hot-headed and hard-drinking forty-four year old who was most at home during a fight." His men in the Third Division of the Second Corps reportedly idolized him.[13]

Late in the afternoon, the Eighth Ohio Regiment began what would become a devastating flank attack on the left of the Confederate line. General Hays soon added two New York regiments and Andrew's Sharpshooters to the left of the Ohio men.[14] In 1884, Bicknell described the sharpshooters' part in the battle: "When Pickett drove a hole into the 2d Corps, we swung down on the left flank of his supports, and when [A. P.] Hill's men would, in turn, crush in the flank of our line, at the [Bryan] lane, our artillery held them back with grape and canister."[15] He expressed much more passion when, with his wartime diary and letters at his elbow, he penned his private recollections.

LUKE BICKNELL (MEMOIR, PP. 80–95)

Finally, a general . . . rode into the grove and halted at the foot of the ridge . . . beckoning me. I do not remember his name now, if I knew it then, but he wore a flannel shirt, which was opened and turned back till a hairy breast and muscular throat were fully exposed. . . . An orderly who followed was struck by a shell and died as I took him from his horse and laid him on the sward. I buckled his revolver around me, and hitched his horse to a tree. A tiara of shells burst around my head as I finished. When I emerged from the cloud of smoke and dust the general, noticing my fatigue, beckoned me to him and handed me a full canteen of whiskey. I coolly and deliberately drank half its contents.

The fire of our guns began to slacken as the liquor I had drank began to get in its work. I went up on the ridge and carefully studied the whole scene

in front. Nothing but lines of skirmishers lying down; and the opposite slope
of Seminary ridge, covered with guns, almost idle, but few men among the
thousands who lay along the walls and breastworks an hour before, to be
seen now.

I came down and described the situation to the general. He proposed that
I should clear the grove of the men who had sought its shelter, sending men
whose position in line was close at hand to their places, and the rest, up on
the ridge, where he would form them in line. I went around touching each
man lightly with my sword if he lay on his face. All the living that I touched
sprang quickly to their feet and obeyed my orders with a soldiers promptness.

At last the ravine was cleared of all but the dead and the sharpshooters;
and we had some 200 men in line on the crest to the right of a lane [Bryan
Lane] which ran down from the grove to the Emmittsburg road. I went up
on the crest again and saw that the charging line was coming on, well down
the opposite slope already, and extending as far to the right and left as my eye
could reach.

Again, we had a line extending to my left along Cemetery ridge, but not in
its old strength, and I trembled for the result. The general, I have mentioned,
was putting his picked up line through the manual of arms, [near the Bryan
House] to steady and cool them. I shouted "sharpshooters, rally on the left"
and went down in to the ravine to call in the men there. I had not time to get
the men, on the knoll between the ravine and Taneytown road, and in fact I
did not need them for my purpose, which was to pick off general officers as
their lines approached. The sharpshooters promised me to hold their fire for
my order and I directed them to fire all together at whoever I pointed with
my sword.

Their charging lines came steadily, swiftly on, unchecked, unbroken by the
storm of shot and shell our batteries hurled against them. At first the direction taken by the supporting lines indicated that the heaviest blow would fall
upon the 3rd corps, but, as they crossed the Emmittsburg road, under cover
of the smoke of the fire their front line now began to pour out, the supports
concentrated swiftly upon the 2nd [General John Gibbon's] corps, and their
[the Confederates'] line to my far left, was broken by a right oblique movement, as ours was broken at Antietam.

The advance lines of the 2nd corps crumbled before their column like a
rope of sand. In my eagerness to note the further result I stepped forward of
our line and glanced along the line of faces. Every lip compressed to white-
ness, every feature set like granite! I have seen this look before and at once
know that they will die but will not be driven. I wonder if it is so where the

column and the center of the 2nd corps are now covered by one dense, common cloud of smoke.

Suddenly, with a resounding crash, the cloud of smoke is turned to flame enveloping their column, and the volley they gave us at Antietam has been returned. They reel, recoil, recover and begin to drift towards us. It is not so much a regular movement as it is a swift rush of their rear lines to pass behind their front men, and throw themselves in contact with our line nearer and nearer to my position. How I wish now that I had been allowed to stay where I first put the company, in the present very center of it.

Finally a mounted officer gallantly leading in his men comes within range and even as I point to him the ready rifles leap to each shoulder and the brave leader falls. The men, some of whom are bleeding, look at me imploringly and reproachfully when they have loaded for it seems a crime to stand idle where each shot would tell; but I set my lips and shake my head and they stand this highest test of discipline and obey.

It seems as if the smoke which now envelopes all to the left of the lane would never part or lift again, but, at length, it does part before a brigade of the enemy with their general riding in their midst. He halts, on the east side of a log house standing beside the lane, to gather his lines for the rush that is to carry them over the ridge. The rifles of my men already cover him and as I nod to them they fire; and his men gather around him and take him from his horse and steady him up beside it. In vain does leader after leader spring forward to bring order out of the confusion in the brigade. My men now loading and firing at will select such for their aim; and the brigade becomes more and more food for the fire of our line, as the rear regiments press forward.

And now . . . our General [Hays] with the bare breast . . . the general who accosted me in the ravine, appears again and gives the order "left wheel, charge bayonets, and give them hell." We rush down to the [Bryan] lane and pour a flank fire into the crowded mass upon its opposite side; who crowd to the fence and pour it back at us, muzzle to muzzle. I can now see below the smoke clear up to the apple trees back of the wall where I first located. We no longer hold the slope behind the wall alone. It is covered with a mingled mass of blue and gray, lines wedged into each other like the teeth of two gigantic saw blades, struggling in a hand to hand conflict around the silent guns.

At the head of the lane, where our line has not been pushed back from the wall, two guns [from Woodruff's battery] are being hurried into position. I turn to my right and see that the enemy are crossing the lane where the Emmittsburg road cuts it, and are already forming a line and firing into our flank and rear. I run along our line towards the crest of the ridge until I find a Major. He helps me draw our line back a little towards the ridge, so that we are out of the way of the guns at the head of the lane.

The men step backwards, loading and firing still, and the enemy pour over into the lane and choke it, firing from the fence we had left. The two guns pour showers of grape and canister down the lane until there are but few left to fire on us. Again the enemy press forward and crowd the lane, and stand upon the heaps of dead to fire at us. They even mount the fence, intent upon getting at us, when again the two guns pour their double charges of grape down the lane and the grand charge is finished. . . .

Our guns pursued the retreating men with grape and canister and many threw themselves behind a fence beyond the Emmittsburg road. I took five men and, working my way around behind them, sent in one hundred and thirty prisoners, who surrendered with their Colonel without a struggle.[16] I then went along the fence till I was well in front of the 2nd Corps and tried to take some more men prisoners who were lying behind the same fence, but they showed fight, and I soon engaged in a hand to hand conflict in which I knocked away a loaded gun as it was being fired at my breast, and disarmed my antagonist with my sword.

[Alfred A.] Batchelder who was with me received a wound in the shoulder from which he afterwards died, and a skirmish line advancing from a brigade which the enemy had thrown in to cover the retreat, we were driven back to our own lines.[17] We loaded and fired with great rapidity and fatal effect, but they were altogether too many for us. We scattered as we ran back, and the enemy concentrated their fire upon me, until I threw up my arms and fell forward as if shot dead; still some distance from my lines. I laid here until a little rested, for I had used up the strength of the whiskey I had taken. Then I got up and ran in, in zigzags, to our lines, the 2nd division rising to its feet and cheering me on as I ran.

My ruse had deceived friend and foe alike. Seargt. Gilbrath had assembled the survivors of our little band about him in the grove, as he had the survivors of the volley at Antietam, and they were speaking of the coincidence, when my appearance amongst them put a stop to their philosophizing. We had but six cartridges left amongst us all, and could not get a new supply till night; so I led the men back to the Taneytown road. The horse I had hitched in the grove had passed unscathed through it all, and I took him along to ride, in case we had to march that night.

We were soon busy in plain sight of Gen. [George] Meade's head quarters in making coffee, having fasted since morning. My servant, a genuine black diamond, saw us; and I soon had something more staple inside than the whiskey that had carried me through the charge. He had his story of the day to tell. Of how as he lay at the roots of a tree, the bottom of a pile of darkeys, a shell had gone, most clean through the top man.

An aid[e] rode up and inquired why we had left the line. He took the horse away, and soon returned saying that Gen. Meade had ordered an advance on Seminary ridge, and that I was to lead the right of the skirmish line with the sharpshooters. He said I would be furnished with ammunition in the grove. We went back to the ravine, and soon a squad of cavalry who used Sharps Carbines supplied us with ten rounds apiece from their cartridge boxes.

While waiting in the grove I sent for an officer in the 2nd corps, in whose judgement and patriotism I had the greatest confidence, and telling him what I had seen while I was out in front, taking prisoners, convinced that we were about to run our heads into a hornets nest and, at the best, throw away the fruits of the victory we had gained. He urged it as my duty to insist on a personal interview with General Meade. When the aid[e] returned with the squad of cavalry I did so.

The general listened closely and patiently to all I had to say and checked the murmur of dissent and disapproval which arose from many of the officers as I concluded. He rebuked a Colonel who wished to take my place and lead, on the right, with his regiment, and said that I had shown greater bravery in insisting on speaking my convictions to him, than I should, to have simply obeyed without a word. He said that he should closely watch the effect produced on the enemy by the advance of the skirmish line, and that if it appeared, as I supposed, that they were ready to receive an assault, our main line would not be ordered forward, and I was to be content with advancing our skirmish line to a point, desirable for a picket line, that night. But, before I came back in, he wished me to relieve the 2nd corps from the annoyance of a line of men who occupied a stone wall in their front. He, at first, supposed these to be a lot of men who had halted here as they retreated, but when I told him that it was a regular officered organization, he ordered part of a regiment, detailed, and, with their officers, placed under my orders. I suppose the force to have been that referred to in history as "the shattered remnant of Wright's Georgia Brigade" and they certainly were the same men who had driven me from the field after the assault.

I placed the men who had been added to my squad on my right, and at 5 P.M. moved out of the grove and to the foot of the slope without deploying. At this moment the same Aid[e] I have referred to overtook me and said that Gen. Meade desired to avoid another engagement, that night, and trusted to my discretion to manage the affair so that the result would be in accordance with his wishes. I can see now, that if I had kept quiet I should have got this same order, all the same, at the same moment. Ten cartridges apiece [didn't] mean Seminary ridge nor half way there. But, when I insisted on the interview, I didn't know but what we were to have a box full apiece.

I waited till the movement was taken up and skirmishers thrown out along the entire front of the 2nd Corps, when I advanced to the Emmittsburg road. Two men from the regiment had been struck as we advanced, and they were nervous about standing as a target for the men in the rifle pits across the road. I had most of them lay down in the road, which had a slight bank, and told them to open fire on the pits in this position. The rest I sent down the lane to crawl along the fence and put in a flank fire upon the pits. It was not any use to charge the pits, for they had a strong line of supports, as well as artillery, in their rear. I wished however to pass their flank without being annoyed by their fire. Then I crossed the lane, to the left, with my fourteen sharpshooters, deployed, and connected with the right of the 15th Mass which had advanced as skirmishers in front of the 2nd corps.

Up to this time I had been so dilatory in all my movements that I have no doubt that in the main line, back of me, which was all impatient to follow, and which consisted largely of men who had arrived just in season to see the enemys coat tails, I had been cursed, long and loud, as a coward.

When I had crossed the lane I had a fine view of an extended and animated scene. Our main line along the ridge was standing ready dressed for the charge. Shells were coursing back and forth overhead along the center of both armies. As far to the right, as the Seminary itself, the enemy was showing double and triple lines. In my front he was moving a long line part way down the slope, to the support of his advanced brigade; and the edge of his woods, beyond, fairly bristled with bayonets. To the left, only, did he show weakness. There, he advanced no line to the support of a battery, which was rapidly being driven back.

It was just as I had supposed. He had concentrated his forces to repulse an expected, and desired, charge upon his center. If Gen. Meade wished to try it, it was time for the main line to be coming on. I consulted with the officer in charge of the 15th, and ordered a halt.

The brigade in our front was firing rapidly, and wild. Evidently, far from cool, they were filling the air overhead with bullets. Protected by the fire of the 15th, I ran down with the sharpshooters to a fence close in their front, their skirmishers having been drawn in. Throwing ourselves flat behind the fence and selecting officers as much as possible, we poured in a volley from the lower rail which seemed to set them wilder than ever. Directing the men to husband their cartridges, with a view of holding the position till dark, I looked back to our line, and saw that it had disappeared, as if by magic, and concluded that the bullets passing high over our heads must be dropping, back there, somewhere.

One by one, as their ammunition gave out, the men stole back to the grove till finally I was left alone. I then approached the rifle pits to see how it fared with the men from the regiment I had left around them. My approach drew out so hot and personal a fire from the pits that I sheered off without opening communication. I saw that I should lose many men if I withdrew them now; it would be better to let them lay there till dark, when, I supposed, their own officers would withdraw them.

Bicknell's story about the wounded general in the following passage is probably a fabrication. It bears a striking similarity to the story of Confederate General Lewis Armistead, who was wounded almost a half mile south of Andrew's Sharpshooters' position in the battle. Or perhaps Bicknell's memory had faded and the encounter had involved a lower-ranking Confederate officer.[18]

I have already mentioned a log house standing on the south side of the [Bryan] lane. As I came in I found a dying Confederate general on the north side of it. He begged me to take him inside our lines to die, offering me his gold watch, which I put back into his pocket, his fingers already wandering in a vain effort to accomplish the task. I told him that my duty would not allow me to attend to his request, and his effort to buy me, caused me to forget his condition, and to utter words of reproach. He begged my pardon, and said he bitterly regretted that he had ever raised his hand against his country, and hoped that there would be no more fighting. He spoke of Gen. Hancock, and other personal acquaintances fighting on our side, and wished that he could see them before he died. I reported his name, condition and wishes, to officers of the 2nd corps and he was soon brought in.

Seargt. Gilbrath, who had returned before me had brought in a young Confederate officer who fell in the lane gallantly leading on his men in the last desperate rush. We had made him as comfortable as possible, and, at his request, had planted the stars and stripes at his side. Just before he died he thanked us all in well chosen words for our care, and declared that approaching death had enlarged his vision so that he saw the South was in the wrong. That he saw, as if it already were, the star spangled banner floating again over the whole United States. At last, raising his hand to heaven by a mighty effort, he thanked God that he had been struck down now, instead of being left to strike another blow against the right; and while the words still trembled on his lips, his spirit took [its] flight, while, to us standing uncovered around, heaven's gates swung wide open for a moment.

About 9 o'clock an Aid[e] said I was wanted again. I followed him to where the general [Hays] who had begged our services that morning was standing waiting to thank the sharpshooters for their services during the day, and by order of Gen. Meade to thank me for the manner in which I had carried out his wishes in my last duty. He then inquired if it were not time for me to bring in the men I had left around the rifle pits.

I had forgotten that sharpshooters, alone, are privileged to leave their position as darkness gathers around them. As I walked down the slope it brought to mind places traversed, at this hour, in childhood. With something of the old dread oppressing me I sought to penetrate the gloom beyond and learn what terrible imminent danger it concealed. Something of this same feeling shared by both picket lines made my mission a very delicate one. As I picked my way amongst the fallen, the moans of the dying rose from all around and filled the air. I wondered if this scene were present in the mind of God when he created man. The dim planets above and all pulseless voiceless nature beneath seemed to unite with the dead in silent protest; but reason answered, Yes! It must be his will that all created things that think, and act at will, should differ and contend, else it had not been so. Had you been Southern born and taught you would have been watching from the opposite heights tonight.

When I returned the men reported that the rest of the company under charge of the Orderly [Oscar Clement] were down by the Taneytown road. We took up the body of [George P.] Roundy and joined them.[19] Roundey had been our teamster as long as we had a team and afterwards had served the brigade in the same capacity until our last march. He had marched to Gettysburg with his bleeding feet bound up in rags in lieu of shoes which had given out. I had stationed him on the knoll between the ravine and the road, as being the safer place, and cautioned his comrades to hold him back and look to his safety. From this position he had seen me go down to the line into the thick of it, and calling on his comrades to follow, he had reached the crest and was searching for us in the boiling hell beneath, when he was seen to fall.

He had ever been my friend, and they laid him by my side as he would have chosen to lay in life, next to the enemy. At frequent intervals the men in the rifle pits sent spiteful vollies through the ravine, and, in the morning, it was seen that his body had been a needed bulwark for me during the night.

The sharpshooters had made a grand record this day. With timely help from the artillery at the Cemetery during the charge, the company had held at bay ten times our numbers along a line extending from the Cemetery itself to the ridge west of the ravine. We had rendered timely assistance in repelling the charge, and to say nothing of the prisoners taken, or of our part in the demonstration afterwards, they well deserved the commendation they had received. As usual, the bloodiest work had fallen to my share. The captain and orderly, in charge of the major part of the company, in the Cemetery, had lost but one man, killed, two fatally wounded.[20]

The next day, July 4th, the enemy having abandoned the rifle pits near the grove, we reoccupied our first chosen position at the stone wall. I was sitting on an ammunition box chatting with a group of officers who reclined around me, when two men advanced, together, to the run between the two heights, and one, raising his rifle, put a bullet through the branches of the apple tree under which I sat. His next shot went in to the body of the tree and his next clipped the hair over my ear as smooth as a razor could have done the job. I had not fired at a man since the battle of Antietam, but did not feel at liberty to decline this personal challenge. I took a Sharpes Rifle, rested on the wall, aimed at a tall blasted pine behind him on the ridge, and dropped him at the first shot. As a question of skill, however, his was the best shooting, for he fired from the shoulder.

The next morning we buried Roundy in the ravine, marking his resting place. The men all waited for me to say a word as we stood around his open grave, but I could not.[21]

Luke Bicknell led Andrew's Sharpshooters during the pursuit of the retreating Confederate Army, but his thoughts clearly were on resigning from the army:

Now that the excitement of the battle was over I could scarcely drag my sore and aching limbs along and was forced to ride in an ambulance until we reached Williamsport. I heartily detested this method of getting along being strongly of the opinion that officers who could not march had better resign and leave the ambulances for the sick and wounded soldiers. . . .

While we were at Williamsport I learned that Governor [John A.] Andrew had sent out a First Lieutenants commission to Mr. Clemans [Clements], our orderly, who would not accept it, or muster, as long as it would place him in command over me; but if the captain would resign, and the Governor commission me as Captain, he would be happy to muster and attend to the company until I could get rested up in hospital.

I footed it to Sandy Hook, sauntering along and resting as I needed, the company getting in a day ahead of me. As I journeyed I thought it all over. I did not believe I could rest up so as to be fit for marching again. Pride and common sense said get out of the way of the man whom your comrades and the Governor of your state have united in preferring above you, You have done your part well, till now, don't stay and spoil your record. The decision made I wrote and sent in my resignation the night I reached our camp at, or near, Sandy Hook.

Next morning I was summoned to corps head quarters, where I found a large number of general officers, who were kind enough to join in hoping that I would withdraw my resignation, and take a rest in hospital while the Governor's mistake, as they termed it, could be rectified. They added so many compliments, and put it so strongly to me as, a duty to the cause, that I should continue to put in practice the special knowledge of sharpshooting I had gained; that I could but offer to leave it to the corps surgeon who was present. As soon as I disrobed the surgeon exclaimed that the youngest soldier in the service would die, gray headed, before I should be fit to march again, so he made out my discharge.

While waiting at Harpers Ferry for the train to Washington, I sat on the balcony of a house while the corps marched past; receiving many a friendly salute, and the honor of a shoulder arms from the sharpshooters, as they passed. My heart was like lead in my bosom, and my eyes dim with tears, as I watched their receding banners.

One of those badly wounded at Gettysburg was Brigadier General John Gibbon, who took a bullet just behind his left shoulder. Gibbon did not return to the Second Division, Second Corps until April 1864. Andrew's Sharpshooters thereby lost not only another patron and protector, but also much of their independent status. In August 1863, Andrew's Sharpshooters were attached to the Twentieth Massachusetts Infantry.[22] But they seem to have retained some degree of autonomy. John Gardner Perry, a surgeon with the Twentieth Massachusetts, noted that "the sharpshooters . . . are not under its absolute control. They form an independent organization, going where they can most injure the enemy." Luke Emerson Bicknell insisted that the unit "still retained . . . its individuality as a company, and was led, to the end of the war, by men who joined it at the start [such as Isaac Mudgett, who was captain until August 1864]."[23]

From mid-July 1863 to the end of Andrew's Sharpshooters' tour of duty in the fall of 1864, the only surviving participant's account of the company's actions is that of the Sutton farmer, Ferdinand Crossman. Crossman fell ill in July and was hospitalized until March 1864, so the record for this period is quite thin.

FERDINAND CROSSMAN

Sandy Hook MD, July 17th /63

Dear Adda,

I take my first opportunity to write you a few lines to let you know I am still alive & like to live.

I have passed though all the Battles & skirmishes safe so far. We have succeeded in driving the Rebs from Maryland, only what we have killed & taken prisoners.

I have been sick since the 9th but not so as to prevent my keeping up with the army & Company until the Enemy had crossed the Potomac. The next day I fell out the ranks & did not join them until last night. I was only 1 day behind.

I have had a bad Bowell complaint & vomiting & I am verry weak. I do not think I shall leave here until I get rested and stronger. I have sent for Dr Clark. He was to Harpers Ferry yesterday but I could not get across the pontoon Bridge as the Cavalry were crossing (Sandy Hook is only 1½ miles from Harpers Ferry). The Company have been verry kind to me on the march carrying my Gun when I was tired out. One of the non commishions officer helped me along & staid with me when I fell out.

If you have any money you had better keep it until you hear from me as I have only a little left. I have bought my meals nearly all the time. It has been rather expensive, but I could not eat army rations & keep up. If I keep up with the Company I shall not want any as I can get all I want & not run the risk of loosing it by mail. . . .

I have received nearly or quite all your letters [and] the one with the intelligence of Lysanders death the 8th or 9th. I little expected to hear sad news of him. Give my respect to his folks. Tell them the Company feel his loss. . . . I learned last night Alfred [Batchelor] was dead. He died in Baltimore the 9th. The rest of our wounded are doing well.

You want to know the reason I cannot write as often as others. When in camp I have *more* time, but when on the march & near the Enemy the Sharpshooters always go immediately to the extreme front, so I do not have a chance to write or know when the mail goes, but after this you will hear from me often & when I have a chance I will give you some of the particulars of the march. . . .

You must not think I am *verry sick* for I walked 9 miles yesterday.

I am only weak & tired out. . . .

Hospital Harpers Ferry Va Aug 1st [1863]

Dear Adda,

I take the present opportunity to write a few lines. . . . I am feeling better this morning than any time since I came here. I think I have been quite sick some of the time. If I can only get an appetite I think I shall pick up slowly but my appetite is verry poor. I could get a plenty to eat if I could only eat it. I guess it wants *you* to cook it for me. . . .

You had better send the money if you have any by John Putnam or bring it *Yourself* if you want to come & see me & the country, as there is no prospect of my getting home at present. . . . I should like to have you take care of me a few weeks & it might do you good as it is verry Healthy country here. . . . We can get a room in a private house here for a few weeks I think for a fair price. Bring a bottle of Wine if possible. . . .

Crossman's wife, Adelaide, did visit, and returned home pregnant. He did not return to the company until March 1864.

John Smith's Tale

In August 1863, Andrew's Sharpshooters executed a fellow rifleman convicted of desertion. Earlier, in the winter of 1862–63, morale in the Union army camped in Falmouth had been low, and the rate of desertion high. One of those who deserted was John Smith (probably a pseudonym). Smith had enlisted in Boston at the end of November, and had been with Andrew's Sharpshooters only a short time.[24] A Boston newspaper recounted his fate.

BOSTON JOURNAL, SEPTEMBER 1, 1863

Last Friday, [August 29] . . . Wm. H. Hill of Co. K, 20th Massachusetts Regiment, and John Smith of the first company of Andrew (Mass.) Sharpshooters, were shot near the headquarters of the Second Army Corps in Virginia for desertion. . . .

John Smith, according to the account of himself, was a native of Philadelphia, was a tailor by trade, and resided in Boston, Mass., when the war broke out. He was 37 years of age last February. Smith was a married man, but had no children. His father and five brothers are living, some of the latter being in the service. He enlisted in Captain Plummer's company of Andrew Sharpshooters about the 1st of December, 1862. He said that he was in the battle of Fredericksburg, "and did my duty, as the officers will say at any time."

About the middle of January, 1863, he deserted his company, which was then at Falmouth, attached to the 15th Massachusetts. He said that large numbers were deserting about that time, and when he left his company he did not think of the consequences. The morning that he deserted he fell into the company of some men who had liquor. He drank to excess, and while intoxicated said that he should like to get home, when his new friends answered that that was easy enough, for all that he had got to do was to start now he had the chance. He said that the men were unknown to him, and even if he knew them he would not expose them. When he reached home he did not feel satisfied, and felt that he ought to get back to the army again, and had made up his mind to re-enter the service by joining Col.[Jones] Frankle's artillery regiment [Second Massachusetts Heavy Artillery], as he had a particular friend there. This friend advised him not to enlist at that time. . . .

About this time, Mr. William Ayers, a carpenter, . . . was drafted. He met Smith, and proposed paying him the sum of three hundred dollars as a substitute, preferring to do this to going to the substitute office. Smith said after some persuasion he took the money and agreed to go as a substitute, though he did not want to go as such. He gave his name as Thomas Waters. He said that his intentions were good at the time; but they (the officers) do not look at it in that way. He at once applied to Col. Frankle to be mustered into his regiment, and the Colonel gave him a note to the Provost Marshal General, making the request, which . . . [the] Provost Marshal . . . , August 3, endorsed. Stating that Waters (or Smith) appeared worthy and deserving, and has conducted himself well since his enlistment. . . . Accordingly, on 8th August, Smith and about one hundred others started for the Army of the Potomac, with orders to report to the Nineteenth Massachusetts Regiment; but to his surprise he found himself face to face with his old comrades, the company of Andrew Sharpshooters. . . . He was immediately recognized and arrested, the Lieutenant [Oscar H. Clement] of the Sharpshooters saying that he had no doubt all would be right, but that he wanted him back to his old company.

Smith said that when he deserted he went to Boston to his friends, and remained there up to the time of his coming away as a substitute; that no one interfered with him, and that no one said a word to him about his desertion, and that he had no fear of being arrested as a deserter. Officers of Smith's regiment say that he deserted several times. He had $300 when arrested, which he wished sent back to Mr. Ayers, whose substitute Smith had engaged him to be, but the government took possession of the amount. . . .

The execution took place . . . in front of the Division headquarters, at three o'clock in the afternoon. The preparations were of the usual character. The condemned men were taken from their prison, an old barn—the Second Corps having been previously disposed so as to form three sides of a square—and marched to the open side of the square, where their graves were already dug, and near which their coffins were placed. A Sergeant and sixteen men of the Andrew Sharpshooters, commanded by Lieut. Back, formed the firing party.

The men walked to the place of execution with slow and steady steps. Rev. Mr. Collins of the 72d Pennsylvania volunteers attended the condemned in their hour of extremity. The religious services being over and the last farewells being expressed, the men were blindfolded and knelt before their coffins, when Lieut. Black [?] shook them by the hand and hastily turned a few paces to the left, at the same time giving the command, "Ready, aim," and then instantly, before the word "fire" could be given, the rifles had belched forth their contents in one report, and the same instant two unfortunate men fell forward, Smith on the left and Hill on the right. The former lay motionless on his back, at full length, with his arms partly folded over his breast; the mouth opened and shut a few times, a heave and a sigh followed, and he was dead. Between the time Lieut. Black shook him by the hand and the firing of the volley he raised both his arms to Heaven and casting up his face, exclaimed twice, "Oh God have mercy upon us!" Hill said nothing.[25]

The Murder of Thomas McKay

In early October 1863, Andrew's Sharpshooters' Lieutenant Oscar H. Clement, a young shoemaker from Stoneham, was implicated in the killing of Captain Thomas McKay of Company F, Twentieth Massachusetts. Regimental Surgeon John Gardner Perry recalled the incident:

Our [Second] corps was encamped in a thick wood within a few miles of Culpeper. . . . On the evening of October 5th, taps had sounded in the Twentieth Massachusetts, lights were out, every man was in his tent, and the silence of the night was broken only by the wind which swept fitfully through the pines. Only the officer of the day and I were in camp, the others being on a visit to another regiment. And the soft little glimmer of light which shone forth in the prevailing darkness came from the tent outside of which Captain McKay and I were seated. . . . The Captain had enlisted as a private when the regiment was first organized, and by his intelligence, bravery, and good fellowship had reached his present rank. Company F, which he commanded, was made up of the worst elements in the regiment. . . .

We sat talking of the incessant delays in hostilities, when a shout interrupted us, followed by yells and drunken laughter.

"The fellows in our rear," I said, after a moment's pause; but the Captain's face was anxious.

"No," he answered, "those are my men; they are drunk and quarrelsome; something tells me there is trouble brewing to-night; ever since I punished the ringleaders in those rows they have been sullen and out of temper. In the drill this afternoon I did not like their mood," and asking me to stand ready in case of need, he left and sauntered towards the company's tent.

I heard the Captain order his men to their quarters, but in so calm a voice that it seemed to me he dealt too gently with the brutes; and on the instant there was a shot and then a moan. I reached the spot in time to see the Captain leap into the air and fall, and to hear him cry, "Doctor, I am murdered!"

By the flickering light of the same little candle by which we had just sat, we bore him into the tent; but he was dead when we reached it. . . .

Instantly the sergeant, then aroused, ordered the men of the Captain's company into line; the officers were sent for, and, on their quick return, the roll was called, and every gun examined. Every man was present, and each had his gun, but many of them were so drunk they could barely stand. Those who were sufficiently sober knew that they stood not only in the presence of a crime, but of their murdered captain, whose body was now stretched upon the ground before them.[26]

Suspicion first fell upon an "Italian boy," who was a "raw recruit" and whose rifle had been fired moments earlier. But the officers judged the boy innocent and agreed that someone had taken the young private's gun while he slept. The next day, Perry reported, McKay's company was subjected to an unusual ritual:

After long deliberation it was decided that the men of Company F should march into the tent one by one, kneel, kiss the Bible, and, with one hand on the heart of the murdered man, each should swear before God that he was innocent of all implication in the crime. . . .

[E]ach man faced the ordeal without flinching, with no sign of guilt; and many bore themselves with the dignity of honest freedom. . . . The experiment was a failure, and hours passed in which all means to discover the assassin were fruitlessly tried. Even the lawless men of the Captain's company were shocked into good behavior, and in their bearing expressed respect and love for their dead commander. Indeed, the Captain's death has cast a deep gloom over the entire regiment. The old Twentieth, which has so long borne the name of "Gallant," now bears the burden of this stigma.[27]

Suspicion next fell—briefly—on another recruit who deserted two days after
the shooting. Rewards were offered and detectives hired. Ultimately Surgeon
Perry and others deduced that the killer was Andrew's Sharpshooters' First
Lieutenant Oscar Clement. Clement had faced court-martial in late September for "conduct prejudicial to good order and discipline," and he was
formally dismissed from the service the morning of McKay's murder.[28] Perry
recounts:

The sergeant and I carefully watched the placing of the Captain's body in an
ambulance bound for Alexandria, where the remains would be embalmed
before the journey home. . . .

As we were about to start we saw a stranger in officer's uniform approaching us, who asked where he could find the officer in command of the regiment. The Major, who happened to be near, heard the question, and said,
"What is your business with me?"

"I hail from the same place as the Captain who was killed last night," answered the man. "I've served my time and am on my way home, and, if you
like, will take charge of the body and see that it arrives safely."

The Major seemed interested. It seemed a most fortunate arrangement. . . .
A sufficient sum of money was raised to cover all expenses, as well as to rec-
ompense the man for his trouble, and the ambulance, with its solitary burden,
was delivered into his hands to begin the long and tedious journey towards
the New England town.[29]

Dr. Perry marched part of the way with the ambulance.

Walking by the side of the vehicle was the Captain's friend [Clement], who,
seeing that he was recognized, joined me. He told me that he had served his
time, was sick and tired of the life, and glad enough to go home. The man's
voice was sullen, and his head hung forward and down.

A noise in the ambulance turned my attention to a water-cask, which I
saw had broken loose, and was rolling over the body.

"Fasten that cask, will you," I said to the man at my side, "or it will injure
the Captain's body."

"D— the Captain!" came like a flash from the lips of the man; but with
an instantaneous glance at me he mumbled: "Oh, what did you say, Doc?
Oh, the water-cask! Yes, I'll fix it"; and he jumped inside of the wagon and
fastened the keg in its place.

This oath, flung out in hate and scorn from the lifelong friend and neigh-
bor of the Captain, was startling to say the least. I turned and looked the man

well over. The more I looked, the more I shrank from something despicable in his gait and aspect; a sneak, and a cowardly bully, I'll be bound, I thought. . . .

As soon as possible the circumstance [was] reported to the officer in charge, but although it was certainly considered suspicious, there did not seem sufficient evidence to act upon.[30]

Letters from McKay's fiancée pointed to a possible motive for the killing:

Some time ago she had refused his [Clement's] offer of marriage and, when he heard of her engagement to the Captain, he swore he would kill him. . . . The contents of the letter soon spread among the men of the regiment, and those concerned in the drunken brawl on the night of the murder finally confessed that the man who traveled from camp with the dead captain was the same who gave them whiskey the night he was shot; that this man did his best to incite them to the murder, and, when he failed in this, grabbed the boy's gun, crouched in the bushes, and fired the fatal shot himself.[31]

Oscar Clement was arrested for McKay's murder, though the outcome of the case is unclear.[32] In any event, by 1880 Clement was an inmate of the Worcester Lunatic Asylum.[33]

The Army of the Potomac fought two brief, minor battles in the fall of 1863 before settling into winter camp in Stevensburg, Virginia, just outside of Culpeper.[34] The Battle of Bristoe Station (October 14), marked an important "first" for Andrew's Sharpshooters: the capture of enemy guns. The historian Richard Miller writes that they "perpetuated a time-honored battlefield fraud": they pretended that they had a large force coming up just behind them and frightened away the few Confederates defending the battery.[35] Major Henry Abbott of the Twentieth Massachusetts reported:

The First Company of Andrew Sharpshooters, attached to this regiment, were thrown out as skirmishers immediately after the enemy retired, gradually advancing at first, finally at a run, captured two pieces of a battery which the enemy had placed in front of our line, but which had been deserted except by a few skirmishers. The first man at the guns was Corpl. George Curtis, of same company, to whom belongs the credit of originating and effecting the capture of these two guns, the first which were taken from this battery.

Although these skirmishers suffered no loss in this attempt, I think they deserve the highest praise for the well-timed audacity of a scheme which only a very brave man could have originated and been the first to execute, since the enemy's skirmishers could still be seen among the trees about the battery, and were very likely to be there in force sufficient to repel such an assault, as, in fact, they were shortly afterward.[36]

Years later, Luke Emerson Bicknell proudly recalled the incident:

To capture a battery, was the life long ambition of the company, born even before it left the state. Back at Camp Benton we had around our camp fires, dragged off and turned many a gun upon the foe. At Bristow Station Curtis and [Samuel] Gilbrath realized the dream, capturing and holding three guns. They both died in the service, and I have no doubt their last moments were brightened by memories of this triumph, for they were both of the spirit of [Lysander] Martin, at Deep Run, who counted his life as well exchanged for a score of the foe.[37]

By early March 1864, Ferdinand Crossman was well enough to return to Andrew's Sharpshooters, who were encamped with the Twentieth Massachusetts near Stevensburg. He clearly was unhappy with the company's loss of independence.

FERDINAND CROSSMAN

Sunny South, Va 11th [March] 1864

Dear Adda,

... I was about to leave Camp Distribution [near Washington, D.C.] for the Front. I left Armory Square the 3rd March & went to the Soldiers rest ... where we were *supposed to stay* until the morning of the 4th but I was up to my *old tricks* & ran the Guard & went back to the Hospital & staid "the *first night I left.*" I sent you $20 the 3d. ... The 4th I was just in time to go with the squad to Camp Distribution Va. ... I did not like that place at all & came away as soon as I could. ...

This company is not what it was when I left it last summer. ... I marched *under guard* to Alexandria where we took the cars ... 60 miles to Brandy Station. ... Several are home on Furlough [and] reinlisted. I shall re-enlist if I am *Drunk* or *crazy.* ...

Picket post near the Rappidan, Mar 15th 1864

Dear Adda,

... My health continues very good. ... I came out on picket the 13th & shall go in tomorrow. ... The first thing after I got here I had to draw *new pants*

Blouse & Cap. They will not let me weare a Hat out side the tent & my dark pants will not do for Dress parade, my *coats* also. . . . I expect they will take my pay from me in fines &c. The Lieut told me he should report me today for not being in *line soon enough* when he called. But it is only 5 *months & a Bit* now & I guess I can stand it. The order of exercise in camp is roll call at 6 A.M. —7 guard [mounting?], 8½—*drill from 10 to 12;* Dress parade at 5½ P.M. when we have to appear with Boots blacked, Buttons shined, hair combed, Teeth brushed, clothes free from Dust, *Blouses* on & Buttoned . . . Waist Belt blackened . . . *White gloves* on & face clean, and gun bright &c. A roll call at 8 P.M. At *every* roll call we have to have our *over coats* & equipments on & stand at attention while the Drum beats.

The 34th Mass Regt is *no where* as regards show & nonesence. But the worst of all is we have nearly all Drunken Irish officers as the 20th is an Irish Regt. The consolation . . . *it is only 5& a bit* keeps us in humor. God pity those who have *re-enlisted. I* don't. If I am so unlucky as to be killed before my time expires, it would have been better to have re-enlisted by $700 for you. But *I* would not have the feelings that I had got to stay in this cussed show more than 5 & a bit for all the money the I ever made & I am shure *You* would not either, so keep up good courage. . . .

Camp near Stevensburg, Va March 21st 1863

Dear Adda,

. . . I have not felt verry well for a few Days. I had a Diarhea 3 days but it is no better & I have not taken anything for it either, so you see it was not verry bad. . . . I believe I have written you what *our style* is, and on the whole, I rather like it for a change. *Discipline* is a very necessary article in the Army to govern *some* and all must share in it. But some things are more show & gotten up to serve the caprice of some petty officers that before the war came could not Drive a yoke of oxen, or, not fit to pick up cobble stones, but here they are "*Some & more.*" Well, in 5 & a bit. . . .

Camp near Stevensburg, Va April 1st [1864]

Dear Adda,

. . . We have so much Duty to do—drilling &c that I hardly get time to wash me except—Saturdays and then I have to do it under guard. . . . Happy to say I still live. . . . You wanted to know how I came out with that Lieutenant for not falling out on Picket: I told Jim Williams about it & the Lieut went to get shaved & Jim spoke of me—told him $13.00 was of no account to me—that I had money & property enough to *buy* the 20th Regt officers and all &c. You know what Jim is to tell a story. I have had to help get wood &c. . . .

Yesterday a regiment of Heavy Artillery of 2365 men joined this corps. They have been in the fortifications near Washington for 2½ years & most of them have reenlisted as they have had an easy time & expected to stay there until the warr closed. But they are today disappointed—for they were told they were to man some *siege guns* for a few months here and now find they have nothing but infantry. I really pity the poor devils as they left good Barracks & now have nothing but shelter tents on the wet ground. Their camp is just across the ravine & in sight of us and makes quite an addition to our canvas city. . . .

                                        Near Stevensburgh, Va Apr 26th 1864
Dear Adda,

. . . I did not get away from camp until late Sunday. I had just finished the letter & sealed it, when we were ordered to *fall in* & be inspected. As I had no pass, I was obliged to be back here before Dress Parade & you had better believe I made a *good* appearance limping up to parade. . . .

Yesterday we were called out at 7½ A.M. in the mud (it rained Sunday night) to drill 2 hours & at 10¼ A.M. formed a line to go & see the man hung. The show came off on a large plain about ¾ of a mile from our camp. We could see them setting up the gallows while we were drilling. Nearly all the Division were present forming a hollow square or 2 lines or 4 deep. Our Brigade formed a part of the 2nd line. About ½ past 12 the fellow was drawd onto the grounds and between the 2 lines around the entire square & to the gallows. He was *sitting on his coffin* with the rope around his neck & his arms tied behind. He looked at the crowd as he passed. Was quite a good looking man but rather care worn. When they arrived at the *spot,* he got up & jumped out of the wagon and walked up the stairs without help after the orders were read & prayer. He was asked if he had anything to say. He looked around and said, "When this rope breaks *my neck* it breaks the neck of an *innocent man.*" He was then asked to step forward onto the drop & the rope thrown over the beam. Just as the cap was drawn over his face, he said, "I am innocent." The Provost Marshall was master of proceedings & as soon as the rope was adjusted on the man's neck, he cut the *rope that held* the drop & the poor fellow was launched into eternity Double Dutch. Worst of all was they gave him too *much* rope & his toes just touched the ground & they had to draw him up a little & shorten the rope while he was struggling. He took out his handkerchief while they were on the scaffold & held on to it all through. He did not struggle but very little & only with his *hands.* His grave was dug *just by the scaffold.* We were marched off before they cut him down, but he was dead as soon as he dropped, but I guess this is enough of hanging. . . .

Picket near the Rappidan, Va May 1st /64

Dear Adda,

... My health continues very good with as good appetite for *coffee Hard Tack* & anything better that I can get. ... It is only 4 & 2 now. You had better believe we keep a good count of the Days. Every night we have a *caucus* & cross out one from the almanac.

Camp near Stevensburgh, Va May 3d 1864

Dear Adda,

I will just write you a word. We expect to march tonight & Cross the Rappidan. You will know all about it by the papers befor this reaches you. I wrote only last night. We have 6 days rations & 50 rounds of ammunition. I send you some pictures. The ones I *lost* in Washington I found again, or rather a [hospital] ward-Master found them in the bath room. ... I have a Photograph of you Dearest & the children ... & one of mine to send to Asa ... Write often & I will do the same for the next 4 *Months*.

Dear Wife, I am ever your
Ferdinand

Crossman went missing May 12, during the long Battle of Spotsylvania Court House. He had been captured by Confederates and shipped to Andersonville Prison in Georgia.[38]

The Andrew's Sharpshooters fought at Cold Harbor, Petersburg, and Ream's Station before their thirty-two survivors mustered out in early September 1864. Men who reenlisted or whose time had not yet expired were transferred to the Nineteenth Massachusetts Regiment.[39] Luke Emerson Bicknell later studied the company's records and calculated that "but seven of the men who followed Capt. Saunders from Lynfield served out the three years of their enlistment in the company."[40]

The last detailed account of Andrew's Sharpshooters describes the death of Samuel G. Gilbreth, a sailor from Belfast, Maine. Gilbreth, Bicknell's good friend, had been promoted to first lieutenant in September 1863. He replaced the disgraced Oscar Clement. Lieutenant Gilbreth died June 18, 1864, during an assault at Petersburg.[41] Surgeon John G. Perry of the Twentieth Massachusetts reported:

Yesterday another brave officer, Lieutenant G—— of the Twentieth Regiment, was killed, and so uselessly, too.

Lieutenant G—— was in command of the sharpshooters attached to the regiment. ... We had been fighting for several days in the most advanced trenches amidst persistent firing from both sides, which, however, did little damage, except to prevent all rest and sleep. Finally both armies saw the folly of such warfare and desisted. Towards noon yesterday, weary, I suppose, of the inaction, a Confederate sharpshooter mounted his earthwork and challenged any one of our sharpshooters to single combat. Lieutenant G——, a fine fellow, standing at least six feet two in his stockings, accepted the challenge, and they commenced what to them was sport. Life is cheap in this campaign! Both fired, and the Confederate dropped. G——'s great size was so unusual that his opponent had the advantage, and our men tried to make him give way to a smaller man. But, no! He would not listen, became very excited as his successes multiplied, and when darkness stopped the dueling he remained unscathed, while every opponent had fallen victim to his unerring aim.

The lieutenant was so exhilarated that he claimed with much bluster a charmed life; said nothing would kill him; that he could stand any amount of duelling, and this he would prove in the morning. When he was in his tent for the night, we officers used every argument and entreaty to convince him of the foolhardiness and criminality of such a course, and also assured him of the certainty of his death. But the man seemed crazed with the faith in his charmed life. He would not yield his determination, and when we left him was simply waiting, as best he could, for daylight to begin the duelling again.

As we all foretold, he was finally killed, but his death was due to treachery. In the morning, true to his mistaken conviction, he stood upon the works again and challenged an opponent. Instantly one appeared, and as both were taking aim, a man from another part of the Confederate line fired and shot G—— through the mouth, the ball lodging in the spinal vertebrae, completely paralyzing him below the head. We dragged the poor, deluded fellow to his tent, where, after uttering inarticulately, "I hit him any way, Doctor," he died.

We then heard a tremendous uproar outside, and found that our men were claiming the murderer of their lieutenant; but the Confederates shouted that they had already shot him for a cowardly villain, and then came praises across the line for Lieutenant G——'s pluck and skill.[42]

CHAPTER

AFTER

The curtain which God's hand has hung between the living and the dead is never drawn aside by any hand but His.

—Luke Emerson Bicknell

Corporal Hill

Moses Hill "fell out" near Rockville, Maryland, just before the Battle of Antietam in mid-September 1862. He was taken to Harewood Hospital near Washington, D.C., where he continued to waste away from chronic dysentery. In October his wife, Eliza, dispatched a friend to bring him home. When Moses arrived in East Medway, his appearance must have shocked his family. The stalwart five-foot, six-inch corporal who had once boasted of weighing nearly 155 pounds was a fevered, emaciated wreck. Despite the frantic efforts of his wife, family, and doctor, he died on October 29, 1862, in the big farmhouse owned by George Harding, his wife's former guardian. He had been home less than two weeks.[1]

Hill's burial at the ancient East Medway Prospect Hill Cemetery was well attended, and was no doubt typical of many of those of the state's volunteer "Boys of '61," as its early Union recruits were sometimes called. His wife's family reached back to the seventeenth century in the area, and his own clan counted many friends and relatives there, too. Adin Ballou's dwindling Hopedale Community likely sent members to comfort their "sister" Eliza. And surely the ladies and gentlemen of Medway's Soldier's Aid Society turned out to support their bereaved president.

As the town's Congregationalist minister spoke his final words, many in the crowd surely must have been aware of other soldiers' graves nearby. Like Eliza, other women there wore the black of mourning. Just before the coffin was lowered into the grave, someone pried off its oval, silver-plated, engraved name plaque and handed it to the widow. No description of that moment survives. Most likely Eliza Hill silently wrapped the relic in a linen handkerchief and tucked it away in a pocket. She cherished it along with the dozens of elaborately printed cards and letters of condolence she received. One letter, written by Martha Gale, a schoolteacher, was a model of middle-class Victorian sensitivity, sincerity, and piety:

November 3, 1862

My Dear Friend,

Please accept the enclosed lines as a slight tribute of sympathy and affection. How feebly they express what I would say to you! Words always seem vain, empty, when the heart is full. And when we would come near to a soul on which God's hand in chastening has been laid, what can we say? There is a sacredness in grief to which words seem like idle intruders; and we can best offer our sympathy in silence and in tears. . . .

I know full well that I can form no just idea of sorrow such as yours! I cannot appreciate it as others may who have known a like bereavement—but I know that life has been bereft of much of its brightness and its joy, that henceforth there is a vacant place in your heart and by your fireside which none can fill, and that you must bear with you an aching void and a weariness which only the Infinite Father can comprehend and assuage. I know, too, that your faith in Him will cheer and uphold you, that to you the Spirit World is not a far-off dream, but a living present reality, and that the loved who tread the eternal night come near to cheer and bless you. I know that the pitying Father will lead you on, that he will fold you the closer to His Infinite bosom for the pain and the loneliness of your life, and that he will comfort and sustain you.

I do not forget Lucina, and little Georgie. Over her young & glad life has crept a dark cloud, whose shadows fall heavily upon her; but rifts will break through the cloud, I trust, revealing its "silver lining," and letting in upon her saddened spirit heavenly love and brightness. It will comfort her to know that her father's life has not been sacrificed in vain—that the very life so bravely given to the cause of Truth and Freedom, is fraught with the power to sustain the Right, and to weaken and destroy the Wrong: though perhaps our human vision may not always see it clearly.

A mother's love is still spared to her, to guide and bless her; and she will feel that her father, though unseen, still watches over his child with undying love, and seeks to lead her steps in the path of duty.

Little Georgie looks with childhood's wondering eyes into the face of his great grief, scarcely comprehending his loss, yet feeling it press hard on

Figure 13. Eliza (Arnold) Hill, c. 1862. MHS Photo Archives,
Massachusetts Historical Society.

his little life. Yet he will learn from his mother and sister to remember and love his father, who died for his country, who yielded up his life for Freedom's holy cause.

Someone provided a memorial poem for Moses Hill that may have been read aloud at the burial service. In any event, Eliza liked it so much she had one stanza chiseled on Moses's headstone that faces west into the setting sun:

> He fills a Patriot's honored grave;
> Life's battle stern for him is o'er,
> And in the Land of Rest and Peace
> His spirit dwells forevermore.

Eliza continued to work for the Medway Soldier's Aid Society. Under her guidance, the town sent barrels of clothing and other articles to Union military hospitals in the South. Late in the war she also raised clothing and money to donate to the Freedmen's Bureau for distribution among former slaves in the South. She lived with her earlier guardians, the Hardings, until the 1870s when she purchased a modest cottage in downtown East Medway. She occasionally worked as a nurse to supplement her eight-dollar-a-month war widow's pension. She never remarried.[2]

Private Crossman

In the spring of 1864, Adelaide Crossman was pregnant—or "sick" as she termed it. She struggled to supplement the family income by taking in piece-work, sewing shirts and trousers for pay. Her brief diary entries express a sense of monotony, weariness, and helplessness, especially after Ferdinand's letters stopped coming in May.

ADELAIDE CROSSMAN
March [1864]

Thurs 3. I fixed the Cradle & Chare Cushion. Got a letter [from] Ferd. Eve. I wrote to him . . . Monday 7. I made 5 pairs drawers. Tues 8. Got a letter Ferd. He sent me $20.00. He has gone to the front. I made 3 pairs. Thurs 10 . . . Adda [her daughter] is 7 years old to day. I most sick . . . rec[eiv]ed for drawers .48 cts. Fri 11. I made 5 pairs drawers. Got a letter from Ferd. Sat 12. I baked pies & bread . . . I made 4 pair drawers. I got 2 books . . . for Ferd.

Mon 14. I made 5 pair drawers . . . Tues 15. I paid saw bill to Whitins 1.73. I made $5. Got a letter Ferd. Wed 16. I made 4 pair drawers, finished my 2 doz. Eve. Wrote to Ferd. Thurs 17. Worked . . . Thurs 24. I made 6 pair. Finished up 3 doz . . .

April [1864]

Friday 1. We washed & mopped.[3] I filled Childrens bed & cleaned kitchen . . . I finished off drawers. Made 3 pair. I have made 3 doz. in 4 days. Tues 5. I made 7 pair & hemmed 2 pair more. Not any one here to day. Cold. Wed 6. I had letter Ferd. I wrote to him. Made 5 pair drawers. Friday 22. Very warm & pleasant. I made 7 pair. Sold the heifers $50.00 . . . Ferd is 30 years old to day (I wrote to Ferd). Sat 23. I paid Walker for horse 75 cts. I had out 1 tooth out. Mopped. Baked & ironed. I made 8 pair; finished my 3 doz. Got a letter Ferd. He sent 2 photographs.

May [1864]

Thurs 5. Cleaned chambers & entry. A big fight to day in the army of the Potimac. Sat 7. I baked & ironed. Made 5 pair drawer. Got letter Ferd. Wrote the 2d & [sent] 3 of his pictures & mine & childrens. Thurs 12. I made 6 pair . . . Ferd in battle [at] Spotsilvana today & is killed we expect. Oh what shall I do? Friday 13. I made 5 pair drawers & planted in the garden potatoes and beens (no news from Ferd). Sunday 15. Rained all day. Had head ache . . . No News from Dear Ferdinand. What shall I do? Friday 20. Primed & planted beens &c . . . Nothing from Ferd. Tues 24. I planted squashes & Mellons & turnips &c. Mouth verry sore . . . Thurs 26 . . . No news from Dear Ferd. Tues 31. I made Adda's sash . . . No news from Ferd yet.

June [1864]

Friday 3. I most sick . . . Went to Mrs Brown to get Adda's hat sewed. No news from Ferd. One Month today sins I heard . . . Saturday 4. I ironed & baked. Heard by Amos Plimpton that Ferd's gun was found on the Battle field, but cannot find him. Oh Dear what shall I do? Sunday 5. Oh, how lonely. I wrote to Lieut [Samuel] Gilbreth & Geo. Bancroft [Ferdinand's friend in the company] . . . Monday 6 . . . Oh how lonely. Sun 19. Adda went to meeting. Oh how lonely. Mon 20. I washed & made Georgies pants . . . (dreamed about Ferd). Tues 21. I ironed. Got a letter from Lie[utenant] Gilbreth. Mr [?] came & told me about Ferd. Tells me he is dead. He was 30 years & 20 days. Thurs 23. I most sick. I wrote [Lieutenant] Gilbreth. Sat 25. Very hot. I baked beens

&c. Most sick. Tues 23 . . . No news from Ferd. Thursday 30. Heard Ferds name in the paper . . .

July [1864]

Tuesday 5. I washed & cut a dress . . . Eve. Got a letter from Sargent [Isaac] Mudgett. He thinks Ferd is a Prisoner & I think so too. Friday 11 . . . I set out cabbage plants. When shall I hear from Ferd? Wed 20. I washed & mopped & baked bread. Albert called here. Had a talk about Ferdinand. Oh shall I never hear from him again? Friday 22 . . . I ironed & reced a letter from F. Dear Ferdinand, he is a prisoner at Lynchburg Va. It was wrote May 19th . . . Mon 25. (the babie is better.) Sat 30. I baked some & we boiled beef & vegitables for dinner. I have had the babie 1 week . . .

August [1864]

Monday 1. Ferdinand died today about noon in a Southern Prison & Truman Naramore [?] was there & took care of him. Poor man. He had to die away from home & all he loved. Mon 8. I most sick . . . Dr Holbrook here to see babie. I ironed the rest of last weeks wash . . . Wed 10. I did not do much of anything. Babie sick all night . . .

December [1864]

Sunday 11. Eve. Uncle Milton [Crossman] came & brought a letter from Truman telling of Ferdinands death. He died the first day of August in Andersonville, Georgia. Poor man, he is at rest age 30 years 3 months & 10 days. Monday 12. I most sick all day . . . I verry lonely now I know he (Dear one) is gone forever. Oh dear . . .

By the time Adelaide learned of Ferdinand's death, her newborn son, named for his father and conceived during her brief visit to her convalescing husband the previous fall, had died.[4] Ferdinand, one of nearly thirteen thousand Union casualties at the infamous Andersonville Prison in Georgia, died August 8, 1864, of scurvy and chronic diarrhea.[5] Truman, the husband of one of Adelaide's Vermont cousins, was also a prisoner, and was with Ferdinand when he died. The cousin later wrote to Adelaide:

Charlotte, Dec. 11, 1864

Dear Afflicted Cousin Adda,
I felt as though I could not wait a minute, that I must write to you & yet what can I say that will in the least assuage a widow's grief?

Truman came across him in Prison but does not tell where, but we sur-
mise it was that "hellish" Andersonville. And he says that they kept together
until June 28th when Ferd was taken very sick. He does not describe the illness, but he only lived 3 days. He had his senses most of the time. He says he
died in his arms, a very quiet easy death, and said he was perfectly resigned to
his fate. He wanted to have Tru[man], if he lived through his imprisonment,
"remember him to all his friends . . . & left kind messages to his dear wife &
little ones . . ." Adda, what must be your bitter disappointment. . . . Your last
ray of hope is gone. Agonizing anxiety is over with & nothing is left to you
but the deepest grief. Dear Adda, the tears have flowed for you nearly all
night. . . .

Tru[man's] disease has been the scurvy in the worst form; [he] is in Annapo-
lis Md hospital. . . . He could only write you a few words . . . as he was so weak.
We are glad Ferd had a kind friend with him & that he could be spared to tell
the story. We expect perhaps his health is destroyed for life. . . .

Your affectionate cousin Mary[6]

Ferdinand Crossman was buried in Andersonville, but his wife arranged for
a funeral service at the nearby Baptist church, and erected a memorial headstone for him in the South Sutton cemetery. It stands only a few steps away
from the grave of his best friend and fellow sniper, Lysander Martin, who fell
at Deep Run. Adelaide recorded in her journal:

1865 Firs[t] day of Jan/65. Had a funeral for Ferd today. Had a prayer to the
house, had an excilent sermon. A great many there. 14 came later to tea.

FJF Crossman was born & brought up here & has lived here except a short
time in his infantsys. His request was 1st be brought home, but had to die on
rebbel soil.

At twenty-seven, Adelaide was still relatively young when she became a widow
in 1864. Her large farm was a major asset, and it was not long before a local
suitor asked for her hand. In January 1866, Adelaide married Frederick P. Burr.
Burr came from a solid, middling farm family and was a veteran of the Fourth
Massachusetts Cavalry. But tongues likely wagged in South Sutton, for Burr
was a teenager almost ten years her junior.[7]

"Fred" and Adelaide seem to have been happy together. Beyond his regular farm chores, Fred—like his predecessor Ferd—busied himself with cutting and hauling timber and ice for market and doing odd jobs. But he had
plenty of time to hunt rabbits and quail in Sutton's hills, and to go to dances

with his wife. Adelaide no longer had to labor with needle and thread to sustain the family. Instead, her 1867 journal expressed stability and abundance:

May 17 [1867]. Fred plowed H[oughton's] garden. $1.25. His father here to work. We planted beets, onions & parsnips . . . Tues 21. Fred & Father planted corn. I cleaned the but[t]ery. Got 31 chickens . . . Fri 24. I cleaned the sitting

Figure 14. Ferdinand Crossman headstone, South Sutton, Massachusetts.
Photo by the author.

room . . . The Old Cow has got a little black calf. Sat 25. I baked & helped plant the garden . . . I sol[d] 2 pigs for $7.50.

Sometime after the birth of their daughter Ida in 1870, Fred and Adelaide left South Sutton for a new farm in central Kansas.[8]

Private Hixon

Egbert Oswald Hixon, Moses Hill's Medway comrade, disappeared from camp near Washington, D.C., on September 4, 1862, the day before the long march to Antietam.[9] He made his way to Cleveland where his wife, Louise, was boarding with her sister and struggling to support their children. He changed the family name to Hicks, and in 1863 enlisted under that name in Company C of the 124th Ohio Infantry.

The handful of letters Hixon wrote to his family in 1864 suggest that he was determined to serve out his tour of duty. He was sick—possibly with malaria—during his first nine months with the 124th. In the spring he wrote his wife, "I expect my blood is very poor for my feet & hands are cold all the time. If you know of anything that would do me good send [it] in a letter . . . & I will take it. I hate to go to the doctor, the boys laugh if any one does & say they are playing off." Partly because he was older (almost forty) and partly because most of his company were Irish, he was socially isolated and often subject to the "blues," his term for his bouts of depression. He told his son: "I'm not very well & have no one to associate with & I get very lonesome indeed & sometimes get downhearted a little. If I have plenty of reading & tobacco I can light my pipe & read stories & pass off the time. . . . It [makes] these long days a great deal shorter." Hixon's military service contributed significantly to his family's support. As he put it, "I have no doubt that I manage [the family's financial affairs] a great deal better here than I should if I were home."[10]

In November 1864, the 124th Ohio marched from northern Georgia to central Tennessee, near Nashville. After two weeks of marching and camping in the cold and wet, Hixon was struggling with the great scourge of the army—severe diarrhea. On November 12, he was sent to his division's hospital in the small town of Pulaski, south of Nashville, and was lost during the chaos of a rapid Union retreat. One of his officers later recounted that Hixon was shipped north from Pulaski: "He was found at the depot . . . in an insensible condition & the surgeon who was present said he could not live more than an hour or two." He died November 22, 1864, likely at the "depot" in the tiny town of Lynnville, Tennessee. The officer added: "He doubtless died and was buried without being identified." Egbert Hixon suffered a fate much dreaded by soldiers: to be sick or injured and abandoned by one's comrades, left to die alone along some remote road, left to be rolled into a hastily dug, unmarked, quickly forgotten grave. Later, his name was included on a Civil War monument in Cleveland.[11]

Lieutenant Bicknell

Luke Emerson Bicknell survived the war and returned to a busy civilian life in the foothills of the Berkshires. During his furlough in the winter of 1863, he married his schoolteacher sweetheart, Lucretia Pierce. They had nine children (a "tribe," he called them). For a brief time Bicknell tried his hand at flour milling in Iowa, Illinois, and Michigan, but he soon returned to his beloved Windsor, Massachusetts, and purchased a farm. "He was not physically adapted for farm life and he abandoned it and bought the store on the hill, and while there established a larger trade than that store has before or since enjoyed." He also served as town clerk. In 1872 he bought a store in nearby West Cummington and ran it successfully until his death. He also served as the town's postmaster.[12]

Bicknell was, as one West Cummington resident remarked after his death "a natural leader among his contemporaries":

Being possessed of a fine business ability, firm integrity and an easy command of language, his society and counsels were frequently sought. As a business man, he was honest, upright, and as a merchant he never resorted to tricks and dodges used by some to display his goods and strictly adhered to the one price system [he did not charge more for items purchased on credit]. As a debater in the local lyceum, he was a formidable opponent, presenting clean-cut, scathing arguments. As a writer, he enjoyed a local reputation, frequently furnishing articles for the local press.

Of his seven surviving children, the oldest two (daughters) followed in their mother Lucretia's footsteps and became "eminent teachers" in local schools.[13]

Unlike many other Massachusetts units, Andrew's Sharpshooters did not form a veteran's society or organize reunions and group trips to battlefields. Bicknell, however, did accompany an "excursion of Massachusetts veterans to Gettysburg." He probably went with the Fifteenth Massachusetts Regiment Association, which gathered in Worcester in the spring of 1886. At the battlefield, Bicknell revisited Ziegler's Grove, where he and twenty Andrew's sharpshooters had fought so desperately on the final day of the battle. He may have been the only Andrew's Sharpshooter who made the trip. Bicknell remarked that after the war he heard from only two of his former comrades, "both contented and honored citizens of the great North West." He added, "I have never met since the day I left the army any one of the men who stood firmly by my side in the scenes I have depicted, but I love to fancy that I shall find many of them drawn up in line on the other shore, to welcome an old comrade."[14] Not long before he died, Bicknell reflected: "Since the war my life has been so quiet that it often seems like a dream that I took an active part in its stirring scenes. To reassure myself, as I write, I have drawn the sword I carried at Gettysburg from its scabbard and laid it on the table where I can look upon its edge, dented by the gun barrel I struck away. Though uncared for, its blade has not rusted."[15]

Bicknell died of "bronchial consumption" in West Cummington in April 1888. He was forty-nine years old.

From 1883 to 1885, both Bicknell and Captain William Plumer corresponded with John B. Bachelder, a New Hampshire artist and amateur historian. Bachelder hoped to write an extensive history of the Battle of Gettysburg and was in contact with many veterans of that fight. In the 1880s he headed the Gettysburg Battlefield Memorial Association, and Bicknell and Plumer helped to clarify the locations and movements of Andrew's Sharpshooters during the three-day battle.[16] Bicknell clearly was dissatisfied with the outcome. In mid-1884 he recorded privately:

I find that my nerve, energy and ambition have failed me. My desire to accomplish does not hold out to the end as well as formerly. . . . I think if I had not gone back to the army after the battle of Antietam, had accepted the advice of all physicians to call it,—that I had done enough—that I might have retained my business ability twenty years longer. . . . I find that I do not any longer care to have the part I played at Gettysburg established and admitted. Let them mark the field as they choose and tell the story of the battle as they have heretofore done. What matters it to me?[17]

By 1885, arrangements were well under way to erect a monument on the battlefield to the sharpshooters. The spot chosen for it did not correspond with Bicknell's account of the company during the battle. Captain Plumer notified Bachelder: "I have ordered a monument of Italian marble from Torrey, N.C. It is to be a rough flank, ten feet high. . . . On one face a figure erect, of a sharpshooter in the act of firing his telescopic rifle, cut in bas-relief. The Inscription is as follows. '1st Andrew Sharpshooters, Mass. Vols.'" Then Plumer asked Bachelder's opinion:

The motto either:

"Our aim was man,
We rarely missed the mark,"
or
"In God we put our trust,
But we kept our powder dry."

Which of the two do you think better?[18]

Bachelder's response has not survived. The second motto appears on the monument.

The first, a reflection of the sniper's "cool blooded" pride, was forgotten.

ABBREVIATIONS AND SOURCES

CFD   Crossman Family Diaries, 1855–57, 1864, 1867. Manuscript Collection, American Antiquarian Society, Worcester, Mass. All diary entries by Ferdinand and Adelaide Crossman quoted in the text are from this collection.

EOH   Civil War diary and letters of Egbert Oswald Hixon. Private Collection of John Robinson. All documents by Hixon quoted in the text are from this collection.

FC   Civil War letters of Ferdinand J. F. and Adelaide Crossman. Crossman Papers, 1855–1875. James S. Schoff Civil War Collection, William L. Clements Library, University of Michigan, Ann Arbor. All letters to and from the Crossmans quoted in the text are from this collection.

LEB   "The Sharpshooters," by Luke Emerson Bicknell. Microfilm P-376, reel 1, Massachusetts Historical Society, Boston. Passages from Bicknell's memoir cited by page number in the text are from this document.

LEBD   Bicknell Papers. Private Collection of Evangeline (Bicknell) Dollemore. The collection includes all of Luke Bicknell's wartime letters to his fiancée (and later wife), Lucretia, quoted in the text, as well as a first draft of "The Sharpshooters" and a number of other documents and clippings.

LEW   Lewis E. Wentworth Civil War Journal, 1861–1863 (Journal of the Second Company, Massachusetts Volunteer Sharpshooters). Microfilm P-376, reel 1, Massachusetts Historical Society.

MH   Moses Hill Letters. Frank Irving Howe, Jr. Family Papers, Series 1: Hill-Howe Family Papers, 1839–2000. Ms. N-2371, Massachusetts Historical Society. All letters to and from Hill family members quoted in the text are from this collection.

MSSM   Massachusetts Adjutant General, *Massachusetts Soldiers, Sailors, and Marines in the Civil War*. 8 volumes. Norwood, Mass.: Norwood Press, 1931.

OR   U.S. War Department, *The War of the Rebellion: A Compilation of the Official Records of the Union and Confederate Armies*. 128 vols. Washington, D.C.: Government Printing Office, 1880–1901.

NOTES

Introduction

1. Gary L. Ecelbarger, *Frederick W. Lander: The Great Natural American Soldier* (Baton Rouge: Louisiana State University Press, 2000), 126–27. See also LEB, 3–4; Phineas C. Headley, *Massachusetts in the Rebellion: A Record of the Historical Position of the Commonwealth and the Services of the Leading Statesmen, the Military, the Colleges, and the People, in the Civil War of 1861–65* (Boston: Walker, Fuller, 1866), 474; John L. Parker, *Henry Wilson's Regiment: History of the Twenty-Second Massachusetts Infantry, the Second Company Sharpshooters, and the Third Light Battery, in the War of the Rebellion* (Boston: Rand Avery, 1887), 20; James L. Bowen, *Massachusetts in the War, 1861–1865* (Springfield, Mass.: Clark W. Bryan, 1889), 862; Andrew Elmer Ford, *The Story of the Fifteenth Massachusetts Volunteer Infantry in the Civil War, 1861–1864* (Clinton, Mass.: W. J. Coulter, 1898), 145; David M. McGlaughlin, "The 1st Company Andrew Sharpshooters in the Civil War," 15th Massachusetts Volunteer Infantry website, www.nextech.de/ma15mvi/.

2. William Schouler, *A History of Massachusetts in the Civil War*, 2 vols. (Boston: E. P. Dutton, 1868–1871), 1:225. Schouler reports: "The Governor telegraphed to Colonel Dalton, at Washington, to find out whether 'a company of sharpshooters, for one year or the war, would be accepted, — to be raised in four divisions of twenty-five men each, with four lieutenants and four sergeants. They should have twenty-five dollars a month. Their rifles will cost one hundred dollars each: will the Government pay for them?'"

3. Quoted in Parker, *Henry Wilson's Regiment*, 20. See also C. A. Stevens, *Berdan's United States Sharpshooters in the Army of the Potomac, 1861–1865* (St. Paul, Minn.: Price-McGill, 1892; repr., Dayton, Ohio: Morningside, 1984), 2–5, 205; Wiley Sword, *Sharpshooter: Hiram Berdan, His Famous Sharpshooters, and Their Sharps Rifles* (Lincoln, R.I.: Andrew Mowbrey, 1988), 84.

4. Both names were in use, even among the company's sharpshooters (and their relatives) from the same town. For instance, the headstones of Ferdinand Crossman and Lysander Martin, buried just a few yards apart in the small cemetery in South Sutton, Massachusetts, display both versions of the company's name. Although Crossman and Martin

had been neighbors and close friends before the war, and were tentmates while campaigning in Virginia, Crossman's wife had "Andrew's Sharpshooters" engraved his headstone,
while Martin's parents chose "Andrew Sharpshooters" for their son's inscription.

5. Martin Pegler, *Out of Nowhere: A History of the Military Sniper* (Oxford: Osprey,
2004), 63 (quotation); Martin Pegler, *Sniper: A History of the US Marksman* (Oxford:
Osprey, 2007), 66–78. See also Philip Katcher, *Sharpshooters of the American Civil War*
(Oxford: Osprey, 2002), 4–5.

6. Earl J. Hess, *The Rifle Musket in Civil War Combat: Reality and Myth* (Lawrence:
University Press of Kansas, 2008), 175.

7. Heinz K. Meier, *Memoirs of a Swiss Officer in the Civil War* (Bern, Switzerland: Herbert Lang, 1972), 14–15; see also Hess, *The Rifle Musket in Civil War Combat*,
127–30; Sword, *Sharpshooter*, 11; Fred L. Ray, "Civil War Sharpshooters," *Infantry* 95, no.
3 (May–June 2006): 18–20. In the early nineteenth century, the French army deployed
companies of sharpshooters (called *voltigeurs* and equipped with special uniforms and
weapons) as skirmishers. In 1847, the U.S. Army raised a voltigeur regiment to fight in
the Mexican-American War. Erik D. France, "The Regiment of Voltigeurs, U.S.A.: A
Case Study of the Mexican-American War," paper presented at the Second Palo Alto
Conference, Brownsville, Texas, February 1994, available at https://sites.google.com/site/
efrance23/theregimentofvoltigeurs,usa. See also Philip Katcher, *The Mexican-American
War, 1846–1848* (Oxford: Osprey, 1976), 8, 13, 24.

8. William F. Fox, *Regimental Losses in the American Civil War, 1861–1865* (Albany,
N.Y.: Brandow Printing, 1898; repr., Dayton, Ohio: Morningside, 1974), 418–19. See also
Meier, *Memoirs of a Swiss Officer*, 14–15; and Sword, *Sharpshooter*, 8. On Berdan and his
sharpshooters, see Stevens, *Berdan's United States Sharpshooters*; William H. Hastings,
ed., *Letters from a Sharpshooter: The Civil War Letters of Private William B. Greene, Co.
G, 2nd United States Sharpshooters (Berdan's), Army of the Potomac, 1861–1865* (Belleville,
Wis.: Historic Publications, 1993); Hess, *The Rifle Musket in Civil War Combat*, 127–30;
Katcher, *Sharpshooters of the American Civil War*, 6–29; Roy M. Marcot, *U.S. SharpShoot-
ers: Berdan's Civil War Elite* (Mechanicsburg, Pa.: Stackpole, 2007); R. L. Murray, *Letters
from Berdan's Sharpshooters* (Wolcott, N.Y.: Benedum, 2005); William Y. W. Ripley, *Ver-
mont Riflemen in the War of the Union, 1861 to 1865: A History of Company F, First United
States Sharp Shooters* (Rutland, Vt.: Tuttle, 1883); Russell C. White, ed., *The Civil War
Diary of Wyman S. White, First Sergeant of Company F, 2nd United States Sharpshooters
Regiment, 1861–1865* (Baltimore: Butternut and Blue, 1991); and Andy Dougan, *Through
the Crosshairs: A History of Snipers* (New York: Carroll and Graf, 2004), 99–130.

9. Stevens, *Berdan's United States Sharpshooters*, 9.

10. Ibid., 9–12; *Harper's Weekly*, 24 August 1861. For other examples of *Harper's Weekly*
coverage of Berdan's Sharpshooters, see 26 April 1862, 3 May 1862, and 2 August 1862. See
also *New York Times*, 9 April 1862, 12–13 April 1862, 19 April 1862, and 23 April 1861; and
Ned H. Roberts, *The Muzzle-Loading Cap Lock Rifle* (Manchester, N.H.: Granite State
Press, 1940; repr., Mechanicsburg, Pa.: Stackpole, 2009), 125–29.

11. For a list and brief descriptions of Union sharpshooter units, see Katcher, *Sharpshooters of the American Civil War*, 8–9. See also Hess, *The Rifle Musket in Civil War
Combat*, 128, 180–81. Others might be added to the list, such as the Second Company
Minnesota Sharpshooters, which was originally raised for Berdan's Sharpshooters. The
company, however, served with Berdan's First U.S.S.S. only for about a month, when it
was permanently assigned to the First Minnesota Infantry in General John Sedgwick's

division, Willis Gorman's brigade. The Second Minnesota Sharpshooters were armed with Sharp's breech-loading rifles and seem to have served primarily as skirmishers. Board of Commissioners, *Minnesota in the Civil and Indian Wars, 1861–1865*, vol. 1 (St. Paul: Pioneer Press, 1890), 513–16.

12. Notable exceptions include Raymond J. Herek, *These Men Have Seen Hard Service: The First Michigan Sharpshooters in the Civil War* (Detroit: Wayne State University Press, 1998); McGlaughlin, "The 1st Company Andrew Sharpshooters"; and Alden C. Ellis Jr., *The Massachusetts Andrew Sharpshooters: A Civil War History and Roster* (Jefferson, N.C.: McFarland, 2012). For standard treatments of Union sharpshooters, see, for example, Joseph G. Bilby, *Civil War Firearms: Their Historical Background, Tactical Use and Modern Collecting and Shooting* (Conshohocken, Pa.: Combined Books, 1996), 103–16; and Pegler, *Out of Nowhere*, 63–66.

13. Hess, *The Rifle Musket in Civil War Combat*, 176.

14. Ibid., 121–74. See also Katcher, *Sharpshooters of the American Civil War*, 9–13; and Marcot, *U.S. SharpShooters*, 24.

15. Hess, *The Rifle Musket in Civil War Combat*, 124.

16. Parker, *Henry Wilson's Regiment*, 60. See also George A. Bruce, *The Twentieth Regiment of Massachusetts Volunteer Infantry, 1861–1865* (Boston: Houghton, Mifflin, 1906), 18; Herek, *These Men Have Seen Hard Service*, 102–3, 171.

17. Pegler, *Out of Nowhere*, 64. Pegler also notes that although Confederate sharpshooters were used "more often in the traditional role of line infantry, they were normally the first troops in action during an engagement." *Sniper*, 126. See also Bilby, *Civil War Firearms*, 104.

18. Hess, *The Rifle Musket in Civil War Combat*, 103. The term "sharpshooters" was not derived from the Sharps rifle. In fact, a wide variety of rifles were used by sharpshooters in the Civil War.

19. Bilby, *Civil War Firearms*, 103–28; Joseph G. Bilby, *Small Arms at Gettysburg: Infantry and Cavalry Weapons in America's Greatest Battle* (Yardley, Pa.: Westholme, 2008), 170; Hess, *The Rifle Musket in Civil War Combat*, 130; Sword, *Sharpshooter*, 14, 41–42, 63–90; Hastings, *Letters from a Sharpshooter*, 2–3; Katcher, *Sharpshooters of the American Civil War*, 17–19; Marcot, *U.S. SharpShooters*, 44–67.

20. See, generally, Stevens, *Berdan's United States Sharpshooters*; and Katcher, *Sharpshooters of the American Civil War*.

21. Hess, *The Rifle Musket in Civil War Combat*, 130. Hess notes that independent Confederate sharpshooting units similarly devolved: "They all shared the same fate . . . , serving in the dual role of line infantry and occasional skirmisher. The units simply merged into the mainstream order of battle, assigned to brigades and fighting like any other state-sponsored unit with the same type of weapons" (132).

22. Pegler, *Out of Nowhere*, 16.

23. Marcot, *U.S. SharpShooters*, 24, 44–45; McGlaughlin, "The 1st Company Andrew Sharpshooters." For the origin of the term "sniper," see Pegler, *Out of Nowhere*, 16. For an overview of the development of telescopic sights for muzzle-loading rifles, see Roberts, *The Muzzle-Loading Cap Lock Rifle*, 35–40.

24. Bowen, *Massachusetts in the War*, 842. For a detailed discussion of the construction, equipage, firing, and performance of the target rifle, see H. W. S. Cleveland, *Hints to Riflemen* (New York: D. Appleton, 1864), 36–69; and Roberts, *The Muzzle-Loading Cap Lock Rifle*, 29–31, 45–51, 66–75.

25. Peter H. Buckingham, ed., *All's for the Best: The Civil War Reminiscences and Letters of Daniel W. Sawtelle, Eighth Maine Volunteer Infantry* (Knoxville: University of Tennessee Press, 2001), 133; MH, 21 September 1861, 24 September 1861, 17 October 1861; Luke Bicknell to Lucretia, 21 August 1861, LEBD; Cleveland, *Hints to Riflemen*, 43–44. Ned H. Roberts says he has found "frequent records" of shots from 550 to 1,100 yards made with target rifles at shooting matches (*The Muzzle-Loading Cap Lock Rifle*, 119–21).

26. Ripley, *Vermont Riflemen in the War of the Union*, 11–12.

27. Cleveland, *Hints to Riflemen*, 45–46; see also McGlaughlin, "The 1st Company Andrew Sharpshooters," 3–4. Luke Bicknell listed some of the target rifle's gear: "each had its own false muzzle, starter, powder flask, charger, bullet molds, swedge [a tool for finishing bullets], box of caps, box of patches, etc. . . . The state furnished a box for each rifle and its numerous fixtures." Luke Bicknell, "A Sharpshooter's Experience with Rifles Weighing 40 Pounds," *Springfield (Mass.) Republican*, February 21, 1887.

28. Stevens, *Berdan's United States Sharpshooters*, 205.

29. See, for example, Sword, *Sharpshooter*, 84; Marcot, *U.S. SharpShooters*, 46; Bilby, *Civil War Firearms*, 113–14; McGlaughlin, "The 1st Company Andrew Sharpshooters"; Ellis, *The Massachusetts Andrew Sharpshooters*, 36–39.

30. Hess, *The Rifle Musket in Civil War Combat*, 176 (quotation); Pegler, *Out of Nowhere*, 22–23.

31. Kathryn Shively Meier, *Nature's Civil War: Common Soldiers and the Environment in 1862 Virginia* (Chapel Hill: University of North Carolina Press, 2013).

32. An important supplemental source on the experiences of target-rifle sharpshooters is the diary of an unidentified member of the Second Company Massachusetts Sharpshooters from 8 October 1861 to 18 April 1863. He seems to have used his field diary to produce a neater—and perhaps more elaborate—manuscript after the war. He also seems to have been a friend of Sergeant Nathan W. Haynes, a carpenter from Haverhill, who died of wounds on 3 January 1863 (*MSSM*, 2:715), and he inserted a large section of Haynes's diary into his own manuscript. The author never mentions the First Company (Andrew's Sharpshooters), but the two units did fight in some of the same campaigns, though not side by side, and thus shared common experiences. The author may well have been acquainted with Moses Hill and Egbert Hixon, for his tentmate was George O. Pond of Medway (LEW, 20 January 1863). Ellis, *The Massachusetts Andrew Sharpshooters*—which provides the only published account of the Second Massachusetts Sharpshooters to date—relies heavily on this diary.

33. Battles, moreover, often included mass firing "into often dimly seen enemy lines, with relatively little opportunity to aim at individual targets." Convention thus held that "a soldier was not personally responsible for the effect of his fire." Earl J. Hess, *The Union Soldier in Battle: Enduring the Ordeal of Combat* (Lawrence: University Press of Kansas, 1997), 106–7. See also Gerald F. Linderman, *Embattled Courage: The Experience of Combat in the American Civil War* (New York: The Free Press, 1987), 68, 147–49. Stealth was an element of guerrilla warfare that similarly caused it to be judged unfair. See, for example, Michael Walzer, *Just and Unjust Wars: A Moral Argument with Historical Illustrations* (New York: Basic Books, 1977), 176–96.

34. Benjamin Thompson, "'This Hell of Destruction': The Benjamin W. Thompson Memoir, Part II," *Civil War Times Illustrated* 12, no. 6 (October 1973): 20.

35. Quoted in Michael Stephenson, *The Last Full Measure: How Soldiers Die in Battle* (New York: Crown, 2012), 162–63.

36. LEB, 33. For a brief overview of the ideal of gallantry in the Civil War see James A. Davis, "Music and Gallantry in Combat during the American Civil War," *American Music* 28, no. 2 (Summer 2010): 153–57.

37. Stephenson, *The Last Full Measure*, 162–63. See also Hess, *The Union Soldier in Battle*, 107.

38. Pegler, *Sniper*, 113, 127–28. As Pegler notes, this "dichotomy of attitude" toward snipers proved enduring (e.g., 158). See also Pegler, *Out of Nowhere*, 20–21.

39. Cleveland, *Hints to Riflemen*, 44.

40. MH, 20 April 1862.

41. Quoted in Stephenson, *Last Full Measure*, 163.

42. MH, 28 April 1862. See also Dougan, *Through the Crosshairs*, 145; Luke Bicknell, first draft of "The Sharpshooters," 50, LEBD. Summary execution of captured snipers occurred as late as World War II. Pegler, *Out of Nowhere*, 19–20.

43. Winslow Homer to George G. Briggs, Miscellaneous Manuscripts, Winslow Homer, Archives of American Art, Washington, D.C., quoted in Lucretia Hoover Giese, "Winslow Homer: A Painter of the Civil War" (PhD diss., Harvard University, 1985), 238; Christopher Kent Wilson, "Marks of Honor and Death: *Sharpshooter* and the Peninsular Campaign of 1862," in *Winslow Homer: Paintings of the Civil War*, ed. Marc Simpson (San Francisco: Bedford Arts, 1988), 38. See also David Tatham, *Winslow Homer and the Pictorial Press* (Syracuse, N.Y.: Syracuse University Press, 2003), 124–25.

44. Wilson, "Marks of Honor and Death," 40.

45. Ripley, *Vermont Riflemen in the War of the Union*, 179. Also quoted in Pegler, *Sniper*, 129.

46. LEB, 33.

47. MH, 28 April 1862; Luke Bicknell to Lucretia, 26 April 1862, LEBD.

48. Pegler, *Sniper*, 129.

49. LEB, 31.

50. Pegler, *Sniper*, 129.

51. Buckingham, *All's for the Best*, 116.

52. Lt. Col. Dave Grossman, *On Killing: The Psychological Cost of Learning to Kill in War and Society* (New York: Back Bay Books, 2009), 97–98, 107–12.

53. Hess, *The Union Soldier in Battle*, 133–36.

54. One writer reports that "unlike Berdan's men, the Andrew's Sharpshooters did not bring their own guns into service in exchange for monetary compensation." Instead, he claims the state purchased 112 target rifles from a Boston gun maker, "no doubt for issue to the two Massachusetts sharpshooter companies." Bilby, *Small Arms at Gettysburg*, 177–78. The rifles were said to have been purchased from W. C. Langdon of Boston at an average cost of $70.80 each in 1861, along with "$1,081.00 worth of 'Sundries to Sharpshooters.'" W. C. Langdon produced more "Sniper Rifles and Telescopic Sights" for the government in 1862. George D. Moller, *Massachusetts Military Shoulder Arms, 1784–1877* (Lincoln, R.I.: Andrew Mowbray, 1988), 94. There is, however, no firm evidence that the two sharpshooter companies were entirely equipped with Langdon target rifles. It seems likely that many of the Massachusetts sharpshooters did in fact bring their own rifles. First, the number of Langdon rifles purchased would not have been enough to arm both companies. Second, it appears that the rifles varied in their weight and appearance, indicating diverse manufacturers. A private of the Fifteenth Massachusetts talked to one of the First Company sharpshooters in September 1861, and wrote that "the average

weight is about 35 lbs., the lightest weighing 17 lbs. and the heaviest 50 lbs. These rifles were not all alike as each man found his own and the government allowed each man for the value of his rifle." Gregory A. Coco, ed., *From Ball's Bluff to Gettysburg . . . and Beyond: The Civil War Letters of Private Roland E. Bowen, 15th Massachusetts Infantry, 1861–1864* (Gettysburg, Pa.: Thomas Publications, 1994), 28; see also McGlaughlin, "The 1st Company Andrew Sharpshooters." Luke Bicknell also said of the rifles that they "were being collected from all over the country and fitted with telescopes and boxes as fast as possible." Bicknell, first draft of "The Sharpshooters," 5; on the varying weights of the guns, see LEB, 3. A group photograph of some of the company in March 1862 also shows some variation in the appearance of the rifles. An 1888 history of Massachusetts in the war noted that Andrew's Sharpshooters "were armed with the telescopic rifle, each man providing his own weapon. These, while heavy, were considered the most efficient rifles then known. They weighed from 20 to 70 pounds, and were necessarily fired from a rest. They were made by gunsmiths in various sections of the country to suit the individual." Bowen, *Massachusetts in the War*, 862. Finally, the *Worcester Spy*, 22 July 1863, mentioned that one member of the company, Lysander Martin, "an efficient mechanic . . . , constructed himself a telescopic rifle."

55. Bicknell, "A Sharpshooter's Experience with Rifles Weighing 40 Pounds."

56. LEB, 3. For Berdan's recruitment promises, see, for example, Meier, *Memoirs of a Swiss Officer*, 30; Stevens, *Berdan's United States Sharpshooters*, 3.

57. Buckingham, *All's for the Best*, 134, 166, 291–92.

58. LEB, 3, 5. See also Sword, *Sharpshooter*, 34–35, 46.

59. Parker, *Henry Wilson's Regiment*, 3.

60. LEB, 3.

61. MH, 22 August 1861, 2 September 1861. According to one source, the average Civil War soldier was five feet, eight inches tall and weighed a little more than 143 pounds. Fox, *Regimental Losses*, 62. Some research suggests that nonfarm, urban recruits tended to be significantly shorter than those from rural areas. See Robert A. Margo and Richard H. Steckel, "Heights of Native-Born Whites during the Antebellum Period," *Journal of Economic History* 43, no. 1 (March 1983): 169, 170–71. As many as thirty Andrew's Sharpshooters, however, may have been over six feet tall. Ecelbarger, *Frederick W. Lander*, 144.

62. Parker, *Henry Wilson's Regiment*, 20–21.

63. Sharpshooters' ages were compiled from *MSSM*, 2:206–13. For age statistics for Union soldiers, see, for example, Benjamin Apthorp Gould, *Investigations in the Military and Anthropological Statistics of American Soldiers* (Cambridge, Mass.: Riverside Press, 1869), 35, 82, 88; and Fox, *Regimental Losses*, 62. Andrew's Sharpshooters also seem to have been older on the average than other sharpshooting units; see, for example, Herek, *These Men Have Seen Hard Service*, 21, and Sword, *Sharpshooter*, 34.

64. Forty percent of Union army recruits were "mechanics and laborers." See Fox, *Regimental Losses*, 63.

65. See also McGlaughlin, "The 1st Company Andrew Sharpshooters." It is likely that men who shared the same occupation and hometown formed their own solidary cliques within the company. The later recruits were still relatively urban, but far more men came from Boston and its immediate vicinity than earlier. The proportion of farmers did increase to over one-quarter, but that was still far less than the average for the Union Army as a whole. Other units recruited in eastern Massachusetts were also heavily urban in their

composition. See, for example, the regimental roster in Bruce, *The Twentieth Regiment of Massachusetts Volunteer Infantry*, 445–517.

66. *MSSM*, 2:711–12, 718.

67. Ecelbarger, *Frederick W. Lander*, xi.

68. Richard F. Miller, *Harvard's Civil War: A History of the Twentieth Massachusetts Volunteer Infantry* (Lebanon, N.H.: University Press of New England, 2005), 47; Russel H. Beatie, *McClellan Takes Command, September 1861–February 1862*, vol. 2 of *Army of the Potomac* (Cambridge, Mass.: Da Capo, 2004), 263–64. Ecelbarger's *Frederick W. Lander* is the definitive biography, and provides excellent coverage of Lander's rise to celebrity status. One incident he mentions, for example, occurred while Lander was leading a railroad survey crew in the Rocky Mountains. One day a large grizzly bear charged him; Lander stood his ground and killed it at close range with his revolver. Ever after, he was nicknamed "Old Grizzly" (18–19).

69. Bruce, *The Twentieth Regiment of Massachusetts Volunteer Infantry*, 19; Colonel Lee quoted in Miller, *Harvard's Civil War*, 47.

70. Mark De Wolfe Howe, ed., *Touched with Fire: Civil War Letters and Diary of Oliver Wendell Holmes, Jr., 1861–1864* (Cambridge: Harvard University Press, 1947), 7.

71. Headley, *Massachusetts in the Rebellion*, 630.

72. Ecelbarger underscores Lander's commitment to what at the time were more novel, covert, and unconventional forms of warfare. *Frederick W. Lander*, 94, 131, 144.

73. LEB, 2; Ecelbarger, *Frederick W. Lander*, 126–27. Lander's acquisition of the First Company probably did not pass unnoticed by Hiram Berdan. In February 1862, an anonymous letter, likely penned by one of Berdan's lieutenants, remarked, "The interference of Governors has had its bad effect upon the formation of companies originally designated for this corps, in different States." Anonymous letter quoted in Murray, *Letters from Berdan's Sharpshooters*, 1.

74. Ecelbarger, *Frederick W. Lander*, 144–45.

75. The novelty of sniper units may have been a problem. McGlaughlin remarks, "It seems commanders didn't know what to do with them." David McGlaughlin to the author, 4 October 2007. Berdan's Sharpshooters sometimes encountered the same kind of confusion: "In the beginning, with many commanders unfamiliar with the concept of sharpshooters, attempts were made to utilize the men as regular infantry." Sword, *Sharpshooter*, 45. The most extreme case of the blurring of sharpshooter and infantry roles was in the First Michigan Sharpshooters. The regiment, despite their colonel's repeated requests for appropriate rifles, had to use the same muzzle-loading Springfield muskets as the infantry. The weapon was suited only for close-range fighting (up to 300 yards). The regiment thus only performed skirmishing and was never deployed as snipers. Herek, *These Men Have Seen Hard Service*, 41–42, 102–3, 239–40.

76. Manuscript schedules of the population census for Medway, Mass., 1850.

77. Norfolk County [Mass.] Probate File no. 9485, 1855 (Medway).

78. Schouler, *A History of Massachusetts in the Civil War*, 2:506.

79. Moses Hill was similarly discreet in reporting to his wife about the many Medway men in other Massachusetts regiments whom he visited. Such discretion was likely common among soldiers writing home. As the historian Reid Mitchell notes, "Soldiers knew that their behavior while in service was monitored by the folks back home. The army provided little escape from the prying eyes of small-town America. News of a man's conduct, moral and military, was too easily sent home. And home was where the volunteer expected

to return when the war was done." *The Vacant Chair: The Northern Soldier Leaves Home* (New York: Oxford University Press, 1993), 26.

80. Thomas Williams Bicknell, *History and Genealogy of the Bicknell Family and Some Collateral Lines, of Normandy, Great Britain and America . . .* (Providence, R.I.: Bicknell, 1913), 122; manuscript schedules of the population census for Windsor, Mass., 1860; Josiah Gilbert Holland, *History of Western Massachusetts*, vol. 2, *The Counties of Hampden, Hampshire, Franklin, and Berkshire* (Springfield, Mass.: Samuel Bowles, 1855), 618–19.

81. Bicknell, *History and Genealogy of the Bicknell Family*, 471; William G. Atkins, "Death of L. E. Bicknell," undated newspaper clipping, LEBD.

82. Bicknell, *History and Genealogy of the Bicknell Family*, 471, 508; MSSM, 2:207.

83. LEB, 102. The handwritten drafts of the memoir were transcribed by Helen Bicknell in the early 1960s. She noted that Luke Bicknell made "many changes" to his story as he revised the original manuscript. Some paragraphs, she said, "are changed completely. . . . Much has been left out, several interesting episodes, but not as military in character." A descendant of Luke Bicknell typed a third draft of the memoir, the one that now is at the Massachusetts Historical Society. Helen Bicknell to Robert W. Maynard, 20 April 1960, LEBD. It is impossible to determine whether the changes made to Bicknell's story were entirely his, or whether his descendant added changes of his own.

84. LEB, 5; MSSM, 2:213; Thomas Wentworth Higginson, ed., *Harvard Memorial Biographies*, vol. 1 (Cambridge, Mass.: Sever and Francis, 1866), 404–5.

85. Luke Bicknell to Lucretia, 30 November 1861, LEBD; LEB, 67.

86. Homer W. Brainard, *A Survey of the Ishams of England and America: Eight Hundred and Fifty Years of History and Genealogy* (Rutland, Vt.: Tuttle, 1938), 538; William A. Benedict and Hiram A. Tracy, *History of the Town of Sutton, Massachusetts, from 1704 to 1876* (Worcester, Mass.: Sanford, 1878), 352, 628; manuscript schedules of the population census for Sutton, Mass., 1850, 1860. Town tax records in 1860 reported that Crossman had 100 acres. "Valuation — Highway, State, County and Town Taxes for the Year 1860," Town of Sutton, Mass. His marriage to Adelaide may have been his second. Next to his headstone in the South Sutton cemetery is one inscribed "Sarah E. Crossman, died January 24, 1851, wife F. Crossman." Her age is illegible. Neither her marriage nor her death appears in Sutton's town records.

87. CFD, 1–24 January 1855, 1857.

88. MSSM, 2:208–10; McGlaughlin, "The 1st Company Andrew Sharpshooters"; manuscript schedules of the population census for Sutton, Mass., 1860; LEB, 70.

89. Carol Botteron to the author, 21 August 2014.

90. Carol Botteron to the author, 29 January 2008.

91. E. O. Jameson, *The Biographical Sketches of Prominent Persons, and the Genealogical Records of Many Early and Other Families in Medway, Mass., 1713–1886* (Millis, Mass.: E. O. Jameson, 1886), 161–62, 245; E. O. Jameson, ed., *The History of Medway, Mass., 1713 to 1885* (Providence, R.I.: J. A. and R. A. Reid, 1886), 199–200; Carol Botteron to the author, 28 January 2008; manuscript schedules of the population census for Medway, Mass., 1860.

92. E. O. Jameson, *The Military History of Medway, Mass., 1745–1885* (Millis, Mass.: E. O. Jameson, 1886), 75; Schouler, *A History of Massachusetts in the Civil War*, 2:506–7; MSSM, 2:206–13; LEB, 2. Hixon's dream is described in a letter of 12 September 1864. For expressions of concern over the well-being of families, see, for example, MH, 9 September

1861, 27 October 1861, 10 November 1861, 23 February 1862; and EOH letters, 23 March 1864, 29 July 1864.

93. *MSSM*, 2:209; EOH letter, 16 March 1864; MH, 2 September 1861, 27 October 1861, 26 March 1862, 13 April 1862; Carol Botteron to the author, 26 December 2007, 13 August 2014.

94. LEW, 2 May 1862, 5 May 1862. See also 19 April 1862, 23 April 1862.

95. LEW, 1 August 1862.

96. Bilby, *Civil War Firearms*, 116–22, quotation on 199–20. See also Pegler, *Out of Nowhere*, 68; Hess, *The Rifle Musket in Civil War Combat*, 184–85; Ray, "Civil War Sharpshooters," 19–20.

97. FC, 11 March 1864.

98. McGlaughlin, "The 1st Company Andrew Sharpshooters" (quotation). McGlaughlin also provides brief sketches of the battles in which the company participated and details some of the casualties.

1. Before

Epigraph: From Richard Grant White, ed., *Poetry: Lyrical, Narrative, and Satirical of the Civil War* (New York: The American News Company, 1866), 10.

1. Town History Committee, *History of the Town of Sutton Massachusetts*, vol. 2, *From 1876 to 1950* (Worcester, Mass.: Commonwealth Press, 1952), 319–20; William A. Benedict and Hiram A. Tracy, *History of the Town of Sutton, Massachusetts, from 1704 to 1876* (Worcester, Mass.: Sanford, 1878), 351–52.

2. "Valuation—Highway, State, County and Town Taxes" for the years 1854, 1860, and 1865, Town of Sutton, Mass.

3. Benedict and Tracy, *History of the Town of Sutton*, 628; manuscript schedules of the population census for Hinesburg, Vt., 1850.

4. The historian John L. Brooke underscores how important informal exchanges of labor and resources between kin and friends were for the persistence of middling farm families in a particular town over the generations. He notes, "Given the expense of maintaining a pair of oxen, plowing was a particularly important point in such exchange relationships." *The Heart of the Commonwealth: Society and Political Culture in Worcester County, Massachusetts, 1713–1861* (New York: Cambridge University Press, 1989), 51.

5. CFD, 1855, 1857; manuscript schedules of the population census for Sutton, Mass., 1860.

6. Adin Ballou, *An Elaborate History and Genealogy of the Ballous in America* (Hopedale, Mass.: Ariel Ballou and Latimer W. Ballou, 1888), 357; Norfolk County Probate Court, Guardianship Decree, 7 December 1839, copy in Legal and Financial Papers, 1839–1956, Frank Irving Howe, Jr. Family Papers, Series 1: Hill-Howe Family Papers, 1839–2000, Massachusetts Historical Society.

7. Valuation List, May 1, 1877, Town of Medway, Mass., 34–35; manuscript schedules of the population census for Medway, Mass., 1850, 1860.

8. Maria A. Harding to Eliza and Moses Hill, 10 August 1849, MH.

9. Moses Hill to William Allen, 1 July 1849; Maria Harding to Moses and Eliza Hill, 10 August 1849, MH.

10. From "Masonic Song," *American Masonic Register and Literary Companion* 1, no. 34 (April 25, 1840): 272.

2. Camp Benton

1. Gregory A. Coco, ed., *From Ball's Bluff to Gettysburg . . . and Beyond: The Civil War Letters of Private Roland E. Bowen, 15th Massachusetts Infantry, 1861–1864* (Gettysburg, Pa.: Thomas Publications, 1994), 24, 26.

2. George A. Bruce, *The Twentieth Regiment of Massachusetts Volunteer Infantry, 1861–1865* (Boston: Houghton, Mifflin, 1906), 21.

3. Richard F. Miller, *Harvard's Civil War: A History of the Twentieth Massachusetts Volunteer Infantry* (Lebanon, N.H.: University Press of New England, 2005), 47.

4. Kathryn Shively Meier, *Nature's Civil War: Common Soldiers and the Environment in 1862 Virginia* (Chapel Hill: University of North Carolina Press, 2013), 35–36. See also Alfred Jay Bollet, *Civil War Medicine: Challenges and Triumphs* (Tucson, Ariz.: Galen, 2002); and Paul E. Steiner, *Disease in the Civil War: Natural Biological Warfare in 1861–1865* (Springfield, Ill.: Charles C. Thomas, 1968).

5. James Bickford was the husband of Maria Harding, Eliza Hill's "sister." The couple had moved to Boston from Medway.

6. Samuel G. Gilbreth was a thirty-one-year-old sailor from Belfast, Maine, who had earlier served with Bicknell in Company A, Eighth Massachusetts Infantry. MSSM, 2:208; LEB, 4.

7. In an earlier draft of his memoir, Bicknell wrote that Captain Saunders "was to have four lieutenants and four sergeants and had already selected old friends, who were skilled marksmen, as his sergeants and William Gleason, William Berry, and Charles Ingalls, as his first, second and third lieutenants, leaving one position, fourth lieutenant, to be filled from the men who should join him." Bicknell and his friend Henry Martin campaigned to have a fellow former Eight Massachusetts comrade, John L. Perley (a twenty-four-year-old baker) commissioned as lieutenant. "Martin and I agreed that Perley, who had been with us in company A, and who had served in the Regular Cavalry in actual war with the Indians before the Rebellion, was best entitled to the vacant Lieutenancy. We set to work with a will, to . . . popularize Perley." Luke Bicknell, first draft of "The Sharpshooters," 4–5, LEBD. Perley failed to get a commission, which helped spark an ongoing conflict. This early draft suggests that Bicknell and many others behaved in a hostile fashion to Lieutenant George C. Gray. For example, Bicknell mentioned that after the sharpshooters' first battle at Edward's Ferry in October 1862, "there seemed to be . . . no longer any necessity of ignoring Lieut. Gray, who had behaved splendidly in the engagement," and added, "[I] insisted that he must be treated with the respect due his rank and position . . . both because we should again lose caste in the army if we failed to do this, and on account of his cool behavior under fire." Some in the company—possibly even Captain Saunders—did not like Bicknell's newfound respect for Lieutenant Gray: "The bad news spread amongst the men, some of whom thought my notions absurd, and I soon had to seek the Lieutenant's tent to get any rest or peace at night." What happened next is unclear, but Bicknell said Captain Saunders ordered him placed under arrest, after which Bicknell went over Saunders's head to a higher-ranking officer and asked for a court-martial. In the end, nothing happened. Bicknell, first draft of "The Sharpshooters," 17–18. Interestingly, Lieutenant Gray (a carpenter from Salem who may have been acquainted with Captain Saunders) also had served in the Eighth Massachusetts Infantry—but in a different company from that of Bicknell and his friends. In any event, Lieutenant Gray resigned from Andrew's Sharpshooters in May 1863. Days later his old rival, John Perley, was commissioned as second lieutenant.

8. Bicknell, first draft of "The Sharpshooters," 8–9.

9. *Worcester Spy*, 30 October 1861.

10. Gary L. Ecelbarger, *Frederick W. Lander: The Great Natural American Soldier* (Baton Rouge: Louisiana State University, 2000), 137–40.

11. Hill refers to Henry Jenkins, a fifty-two-year-old miller from Reading. *MSSM*, 2:210.

12. Thomas Wentworth Higginson, ed., *Harvard Memorial Biographies*, vol. 1 (Cambridge, Mass.: Sever and Francis, 1866), 407–8.

3. Winter Quarters

Epigraph: From Richard G. White, ed., *Poetry: Lyrical, Narrative, and Satirical of the Civil War* (New York: The American News Company, 1866), 226.

1. Reid Mitchell, *The Vacant Chair: The Northern Soldier Leaves Home* (New York: Oxford University Press, 1993), 47; Robert Garth Scott, ed., *Fallen Leaves: The Civil War Letters of Major Henry Livermore Abbott* (Kent, Ohio: Kent State University Press, 1991), 4.

2. Andrew Elmer Ford, *The Story of the Fifteenth Massachusetts Volunteer Infantry in the Civil War, 1861–1864* (Clinton, Mass.: W. J. Coulter, 1898), 128; Scott, *Fallen Leaves*, 79; Lyman Richard Comey, ed., *A Legacy of Valor: The Memoirs and Letters of Captain Henry Newton Comey, 2nd Massachusetts Infantry* (Knoxville: University of Tennessee Press, 2004), 26–27. A private in the Tenth Massachusetts Infantry at Camp Brightwood wrote home: "It has been quite like Thanksgiving at home. We had a roast Turkey and Oysters, Cranbery Sauce Sweet Potatoes &c& . . . so we had all that anyone has. . . . The boys all had roast Turkey, and we have no drill, and have passed the day very agreeably indeed. . . . Company I from Holyoke & W Springfield had an enormous quantity of things sent them. They had 80 chickens 20 Turkies with Mince Pies, plus Cakes plus Cheese. It made a pile about as big as a tent. It was all cooked, so they rigged up a long table on their Co Parade, and all ate dinner together, so you see we have made out quite a Thanksgiving." David W. Blight, ed., *When This Cruel War Is Over: The Civil War Letters of Charles Harvey Brewster* (Amherst: University of Massachusetts Press, 1992), 58–59.

3. Scott, *Fallen Leaves*, 79–80.

4. Thomas Wentworth Higginson, ed., *Harvard Memorial Biographies*, vol. 1 (Cambridge, Mass.: Sever and Francis, 1866), 408.

5. Because of its distinctive hopper and crank mechanism, this primitive machine gun was nicknamed the "coffee mill gun."

4. The Winter Campaign

Epigraph: Reprinted in Gary L. Ecelbarger, *Frederick W. Lander: The Great Natural American Soldier* (Baton Rouge: Louisiana State University Press, 2000), 313.

1. Ecelbarger, *Frederick W. Lander*, 132, 148, 181–83, 199–200; Russel H. Beatie, *McClellan Takes Command, September 1861–February 1862*, vol. 2 of *Army of the Potomac* (Cambridge, Mass.: Da Capo, 2004), 467–70, 477, 483. On General Jackson's actions during the period of Lander's command, see Robert G. Tanner, *Stonewall in the Valley: Thomas J. "Stonewall" Jackson's Shenandoah Valley Campaign, Spring 1862* (Garden City, N.Y.: Doubleday, 1976), 69–93.

2. Ecelbarger, *Frederick W. Lander*, 169.

3. Paul E. Steiner, *Disease in the Civil War: Natural Biological Warfare in 1861–1865* (Springfield, Ill.: Charles C. Thomas, 1968), 7.

4. MH, 1 March 1862; Ecelbarger, *Frederick W. Lander*, 258; OR, series 1, vol. 5, 86; William F. Fox, *Regimental Losses in the American Civil War, 1861–1865* (Albany, N.Y.: Brandow Printing, 1898; repr., Dayton, Ohio: Morningside, 1974), 49; Steiner, *Disease in the Civil War*, 8–10. See also Alfred Jay Bollet, *Civil War Medicine: Challenges and Triumphs* (Tucson, Ariz.: Galen, 2002).

5. Kathryn Shively Meier, *Nature's Civil War: Common Soldiers and the Environment in 1862 Virginia* (Chapel Hill: University of North Carolina Press, 2013), 6–7, 37, 41–42.

6. LEB, 18–19.

7. OR, series 1, vol. 5, 405–6; Ecelbarger, *Frederick W. Lander*, 248–49; Beatie, *McClellan Takes Command*, 499.

8. The soldier was John Price, a thirty-two-year-old carpenter from South Danvers. *MSSM*, 2:211.

9. Edward A. Andrews was a twenty-six-year-old farmer. He died of diphtheria. *MSSM*, 2:206; *Massachusetts Vital Records, 1841–1910*, available online through the New England Historic Genealogical Society, www.AmericanAncestors.org.

10. LEB, 27. On the Battle of Kernstown, see Tanner, *Stonewall in the Valley*, 110–35.

11. William Gleason was first lieutenant until April 1862. He was a fifty-four-year-old farmer from Lexington. *MSSM*, 2:209.

12. Hatch was a shoemaker from Middleton, and was thirty at the time he enlisted. *MSSM*, 2:209.

5. The Peninsula Campaign

1. Richard Elliott Winslow III, *General John Sedgwick: The Story of a Union Corps Commander* (Novato, Calif.: Presidio, 1982), 1–2 (quotation), 167–78.

2. LEB, 35–36, 72. The other regiments in Gorman's Brigade were the First Minnesota, Thirty-Fourth New York, and Eighty-Second New York.

3. This was the Forty-Second New York "Tammany" Regiment, composed mainly of Irish recruits from New York City. See Moses Hill's letter of 26 March 1862: "The N.Y. 42 rigement is with us."

4. George A. Bruce, *The Twentieth Regiment of Massachusetts Volunteer Infantry, 1861–1865* (Boston: Houghton, Mifflin, 1906), 82.

5. Ernest Linden Waitt, comp., *History of the Nineteenth Regiment, Massachusetts Volunteers, 1861–1865* (Salem, Mass.: Salem Press, 1906), 60.

6. Thomas Wentworth Higginson, ed., *Harvard Memorial Biographies*, vol. 1 (Cambridge, Mass.: Sever and Francis, 1866), 409–10.

7. Alexander Gardner, *Gardner's Photographic Sketch Book of the War*, vol. 1 (Washington, D.C.: Philip and Solomons, 1866), plate 15, "The Moore House near Yorktown." On the location of Sedgwick's division at Yorktown, see Winslow, *General John Sedgwick*, 9–11.

8. Higginson, *Harvard Memorial Biographies*, 1:410.

9. Anonymous, "Who Raised the Flag at Yorktown?," in *The Rebellion Record: A Diary of American Events, with Documents, Narratives, Illustrative Incidents, Poetry, Etc.*, ed. Frank Moore, vol. 5 (New York: G. P. Putnam, 1863), 40–41.

10. Stephen W. Sears, *To the Gates of Richmond: The Peninsula Campaign* (New York: Ticknor and Fields, 1992), 55–56, 66.

11. Higginson, *Harvard Memorial Biographies*, 1:410–11.

12. David Littlefield was a twenty-three-year-old farmer from Lowell when he enlisted with the Andrew Sharpshooters. Like Bicknell and several other sharpshooters, he had previously served three months in the Eighth Massachusetts Regiment. *MSSM*, 2:210.

13. MH, 8 March 1862, 28 April 1862; EOH diary, 1–2 April 1862.

14. See also Luke Bicknell, first draft of "The Sharpshooters," 50–52, LEBD. The company roll lists two machinists serving at the time of the incident. According to Bicknell, the artificer was later killed at the battle of Antietam. The other machinist survived; thus it appears that he was Martin V. Strong of Lowell, who was twenty-five at the time he enlisted. *MSSM*, 2:212. It is highly probable that the "discreet man" Bicknell placed to guard Strong was drawn from the ten men with whom Bicknell had served in Company A of the Eighth Massachusetts.

15. John L. Parker, *Henry Wilson's Regiment: History of the Twenty-Second Massachusetts Infantry, the Second Company Sharpshooters, and the Third Light Battery* (Boston: Rand Avery, 1887), 94. He added, "Warned by this disaster, we proceeded with great caution, and wherever the ground appeared to have been recently broken we gave it a wide berth. The gate of the fort stood invitingly ajar, but we declined to enter that way; and it was well we did, for a heavy shell was planted there, which the opening of the gate would have exploded."

16. LEW, May 4, 1862.

17. See also Bicknell, first draft of "The Sharpshooters," 53–55.

18. A member of the Twenty-Second Massachusetts Infantry also mentioned this. He noted: "The dead were not buried when we arrived, but were laid out preparatory to the last rite. What deeply impressed us, however, was the condition of the bodies, which had been mutilated by the savage foe. A large proportion of the dead had their throats cut from ear to ear. Whether this was done before or after death we did not know, but the act showed a degree of savagery we did not expect of an enemy that not only claimed to be civilized but chivalrous." Parker, *Henry Wilson's Regiment*, 100.

19. Blacks in fact did serve alongside the Confederate army. Some worked for wages as body servants, cooks, and teamsters. Others helped build fortifications and served as pickets, and a few may have fought alongside white Confederates, as a number of Union eyewitness accounts claim. Most were coerced into these roles. On African Americans working for both sides during the siege at Yorktown, see Glenn David Brasher, *The Peninsula Campaign and the Necessity of Emancipation: African Americans and the Fight for Freedom* (Chapel Hill: University of North Carolina Press, 2012), 102–15. A few blacks even served as sharpshooters for the Confederates. See, for example, David Herbert Donald, ed., *Gone for a Soldier: The Civil War Memoirs of Alfred Bellard* (Boston: Little, Brown, 1975), 56–57; R. L. Murray, *Letters from Berdan's Sharpshooters* (Wolcott, N.Y.: Benedum, 2005), 21; Brasher, *The Peninsula Campaign and the Necessity of Emancipation*, 110–11. On white Union soldiers' changing views on race and slavery, see, for example, Chandra Manning, "A 'Vexed Question': White Union Soldiers on Slavery and Race," in *The View from the Ground: Experiences of Civil War Soldiers*, ed. Aaron Sheehan-Dean (Lexington: University Press of Kentucky, 2007), 31–66. Moses Hill was likely wrong that a whole brigade of blacks was present in the Yorktown vicinity, but they certainly were numerous

and visible. One of Berdan's Sharpshooters wrote home: "The rebels have not been idle, and have kept their darkies busily employed. Negroes can be seen with the aid of glasses, carrying bags, working the guns, and they also do picket duty." Another wrote: "The rebels had 4,000 negroes at Yorktown. They are twelve miles from us now with thousands and thousands of Negroes hard at work." Murray, *Letters from Berdan's Sharpshooters*, 21, 29.

20. Whittling and carving rings, pipes, and other items from laurel roots became a major pastime for soldiers. Parker, *Henry Wilson's Regiment*, 90.

21. John Sedgwick, *Correspondence of John Sedgwick, Major-General*, vol. 2 (New York: De Vinne Press, 1903), 58.

22. Winslow, *General John Sedgwick*, 17.

23. Donald, *Gone for a Soldier*, 84–85. For a description of the Battle of Fair Oaks, see Sears, *To the Gates of Richmond*, 117–45; Winslow, *General John Sedgwick*, 15–20.

24. Higginson, *Harvard Memorial Biographies*, 1:413.

25. John T. Hubbell, "The Seven Days of George Brinton McClellan," in *The Richmond Campaign of 1862: The Peninsula and the Seven Days*, ed. Gary W. Gallagher (Chapel Hill: University of North Carolina Press, 2000), 28–43, quotation on 35.

26. David W. Blight, ed., *When This Cruel War Is Over: The Civil War Letters of Charles Harvey Brewster* (Amherst: University of Massachusetts Press, 1992), 163–64.

27. For a book-length treatment of the campaign, see Sears, *To the Gates of Richmond*. See also Jeffry D. Wert, *The Sword of Lincoln: The Army of the Potomac* (New York: Simon and Schuster, 2005), 52–134. On conditions at Harrison's Landing, see Sears, *To the Gates of Richmond*, 347–48; Heinz K. Meier, *Memoirs of a Swiss Officer in the American Civil War* (Bern, Switzerland: Herbert Lang, 1972), 78–80. Henry Livermore Abbott, an officer in the Twentieth Massachusetts, summed up conditions at the camp: "Even I, who was at first entirely prostrated by the horrible heat & the swarms of flies (moskitoes there are now) which cover every thing human & beastly, animate & inanimate, even I have become like the rest & can cheerfully breathe the dust, which covers the ground every wheres, inches deep, eat my breakfast of flies & any thing else, while in revenge the flies are eating me & pleasantly smoke my pipe while the perspiration is melting off me, the normal condition of the body out here." Robert Garth Scott, ed., *Fallen Leaves: The Civil War Letters of Major Henry Livermore Abbott* (Kent, Ohio: Kent State University Press, 1991), 133.

The major infectious diseases during the entire Peninsula Campaign were dysentery and diarrhea. Nearly 50,000 cases occurred—well over one-third of them in July at Harrison's Landing. See Paul E. Steiner, *Disease in the Civil War: Natural Biological Warfare in 1861–1865* (Springfield, Ill.: Charles C. Thomas, 1968), 125. See also James I. Robertson Jr., *Soldiers Blue and Gray* (Columbia: University of South Carolina Press, 1988), 151–52. The scanty provisions during much of the campaign led to scurvy—a vitamin C deficiency disease—which further weakened men. In June, a surgeon for the Nineteenth Massachusetts Regiment reported an increase in cases of scurvy. He noted, "This is owing to a want of fresh vegetables. We have had potatoes issued as a ration but once since we came on the Peninsula, and even vinegar but seldom. We reported cases of scurvy sometime since, but its existence was denied at headquarters of the army." Michael B. Chesson, ed., *J. Franklin Dyer: The Journal of a Civil War Surgeon* (Lincoln: University of Nebraska Press, 2003), 24. See also Richard F. Miller, *Harvard's Civil War: A History of the Twentieth Massachusetts Volunteer Infantry* (Lebanon, N.H.: University Press of New England, 2005), 134–35.

28. Chesson, *J. Franklin Dyer*, 29–30.

29. See also Bicknell, first draft of "The Sharpshooters," 65.

30. On the movements of Sedgwick's division during the Seven Days Battles, see Winslow, *General John Sedgwick*, 21–28; Sears, *To the Gates of Richmond*, 288, 294, 298–300, 305–6.

31. William P. Adams was from Milford, a town near Medway. He died of "congestive fever"—malaria—which was widespread among the troops in this campaign. Calvin E. Phillips, "NY 40th—Mozart Regiment—Civil War Page," www.appliedvb.com/NY40th/.

32. See also Bicknell, first draft of "The Sharpshooters," 67.

33. A soldier in the Tenth Massachusetts wrote home about "the little goodies which have been sent from time to time" for the sick, which "no doubt go to fill the mouths of Hospital nurses, and stewards a great portion of them[;] . . . it seems not exactly right but I see no help for it." Blight, *When This Cruel War Is Over*, 165.

34. Gregory A. Coco, ed., *From Ball's Bluff to Gettysburg . . . and Beyond: The Civil War Letters of Private Roland E. Bowen, 15th Massachusetts Infantry, 1861–1864* (Gettysburg, Pa.: Thomas Publications, 1994), 131. See also Meier, *Memoirs of a Swiss Officer*, 82.

35. Steiner, *Disease in the Civil War*, 132. A surgeon for the Nineteenth Massachusetts observed, "Immense fields of corn on the route were stripped of their ears, much to the gratification and bodily improvement of men almost famishing for vegetable food." Chesson, *J. Franklin Dyer*, 34.

6. Antietam

Epigraph: Reprinted in Faith Barrett and Christanne Miller, eds., *"Words for the Hour": A New Anthology of American Civil War Poetry* (Amherst: University of Massachusetts Press, 2005), 100–101.

1. David M. McGlaughlin, "The 1st Company Andrew Sharpshooters in the Civil War," 15th Massachusetts Volunteer Infantry website, www.nextech.de/ma15mvi/. Lieutenant Colonel John W. Kimball, the regimental commander of the Fifteenth Massachusetts during the Peninsula Campaign, said that the Andrew's Sharpshooters were attached to his unit in July. Andrew Elmer Ford, *The Story of the Fifteenth Massachusetts Volunteer Infantry in the Civil War, 1861–1864* (Clinton, Mass.: W. J. Coulter, 1898), 145.

2. C. A. Stevens, *Berdan's United States Sharpshooters in the Army of the Potomac, 1861–1865* (St. Paul, Minn.: Price-McGill, 1892; repr., Dayton, Ohio: Morningside, 1984), 205; Joseph G. Bilby, *Small Arms at Gettysburg: Infantry and Cavalry Weapons in America's Greatest Battle* (Yardley, Pa.: Westholme, 2008), 176–77.

3. EOH diary, 4 August 1862; LEB, 44–45.

4. As Moses Hill noted, at least thirteen of the target rifles were set aside in August 1862 for possible future use. They apparently were shipped to Washington and put in storage. MH, 14 August 1862.

5. John L. Parker, *Henry Wilson's Regiment: History of the Twenty-Second Massachusetts Infantry, the Second Company Sharpshooters, and the Third Light Battery in the War of the Rebellion* (Boston: Rand Avery, 1887), 127–28, 153.

6. Ibid., 154–55. Parker concluded that "the Sharpshooters subsequently came to like their new arm, admitting that it was better for general service than the old." Except for Luke Bicknell, however, none of the sharpshooters in this book expressed any enthusiasm for the Sharps rifles.

7. "Tortugas" was a much-feared Union prison at Fort Jefferson, situated on a small island not far from Key West, Florida. Surrounded by shark-infested waters (plus a moat stocked with sharks), prisoners performed hard labor on meager rations. See Lonnie R.

Speer, *Portals to Hell: Military Prisons of the Civil War* (Mechanicsburg, Pa.: Stackpole, 1997), 201–3. "Rip Raps" was a prison at Fort Wool, on an island near Norfolk, Virginia, and close to Fort Monroe. See Bell Irvin Wiley, *The Life of Billy Yank: The Common Soldier of the Union* (Garden City, N.Y.: Doubleday, 1971), 215.

8. LEW, 14 July to 1 August 1862.

9. The last quotation in this paragraph and those in the following two paragraphs are from LEB, 44–49; Luke Bicknell, first draft of "The Sharpshooters," 70–72, LEBD.

10. Alden C. Ellis Jr., *The Massachusetts Andrew Sharpshooters: A Civil War History and Roster* (Jefferson, N.C.: McFarland, 2012), 40–41.

11. See also Bicknell, first draft of "The Sharpshooters," 70–72.

12. John Sedgwick, *Correspondence of John Sedgwick*, vol. 2 (New York: De Vinne Press, 1903), 79–80; Richard Elliott Winslow III, *General John Sedgwick: The Story of a Union Corps Commander* (Novato, Calif.: Presidio, 1982), 38–39.

13. Gregory A. Coco, ed., *From Ball's Bluff to Gettysburg . . . and Beyond: The Civil War Letters of Private Roland E. Bowen, 15th Massachusetts Infantry, 1861–1864* (Gettysburg, Pa.: Thomas Publications, 1994), 132.

14. Bicknell was alluding to a speech in which General John Pope drew invidious comparisons between the western soldiers he had previously commanded and the eastern soldiers and their officers. He clearly implied that General McClellan and the Army of the Potomac had been too defensive and timid. His critical attitude was widely resented. See John J. Hennessy, *Return to Bull Run: The Campaign and Battle of Second Manassas* (New York: Simon and Schuster, 1993), 12–13.

15. A widespread but false belief held that General McDowell was a traitor who had secretly signaled to the Confederates to inform them of Union movements during the battle. See Hennessy, *Return to Bull Run*, 465–67.

16. Winslow, *General John Sedgwick*, 43–44; Norman Stevens, *Antietam 1862: The Civil War's Bloodiest Day* (Oxford: Osprey, 2004), 33–45; Stephen W. Sears, *Landscape Turned Red: The Battle of Antietam* (New York: Ticknor and Fields, 1983), 115–49, 177.

17. Marion V. Armstrong Jr., *Unfurl Those Colors! McClellan, Sumner, and the Second Army Corps in the Antietam Campaign* (Tuscaloosa: University of Alabama Press, 2008), 165–206. On the movement of the 34th New York, see 182–84.

18. McGlaughlin, "The 1st Company Andrew Sharpshooters." On the Battle of Antietam, see also David J. Eicher, *The Longest Night: A Military History of the Civil War* (New York: Simon and Schuster, 2001), 335–64. For a detailed account of General Edwin Sumner's Second Corps' experience in the battle, see Joseph Pierro, ed., *The Maryland Campaign of September 1862: Ezra A. Carman's Definitive Study of the Union and Confederate Armies at Antietam* (New York: Routledge, 2008), 253–76; Armstrong, *Unfurl Those Colors!*

19. Coco, *From Ball's Bluff to Gettysburg*, 124.

20. Francis W. Palfrey, *The Antietam and Fredericksburg* (New York: Charles Scribner's Sons, 1882; new ed., New York: Da Capo, 1996), 82–87.

21. Marcus Morton Parmenter, a farm laborer, had enlisted in March 1862. He fell during the first volley at the West Woods, wounded in both the head and abdomen. By the time Union forces were able to gather their dead on September 19, Parmenter's body could not be identified. He and others were buried in shallow graves on the battlefield. Ralph Parmenter Bennett, "Private Marcus Morton Parmenter, First Company Massachusetts (Andrew) Sharpshooters att: 15th Massachusetts Regiment Volunteer Infantry," n.d., Hazen Memorial Library, Shirley, Mass.

22. Thomas Wentworth Higginson, ed., *Harvard Memorial Biographies*, vol. 1 (Cambridge, Mass.: Sever and Francis, 1866), 413–14.

23. Pierro, *The Maryland Campaign of September 1862*, 266–67.

24. This passage also draws on Bicknell, first draft of "The Sharpshooters," 74–76.

25. *OR*, series 1, vol. 4, part 1, 312.

26. David Littlefield was a twenty-four-year-old farmer from Lowell who had previously served with Bicknell in Company A of the Eighth Massachusetts Infantry. Captain Saunders's alleged killer was Martin V. Strong, a machinist, also from Lowell. *MSSM*, 2:210, 212.

27. Sears, *Landscape Turned Red*. Sedgwick's wounds were not life threatening, and he soon returned to the army. Winslow, *General John Sedgwick*, 47–48. On losses in the Fifteenth Massachusetts, see William F. Fox, *Regimental Losses in the American Civil War, 1861–1865* (Albany, N.Y.: Brandow Printing, 1898; repr., Dayton, Ohio: Morningside, 1974), 17, 29, 37, 161, 432. On the Andrew's Sharpshooters' losses see *MSSM*, 2:206–13; Ford, *Story of the Fifteenth Massachusetts Volunteer Infantry*, 210; McGlaughlin. "The 1st Company Andrew Sharpshooters"; Phineas C. Headley, *Massachusetts in the Rebellion: A Record of the Historical Position of the Commonwealth and the Services of the Leading Statesmen, the Military, the Colleges, and the People, in the Civil War of 1861–65* (Boston: Walker, Fuller, 1866), 231. The Second Company Massachusetts Sharpshooters was held in reserve and did not take part in the fighting on September 17. They did, however, accompany troops sent in pursuit of the retreating Confederates. The Second Company—along with Berdan's First U.S. Sharpshooters—harassed the enemy's defensive position on the Virginia side of the Potomac River near Shepherdstown. LEW, 17–19 September 1862. See also Peter S. Carmichael, "We Don't Know What on Earth to Do with Him: William Nelson Pendleton and the Affair at Shepherdstown, September 19, 1862," in *The Antietam Campaign*, ed. Gary W. Gallagher (Chapel Hill: University of North Carolina Press, 1999), 267–69.

7. Fredericksburg

Epigraph: John Greenleaf Whittier, *The Complete Poetical Works of John Greenleaf Whittier, Household Edition* (Boston and New York: Houghton, Mifflin, 1904), 420.

1. For a brief overview of the Battle of Fredericksburg, see Jeffry D. Wert, *The Sword of Lincoln: The Army of the Potomac* (New York: Simon and Schuster, 2005), 74–204. See also George C. Rable, *Fredericksburg! Fredericksburg!* (Chapel Hill: University of North Carolina Press, 2002).

2. "Capt. William Plumer" (obituary), *Boston Advertiser*, 5 December 1896, available at 15th Massachusetts Volunteer Infantry website, www.nextech.de/ma15mvi/; *MSSM*, 2:211.

3. *OR*, series 1, vol. 21, 272.

4. Rable, *Fredericksburg! Fredericksburg!*, 210–11. See also Francis Augustin O'Reilly, *The Fredericksburg Campaign: Winter War on the Rappahannock* (Baton Rouge: Louisiana State University Press, 2003), 112; John Gibbon, *Personal Recollections of the Civil War* (New York: G. P. Putnam's Sons, 1928); Dennis S. Lavery and Mark H. Jordan, *Iron Brigade General: John Gibbon, a Rebel in Blue* (Westport, Conn.: Greenwood Press, 1993).

5. A scan of the portrait is available on the Find a Grave website (www.findagrave .com), under "Capt William Plumer, III."

6. Ford, *Story of the Fifteenth Massachusetts Volunteer Infantry*, 244.

7. Daniel E. Sutherland, *Fredericksburg and Chancellorsville: The Dare Mark Campaign* (Lincoln: University of Nebraska Press, 1998), 158; Gibbon, *Personal Recollections of the Civil War*, 111, 114–17; Richard F. Miller, *Harvard's Civil War: A History of the Twentieth Massachusetts Volunteer Infantry* (Lebanon, N.H.: University Press of New England, 2005), 240. For the Battle of Chancellorsville, see, for example, Stephen W. Sears, *Chancellorsville* (New York: Houghton Mifflin, 1996).

8. *OR*, series 1, vol. 25, part 1, 361.

9. Mrs. John Harris was a member of the Philadelphia Ladies Soldiers Aid Society. Over the course of the war, she distributed bandages, clothing, and other supplies, and saw to the preparation of food for sick and injured soldiers. On many occasions she nursed the wounded and dying at battlefield hospitals. She followed the Army of the Potomac for nearly the entire war and was well known by the Northern public for her tireless service. Frank Moore, *Women of the War: Their Heroism and Self-Sacrifice* (Hartford, Conn.: S. S. Scranton, 1866), 176–212.

10. FC, 11–20 May 1863.

11. Oscar H. Clement was a twenty-four-year-old shoemaker from Stoneham who had enlisted with the first volunteers in 1861. He, along with Bicknell and several other Andrew's Sharpshooters, had previously served in the Eighth Massachusetts. Clement was commissioned as first lieutenant May 30, 1863. *MSSM*, 2:207.

12. James Lorenzo Bowen, *Massachusetts in the War, 1861–1865* (Springfield, Mass.: Clark W. Bryan, 1889), 864.

13. Gregory A. Coco, ed., *From Ball's Bluff to Gettysburg . . . and Beyond: The Civil War Letters of Private Roland E. Bowen, 15th Massachusetts Infantry, 1861–1864* (Gettysburg, Pa.: Thomas Publications, 1994), 157–58.

14. See also Luke Bicknell, first draft of "The Sharpshooters," 93–94, LEBD.

15. William A. Benedict and Hiram A. Tracy, *History of the Town of Sutton, Massachusetts, from 1704 to 1876* (Worcester, Mass.: Sanford, 1878), 352; *Worcester Spy*, 22 July 1863.

16. Benedict and Tracy, *History of the Town of Sutton*, 352. See also LEB, 70; Bicknell, first draft of "The Sharpshooters," 94–95.

17. Coco, *From Ball's Bluff to Gettysburg*, 158.

8. Gettysburg and Beyond

1. For general works on the Battle of Gettysburg, see, for example, Allen C. Guelzo, *Gettysburg: The Last Invasion* (New York: Knopf, 2013); Stephen W. Sears, *Gettysburg* (New York: Houghton Mifflin, 2003); and Noah Andre Trudeau, *Gettysburg: A Testing of Courage* (New York: HarperCollins, 2003). On the importance of securing supplies as a motive for the invasion, see, for example, Kent Masterson Brown, *Retreat from Gettysburg: Lee, Logistics, and the Pennsylvania Campaign* (Chapel Hill: University of North Carolina Press, 2005).

2. Bicknell later published brief descriptions of the company's actions at Gettysburg. These accounts are similar to those in his memoir, but lack the latter's sense of immediacy. See Robert Underwood Johnson and Clarence Clough Buel, eds., *Battles and Leaders of the Civil War: Being for the Most Part Contributions by Union and Confederate Officers*, vol. 3 (New York: The Century Co., 1888), 391–92; David L. Ladd and Audrey L. Ladd, eds., *The Bachelder Papers: Gettysburg in Their Own Words*, vol. 2 (Dayton, Ohio:

Morningside, 1994), 963–65, 969–70, 984–88. See also David M. McGlaughlin, "The 1st Company Andrew Sharpshooters in the Civil War," 15th Massachusetts Volunteer Infantry website, www.nextech.de/ma15mvi/.

3. General Sedgwick was shot dead by a Confederate sharpshooter at Spotsylvania, May 6, 1864. His last words were, "They couldn't hit an elephant at this distance!" On Sedgwick's death, see Richard Elliott Winslow III, *General John Sedgwick: The Story of a Union Corps Commander* (Novato, Calif.: Presidio, 1982), 172–75.

4. Harry W. Pfantz, *Gettysburg: The Second Day* (Chapel Hill: University of North Carolina Press, 1987), 52–53, 61, 63–65.

5. Earl J. Hess, *Pickett's Charge—The Last Attack at Gettysburg* (Chapel Hill: University of North Carolina Press, 2001), 121–23, quotation on 121; George R. Stewart, *Pickett's Charge: A Microhistory of the Final Attack at Gettysburg* (Boston: Houghton Mifflin, 1959), 80.

6. As noted earlier, Andrew's Sharpshooters were often mistaken for Berdan's Sharpshooters. Most of Hiram Berdan's First and Second U.S. Sharpshooters were well to the south of General Hays's position. On July 3, one hundred of Berdan's Sharpshooters were sent to help protect part of General John Sedgwick's Sixth Corps. They remained there all day. *OR*, series 1, vol. 27, part 1, 514–17.

7. Richard S. Thompson, "A Scrap of Gettysburg," in *Military Essays and Recollections: Papers Read before the Commandery of the State of Illinois, Military Order of the Loyal Legion of the United States*, vol. 3 (Chicago: The Dial Press, 1899), 98. Also quoted in Pfantz, *Gettysburg*, 67–68.

8. The Second Minnesota Sharpshooters (Company L of the First Minnesota Infantry) were also posted near Ziegler's Grove. The Minnesota men carried Sharps rifles, and were assigned to protect Lieutenant George A. Woodruff's Battery I, First U.S., at Ziegler's Grove. They remained with the battery all day. Board of Commissioners, *Minnesota in the Civil and Indian Wars, 1861–1865*, vol. 2 (St. Paul: Pioneer Press, 1899), 373; Brian Leehan, *Pale Horse at Plum Run: The First Minnesota at Gettysburg* (St. Paul: Minnesota Historical Society Press, 2004), 34.

9. Benjamin Thompson, "'This Hell of Destruction': The Benjamin W. Thompson Memoir, Part II," *Civil War Times Illustrated* 12, no. 6 (October 1973): 17. On July 3, part of the New York regiment's line occupied the spot Luke Bicknell had selected for his company the day before. For a map showing the location of the N.Y. 111th and other units under Brigadier General Hays on July 3, see Jeffrey C. Hall, *The Stand of the U.S. Army at Gettysburg* (Bloomington: Indiana University Press, 2003), 203, 212, 230.

10. Ladd and Ladd, *The Bachelder Papers* 2:964–65; McGlaughlin, "The 1st Company Andrew Sharpshooters."

11. By the 1880s, Bicknell had identified the general and had contributed a short description of the Andrew's Sharpshooters' part in the fighting on July 3. See Johnson and Buel, *Battles and Leaders of the Civil War*, 3:391–92.

12. Fuller, a thirty-one-year-old blacksmith from Lynn, was one of the original 1861 recruits. He died July 18, 1863, in Baltimore. *MSSM*, 2:208.

13. Larry Tagg, *The Generals of Gettysburg: Appraisal of the Leaders of America's Greatest Battle* (Cambridge, Mass.: Da Capo, 1998), 53–54. See also Wayne Mahood, *Alexander "Fighting Elleck" Hays: The Life of a Civil War General, from West Point to the Wilderness* (Jefferson, N.C.: McFarland, 2005).

14. Hall, *The Stand of the U.S. Army at Gettysburg*, 211–13, 227, 230–31.

15. Ladd and Ladd, *The Bachelder Papers*, 2:985.

16. This incident is mentioned briefly in Phineas Camp Headley, *Massachusetts in the Rebellion: A Record of the Historical Position of the Commonwealth and the Services of the Leading Statesmen, the Military, the Colleges, and the People, in the Civil War of 1861–65* (Boston: Walker, Fuller, 1866), 475.

17. Alfred A. Batchelor was a twenty-year-old wheelwright from Worcester. He died July 10, in Baltimore. *MSSM*, 2:207.

18. Compare, for example, Guelzo, *Gettysburg: The Last Invasion*, 418–19, 421. The first men to have encountered General Armistead were privates of the Seventy-Second Pennsylvania, who began to carry him to a field hospital. They were stopped briefly by the judge advocate of the Second Corps, Henry Bingham, who reported having a conversation very similar to the one Bicknell described.

19. George P. Roundy was a thirty-year-old miner from Lynn, and one of the original Andrew's Sharpshooter recruits of 1861. *MSSM*, 2:211.

20. The company's loss was two killed and six wounded. Headley, *Massachusetts in the Rebellion*, 475.

21. See also Luke Bicknell, first draft of "The Sharpshooters," 106–9, LEBD.

22. John Gibbon, *Personal Recollections of the Civil War* (New York: G. P. Putnam's Sons, 1928; repr., Dayton, Ohio: Morningside, 1978), 152–53, 209–10; Richard F. Miller, *Harvard's Civil War: A History of the Twentieth Massachusetts Volunteer Infantry* (Hanover, N.H.: University Press of New England, 2005), 290.

23. Martha Darby Perry, comp., *Letters from a Surgeon of the Civil War* (Boston: Little, Brown, 1906), 190; LEB, 95.

24. *MSSM*, 2:212.

25. *Boston Journal*, 1 September 1863, available at 15th Massachusetts Volunteer Infantry website, www.nextech.de/ma15mvi/.

26. Perry, *Letters from a Surgeon of the Civil War*, 80–83. For a thorough treatment of the McKay murder, see Miller, *Harvard's Civil War*, 288–91.

27. Perry, *Letters from a Surgeon of the Civil War*, 87–88.

28. Miller, *Harvard's Civil War*, 291.

29. Perry, *Letters from a Surgeon of the Civil War*, 89–91.

30. Ibid., 91–93.

31. Ibid., 94–96.

32. Miller notes that much about Clement's background points to his guilt (*Harvard's Civil War*, 290–91). Perry claims that Clement had enlisted in a "Western regiment," was arrested and returned to Virginia for a court-martial, and "was tried, convicted, and sentenced to be hanged." Much to the outrage of the officers, though, Clement was freed: "A legal flaw has been discovered in the paper sent to Washington which renders it absolutely invalid." Perry added disgustedly, "erelong we saw the murderer leave the camp, heard him jeer his would-be executioners, and with his thumb upon his nose, we saw him wave his fingers in derision and vanish into mystery." *Letters from a Surgeon of the Civil War*, 96–98. There is no way to confirm Perry's account. Perry's friend and fellow officer, Major Henry L. Abbott, for example, mentioned nothing about Clement's capture, trial, and acquittal in his letters home. Robert Garth Scott, ed., *Fallen Leaves: The Civil War Letters of Major Henry Livermore Abbott* (Kent, Ohio: Kent State University Press, 1991).

33. The 1880 U.S. Census lists an Oscar Clement in the Worcester Lunatic Asylum. The occupation given—shoemaker—is the same, and the birth year is about right, 1835.

Finally, the state of birth, New Hampshire, also accords with Clement's background. He was listed as married in 1880. Manuscript schedules of the population census for Worcester, Mass., 1880.

34. For overviews of the fighting at Bristoe Station and Mine Run, see, for example, William D. Henderson, *The Road to Bristoe Station: Campaigning with Lee and Meade, August 1–October 20, 1863* (Lynchburg, Va.: H. E. Howard, 1987); Martin F. Graham and George F. Skoch, *Mine Run: A Campaign of Lost Opportunities, October 21, 1863–May 1, 1864* (Lynchburg, Va.: H. E. Howard, 1987). Miller, *Harvard's Civil War*, 278–313, provides an excellent account of the activities of the Twentieth Massachusetts in the fall of 1863.

35. Miller, *Harvard's Civil War*, 302.

36. *OR*, series 1, vol. 29, part 1, 286. Also quoted in McGlaughlin, "The 1st Company Andrew Sharpshooters." George Curtis was a twenty-two-year-old shoemaker who enlisted with the original company in September 1861. In February 1864 he was promoted to sergeant. *MSSM*, 2:208.

37. *LEB*, 95.

38. *MSSM*, 2:208.

39. McGlaughlin, "The 1st Company Andrew Sharpshooters"; John Heseltine, *Chronological History of 1st Massachusetts Sharpshooters Company* (Kennebunk, Maine: Maine in the Civil War, n.d.), 21.

40. *LEB*, 96.

41. *MSSM*, 2:208.

42. Perry, *Letters from a Surgeon of the Civil War*, 191–93.

9. After

1. Medway town records list his cause of death as "chronic diarrhea & consumption." *Massachusetts Vital Records, 1841–1910*, vol. 157, 280, available online through the New England Historic Genealogical Society, www.AmericanAncestors.org.

2. Manuscript schedules for the town of Medway, Mass., 1880; manuscript schedules for the town of Millis, Mass., 1900; Lieutenant Colonel J. Getman to Eliza Hill, 9 May 1863, MH; Mrs. William Rogers to J. Roberts, 14 March 1864, MH.

3. It appears one of Adelaide's sisters came to help with the household late in her pregnancy. CFD, 1864.

4. After mid-August, no more entries appear concerning the "babie." CFD, 1864. A family historian listed a "Ferdinand Joseph Fuller, b. ——," as the third and last of Adelaide's children with Ferdinand. Homer W. Brainard, *A Survey of the Ishams of England and America: Eight Hundred and Fifty Years of History and Genealogy* (Rutland, Vt.: Tuttle, 1938), 538. For reasons that are not clear, the child's death was not recorded in the Sutton town records, nor is there a marked gravesite for the boy. He does not appear in the 1870 U.S. Census for Sutton (manuscript schedules for the town of Sutton, Mass., 1870).

5. The Sutton town records are likely the most accurate, since Adelaide and those in her network had the best knowledge of the circumstances of Crossman's death. The town listed "chronic diarrhea" as the cause of death. "Deaths Registered in the Town of Sutton for the Year 1864," 20, office of the Town Clerk, Sutton, Mass. Another source lists "scorbutus" (scurvy) as the cause of death. National Park Service, Andersonville Prisoner of War Database (National Prisoner of War Museum, Andersonville, Ga.), available online at www.Ancestry.com.

6. FC, 11 December 1864, Mary to Adelaide Crossman.

7. *MSSM*, 6:445; William A. Benedict and Hiram A. Tracy, *History of the Town of Sutton, Massachusetts, from 1704 to 1876* (Worcester, Mass.: Sanford, 1878), 352; Brainard, *A Survey of the Ishams*, 538.

8. Benedict and Tracy, *History of the Town of Sutton*, 352; manuscript schedules for the town of Sutton, Mass., 1860; Brainard, *A Survey of the Ishams*, 538. Their daughter, Ida, was born 17 November 1870. By 1880, they were living in Bennington Township, and Adelaide's son George and his young wife had a farm there as well. Manuscript schedules for the town of Bennington Township, Kans., 1880.

9. *MSSM*, 2:209. According to his descendants, someone tore out the diary pages from mid-August 1862 onward. Carol Botteron to the author, 11 November 2007.

10. EOH to Electa Louise Hixon, 16 March 1864, 11 August 1864, 11 September 1864.

11. Carol Botteron to the author, 26 December 2007, 6 February 2008. What little information exists on Hixon's end comes from his wife's applications for a widow's pension.

12. William G. Atkins, "Death of L. E. Bicknell," undated newspaper clipping, LEBD (quotation); Thomas Williams Bicknell, *History and Genealogy of the Bicknell Family and Some Collateral Lines, of Normandy, Great Britain and America . . .* (Providence, R.I.: Bicknell, 1913), 471; John H. Lockwood et al., eds., *Western Massachusetts: A History, 1636–1925* (New York: Lewis Historical Publishing, 1926), 601; manuscript schedules of the town of St. Joseph, Mich., 1870.

13. Atkins, "Death of L. E. Bicknell."

14. Robert Underwood Johnson and Clarence Clough Buel, eds., *Battles and Leaders of the Civil War: Being for the Most Part Contributions by Union and Confederate Officers*, vol. 3 (New York: The Century Co., 1888), 391–92; *Worcester Aegis and Gazette*, 29 May 1886, and *Worcester Spy*, 21 May 1886, 4 June 1886, available at 15th Massachusetts Volunteer Infantry website, www.nextech.de/ma15mvi/index.htm; LEB, 97.

15. Luke Bicknell, first draft of "The Sharpshooters," 124, LEBD.

16. David L. Ladd and Audrey J. Ladd, eds., *The Bachelder Papers: Gettysburg in Their Own Words*, vol. 2 (Dayton, Ohio: Morningside, 1994–1995), 963–65, 969–70, 984–88, 1097.

17. L. E. Bicknell, "Reflections," 5 April 1884, LEBD.

18. Ladd and Ladd, *The Bachelder Papers*, 2:1100–1101.

INDEX

Italicized page numbers refer to illustrations.

313

drills, 42–43, 47, 51; bayonet, 23, 202; knapsack, 131; skirmish, 3, 231
Dry Tortugas Prison, 305–6n7

Eagle (steamer), 152
East Medway, Mass., 29, 110–11; illness in, 218, 220, 221
Edwards Ferry, 50, 56–57, 58, 96, 203, 300n7; AS at, 61, 65, 78; LEB makes expedition at, 59–60; environmental features of, 59
ethics. *See* sniping, ethics of
execution, 267–68, 274

Fairfax, Va., 204, 214, 248
Fales, Abijah, 34
Fales, Albert, 221
Fales, James
Falmouth, Va., 224
Faneuil Hall (Boston, Mass.), 139
Farmer's Almanac, 44
farming and gardening, 20, 31, 48, 194, 281–82, 299n4; MH and, 16, 34, 47, 49, 142, 159, 172, 173–74, 184, 187, 191, 193–94, 219; FC and, 28, 29, 229, 240
finances: anxiety over, 21, of LEB, 249, 98, of Crossman family, 28, 29, 233, 241, 272, 273, of Hill family, 33–34, 41, 44, 45, 47, 79, 83, 84–85, 103, 105, 111–12, 131, 135, 192, of EOH, 285, and price inflation, 102–3, 115, 149, 158
First Company Massachusetts Sharpshooters. *See* Andrew's Sharpshooters (AS)
First and Second United States Sharp Shooters. *See* Berdan's Sharpshooters
First Corps, 207
Fisher, James, 218
Fisher, Lewis, 198
Fisher Hill, 123
fishing, 31, 150, 173–74, 197
food, 33, 172, 248; Confederate, 155, 179; diet and health, 111–12, 113, 217; foraging, 65, 68, 85–86, 104, 194–95, 196, 304n35; dining out, 85, 229; at holidays, 70, 72, 73–75, 301n2; at home, 80, 84, 105, 115, 161, 163, 184, 191; from home, 77, 83, 91, 190, 193, 228, 233; at hospital, 214, 217; prices of, 182; rations and provisions, 45, 48–49, 54–55, 90, 93, 129, 134, 186, 188, 192, 231, 236, 250, 275; sale of, 102; scarcity of, 135, 176, 178; spoiled, 76, 81–82; sweets, 46, 69, 126, 185, 187

forestry, 27, 28, 107, 169, 173
Forster, Louisa, 221
fortifications, Confederate, 132–34, 136–38, 141–43, 150, 155, 170, 303n19
Fortress Monroe, 127, 129, 134, 141
Frankle, Brig. Gen. Jones, 267
Franklin, Gen. William B., 153, 156
Frederick, Md., 206, 249
Fredericksburg, Va., environmental features of, 237. *See also* Battle of Fredericksburg
Fremont, Maj. Gen. John, 169
friendly fire, 50, 211
Fuller, Sanford, K., 254, 309n12
funerals, 27, 111, 115, 121, 184, 263, 280, 283

Gale, Martha, 278–80
gambling, 22, 64, 76, 147, 241
games, 75, 188, 218
gardening. *See* farming and gardening
machine gun, 87, 301n5
Gettysburg, Pa., 286–88; environmental features of, 251. *See also* Battle of Gettysburg
Gibbon, Gen. John, 226, 250, 256, 264; and AS, 227, 231, 239, 240; LEB and, 230, 251; orders of, at Battle of Gettysburg, 253
Gilbreth, Lt. Samuel, 40, 59, 248, 253, 281, 258, 261, 272, 300n6; death of, 275–76
Gleason, Lt. William, 118, 131, 138, 300n7
Glendale. *See* Seven Days Battles
Gloucester, Mass., 18
Goddard, A. F., 28
Goose Creek (Va.), 59, 84
Gordon House (Fredericksburg, Va.), 224
Gorman, Brig. Gen. Willis A., 56–57, 64, 128, 133, 163, 183, 188, 195, 212
Gray, Lt. George C., 40, 60, 300n7
Greenwood, Charles, 65, 134, 135
Griswold, Col. Charles E., 201
guard duty, 43, 231, 232; of LEB, 56; of MH, 42, 46, 49, 50, 52, 57–58, 70, 71, 76, 79, 80, 83, 86, 92
gun boats, 127, 150, 155, 157, 190, 196
guns, maintenance of, 51, 75, 84, 212, 236

Hall, Col. Norman J., 234, 235, 237
Halleck, Gen. Henry W., 158, 169
Hampton Roads, Va., 195
Hampton, Va., 131; environmental features of, 134
Hancock, Md., 92, 93, 94, 95, 96, 105, 108, 112, 119, 120

ROBERTA SENECHAL DE LA ROCHE is professor of history at Washington and Lee University. Born in Rumford, Maine, she received a bachelor's degree from the University of Southern Maine and earned a doctorate at the University of Virginia. Senechal de la Roche is the author of *The Sociogenesis of a Race Riot: Springfield, Illinois in 1908* (1990; reprinted 2008 as *In Lincoln's Shadow: The 1908 Race Riot in Springfield, Illinois*). The book was awarded the 1991 Illinois State Historical Society Superior Achievement Award and the 1992 Gustavus Myers Center Award for the Study of Human Rights in the United States. Senechal de la Roche has also published several theoretical works on various forms of collective violence, such as lynching, rioting, vigilantism, and terrorism. She currently lives in Charlottesville, Virginia.